K
N
NA
GI

んなぎ

Crazy Shrine Maidens

2

Eri
Takenashi

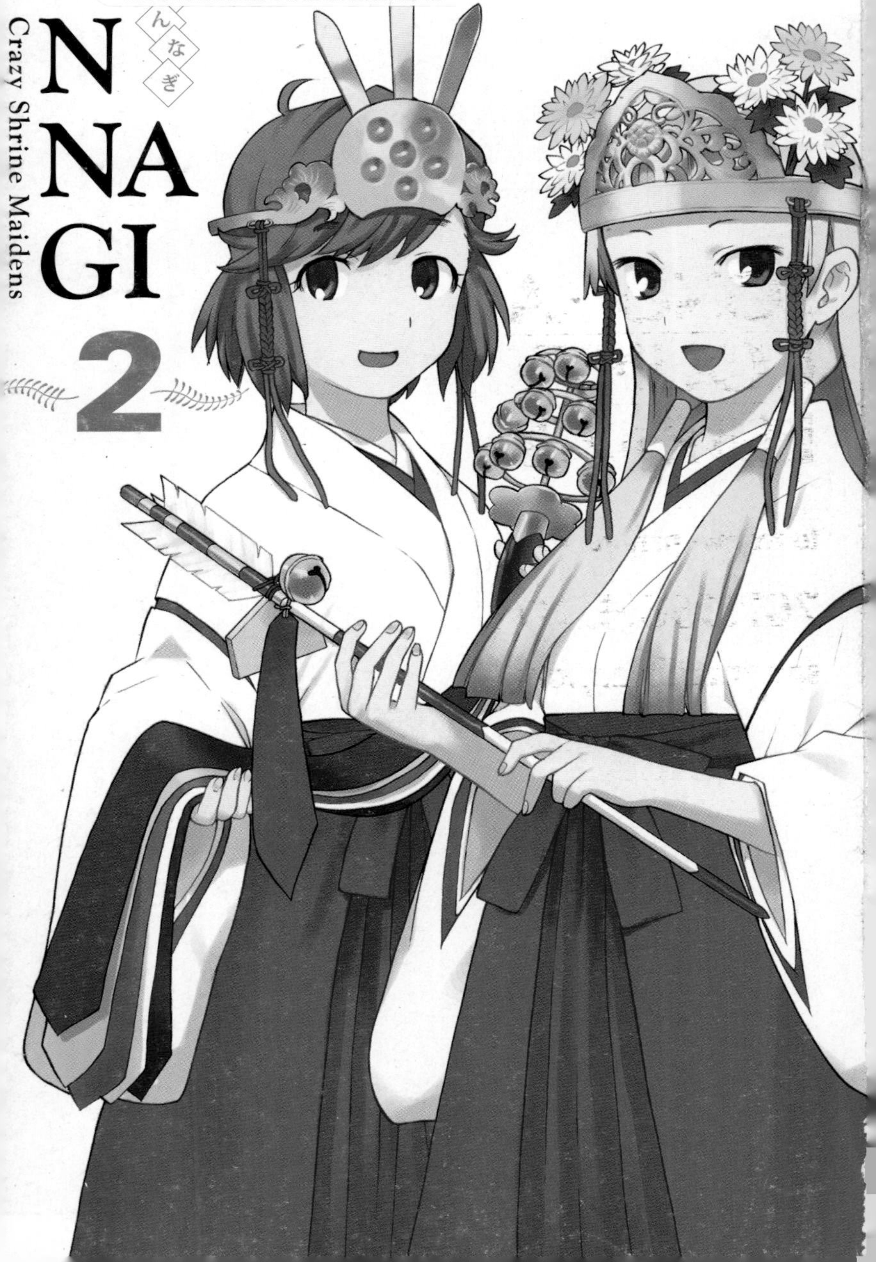

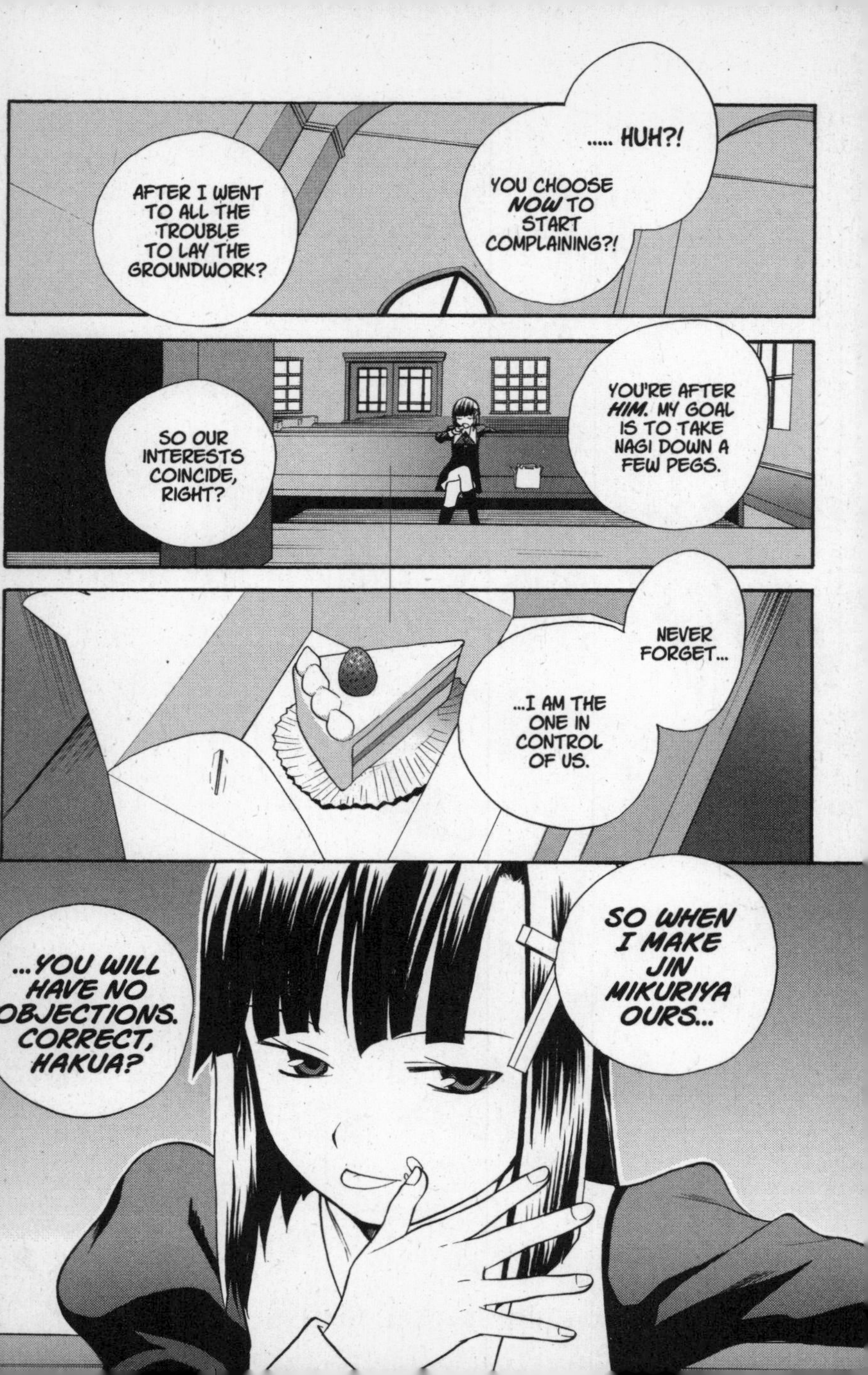

..... HUH?!
YOU CHOOSE NOW TO START COMPLAINING?!
AFTER I WENT TO ALL THE TROUBLE TO LAY THE GROUNDWORK?
YOU'RE AFTER HIM. MY GOAL IS TO TAKE NAGI DOWN A FEW PEGS.
SO OUR INTERESTS COINCIDE, RIGHT?
NEVER FORGET...
...I AM THE ONE IN CONTROL OF US.
SO WHEN I MAKE JIN MIKURIYA OURS...
...YOU WILL HAVE NO OBJECTIONS. CORRECT, HAKUA?

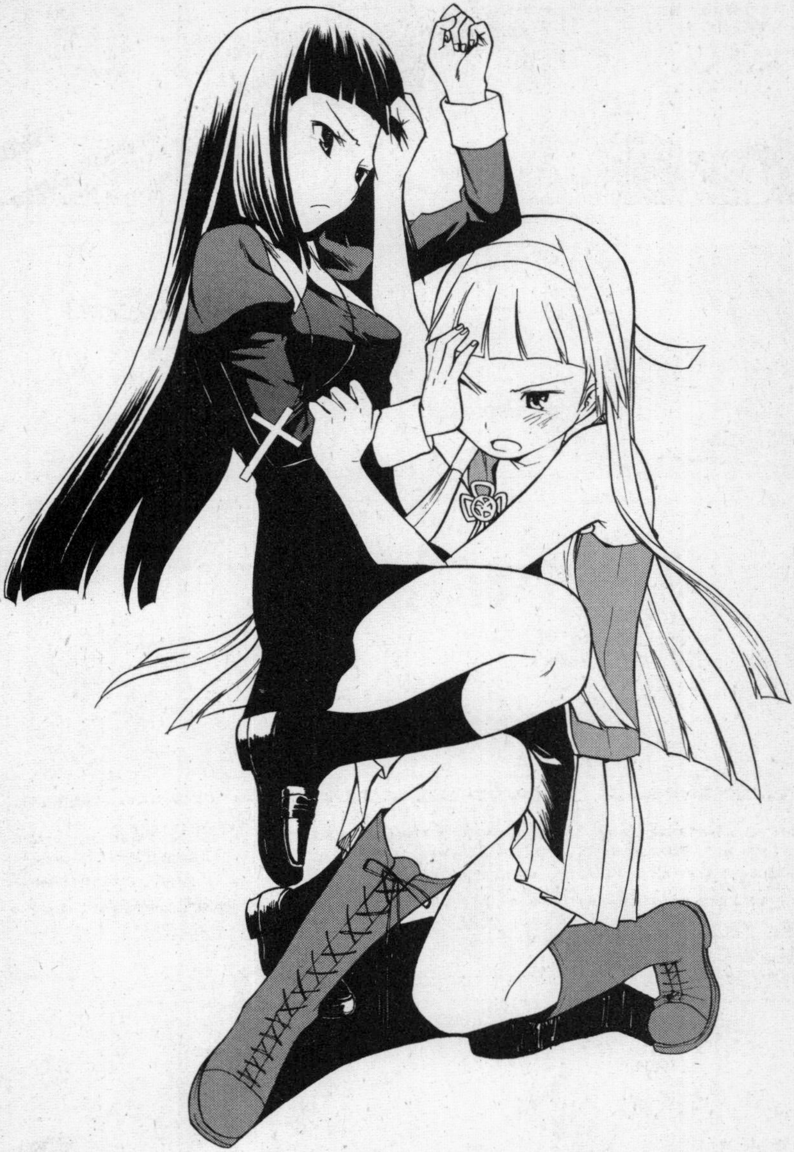

Seventh Chapter Sisters

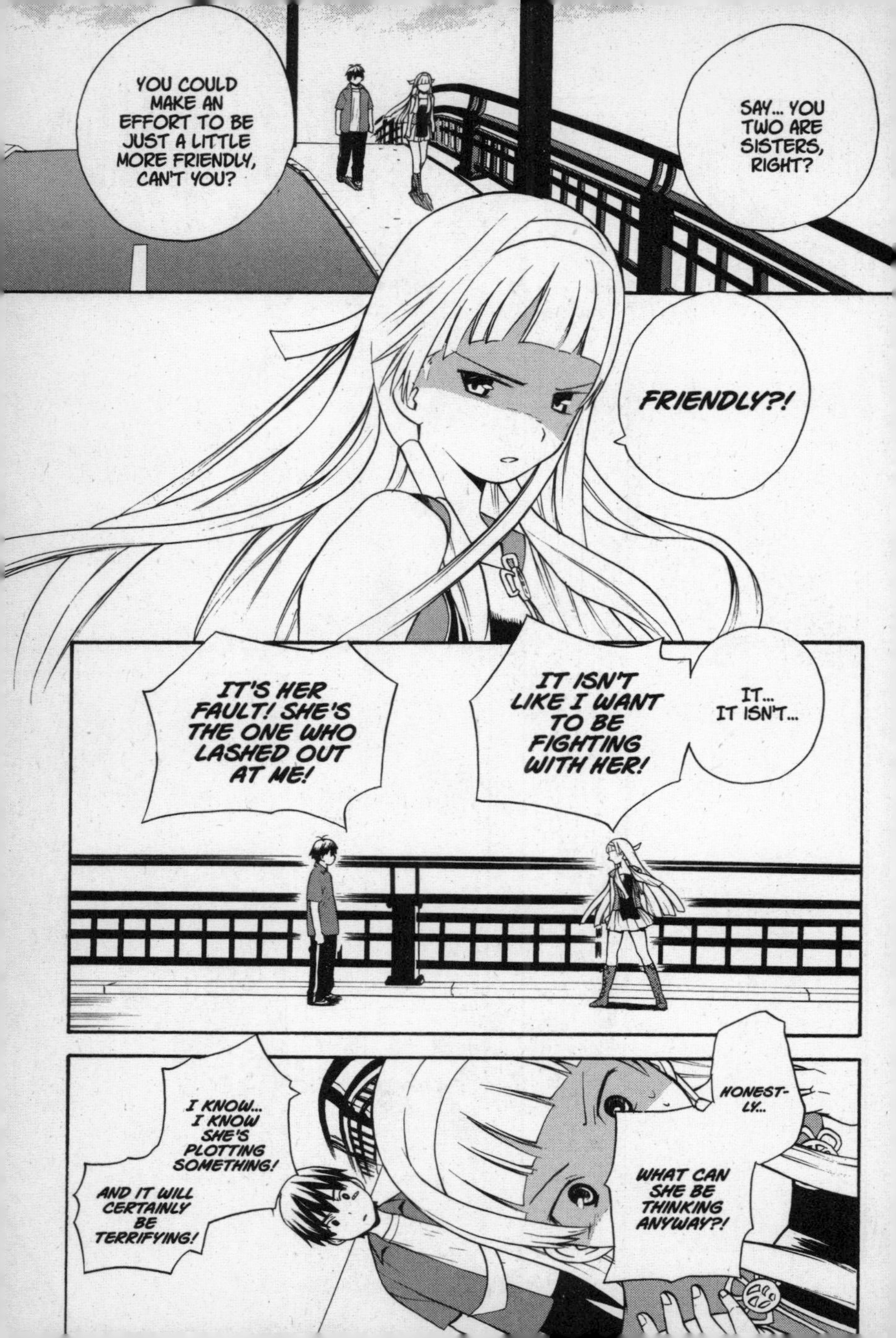
SAY... YOU TWO ARE SISTERS, RIGHT?
YOU COULD MAKE AN EFFORT TO BE JUST A LITTLE MORE FRIENDLY, CAN'T YOU?
FRIENDLY?!
IT... IT ISN'T...
IT ISN'T LIKE I WANT TO BE FIGHTING WITH HER!
IT'S HER FAULT! SHE'S THE ONE WHO LASHED OUT AT ME!
HONEST-LY...
WHAT CAN SHE BE THINKING ANYWAY?!
I KNOW... I KNOW SHE'S PLOTTING SOMETHING!
AND IT WILL CERTAINLY BE TERRIFYING!

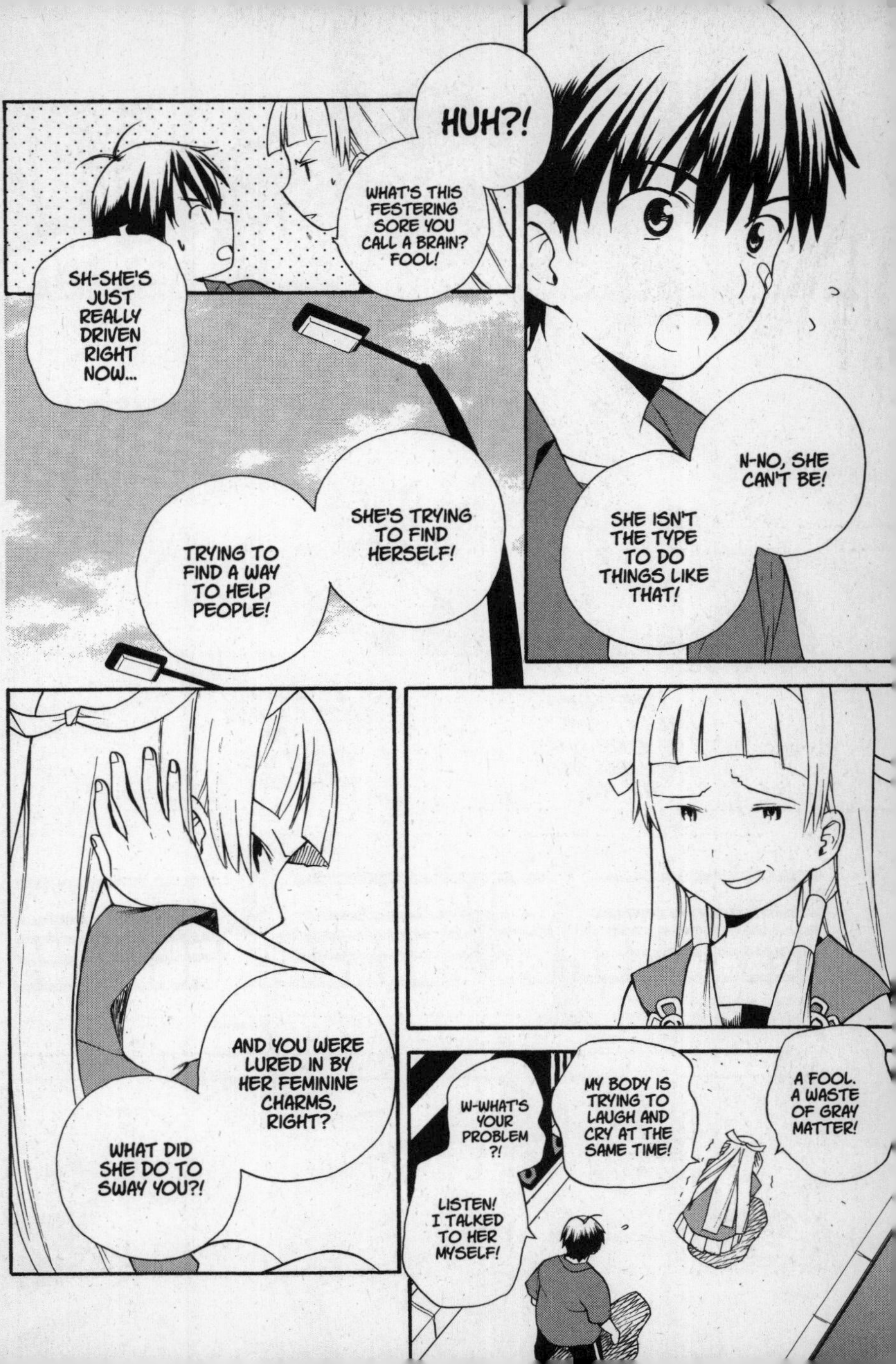
HUH?!
N-NO, SHE CAN'T BE!
SHE ISN'T THE TYPE TO DO THINGS LIKE THAT!
WHAT'S THIS FESTERING SORE YOU CALL A BRAIN? FOOL!
SH-SHE'S JUST REALLY DRIVEN RIGHT NOW...
SHE'S TRYING TO FIND HERSELF!
TRYING TO FIND A WAY TO HELP PEOPLE!
A FOOL. A WASTE OF GRAY MATTER!
MY BODY IS TRYING TO LAUGH AND CRY AT THE SAME TIME!
W-WHAT'S YOUR PROBLEM ?!
LISTEN! I TALKED TO HER MYSELF!
AND YOU WERE LURED IN BY HER FEMININE CHARMS, RIGHT?
WHAT DID SHE DO TO SWAY YOU?!

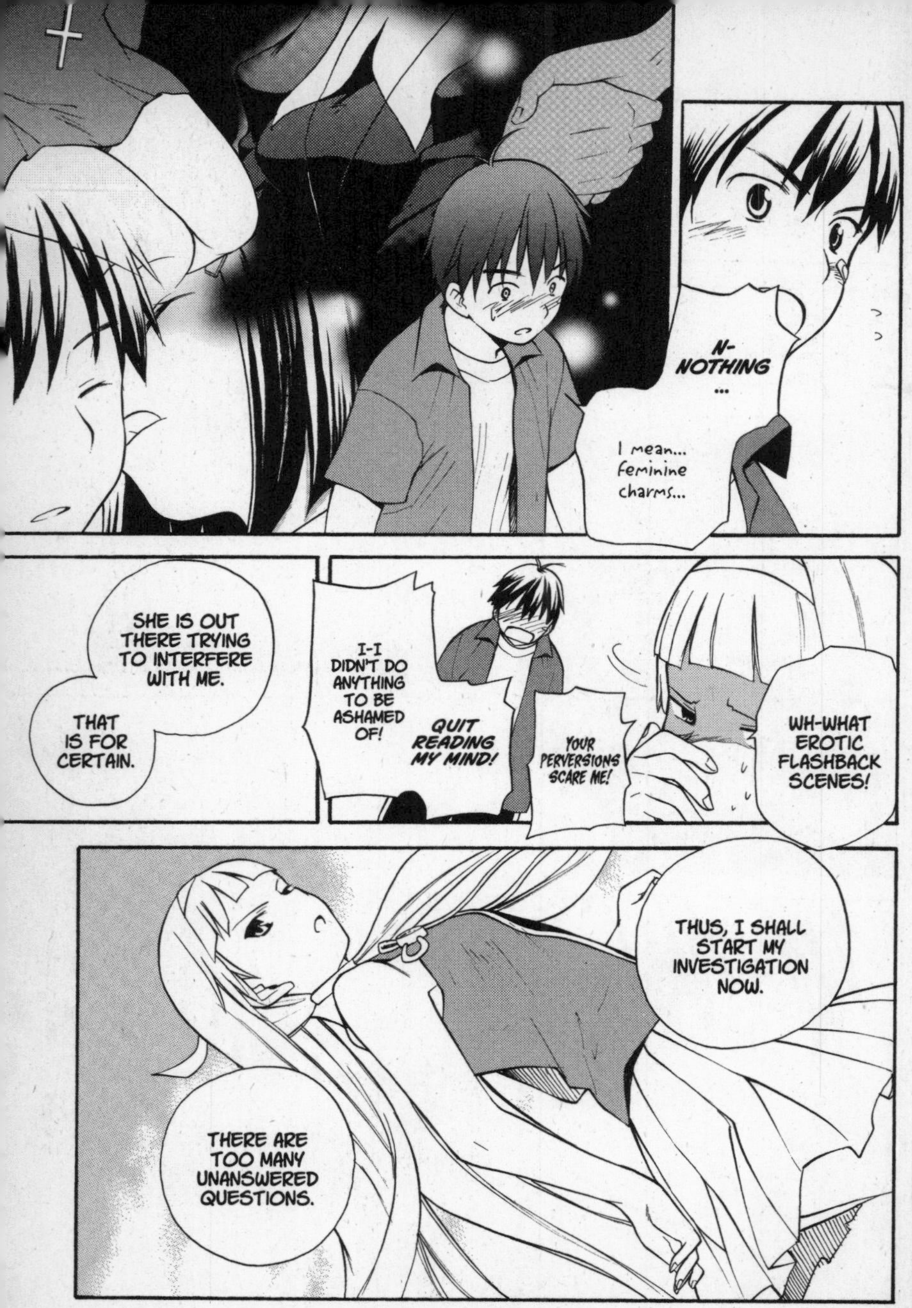
N-NOTHING...
I mean... feminine charms...
WH-WHAT EROTIC FLASHBACK SCENES!
YOUR PERVERSIONS SCARE ME!
I-I DIDN'T DO ANYTHING TO BE ASHAMED OF!
QUIT READING MY MIND!
SHE IS OUT THERE TRYING TO INTERFERE WITH ME.
THAT IS FOR CERTAIN.
THUS, I SHALL START MY INVESTIGATION NOW.
THERE ARE TOO MANY UNANSWERED QUESTIONS.

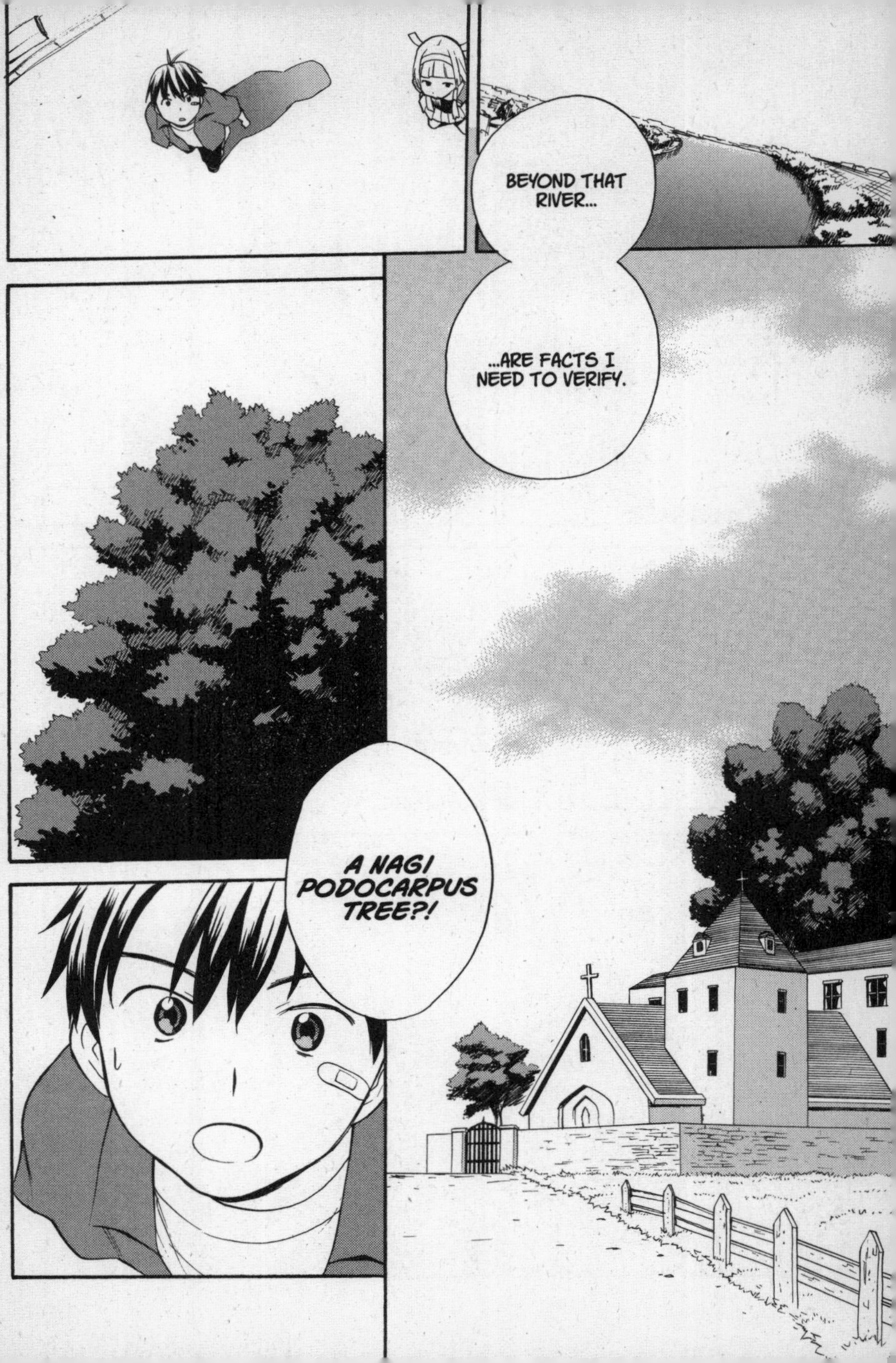
BEYOND THAT RIVER...
...ARE FACTS I NEED TO VERIFY.
A NAGI PODOCARPUS TREE?!

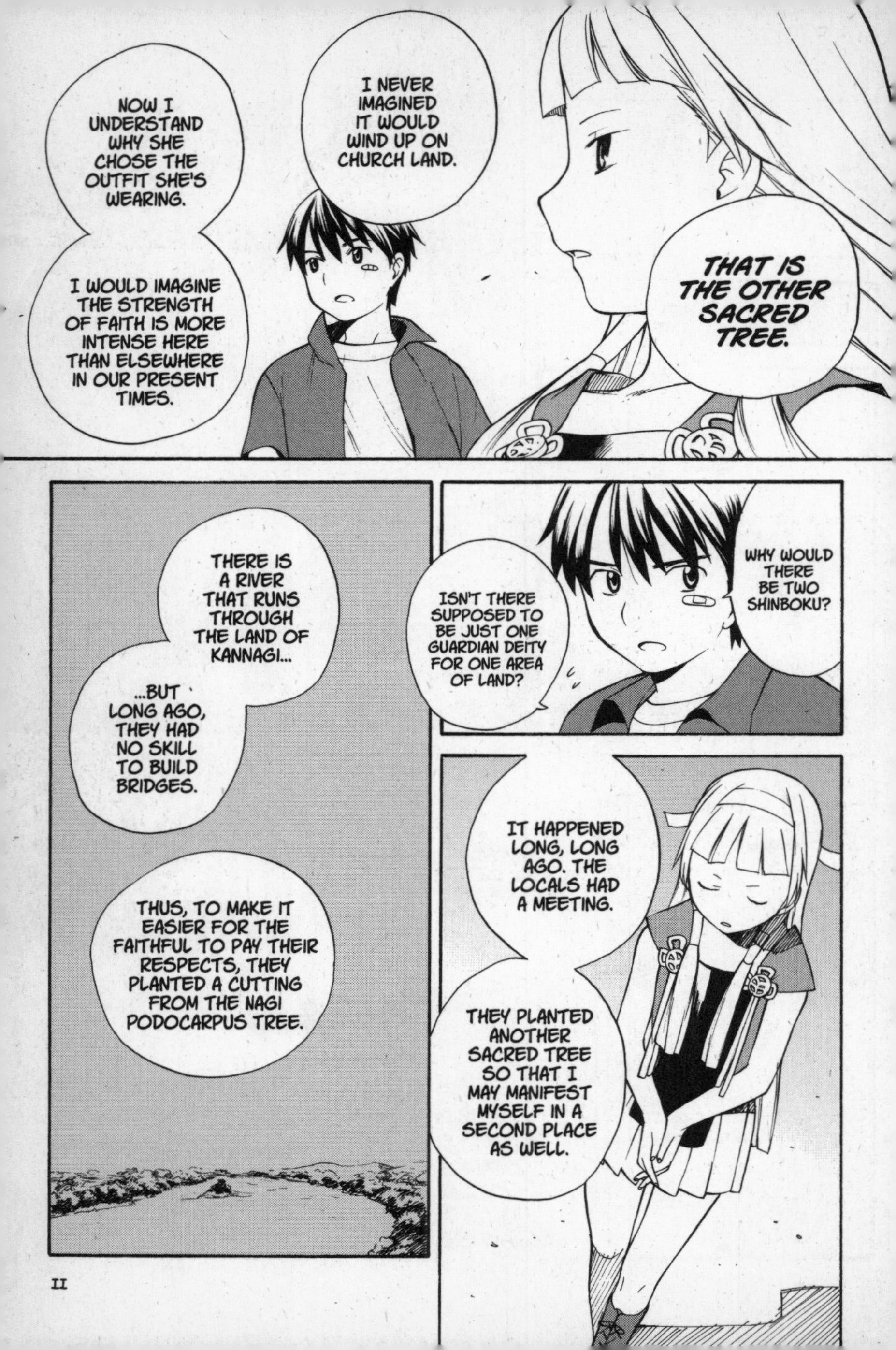
THAT IS THE OTHER SACRED TREE.
I NEVER IMAGINED IT WOULD WIND UP ON CHURCH LAND.
NOW I UNDERSTAND WHY SHE CHOSE THE OUTFIT SHE'S WEARING.
I WOULD IMAGINE THE STRENGTH OF FAITH IS MORE INTENSE HERE THAN ELSEWHERE IN OUR PRESENT TIMES.
WHY WOULD THERE BE TWO SHINBOKU?
ISN'T THERE SUPPOSED TO BE JUST ONE GUARDIAN DEITY FOR ONE AREA OF LAND?
IT HAPPENED LONG, LONG AGO. THE LOCALS HAD A MEETING.
THEY PLANTED ANOTHER SACRED TREE SO THAT I MAY MANIFEST MYSELF IN A SECOND PLACE AS WELL.
THERE IS A RIVER THAT RUNS THROUGH THE LAND OF KANNAGI...
...BUT LONG AGO, THEY HAD NO SKILL TO BUILD BRIDGES.
THUS, TO MAKE IT EASIER FOR THE FAITHFUL TO PAY THEIR RESPECTS, THEY PLANTED A CUTTING FROM THE NAGI PODOCARPUS TREE.

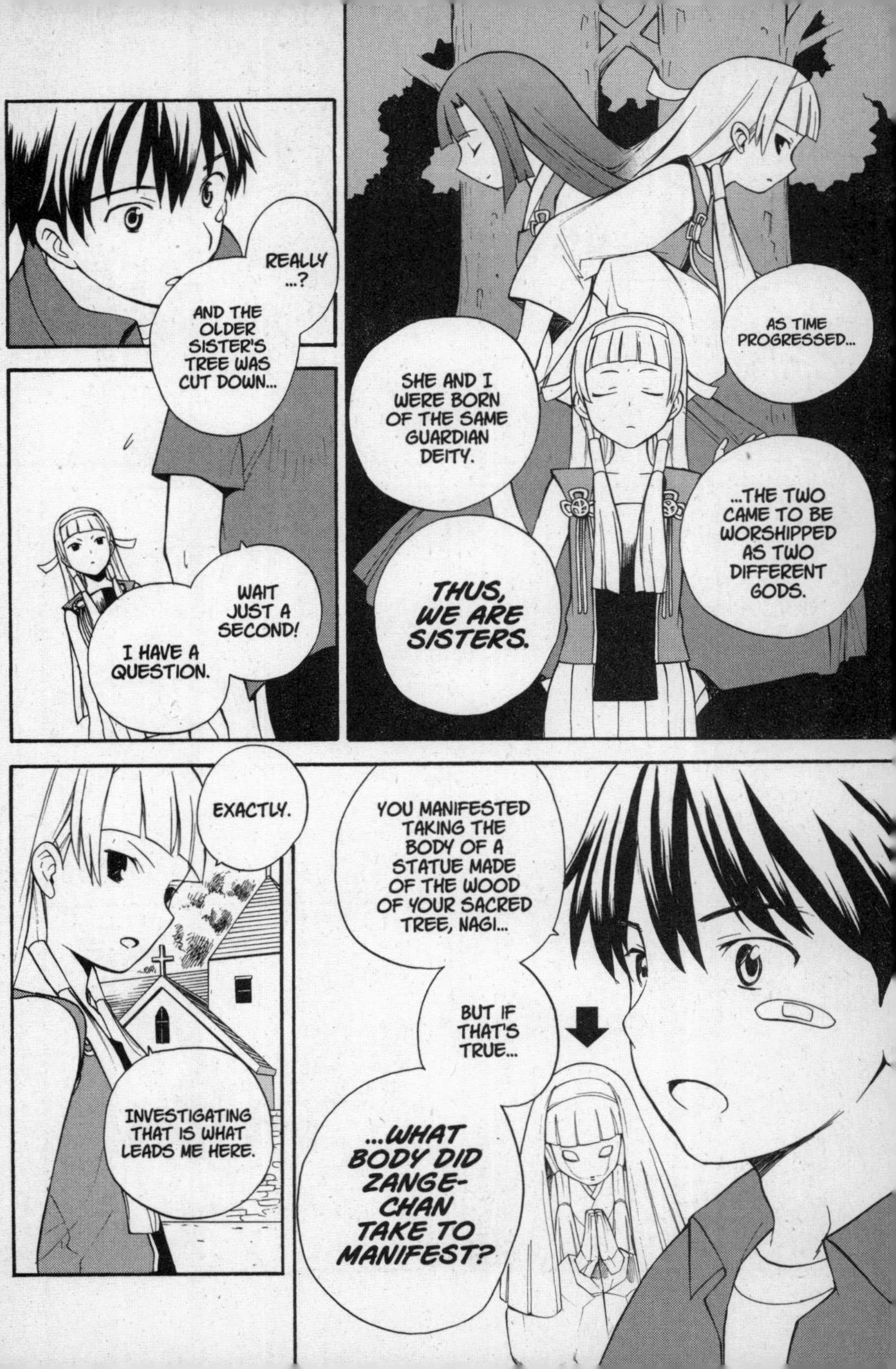
AS TIME PROGRESSED...
...THE TWO CAME TO BE WORSHIPPED AS TWO DIFFERENT GODS.
SHE AND I WERE BORN OF THE SAME GUARDIAN DEITY.
THUS, WE ARE SISTERS.
REALLY ...?
AND THE OLDER SISTER'S TREE WAS CUT DOWN...
WAIT JUST A SECOND!
I HAVE A QUESTION.
YOU MANIFESTED TAKING THE BODY OF A STATUE MADE OF THE WOOD OF YOUR SACRED TREE, NAGI...
BUT IF THAT'S TRUE...
...WHAT BODY DID ZANGE-CHAN TAKE TO MANIFEST?
EXACTLY.
INVESTIGATING THAT IS WHAT LEADS ME HERE.

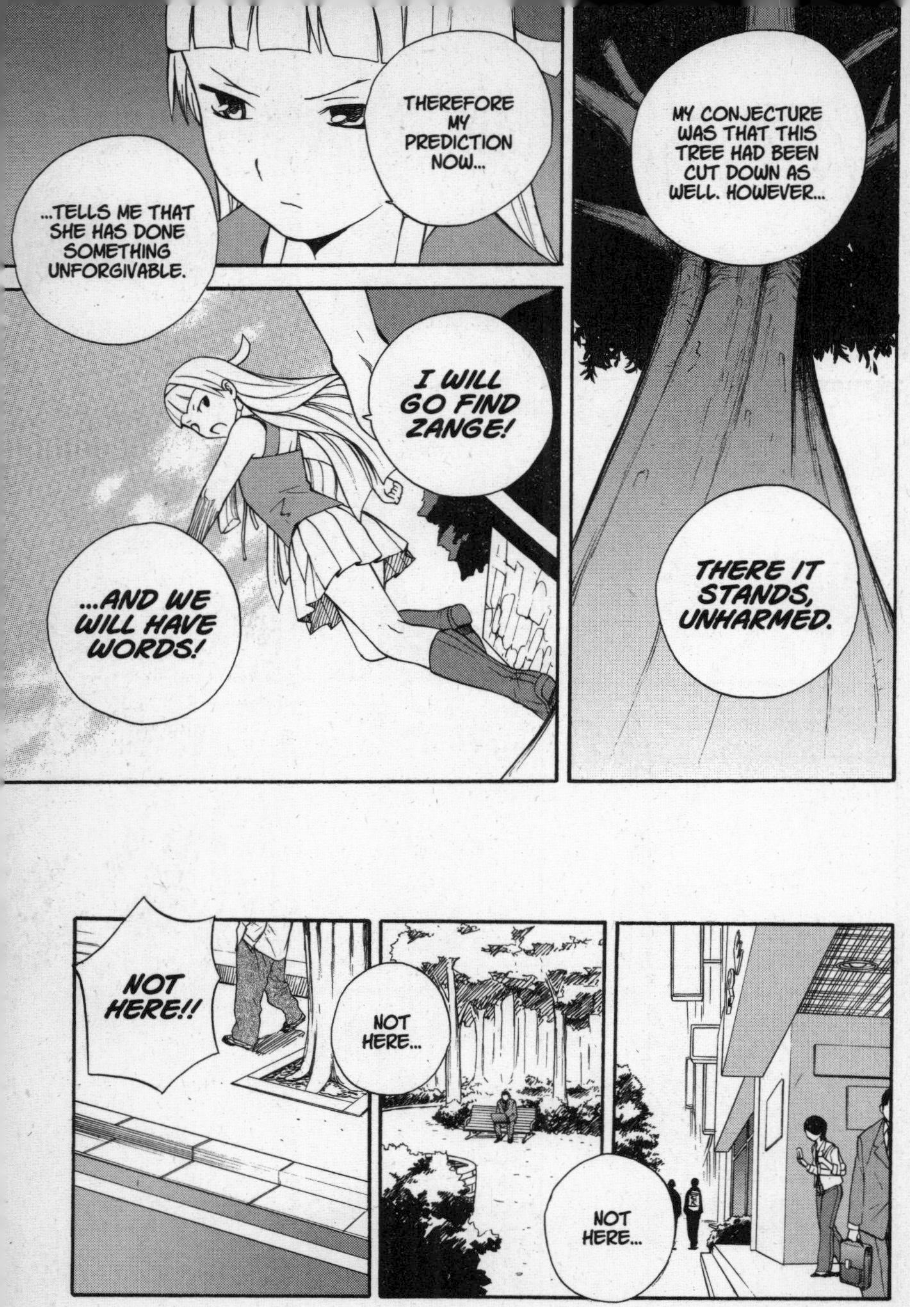
MY CONJECTURE WAS THAT THIS TREE HAD BEEN CUT DOWN AS WELL. HOWEVER...
THERE IT STANDS, UNHARMED.
THEREFORE MY PREDICTION NOW...
...TELLS ME THAT SHE HAS DONE SOMETHING UNFORGIVABLE.
I WILL GO FIND ZANGE!
...AND WE WILL HAVE WORDS!
NOT HERE...
NOT HERE...
NOT HERE!!

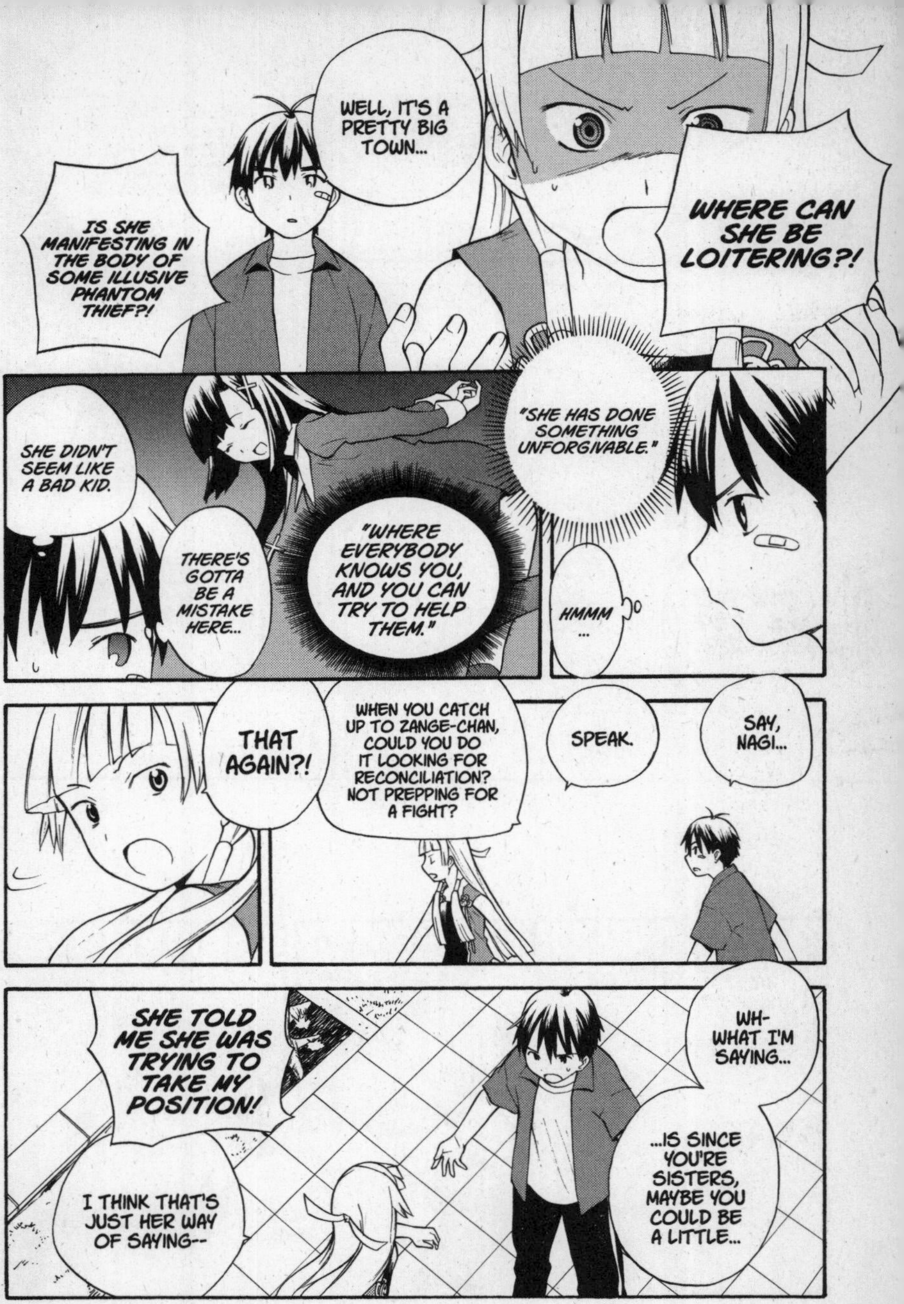
WHERE CAN SHE BE LOITERING?!
WELL, IT'S A PRETTY BIG TOWN...
IS SHE MANIFESTING IN THE BODY OF SOME ILLUSIVE PHANTOM THIEF?!
"SHE HAS DONE SOMETHING UNFORGIVABLE."
HMMM...
"WHERE EVERYBODY KNOWS YOU, AND YOU CAN TRY TO HELP THEM."
SHE DIDN'T SEEM LIKE A BAD KID.
THERE'S GOTTA BE A MISTAKE HERE...
SAY, NAGI...
SPEAK.
WHEN YOU CATCH UP TO ZANGE-CHAN, COULD YOU DO IT LOOKING FOR RECONCILIATION? NOT PREPPING FOR A FIGHT?
THAT AGAIN?!
WH- WHAT I'M SAYING...
...IS SINCE YOU'RE SISTERS, MAYBE YOU COULD BE A LITTLE...
SHE TOLD ME SHE WAS TRYING TO TAKE MY POSITION!
I THINK THAT'S JUST HER WAY OF SAYING--

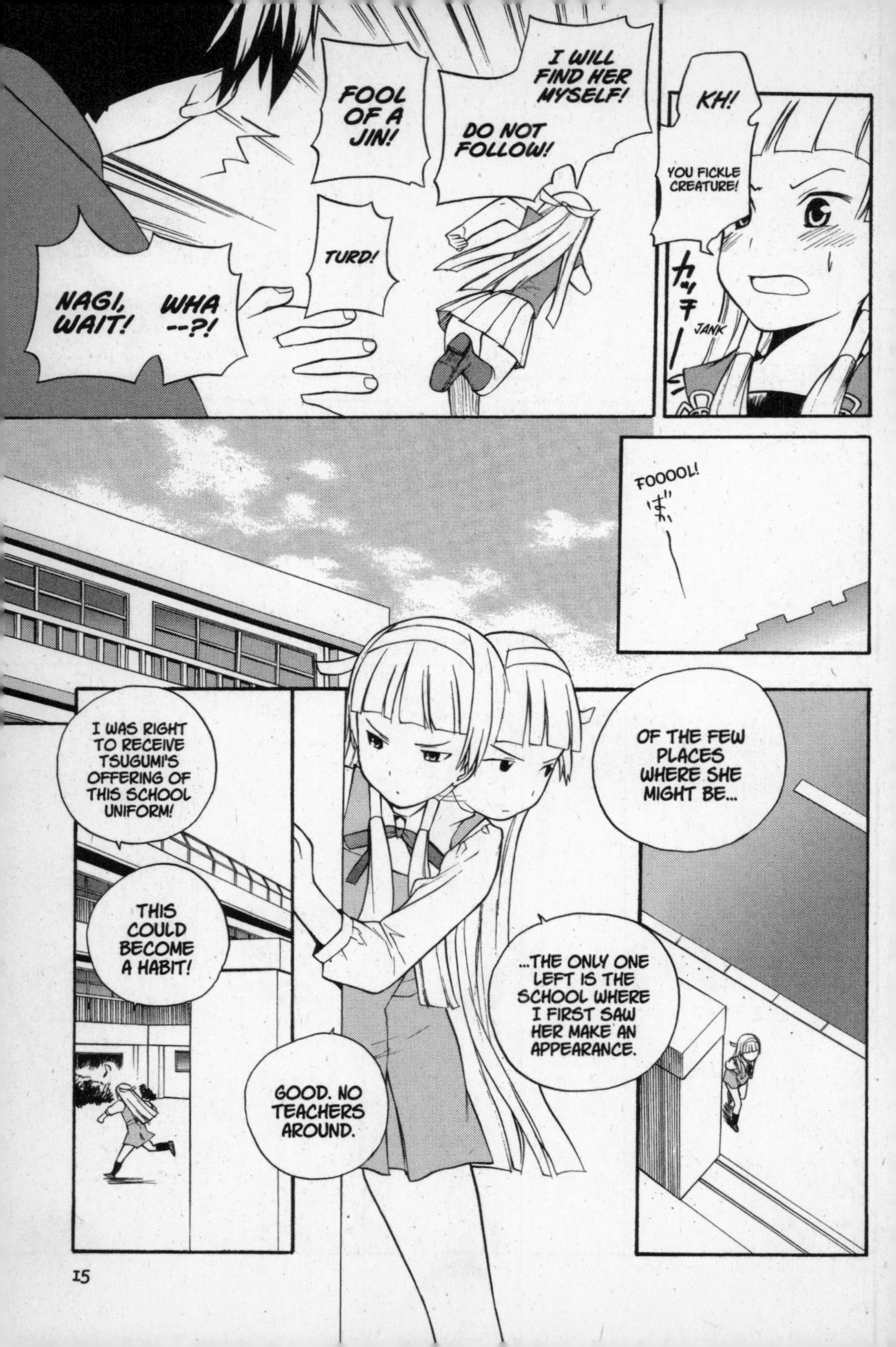
KH!
YOU FICKLE CREATURE!
JANK
I WILL FIND HER MYSELF!
DO NOT FOLLOW!
FOOL OF A JIN!
TURD!
WHA --?!
NAGI, WAIT!
FOOOOL!
OF THE FEW PLACES WHERE SHE MIGHT BE...
...THE ONLY ONE LEFT IS THE SCHOOL WHERE I FIRST SAW HER MAKE AN APPEARANCE.
GOOD. NO TEACHERS AROUND.
I WAS RIGHT TO RECEIVE TSUGUMI'S OFFERING OF THIS SCHOOL UNIFORM!
THIS COULD BECOME A HABIT!

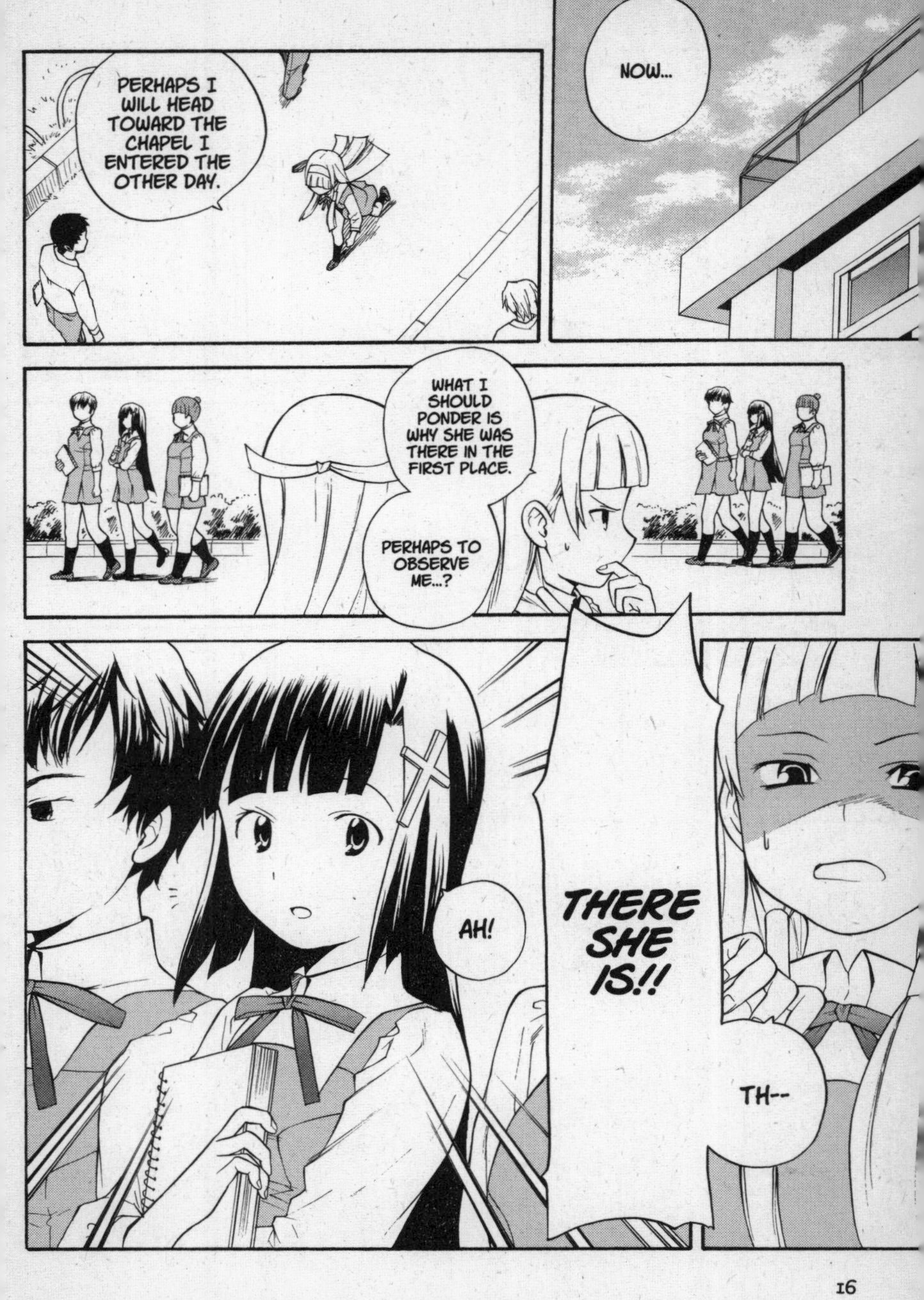
NOW...
PERHAPS I WILL HEAD TOWARD THE CHAPEL I ENTERED THE OTHER DAY.
WHAT I SHOULD PONDER IS WHY SHE WAS THERE IN THE FIRST PLACE.
PERHAPS TO OBSERVE ME...?
THERE SHE IS!!
AH!
TH--

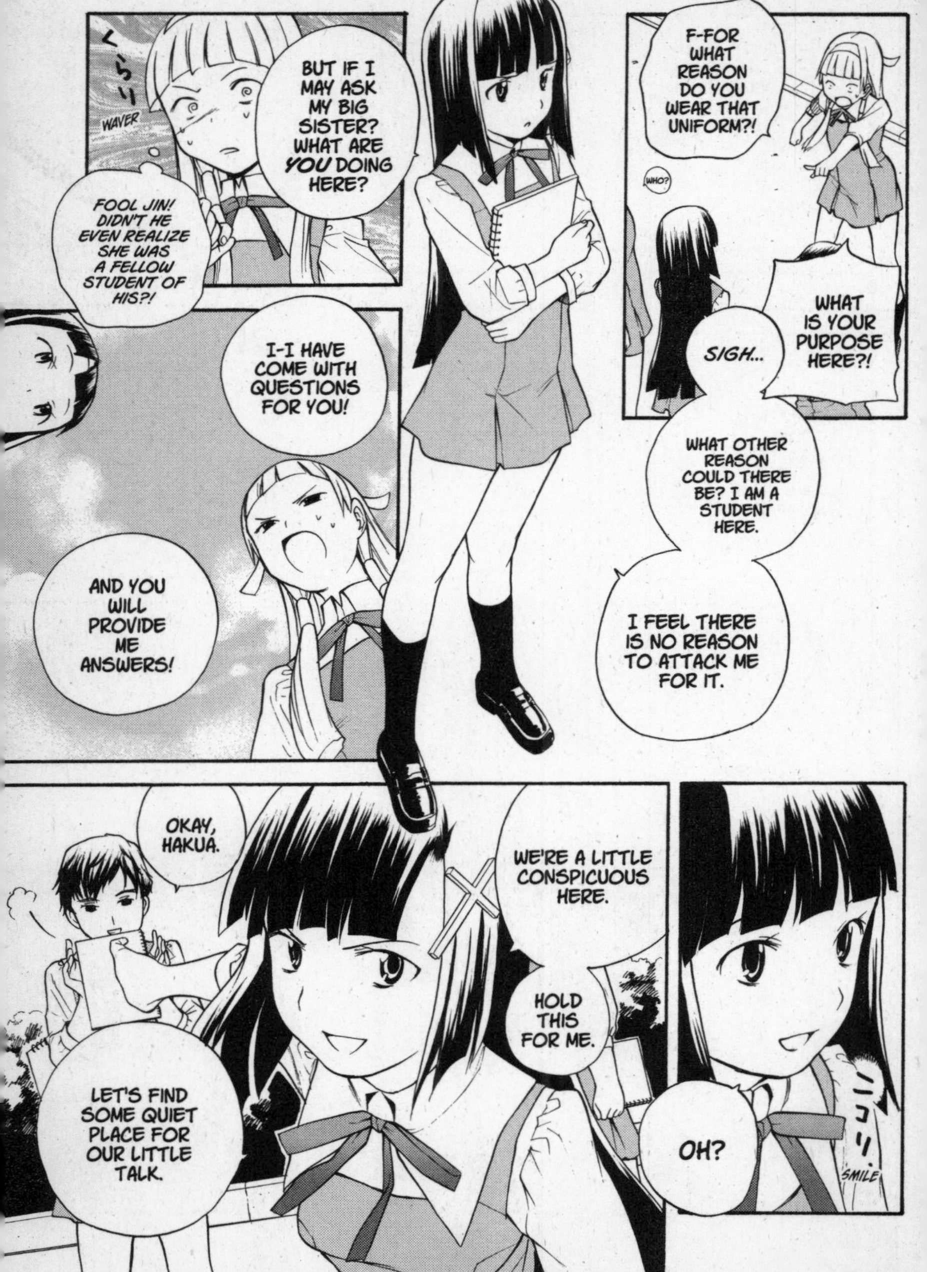

F-FOR WHAT REASON DO YOU WEAR THAT UNIFORM?!
WHO?
WHAT IS YOUR PURPOSE HERE?!
SIGH...
WHAT OTHER REASON COULD THERE BE? I AM A STUDENT HERE.
I FEEL THERE IS NO REASON TO ATTACK ME FOR IT.
BUT IF I MAY ASK MY BIG SISTER? WHAT ARE *YOU* DOING HERE?
くらり
WAVER
FOOL JIN! DIDN'T HE EVEN REALIZE SHE WAS A FELLOW STUDENT OF HIS?!
I-I HAVE COME WITH QUESTIONS FOR YOU!
AND YOU WILL PROVIDE ME ANSWERS!
ニコリ
SMILE
OH?
WE'RE A LITTLE CONSPICUOUS HERE.
HOLD THIS FOR ME.
OKAY, HAKUA.
LET'S FIND SOME QUIET PLACE FOR OUR LITTLE TALK.

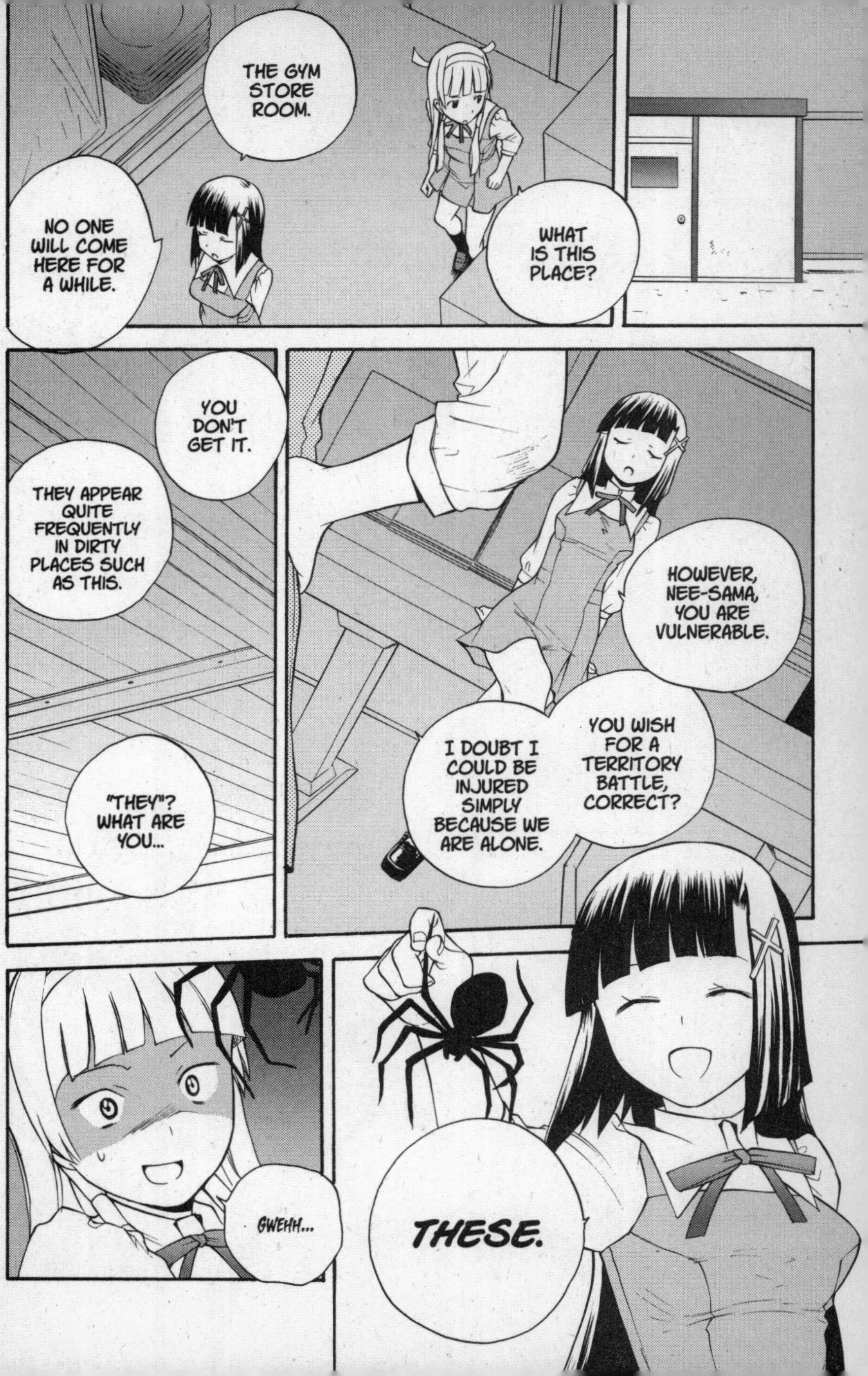
WHAT IS THIS PLACE?
THE GYM STORE ROOM.
NO ONE WILL COME HERE FOR A WHILE.
HOWEVER, NEE-SAMA, YOU ARE VULNERABLE.
YOU WISH FOR A TERRITORY BATTLE, CORRECT?
I DOUBT I COULD BE INJURED SIMPLY BECAUSE WE ARE ALONE.
YOU DON'T GET IT.
THEY APPEAR QUITE FREQUENTLY IN DIRTY PLACES SUCH AS THIS.
"THEY"? WHAT ARE YOU...
THESE.
GWEHH...

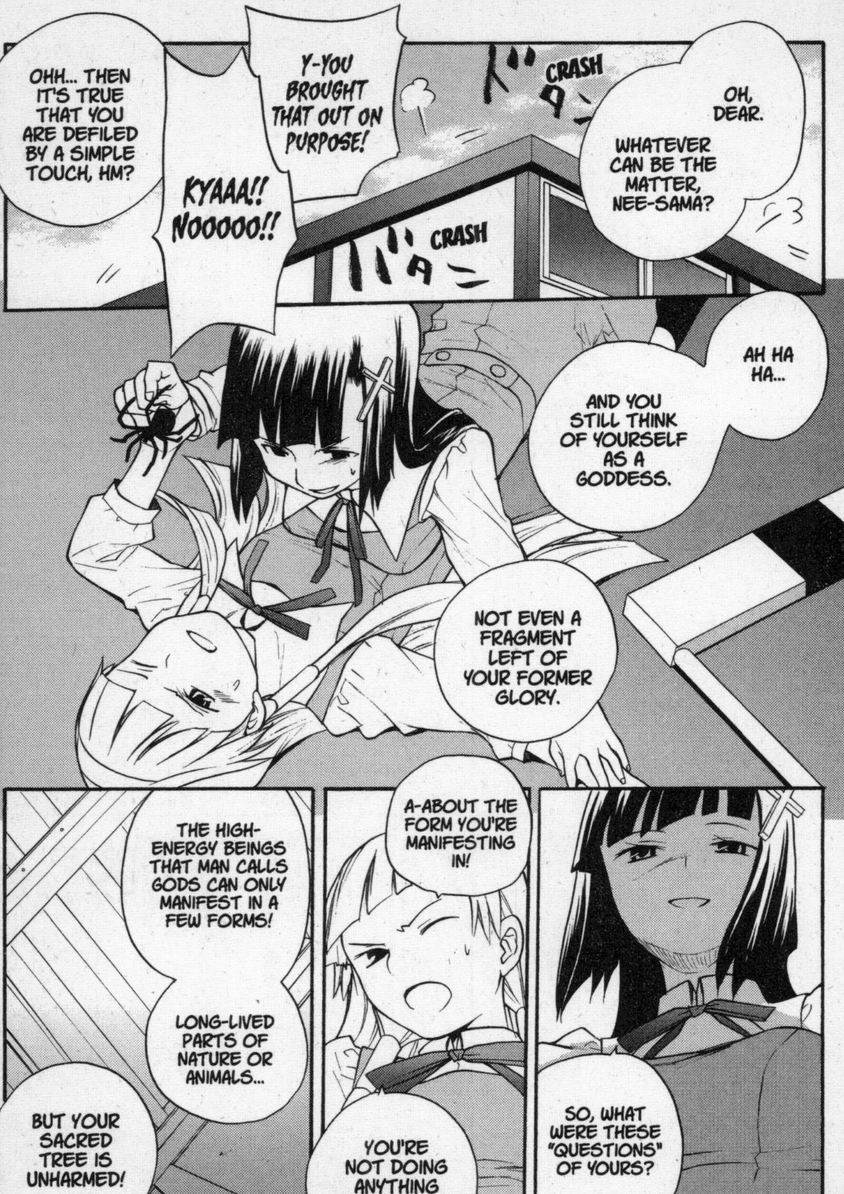
CRASH
OH, DEAR.
WHATEVER CAN BE THE MATTER, NEE-SAMA?
CRASH
Y-YOU BROUGHT THAT OUT ON PURPOSE!
KYAAA!! NOOOOO!!
OHH... THEN IT'S TRUE THAT YOU ARE DEFILED BY A SIMPLE TOUCH, HM?
AH HA HA...
AND YOU STILL THINK OF YOURSELF AS A GODDESS.
NOT EVEN A FRAGMENT LEFT OF YOUR FORMER GLORY.
SO, WHAT WERE THESE "QUESTIONS" OF YOURS?
A-ABOUT THE FORM YOU'RE MANIFESTING IN!
YOU'RE NOT DOING ANYTHING FORBIDDEN, ARE YOU?
THE HIGH-ENERGY BEINGS THAT MAN CALLS GODS CAN ONLY MANIFEST IN A FEW FORMS!
LONG-LIVED PARTS OF NATURE OR ANIMALS...
BUT YOUR SACRED TREE IS UNHARMED!

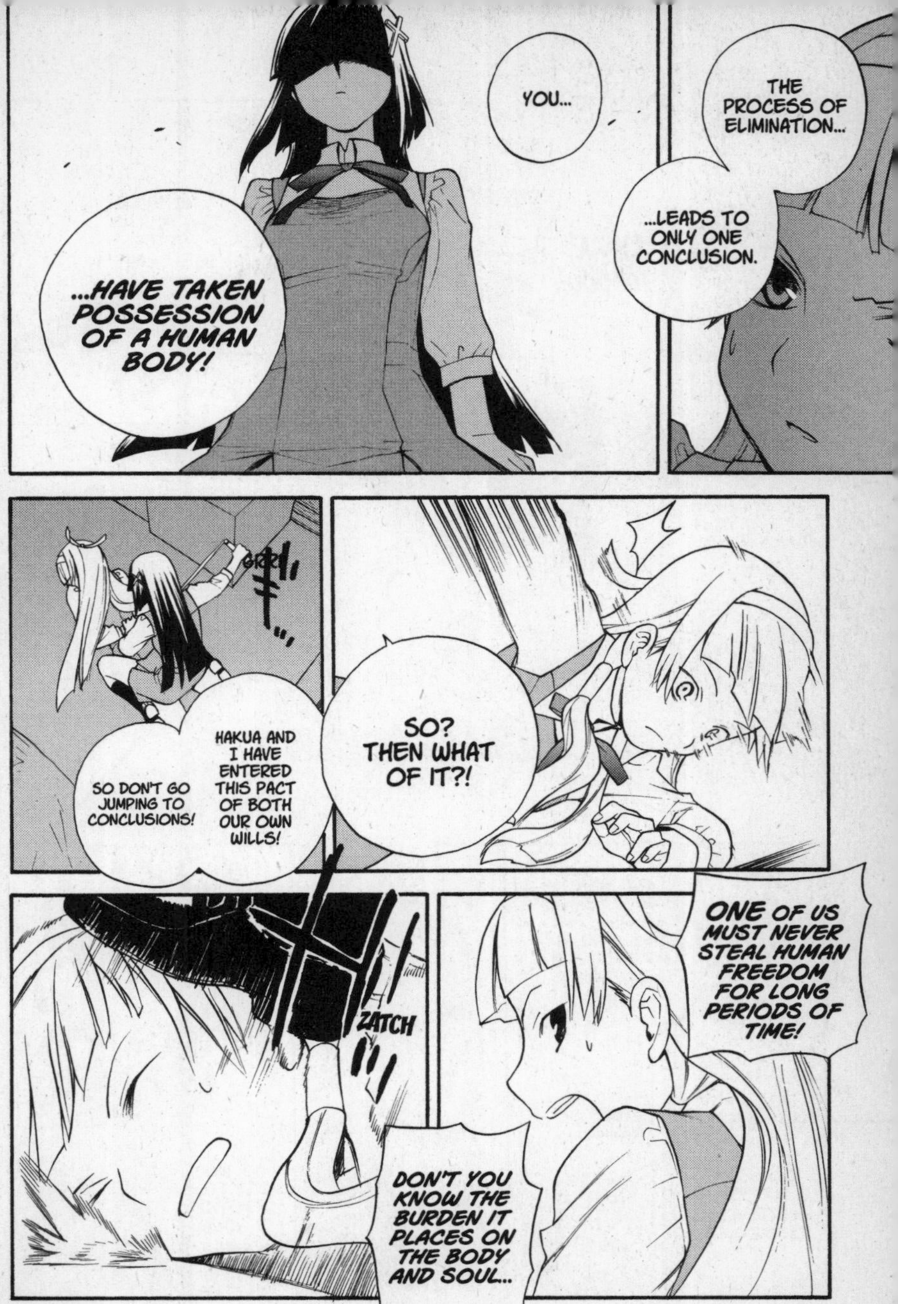
THE PROCESS OF ELIMINATION...
...LEADS TO ONLY ONE CONCLUSION.
YOU...
...HAVE TAKEN POSSESSION OF A HUMAN BODY!
SO? THEN WHAT OF IT?!
GRR
HAKUA AND I HAVE ENTERED THIS PACT OF BOTH OUR OWN WILLS!
SO DON'T GO JUMPING TO CONCLUSIONS!
ONE OF US MUST NEVER STEAL HUMAN FREEDOM FOR LONG PERIODS OF TIME!
DON'T YOU KNOW THE BURDEN IT PLACES ON THE BODY AND SOUL...
ZATCH

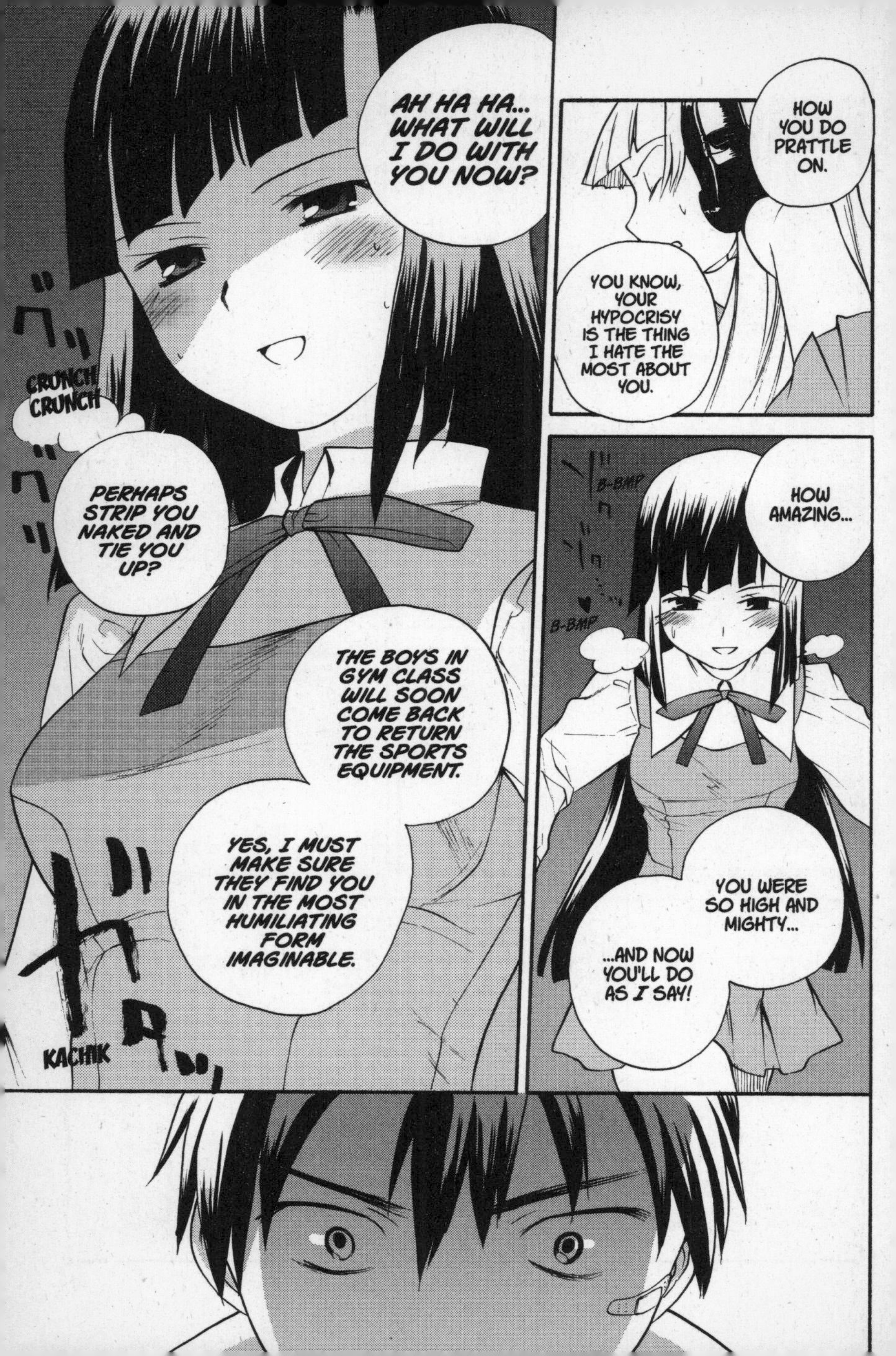

HOW YOU DO PRATTLE ON.
YOU KNOW, YOUR HYPOCRISY IS THE THING I HATE THE MOST ABOUT YOU.
B-BMP
B-BMP
HOW AMAZING...
YOU WERE SO HIGH AND MIGHTY...
...AND NOW YOU'LL DO AS *I* SAY!
AH HA HA... WHAT WILL I DO WITH YOU NOW?
CRUNCH CRUNCH
PERHAPS STRIP YOU NAKED AND TIE YOU UP?
THE BOYS IN GYM CLASS WILL SOON COME BACK TO RETURN THE SPORTS EQUIPMENT.
YES, I MUST MAKE SURE THEY FIND YOU IN THE MOST HUMILIATING FORM IMAGINABLE.
KACHIK

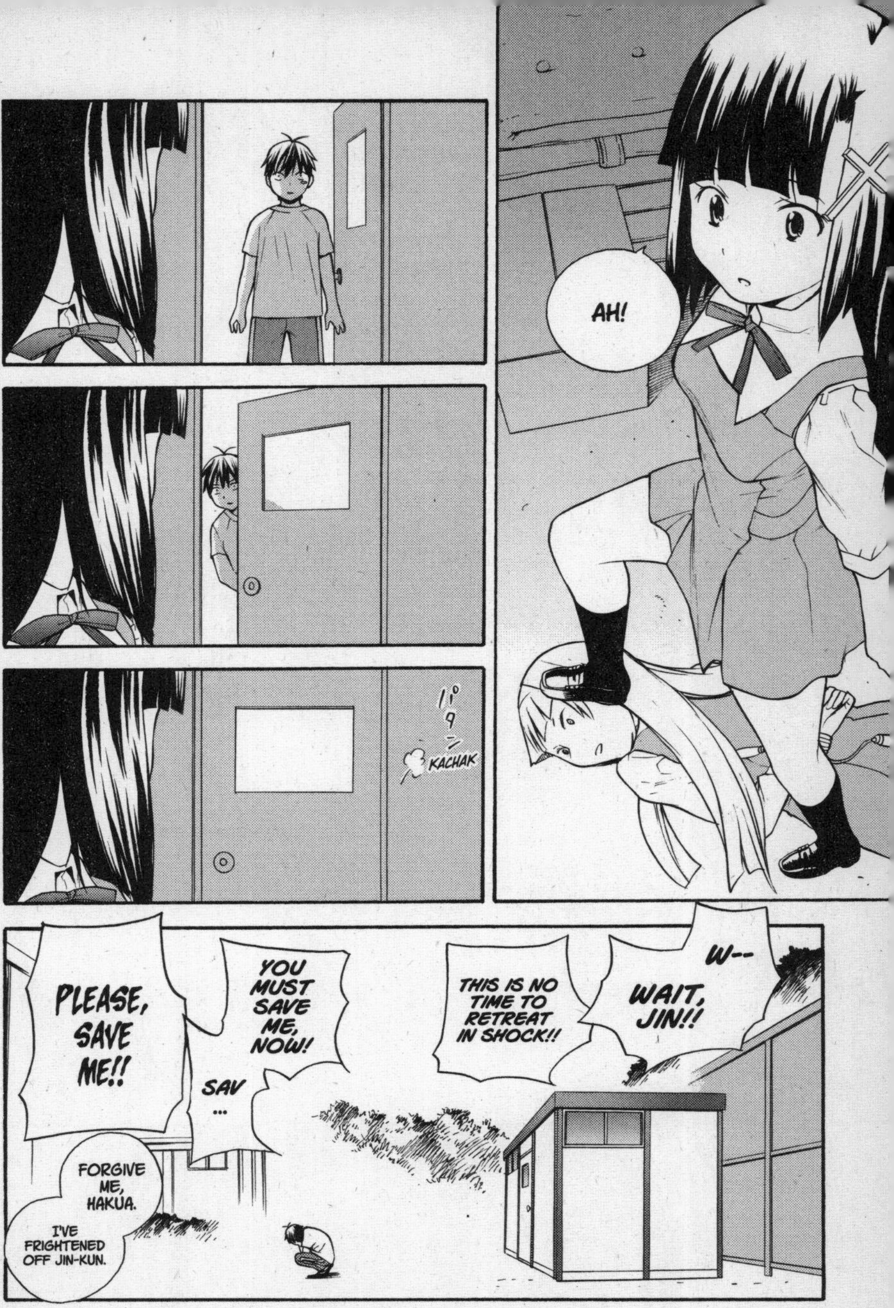
AH!
パタン
KACHAK
W--
WAIT, JIN!!
THIS IS NO TIME TO RETREAT IN SHOCK!!
YOU MUST SAVE ME, NOW!
PLEASE, SAVE ME!!
SAV ...
FORGIVE ME, HAKUA.
I'VE FRIGHTENED OFF JIN-KUN.

KANNAGI

My
friends!

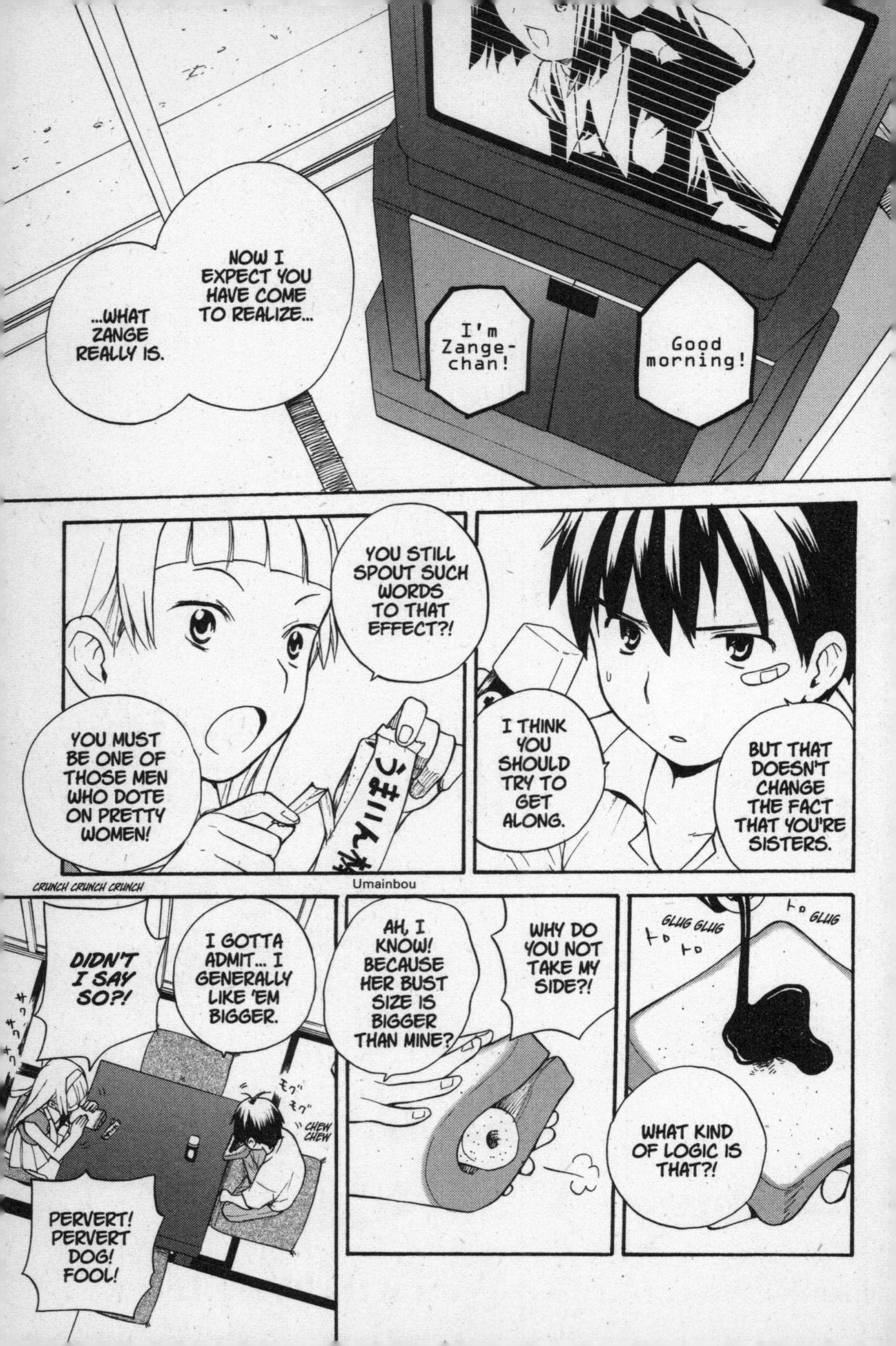
Good morning!
I'm Zange-chan!
NOW I EXPECT YOU HAVE COME TO REALIZE...
...WHAT ZANGE REALLY IS.
BUT THAT DOESN'T CHANGE THE FACT THAT YOU'RE SISTERS.
I THINK YOU SHOULD TRY TO GET ALONG.
YOU STILL SPOUT SUCH WORDS TO THAT EFFECT?!
YOU MUST BE ONE OF THOSE MEN WHO DOTE ON PRETTY WOMEN!
Umainbou
CRUNCH CRUNCH CRUNCH
GLUG
GLUG GLUG
WHAT KIND OF LOGIC IS THAT?!
WHY DO YOU NOT TAKE MY SIDE?!
AH, I KNOW! BECAUSE HER BUST SIZE IS BIGGER THAN MINE?
I GOTTA ADMIT... I GENERALLY LIKE 'EM BIGGER.
DIDN'T I SAY SO?!
CHEW CHEW
PERVERT! PERVERT DOG! FOOL!

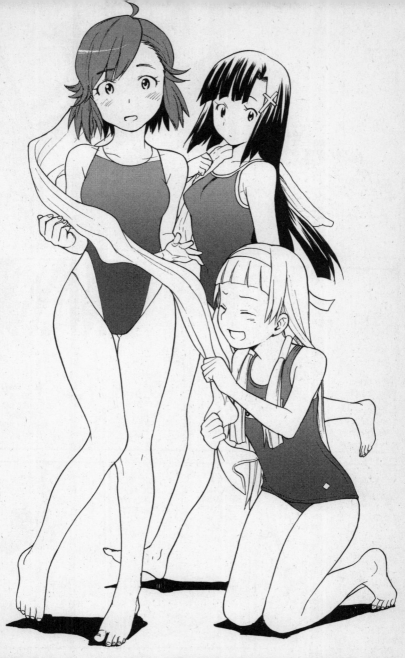

Eighth Chapter The Fiery Gods of the Dinner Table x2+1

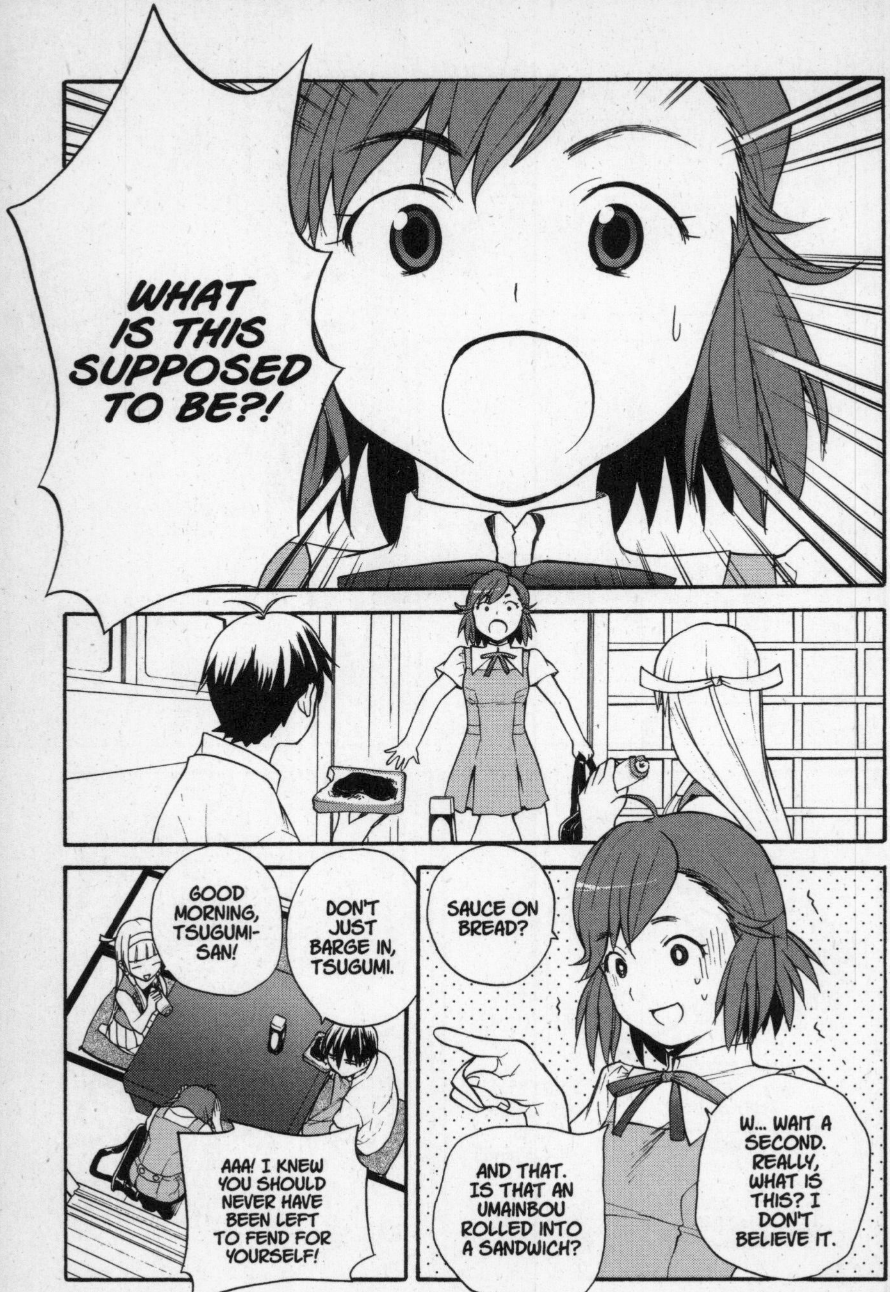
WHAT IS THIS SUPPOSED TO BE?!
SAUCE ON BREAD?
AND THAT. IS THAT AN UMAINBOU ROLLED INTO A SANDWICH?
W... WAIT A SECOND. REALLY, WHAT IS THIS? I DON'T BELIEVE IT.
DON'T JUST BARGE IN, TSUGUMI.
GOOD MORNING, TSUGUMI-SAN!
AAA! I KNEW YOU SHOULD NEVER HAVE BEEN LEFT TO FEND FOR YOURSELF!

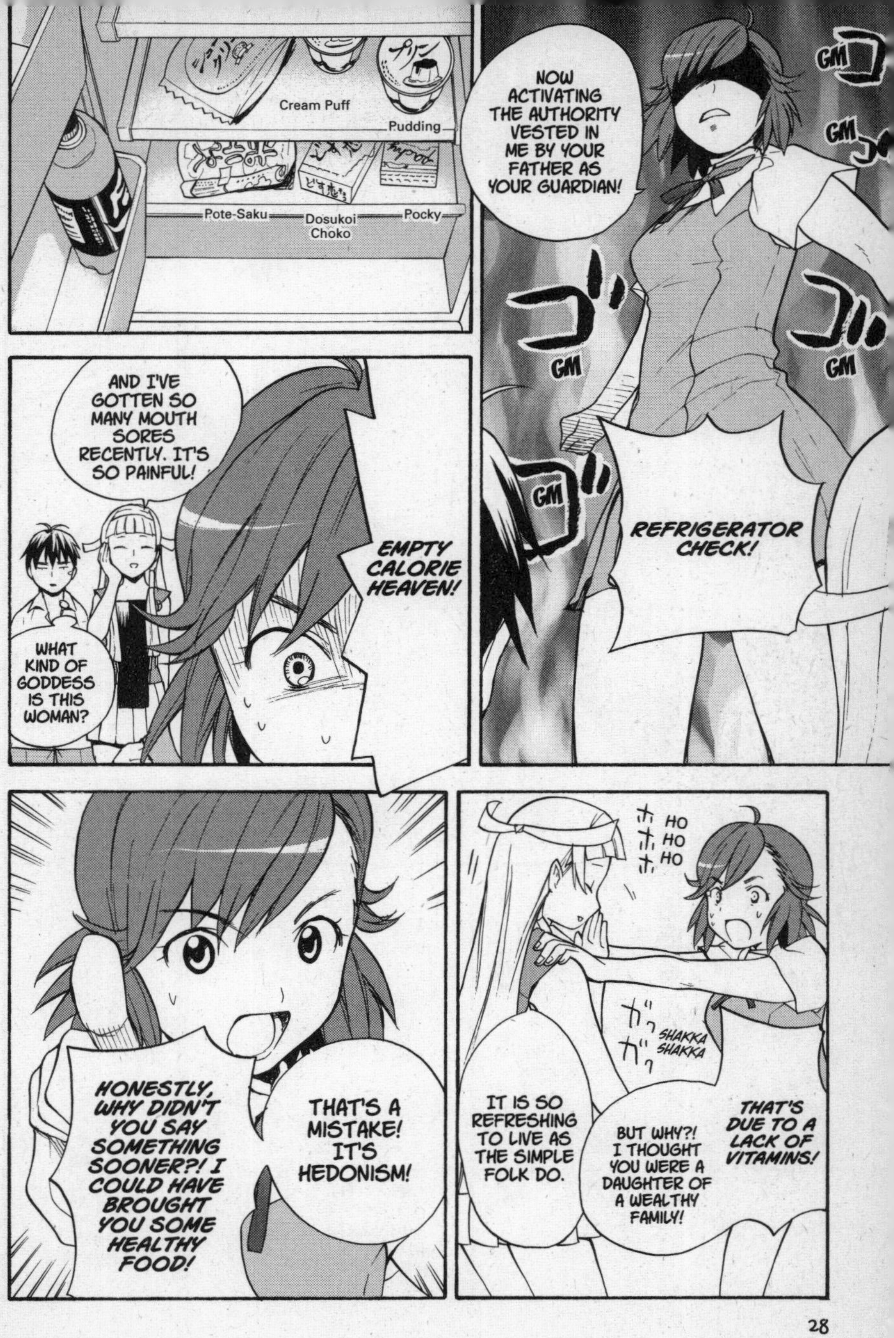
NOW ACTIVATING THE AUTHORITY VESTED IN ME BY YOUR FATHER AS YOUR GUARDIAN!
GM
GM
GM
GM
GM
REFRIGERATOR CHECK!
Cream Puff
Pudding
Pote-Saku
Dosukoi Choko
Pocky
EMPTY CALORIE HEAVEN!
AND I'VE GOTTEN SO MANY MOUTH SORES RECENTLY. IT'S SO PAINFUL!
WHAT KIND OF GODDESS IS THIS WOMAN?
HO HO HO
SHAKKA SHAKKA
THAT'S DUE TO A LACK OF VITAMINS!
BUT WHY?! I THOUGHT YOU WERE A DAUGHTER OF A WEALTHY FAMILY!
IT IS SO REFRESHING TO LIVE AS THE SIMPLE FOLK DO.
THAT'S A MISTAKE! IT'S HEDONISM!
HONESTLY, WHY DIDN'T YOU SAY SOMETHING SOONER?! I COULD HAVE BROUGHT YOU SOME HEALTHY FOOD!

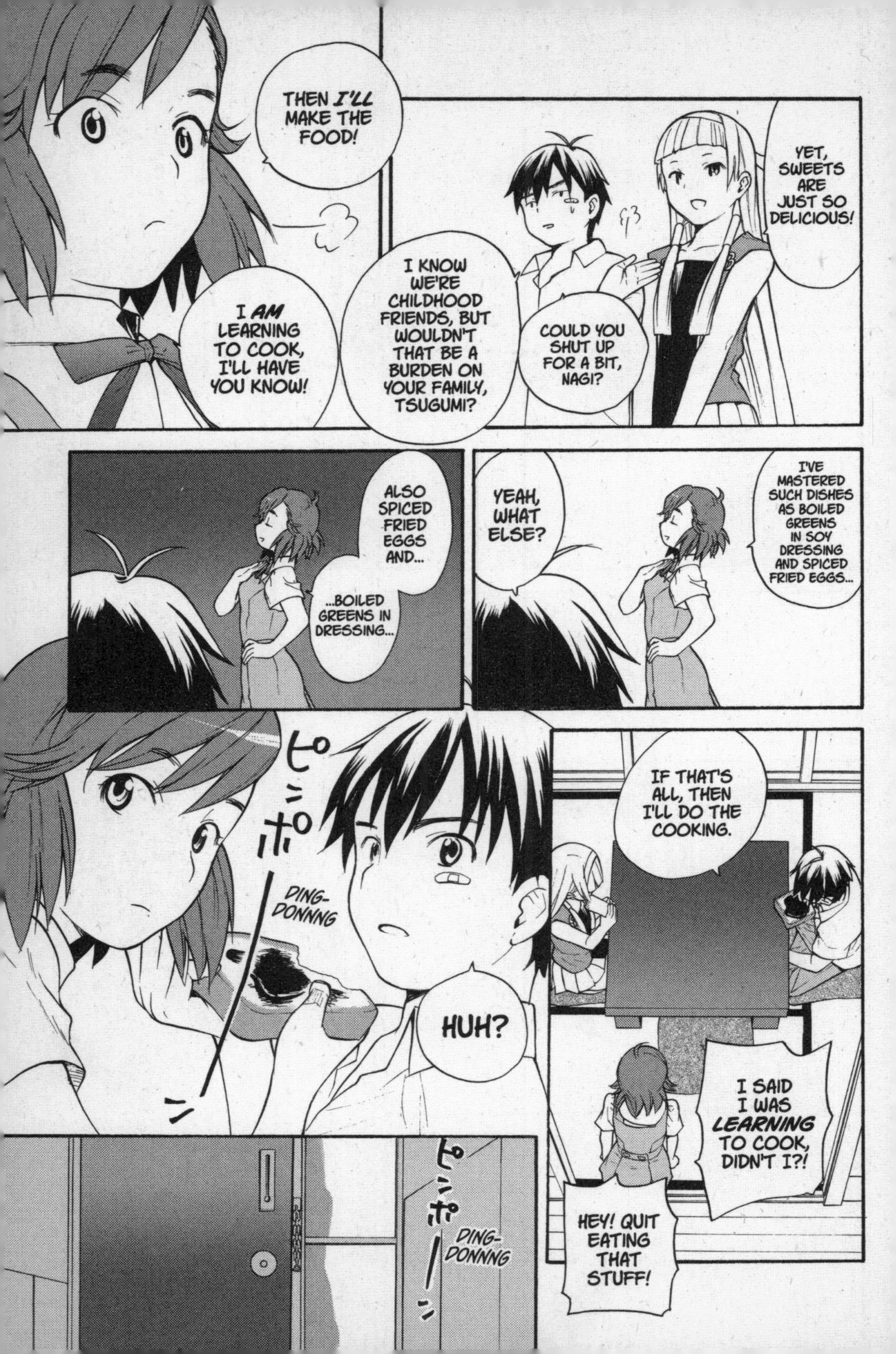
YET, SWEETS ARE JUST SO DELICIOUS!
COULD YOU SHUT UP FOR A BIT, NAGI?
I KNOW WE'RE CHILDHOOD FRIENDS, BUT WOULDN'T THAT BE A BURDEN ON YOUR FAMILY, TSUGUMI?
THEN *I'LL* MAKE THE FOOD!
I *AM* LEARNING TO COOK, I'LL HAVE YOU KNOW!
I'VE MASTERED SUCH DISHES AS BOILED GREENS IN SOY DRESSING AND SPICED FRIED EGGS...
YEAH, WHAT ELSE?
ALSO SPICED FRIED EGGS AND...
...BOILED GREENS IN DRESSING...
IF THAT'S ALL, THEN I'LL DO THE COOKING.
I SAID I WAS *LEARNING* TO COOK, DIDN'T I?!
HEY! QUIT EATING THAT STUFF!
DING-DONNNG
HUH?
DING-DONNNG

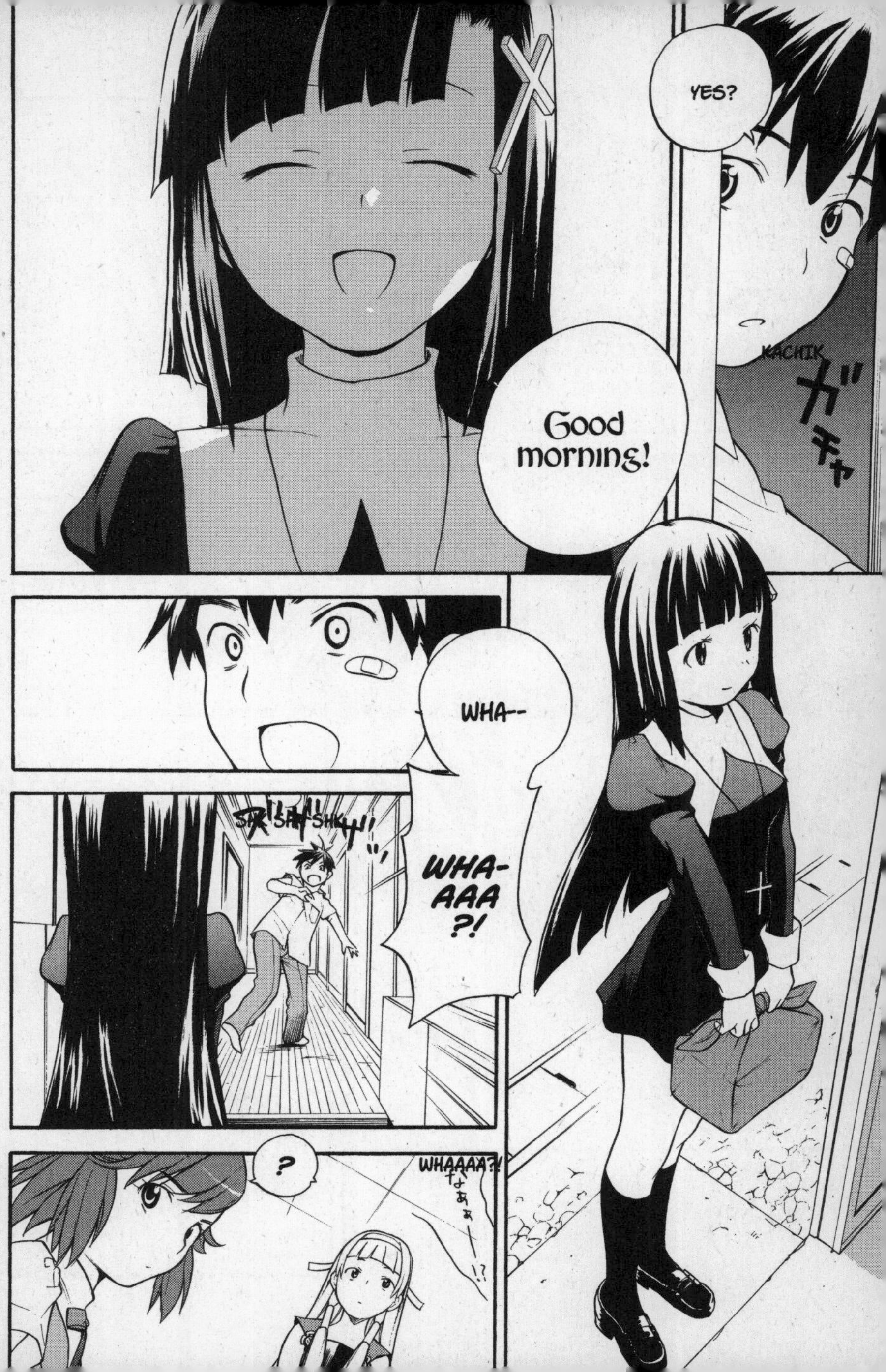

YES?
KACHIK
ガチャ
Good morning!
WHA--
WHA-AAA?!
?
WHAAAA?!

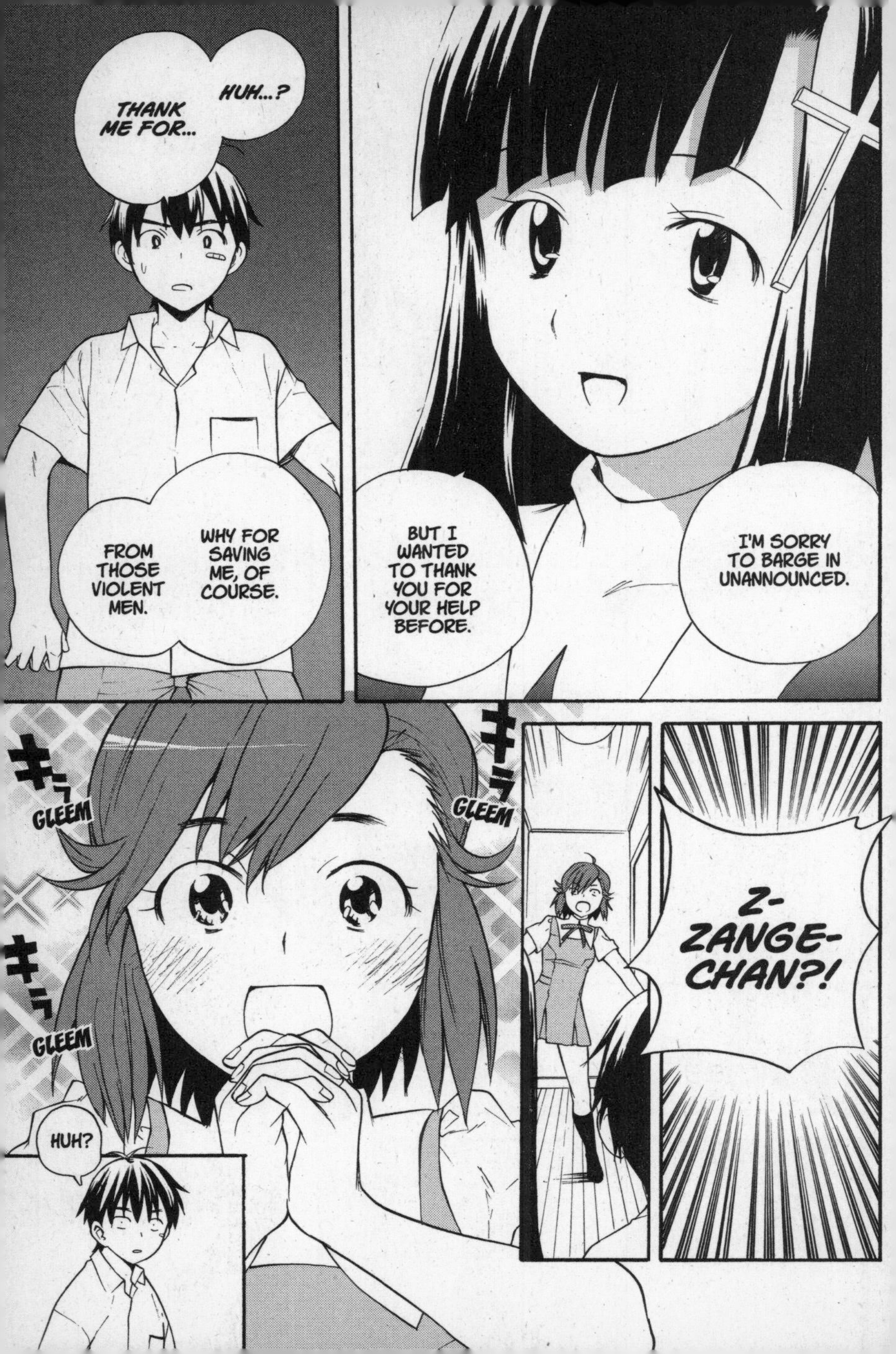
I'M SORRY TO BARGE IN UNANNOUNCED.
BUT I WANTED TO THANK YOU FOR YOUR HELP BEFORE.
HUH...?
THANK ME FOR...
WHY FOR SAVING ME, OF COURSE.
FROM THOSE VIOLENT MEN.
Z-ZANGE-CHAN?!
キラ
GLEEM
キラ
GLEEM
キラ
GLEEM
HUH?

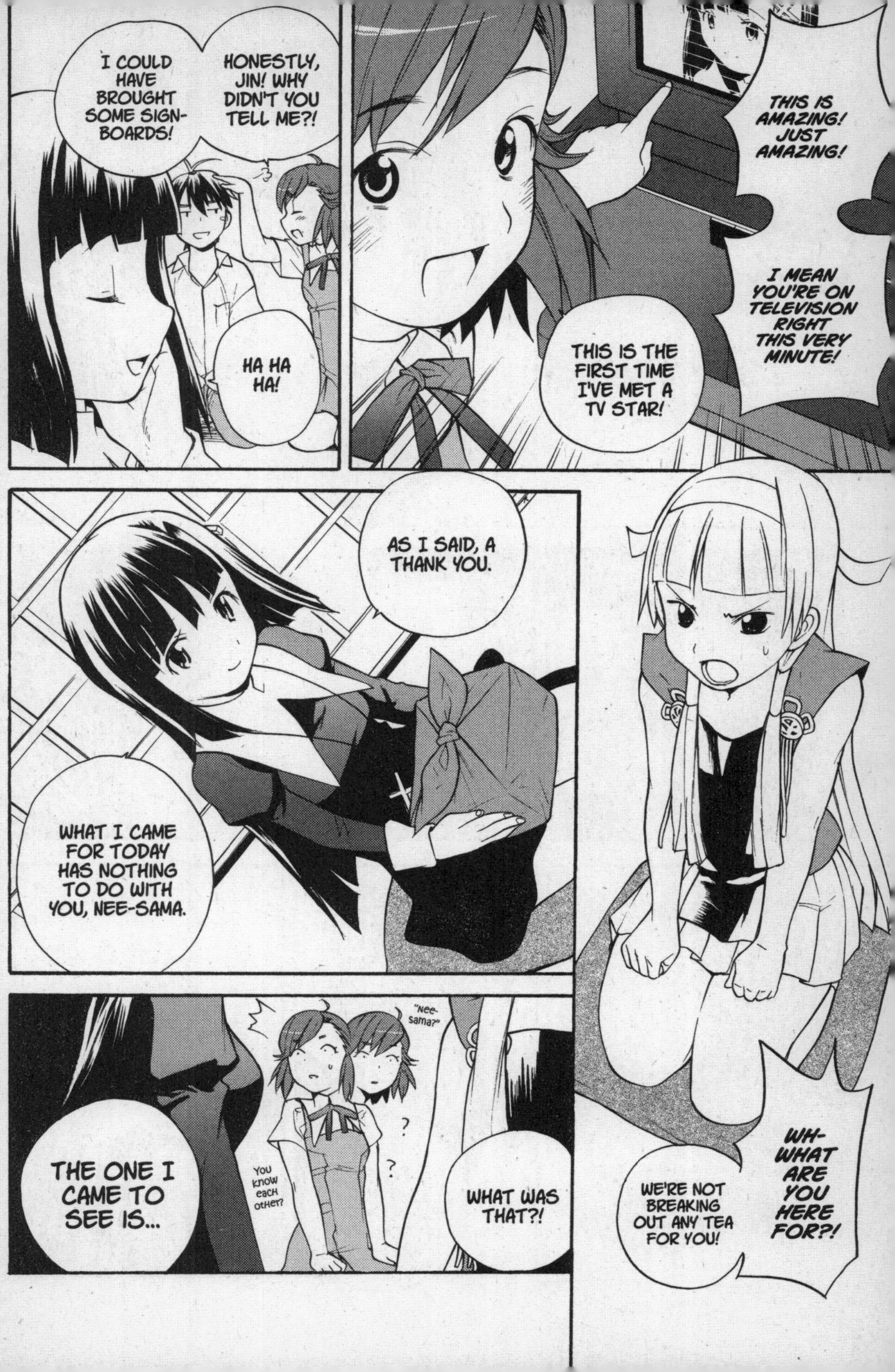
THIS IS AMAZING! JUST AMAZING!
I MEAN YOU'RE ON TELEVISION RIGHT THIS VERY MINUTE!
THIS IS THE FIRST TIME I'VE MET A TV STAR!
HONESTLY, JIN! WHY DIDN'T YOU TELL ME?!
I COULD HAVE BROUGHT SOME SIGN-BOARDS!
HA HA HA!
WH-WHAT ARE YOU HERE FOR?!
WE'RE NOT BREAKING OUT ANY TEA FOR YOU!
AS I SAID, A THANK YOU.
WHAT I CAME FOR TODAY HAS NOTHING TO DO WITH YOU, NEE-SAMA.
WHAT WAS THAT?!
"Nee-sama?"
?
?
You know each other?
THE ONE I CAME TO SEE IS...

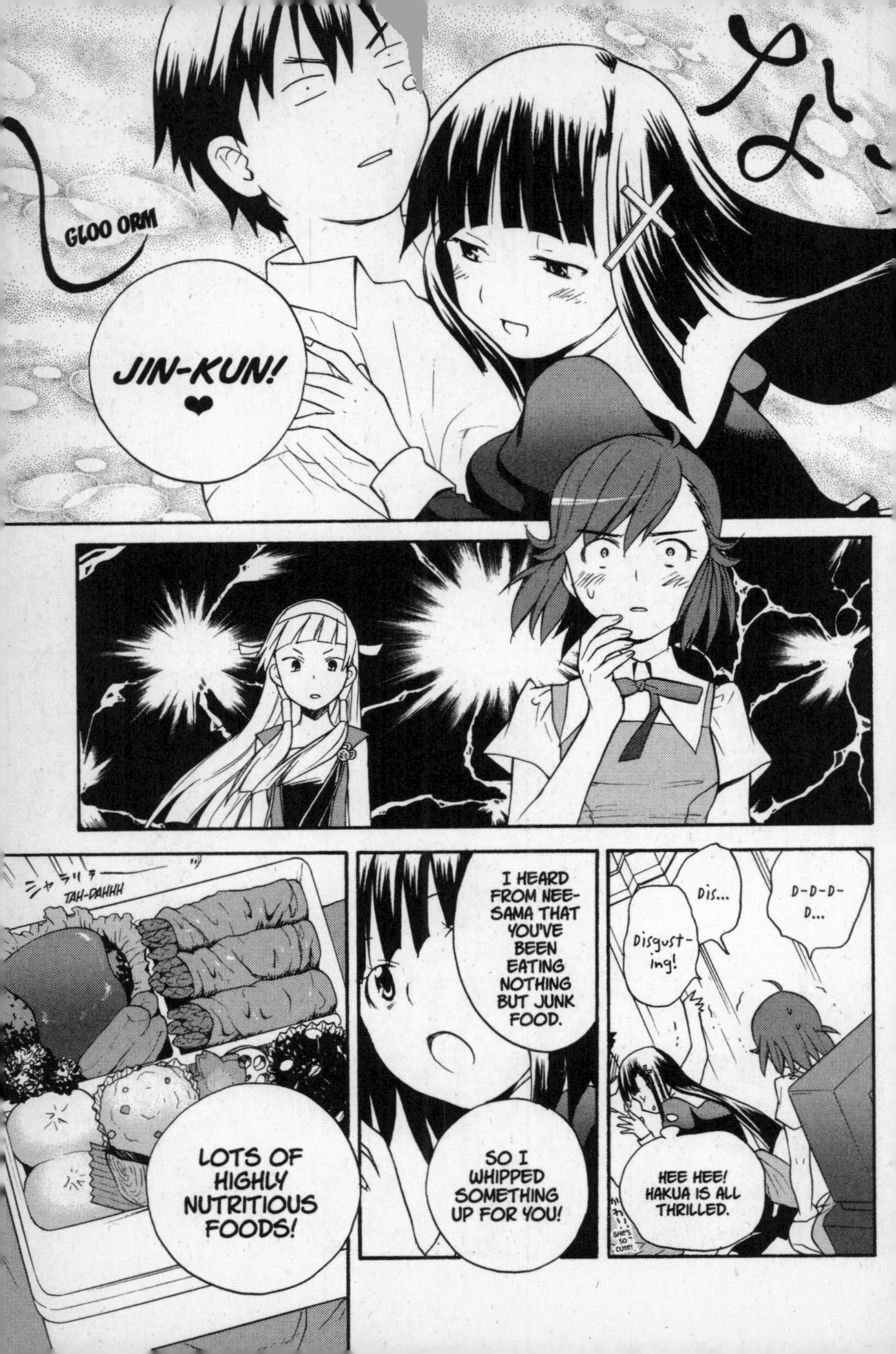
GLOO ORM
JIN-KUN! ❤
D-D-D-D...
Dis...
Disgust-ing!
HEE HEE! HAKUA IS ALL THRILLED.
SHE'S SO CUTE!
I HEARD FROM NEE-SAMA THAT YOU'VE BEEN EATING NOTHING BUT JUNK FOOD.
SO I WHIPPED SOMETHING UP FOR YOU!
シャラリラー
TAH-DAHHH
LOTS OF HIGHLY NUTRITIOUS FOODS!

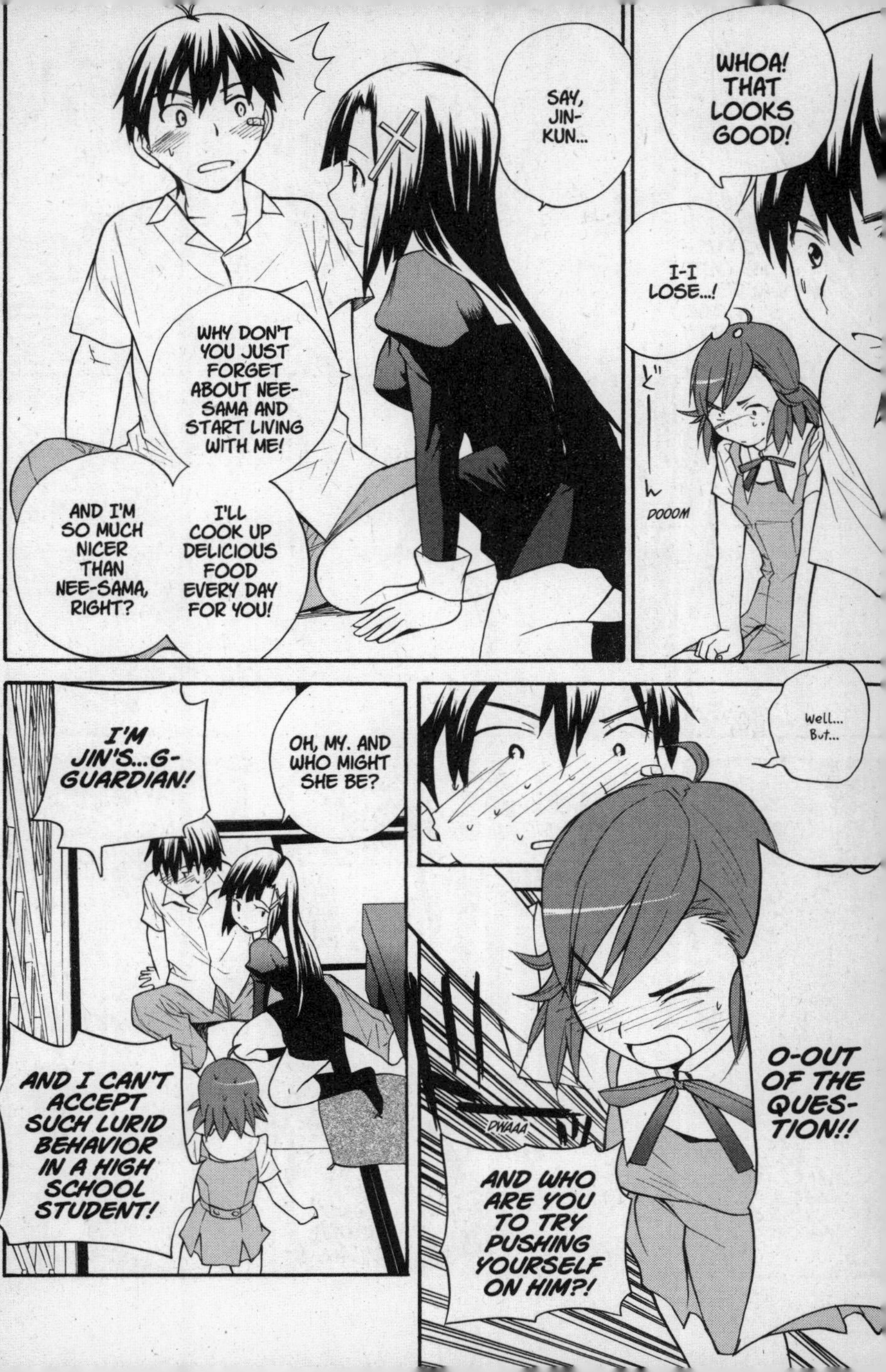
WHOA! THAT LOOKS GOOD!
I-I LOSE...!
DOOOM
SAY, JIN-KUN...
WHY DON'T YOU JUST FORGET ABOUT NEE-SAMA AND START LIVING WITH ME!
I'LL COOK UP DELICIOUS FOOD EVERY DAY FOR YOU!
AND I'M SO MUCH NICER THAN NEE-SAMA, RIGHT?
Well... But...
O-OUT OF THE QUES-TION!!
DWAAA
AND WHO ARE YOU TO TRY PUSHING YOURSELF ON HIM?!
OH, MY. AND WHO MIGHT SHE BE?
I'M JIN'S...G-GUARDIAN!
AND I CAN'T ACCEPT SUCH LURID BEHAVIOR IN A HIGH SCHOOL STUDENT!

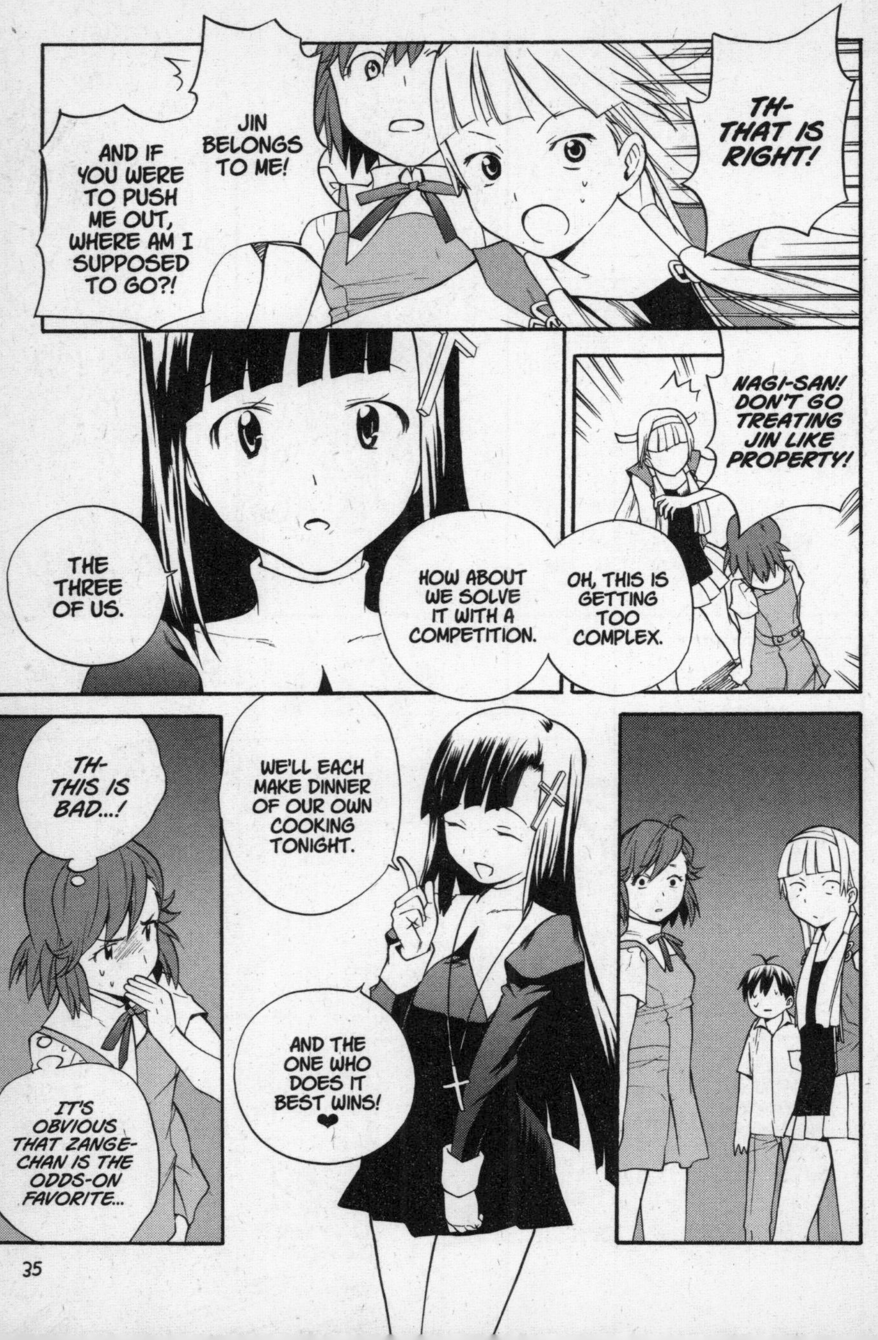
TH- THAT IS RIGHT!
JIN BELONGS TO ME!
AND IF YOU WERE TO PUSH ME OUT, WHERE AM I SUPPOSED TO GO?!
NAGI-SAN! DON'T GO TREATING JIN LIKE PROPERTY!
OH, THIS IS GETTING TOO COMPLEX.
HOW ABOUT WE SOLVE IT WITH A COMPETITION.
THE THREE OF US.
WE'LL EACH MAKE DINNER OF OUR OWN COOKING TONIGHT.
AND THE ONE WHO DOES IT BEST WINS! ❤
TH- THIS IS BAD...!
IT'S OBVIOUS THAT ZANGE-CHAN IS THE ODDS-ON FAVORITE...

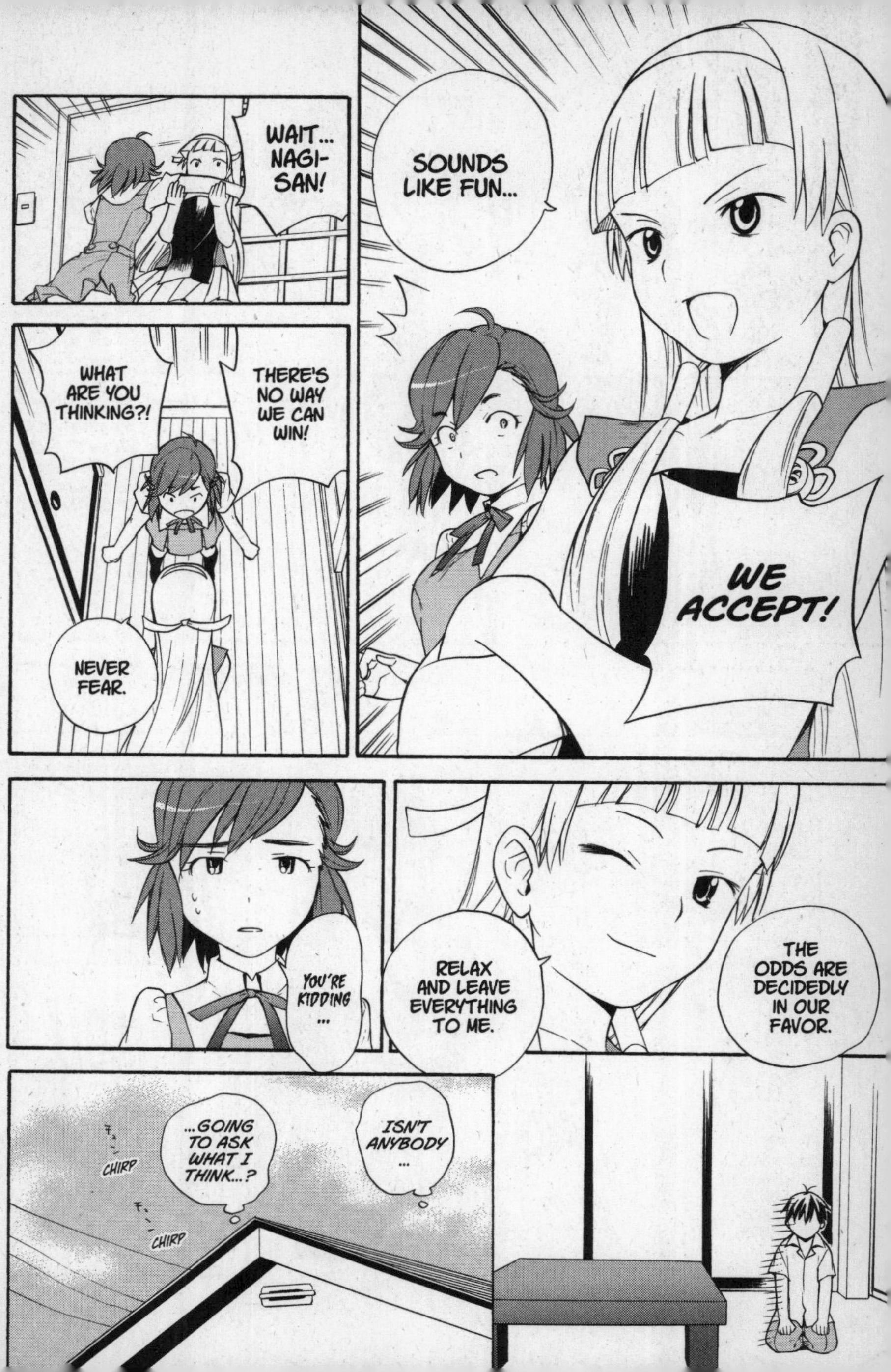
SOUNDS LIKE FUN...
WE ACCEPT!
WAIT... NAGI-SAN!
THERE'S NO WAY WE CAN WIN!
WHAT ARE YOU THINKING?!
NEVER FEAR.
THE ODDS ARE DECIDEDLY IN OUR FAVOR.
RELAX AND LEAVE EVERYTHING TO ME.
YOU'RE KIDDING...
ISN'T ANYBODY...
...GOING TO ASK WHAT I THINK...?
CHIRP
CHIRP

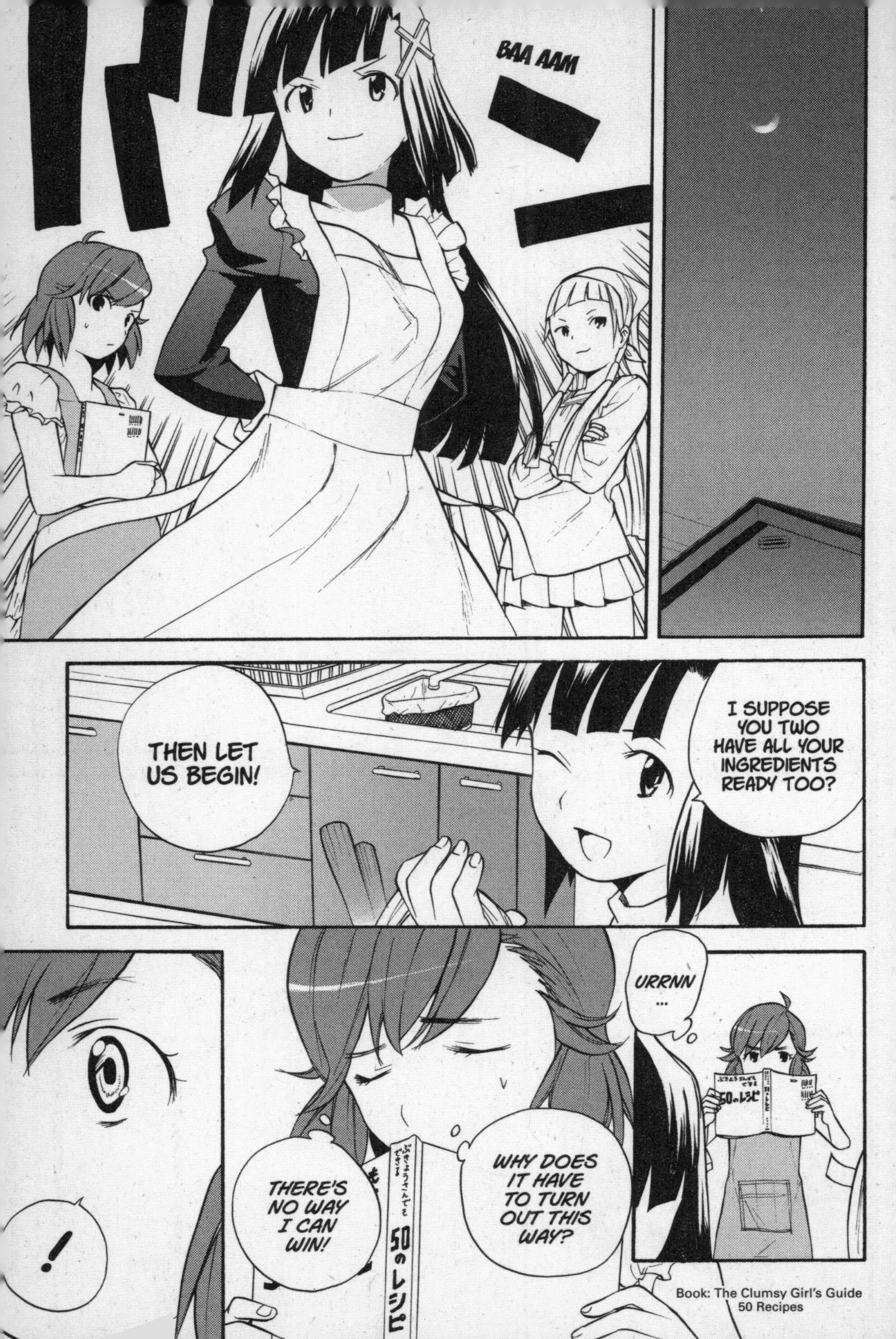
BAA AAM
I SUPPOSE YOU TWO HAVE ALL YOUR INGREDIENTS READY TOO?
THEN LET US BEGIN!
URRNN ...
50のレシピ
Book: The Clumsy Girl's Guide 50 Recipes
WHY DOES IT HAVE TO TURN OUT THIS WAY?
THERE'S NO WAY I CAN WIN!
50のレシピ
!

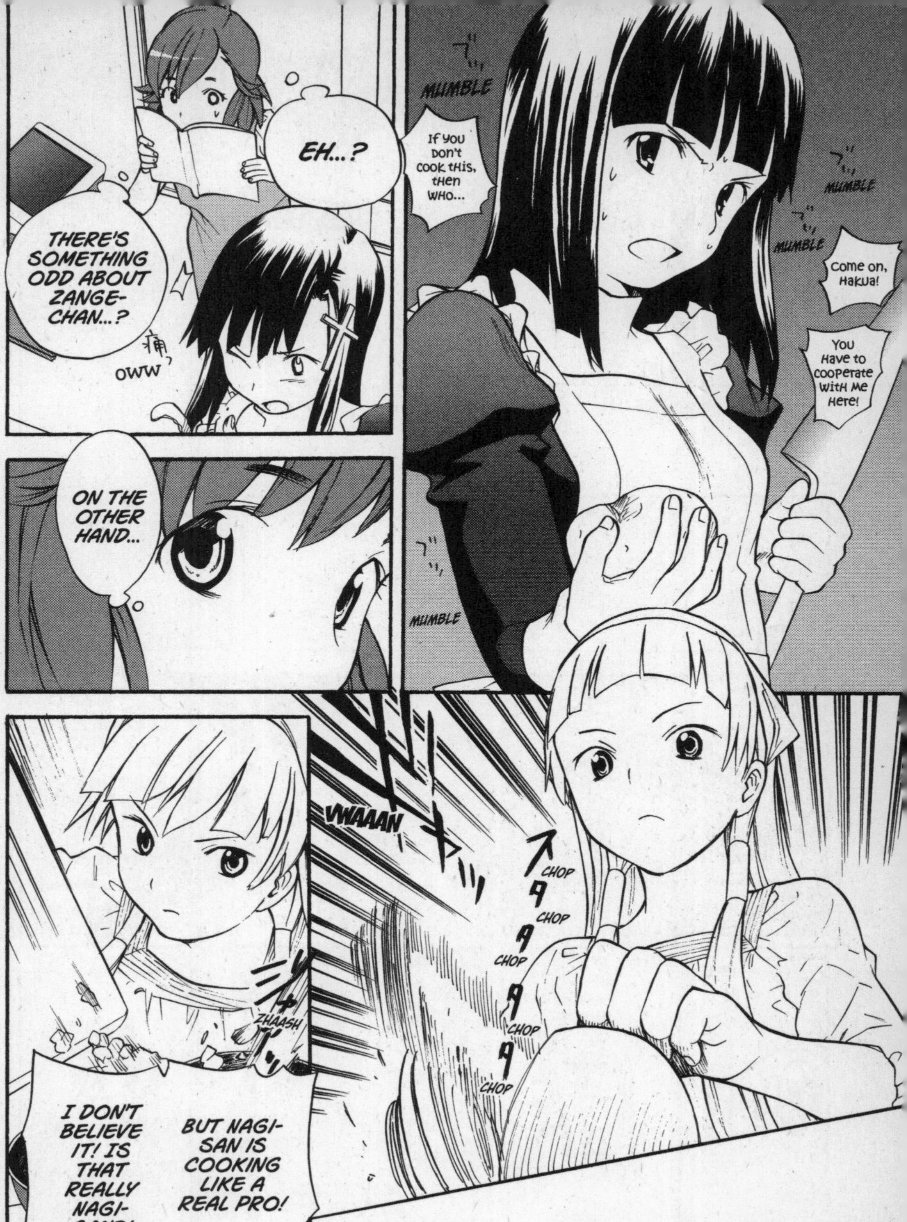
MUMBLE
MUMBLE
Come on, Hakua!
You have to cooperate with me here!
MUMBLE
If you don't cook this, then who...
MUMBLE
EH...?
THERE'S SOMETHING ODD ABOUT ZANGE-CHAN...?
痛
OWW
ON THE OTHER HAND...
CHOP
CHOP
CHOP
CHOP
CHOP
VWAAAN
ZHAASH
BUT NAGI-SAN IS COOKING LIKE A REAL PRO!
I DON'T BELIEVE IT! IS THAT REALLY NAGI-SAN?!

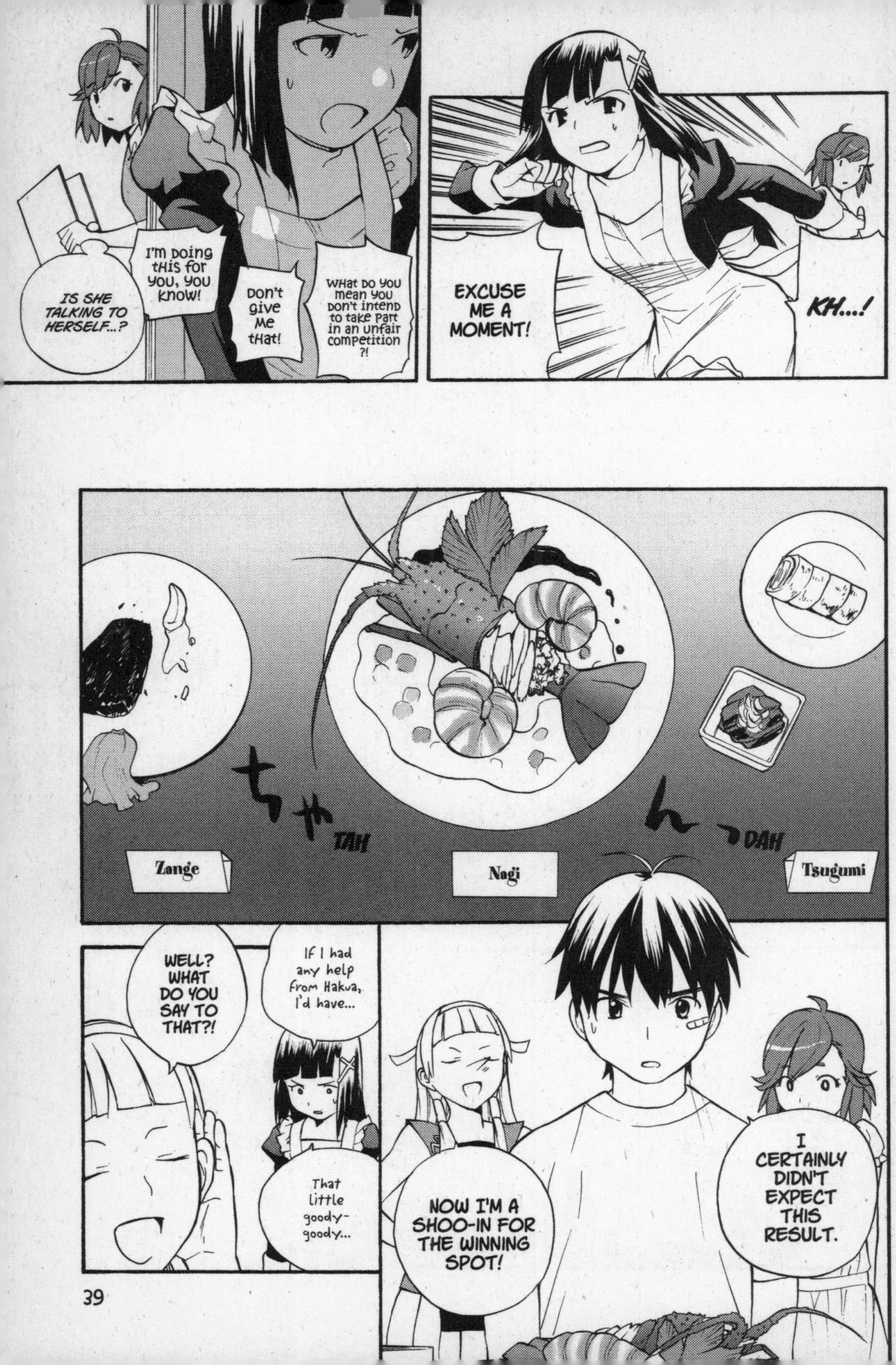
KH...!
EXCUSE ME A MOMENT!
What do you mean you don't intend to take part in an unfair competition?!
Don't give me that!
I'm doing this for you, you know!
IS SHE TALKING TO HERSELF...?
DAH
Tsugumi
Nagi
TAH
Zange
I CERTAINLY DIDN'T EXPECT THIS RESULT.
NOW I'M A SHOO-IN FOR THE WINNING SPOT!
If I had any help from Hakua, I'd have...
WELL? WHAT DO YOU SAY TO THAT?!
That little goody-goody...

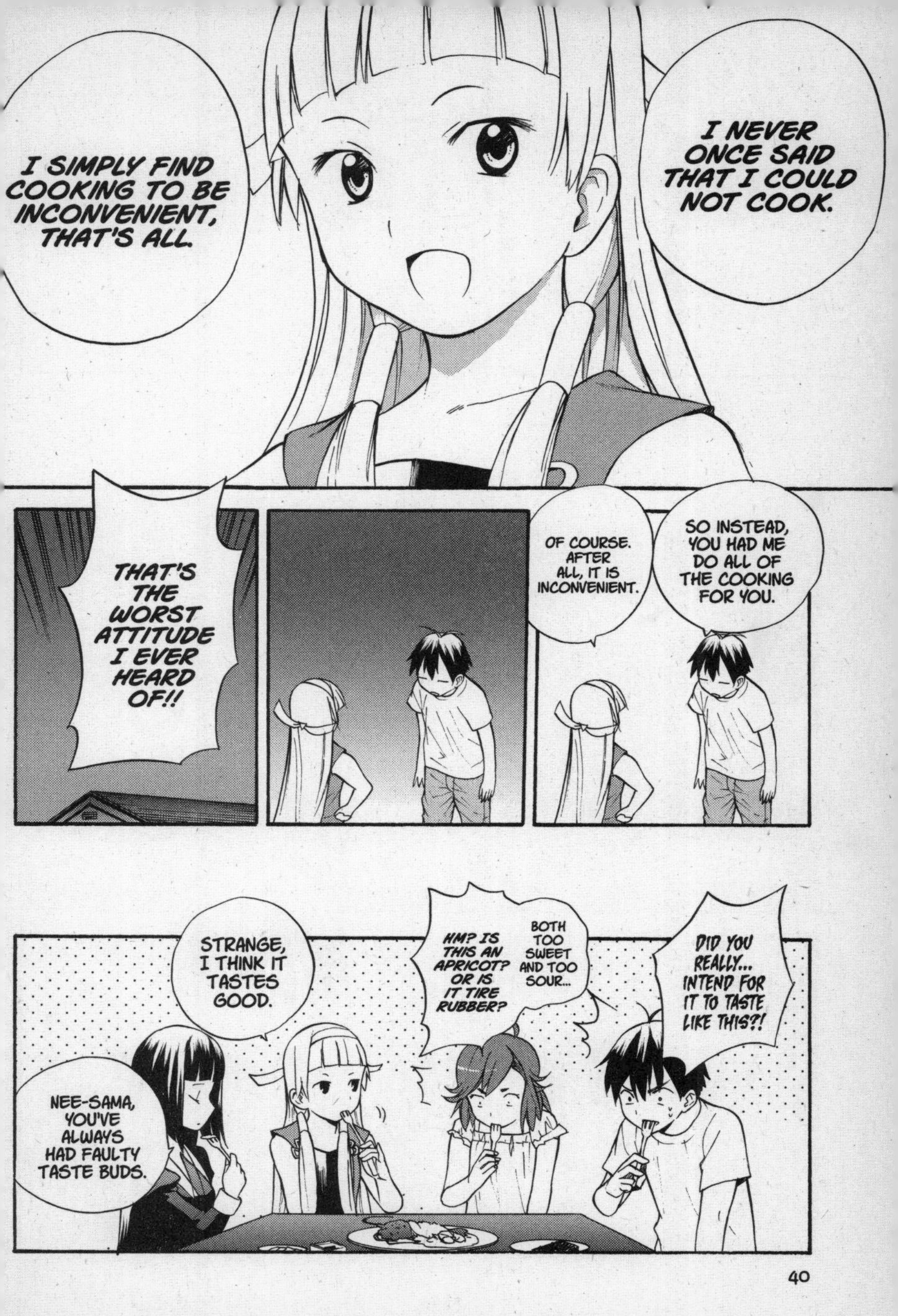
I NEVER ONCE SAID THAT I COULD NOT COOK.
I SIMPLY FIND COOKING TO BE INCONVENIENT, THAT'S ALL.
SO INSTEAD, YOU HAD ME DO ALL OF THE COOKING FOR YOU.
OF COURSE. AFTER ALL, IT IS INCONVENIENT.
THAT'S THE WORST ATTITUDE I EVER HEARD OF!!
DID YOU REALLY... INTEND FOR IT TO TASTE LIKE THIS?!
BOTH TOO SWEET AND TOO SOUR...
HM? IS THIS AN APRICOT? OR IS IT TIRE RUBBER?
STRANGE, I THINK IT TASTES GOOD.
NEE-SAMA, YOU'VE ALWAYS HAD FAULTY TASTE BUDS.

K A N N A G I

Tastes a little like cypress trees... A little like stomach medicine...

AH, but maybe if I got used to it, it could be good?

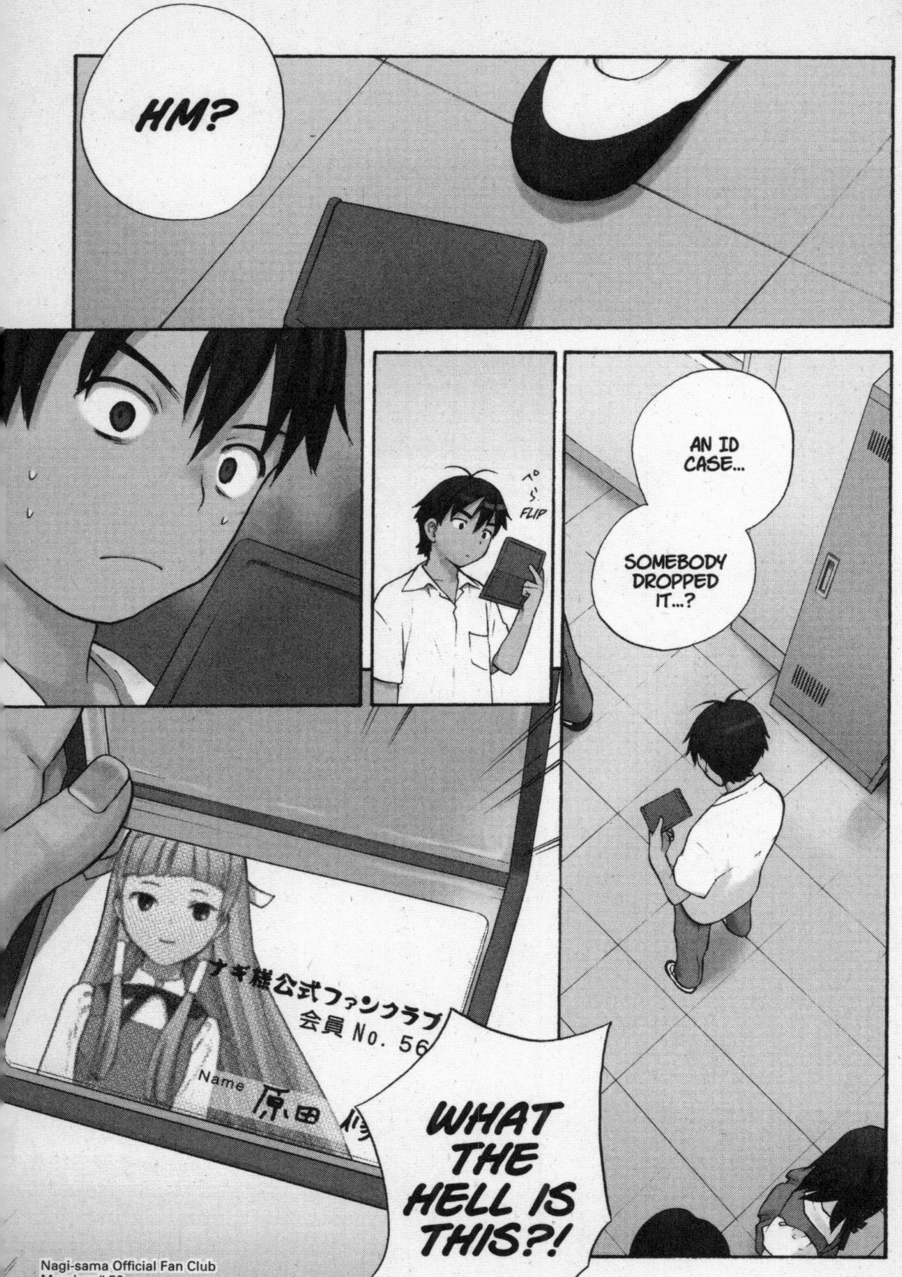
HM?
AN ID CASE...
SOMEBODY DROPPED IT...?
ぺら
FLIP
ナギ様公式ファンクラブ
会員 No. 56
Name 原田
WHAT THE HELL IS THIS?!

Nagi-sama Official Fan Club
Member # 56
[“Name” in English] [hand writing] Herada, Osamu [cut off]

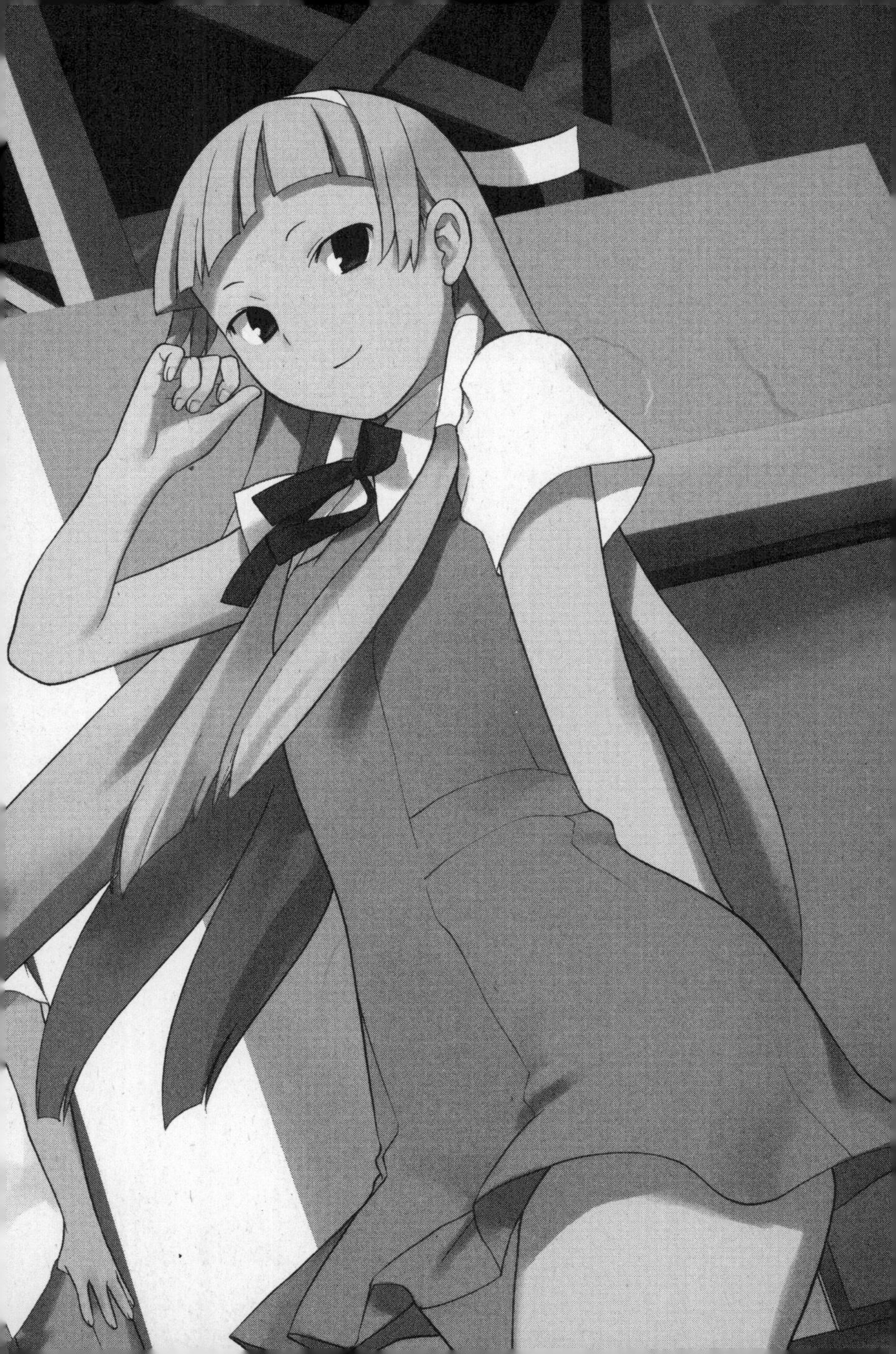

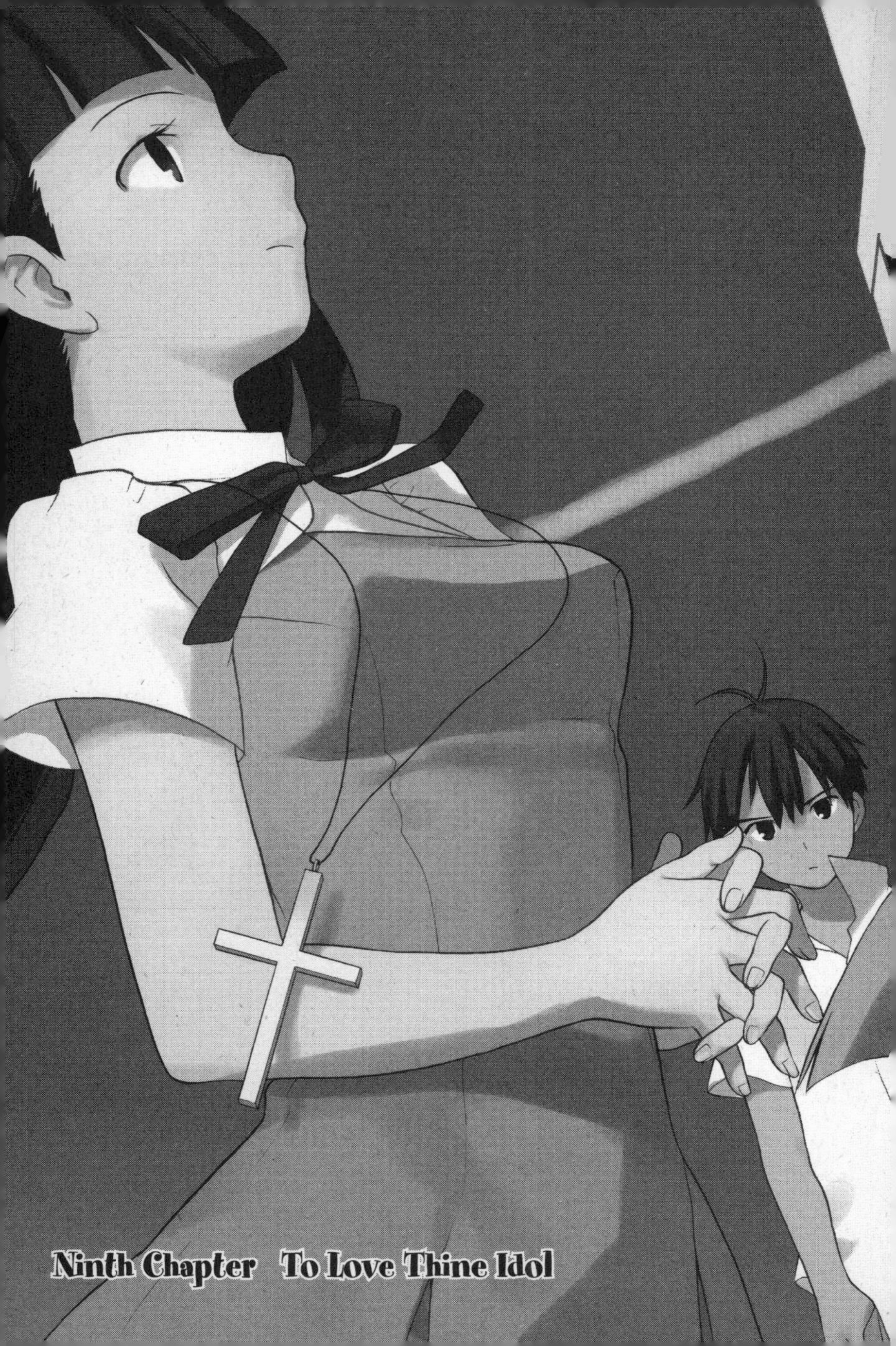

Ninth Chapter To Love Thine Idol

● Nagi-sama Official Fan Club Card

If you go to the Fan Club Home Page and fill in your name and address, they will mail you yours. It's a plastic card.
Special Features: It has no magnetic strip upon which any information is contained. It is simply for you to proclaim your pride in being a fan. You write your own name in the name portion of the card.
Nagi was nice enough to bring one of her own photos for use on the card.

表

Front

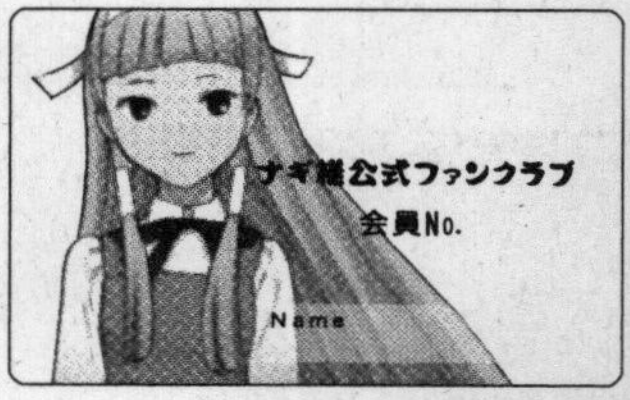

ナギ様公式ファンクラブ
会員No.
Name

Nagi-sama Official Fan Club
Member No.
Name

裏

Back

ナギ様公式ファンクラブ会員カード所持上の注意

1.署名無きカードは会員カードとしての効力を認めません。
2.カードに有効期限はありません。
3.第三者への貸与、譲渡を禁じます。
4.みだりに関係者以外（特に教師）へ公開しないこと。
5.カードの紛失・盗難等について当ファンクラブは
一切の責任を負いません。

Things to be aware of when carrying the Nagi-sama Official Fan Club Membership Card

1. Unsigned cards are not considered official fan club cards.
2. There is no expiration date for this card.
3. It is forbidden to sell this card or transfer membership.
4. Unauthorized revelation of this card to non-members (especially teachers) is strictly prohibited.
5. The Fan Club assumes no responsibility for lost or stolen cards.

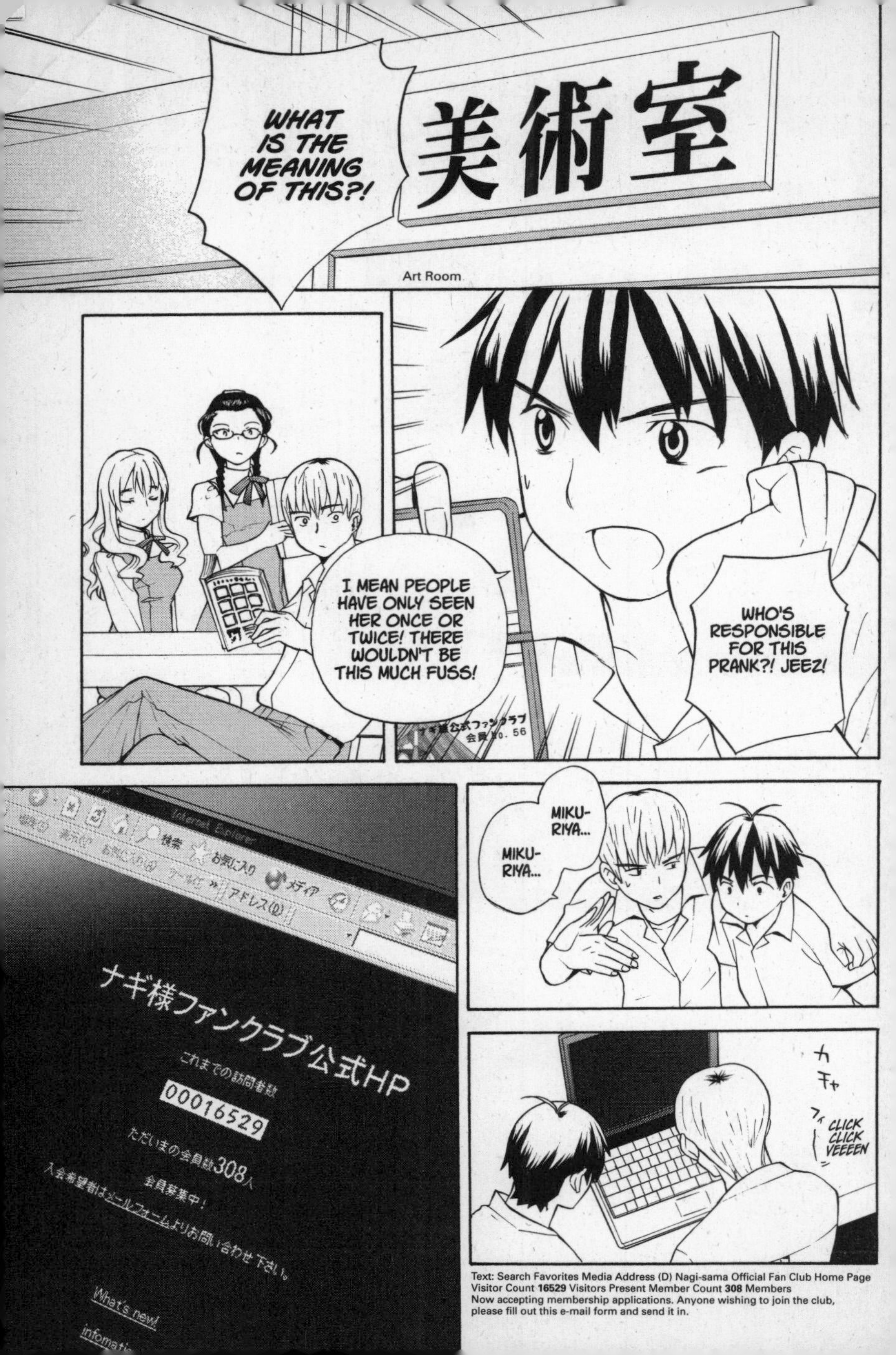
WHAT IS THE MEANING OF THIS?!
美術室
Art Room
WHO'S RESPONSIBLE FOR THIS PRANK?! JEEZ!
ナギ様公式ファンクラブ
会員No. 56
I MEAN PEOPLE HAVE ONLY SEEN HER ONCE OR TWICE! THERE WOULDN'T BE THIS MUCH FUSS!
MIKU-RIYA...
MIKU-RIYA...
カチャ
フィー
CLICK CLICK VEEEEN
Internet Explorer
検索
お気に入り
メディア
アドレス(D)
ナギ様ファンクラブ公式HP
これまでの訪問者数
00016529
ただいまの会員数308人
会員募集中！
入会希望者はメールフォームよりお問い合わせ下さい。
What's new!
Text: Search Favorites Media Address (D) Nagi-sama Official Fan Club Home Page Visitor Count 16529 Visitors Present Member Count 308 Members Now accepting membership applications. Anyone wishing to join the club, please fill out this e-mail form and send it in.

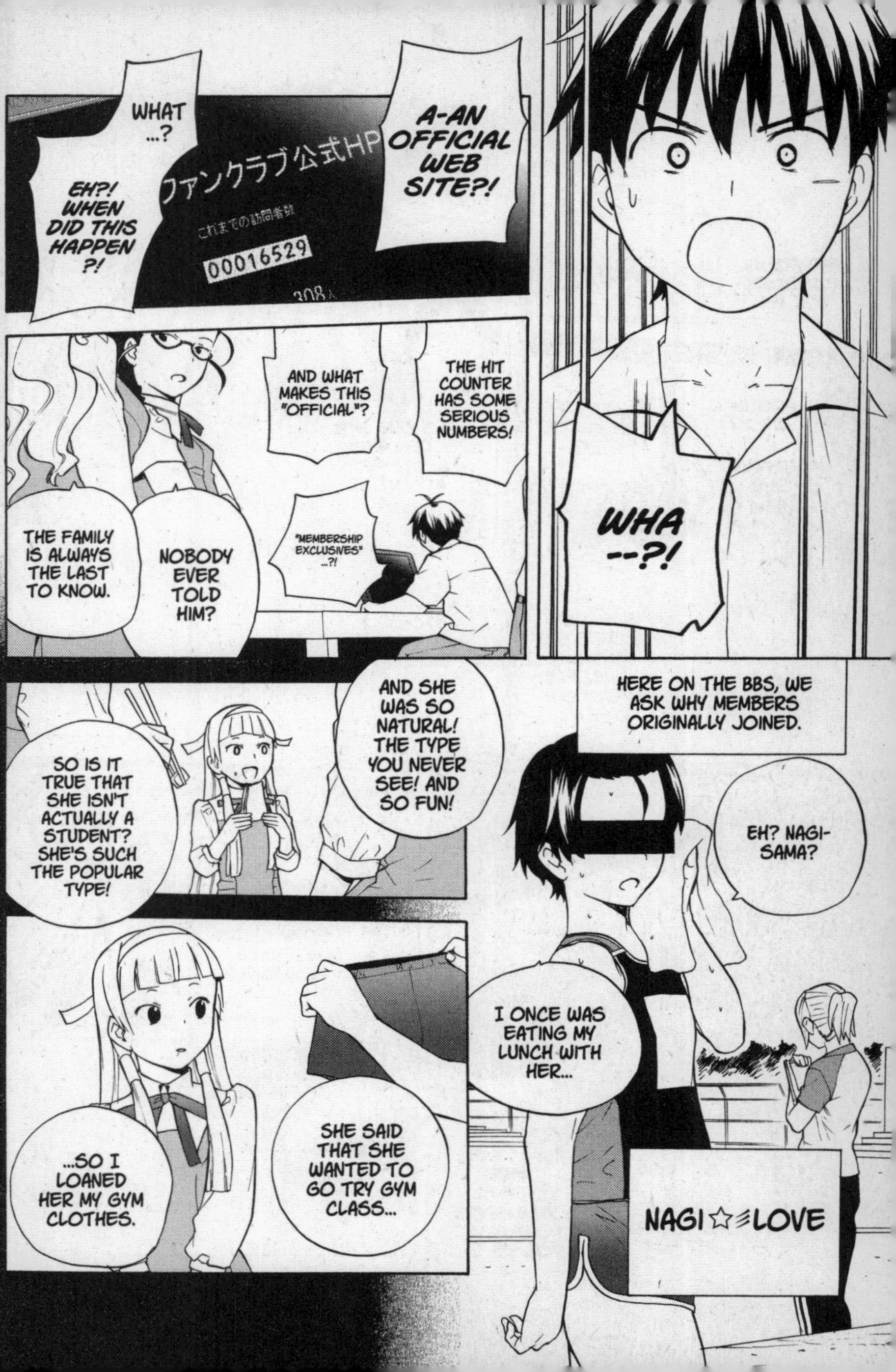
WHA--?!
A-AN OFFICIAL WEB SITE?!
WHAT ...?
ファンクラブ公式HP
これまでの訪問者数
00016529
EH?! WHEN DID THIS HAPPEN ?!
THE HIT COUNTER HAS SOME SERIOUS NUMBERS!
AND WHAT MAKES THIS "OFFICIAL"?
"MEMBERSHIP EXCLUSIVES" ...?!
NOBODY EVER TOLD HIM?
THE FAMILY IS ALWAYS THE LAST TO KNOW.
HERE ON THE BBS, WE ASK WHY MEMBERS ORIGINALLY JOINED.
EH? NAGI-SAMA?
I ONCE WAS EATING MY LUNCH WITH HER...
NAGI☆≡LOVE
AND SHE WAS SO NATURAL! THE TYPE YOU NEVER SEE! AND SO FUN!
SO IS IT TRUE THAT SHE ISN'T ACTUALLY A STUDENT? SHE'S SUCH THE POPULAR TYPE!
SHE SAID THAT SHE WANTED TO GO TRY GYM CLASS...
...SO I LOANED HER MY GYM CLOTHES.

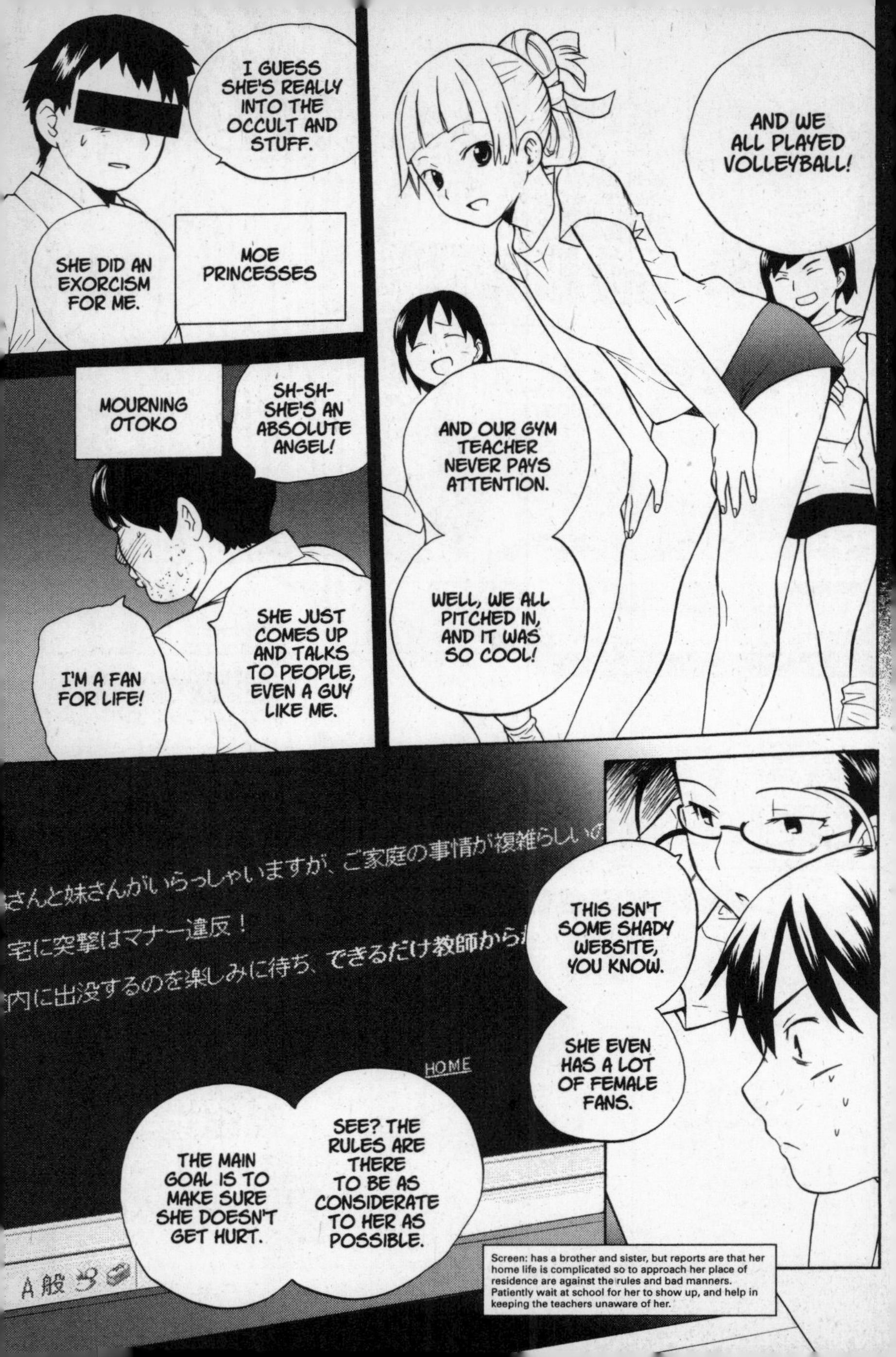
AND WE ALL PLAYED VOLLEYBALL!
AND OUR GYM TEACHER NEVER PAYS ATTENTION.
WELL, WE ALL PITCHED IN, AND IT WAS SO COOL!
I GUESS SHE'S REALLY INTO THE OCCULT AND STUFF.
MOE PRINCESSES
SHE DID AN EXORCISM FOR ME.
SH-SH-SHE'S AN ABSOLUTE ANGEL!
MOURNING OTOKO
SHE JUST COMES UP AND TALKS TO PEOPLE, EVEN A GUY LIKE ME.
I'M A FAN FOR LIFE!
THIS ISN'T SOME SHADY WEBSITE, YOU KNOW.
SHE EVEN HAS A LOT OF FEMALE FANS.
さんと妹さんがいらっしゃいますが、ご家庭の事情が複雑らしいの
宅に突撃はマナー違反！
内に出没するのを楽しみに待ち、できるだけ教師から
HOME
SEE? THE RULES ARE THERE TO BE AS CONSIDERATE TO HER AS POSSIBLE.
THE MAIN GOAL IS TO MAKE SURE SHE DOESN'T GET HURT.
A 般
Screen: has a brother and sister, but reports are that her home life is complicated so to approach her place of residence are against the rules and bad manners. Patiently wait at school for her to show up, and help in keeping the teachers unaware of her.

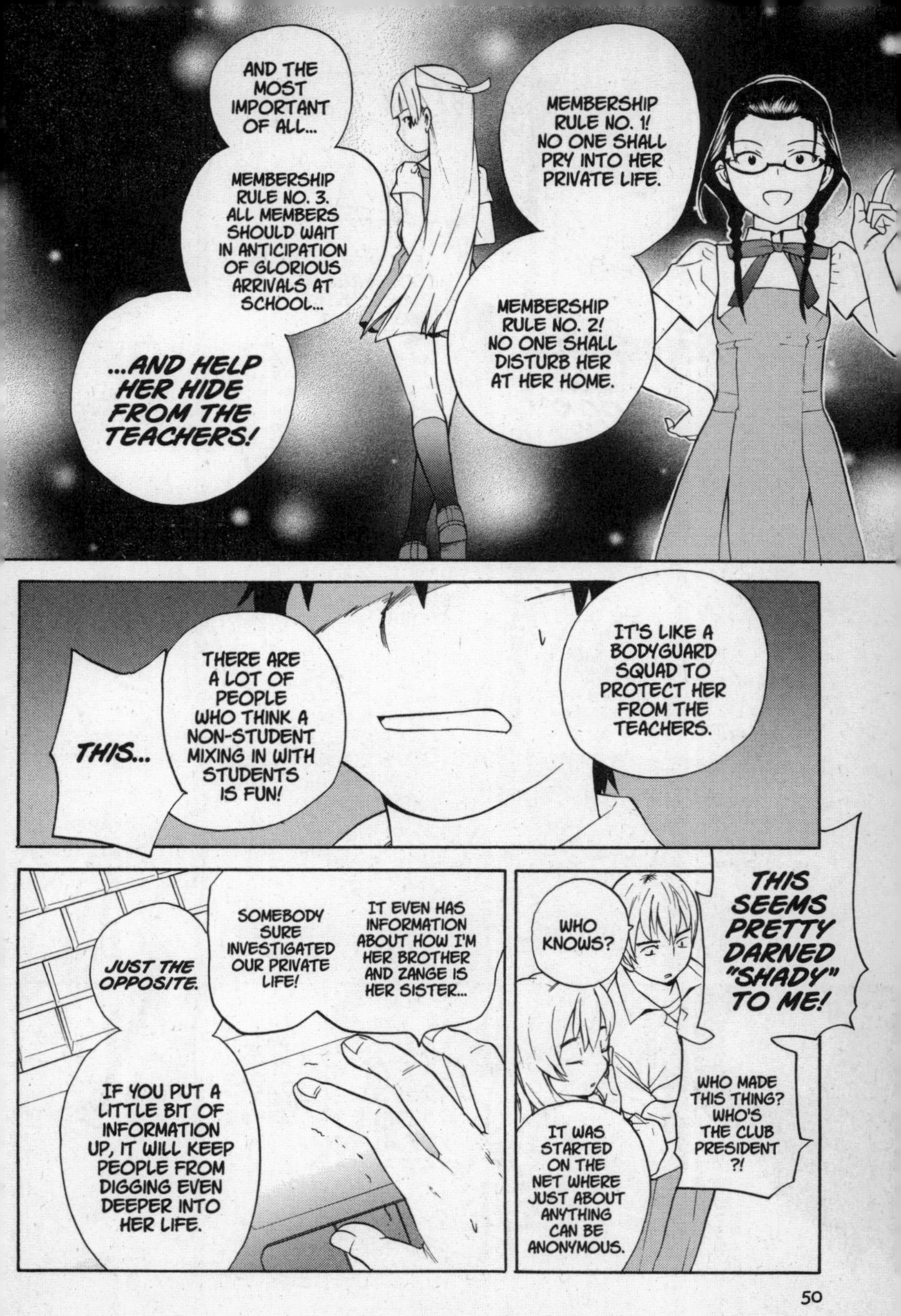
MEMBERSHIP RULE NO. 1! NO ONE SHALL PRY INTO HER PRIVATE LIFE.
MEMBERSHIP RULE NO. 2! NO ONE SHALL DISTURB HER AT HER HOME.
AND THE MOST IMPORTANT OF ALL...
MEMBERSHIP RULE NO. 3. ALL MEMBERS SHOULD WAIT IN ANTICIPATION OF GLORIOUS ARRIVALS AT SCHOOL...
...AND HELP HER HIDE FROM THE TEACHERS!
IT'S LIKE A BODYGUARD SQUAD TO PROTECT HER FROM THE TEACHERS.
THERE ARE A LOT OF PEOPLE WHO THINK A NON-STUDENT MIXING IN WITH STUDENTS IS FUN!
THIS...
THIS SEEMS PRETTY DARNED "SHADY" TO ME!
WHO MADE THIS THING? WHO'S THE CLUB PRESIDENT ?!
WHO KNOWS?
IT WAS STARTED ON THE NET WHERE JUST ABOUT ANYTHING CAN BE ANONYMOUS.
SOMEBODY SURE INVESTIGATED OUR PRIVATE LIFE!
IT EVEN HAS INFORMATION ABOUT HOW I'M HER BROTHER AND ZANGE IS HER SISTER...
JUST THE OPPOSITE.
IF YOU PUT A LITTLE BIT OF INFORMATION UP, IT WILL KEEP PEOPLE FROM DIGGING EVEN DEEPER INTO HER LIFE.

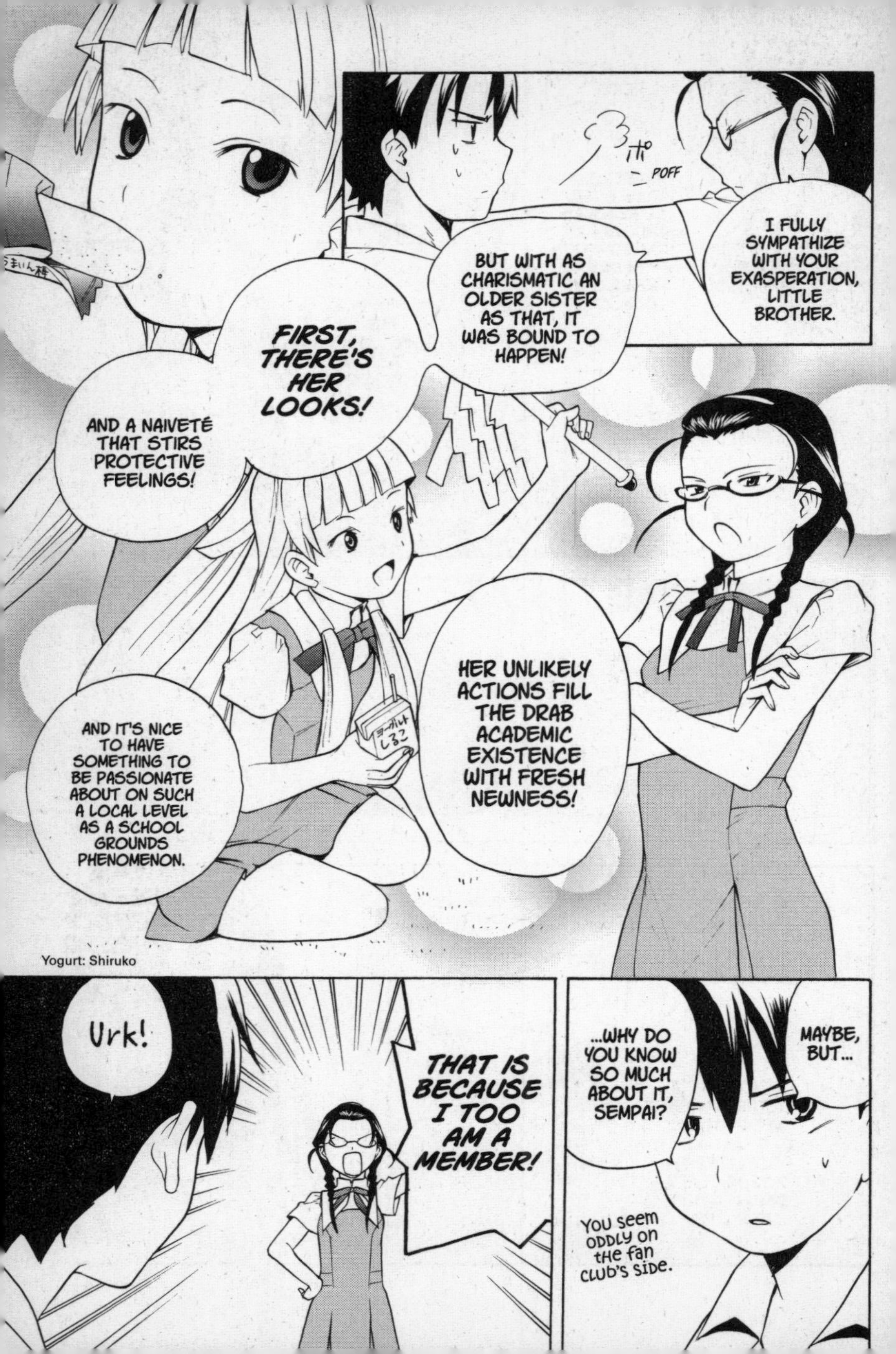
ポ
POFF
I FULLY SYMPATHIZE WITH YOUR EXASPERATION, LITTLE BROTHER.
BUT WITH AS CHARISMATIC AN OLDER SISTER AS THAT, IT WAS BOUND TO HAPPEN!
FIRST, THERE'S HER LOOKS!
AND A NAIVETÉ THAT STIRS PROTECTIVE FEELINGS!
HER UNLIKELY ACTIONS FILL THE DRAB ACADEMIC EXISTENCE WITH FRESH NEWNESS!
ヨーグルト しるこ
AND IT'S NICE TO HAVE SOMETHING TO BE PASSIONATE ABOUT ON SUCH A LOCAL LEVEL AS A SCHOOL GROUNDS PHENOMENON.
MAYBE, BUT...
...WHY DO YOU KNOW SO MUCH ABOUT IT, SEMPAI?
You seem oddly on the fan club's side.
THAT IS BECAUSE I TOO AM A MEMBER!
Urk!
Yogurt: Shiruko

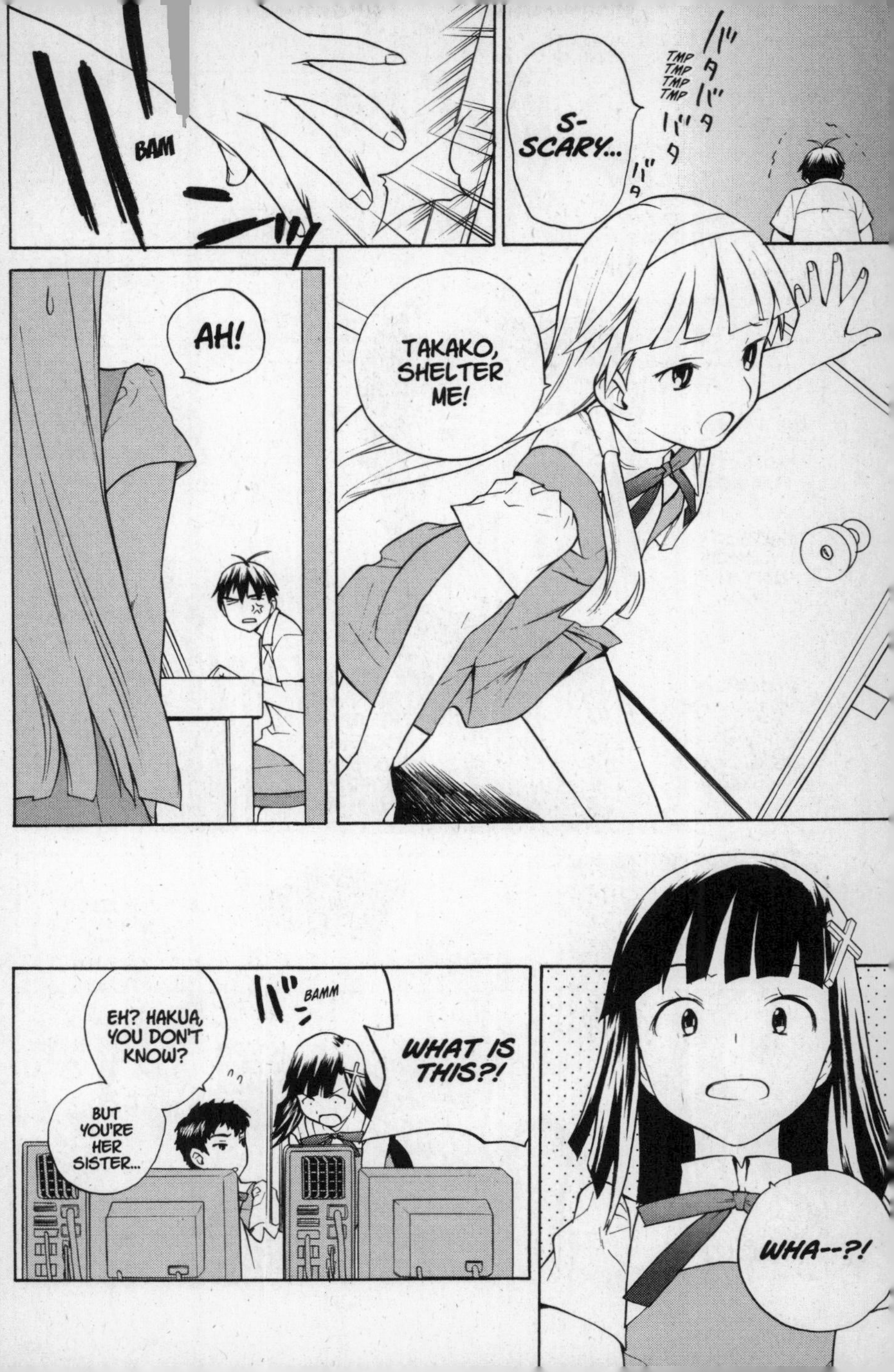
S-SCARY...
TMP TMP TMP TMP
BAM
TAKAKO, SHELTER ME!
AH!
WHA--?!
WHAT IS THIS?!
BAMM
EH? HAKUA, YOU DON'T KNOW?
BUT YOU'RE HER SISTER...

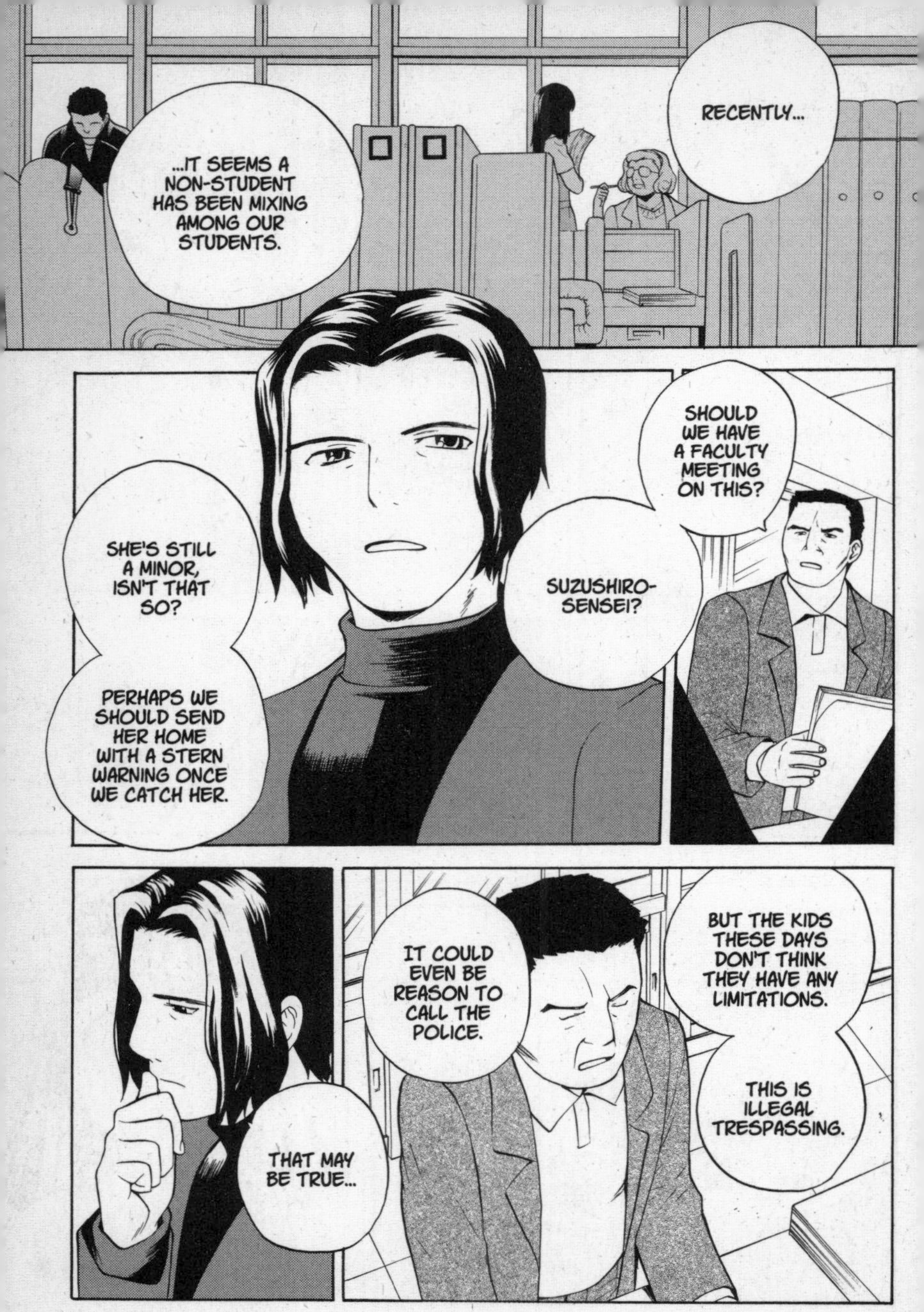
RECENTLY...
...IT SEEMS A NON-STUDENT HAS BEEN MIXING AMONG OUR STUDENTS.
SHOULD WE HAVE A FACULTY MEETING ON THIS?
SUZUSHIRO-SENSEI?
SHE'S STILL A MINOR, ISN'T THAT SO?
PERHAPS WE SHOULD SEND HER HOME WITH A STERN WARNING ONCE WE CATCH HER.
BUT THE KIDS THESE DAYS DON'T THINK THEY HAVE ANY LIMITATIONS.
THIS IS ILLEGAL TRESPASSING.
IT COULD EVEN BE REASON TO CALL THE POLICE.
THAT MAY BE TRUE...

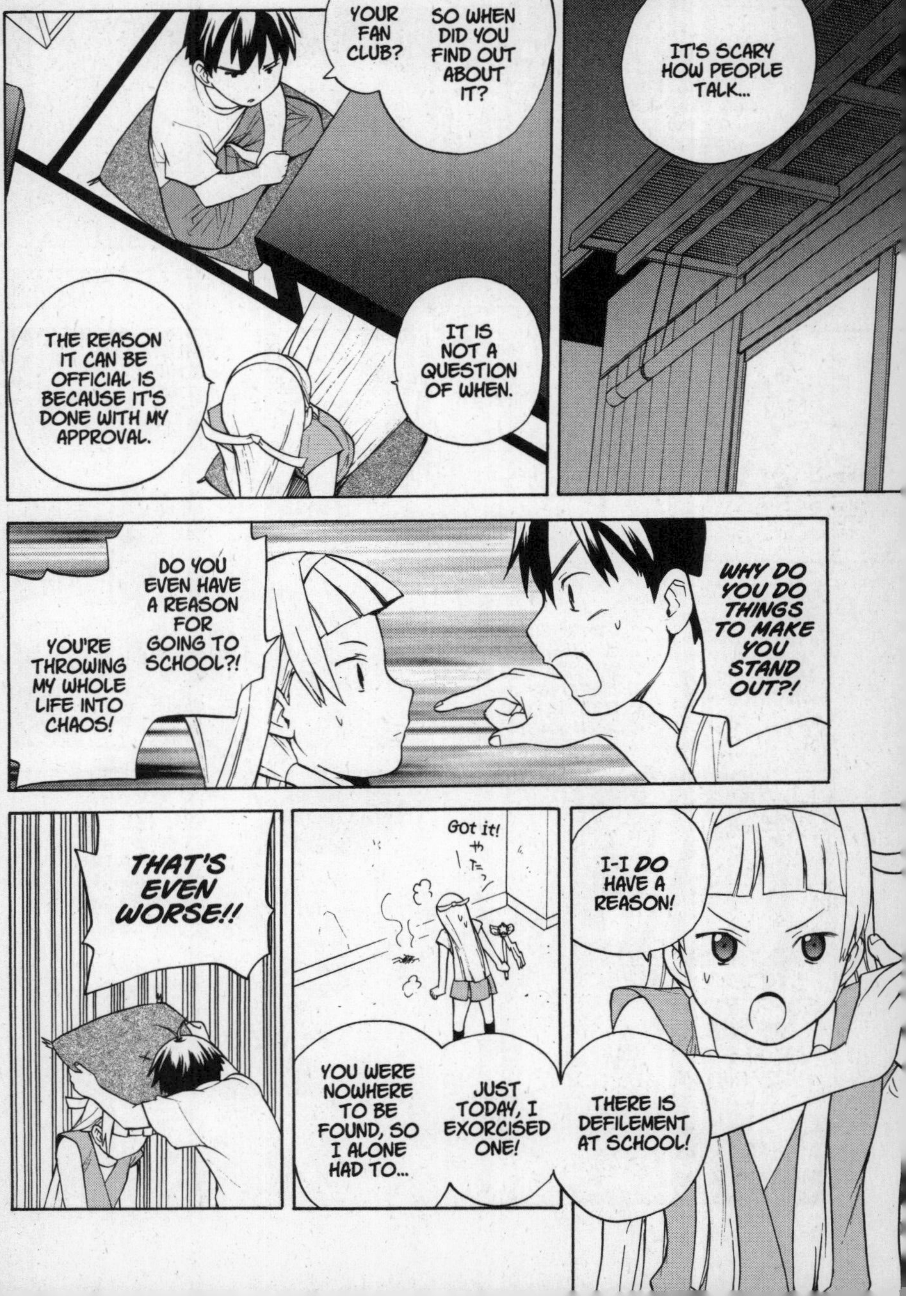
IT'S SCARY HOW PEOPLE TALK...
SO WHEN DID YOU FIND OUT ABOUT IT?
YOUR FAN CLUB?
IT IS NOT A QUESTION OF WHEN.
THE REASON IT CAN BE OFFICIAL IS BECAUSE IT'S DONE WITH MY APPROVAL.
WHY DO YOU DO THINGS TO MAKE YOU STAND OUT?!
DO YOU EVEN HAVE A REASON FOR GOING TO SCHOOL?!
YOU'RE THROWING MY WHOLE LIFE INTO CHAOS!
I-I DO HAVE A REASON!
THERE IS DEFILEMENT AT SCHOOL!
Got it!
JUST TODAY, I EXORCISED ONE!
YOU WERE NOWHERE TO BE FOUND, SO I ALONE HAD TO...
THAT'S EVEN WORSE!!

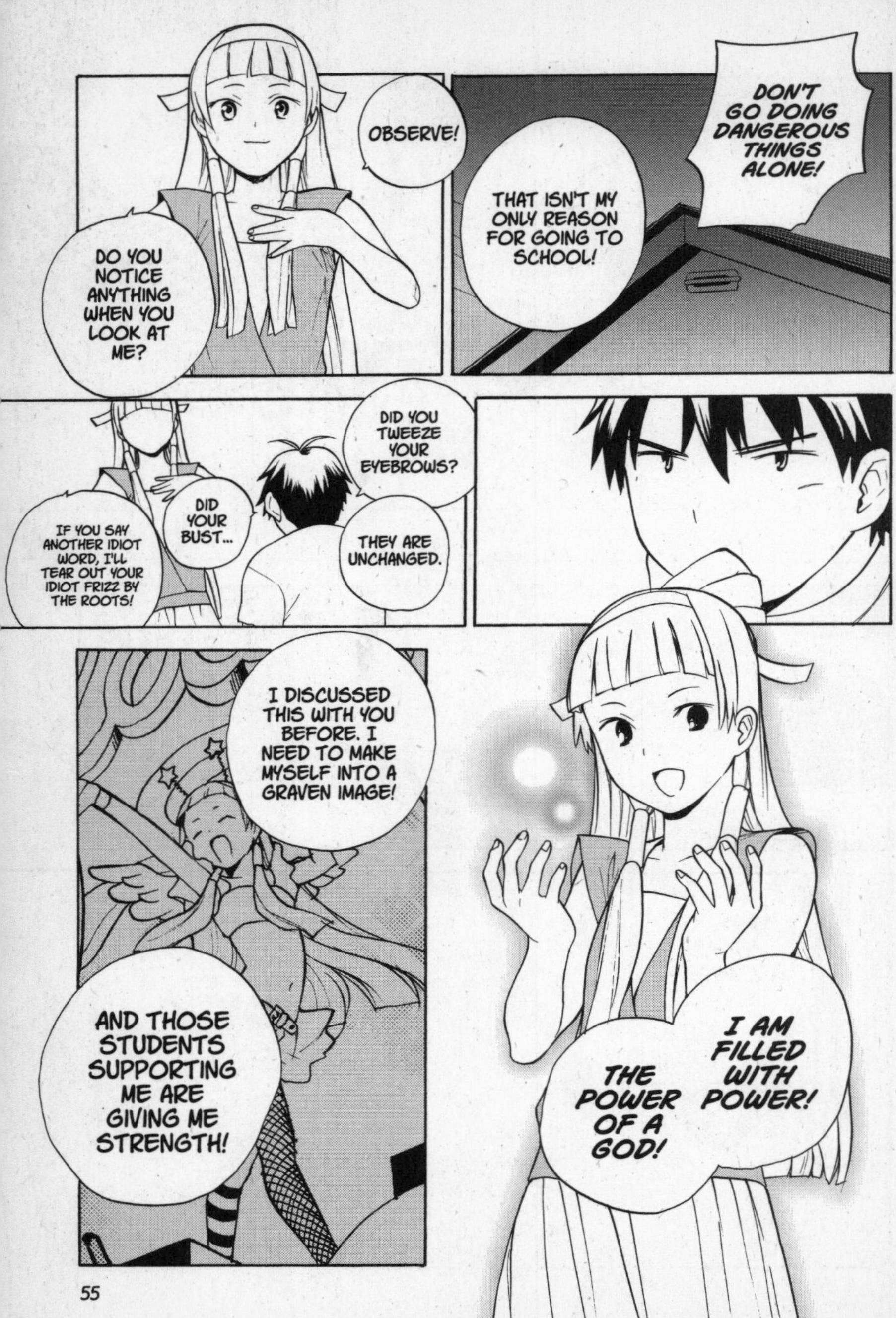
DON'T GO DOING DANGEROUS THINGS ALONE!
THAT ISN'T MY ONLY REASON FOR GOING TO SCHOOL!
OBSERVE!
DO YOU NOTICE ANYTHING WHEN YOU LOOK AT ME?
DID YOU TWEEZE YOUR EYEBROWS?
THEY ARE UNCHANGED.
DID YOUR BUST...
IF YOU SAY ANOTHER IDIOT WORD, I'LL TEAR OUT YOUR IDIOT FRIZZ BY THE ROOTS!
I AM FILLED WITH POWER!
THE POWER OF A GOD!
I DISCUSSED THIS WITH YOU BEFORE. I NEED TO MAKE MYSELF INTO A GRAVEN IMAGE!
AND THOSE STUDENTS SUPPORTING ME ARE GIVING ME STRENGTH!

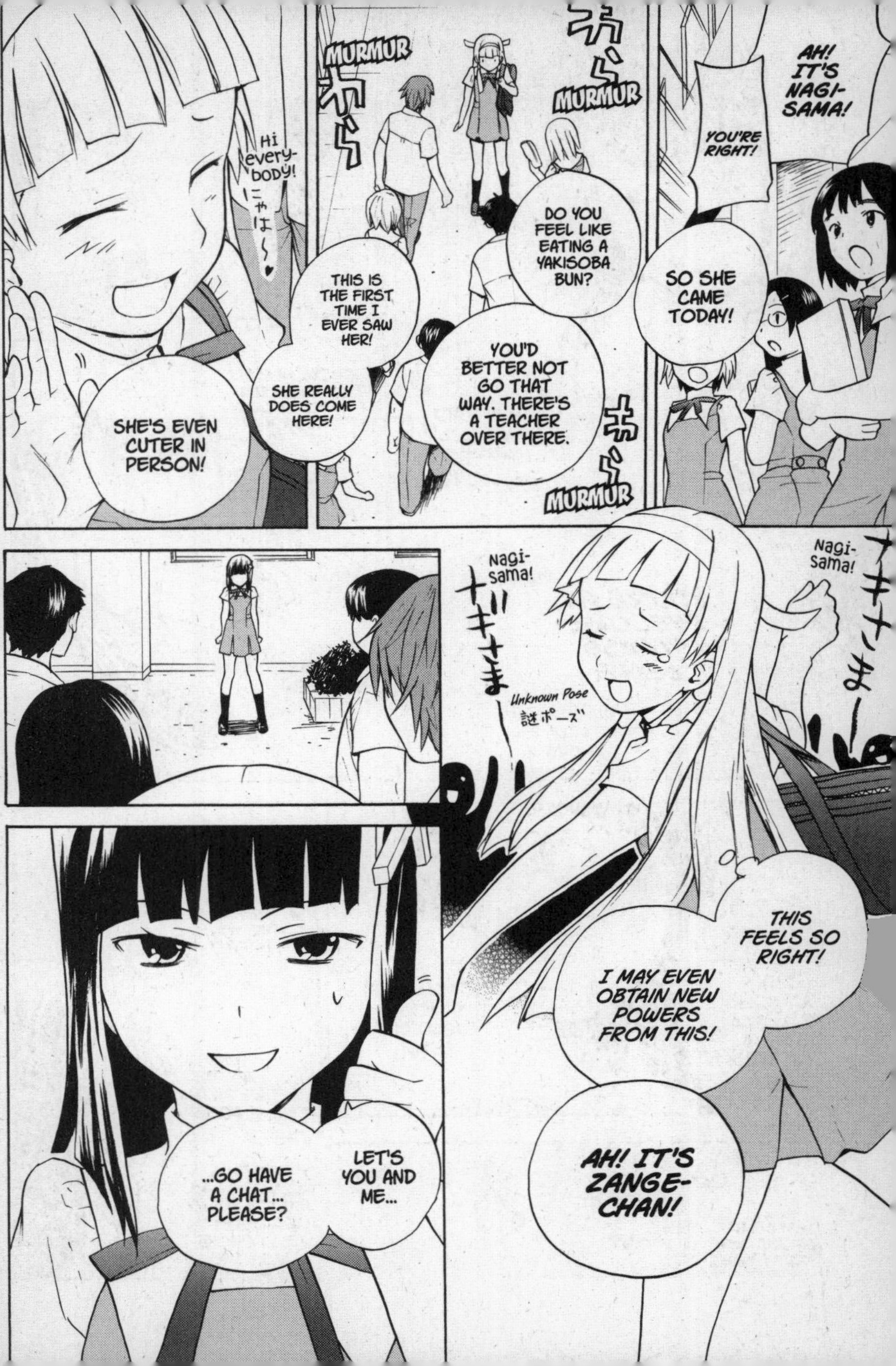
AH! IT'S NAGI-SAMA!
YOU'RE RIGHT!
SO SHE CAME TODAY!
ざわ
MURMUR
ざわ
MURMUR
DO YOU FEEL LIKE EATING A YAKISOBA BUN?
THIS IS THE FIRST TIME I EVER SAW HER!
YOU'D BETTER NOT GO THAT WAY. THERE'S A TEACHER OVER THERE.
SHE REALLY DOES COME HERE!
ざわ
MURMUR
Hi every-body!
にゃは~♥
SHE'S EVEN CUTER IN PERSON!
Nagi-sama!
ナギさまー!
Nagi-sama!
ナギさまー
Unknown Pose
謎ポーズ
THIS FEELS SO RIGHT!
I MAY EVEN OBTAIN NEW POWERS FROM THIS!
AH! IT'S ZANGE-CHAN!
LET'S YOU AND ME...
...GO HAVE A CHAT... PLEASE?

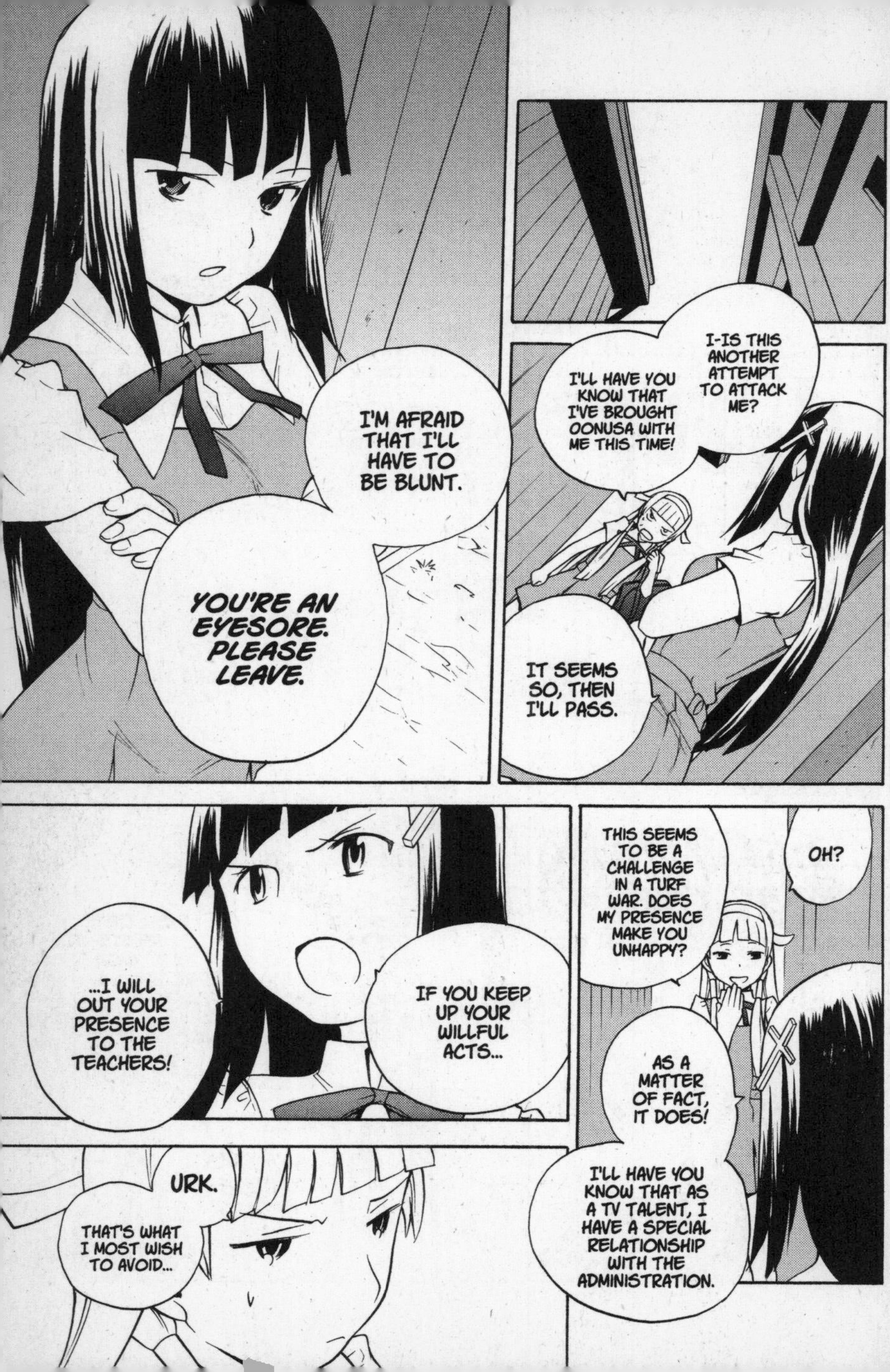
I-IS THIS ANOTHER ATTEMPT TO ATTACK ME?
I'LL HAVE YOU KNOW THAT I'VE BROUGHT OONUSA WITH ME THIS TIME!
IT SEEMS SO, THEN I'LL PASS.
I'M AFRAID THAT I'LL HAVE TO BE BLUNT.
YOU'RE AN EYESORE. PLEASE LEAVE.
OH?
THIS SEEMS TO BE A CHALLENGE IN A TURF WAR. DOES MY PRESENCE MAKE YOU UNHAPPY?
AS A MATTER OF FACT, IT DOES!
I'LL HAVE YOU KNOW THAT AS A TV TALENT, I HAVE A SPECIAL RELATIONSHIP WITH THE ADMINISTRATION.
IF YOU KEEP UP YOUR WILLFUL ACTS...
...I WILL OUT YOUR PRESENCE TO THE TEACHERS!
URK.
THAT'S WHAT I MOST WISH TO AVOID...

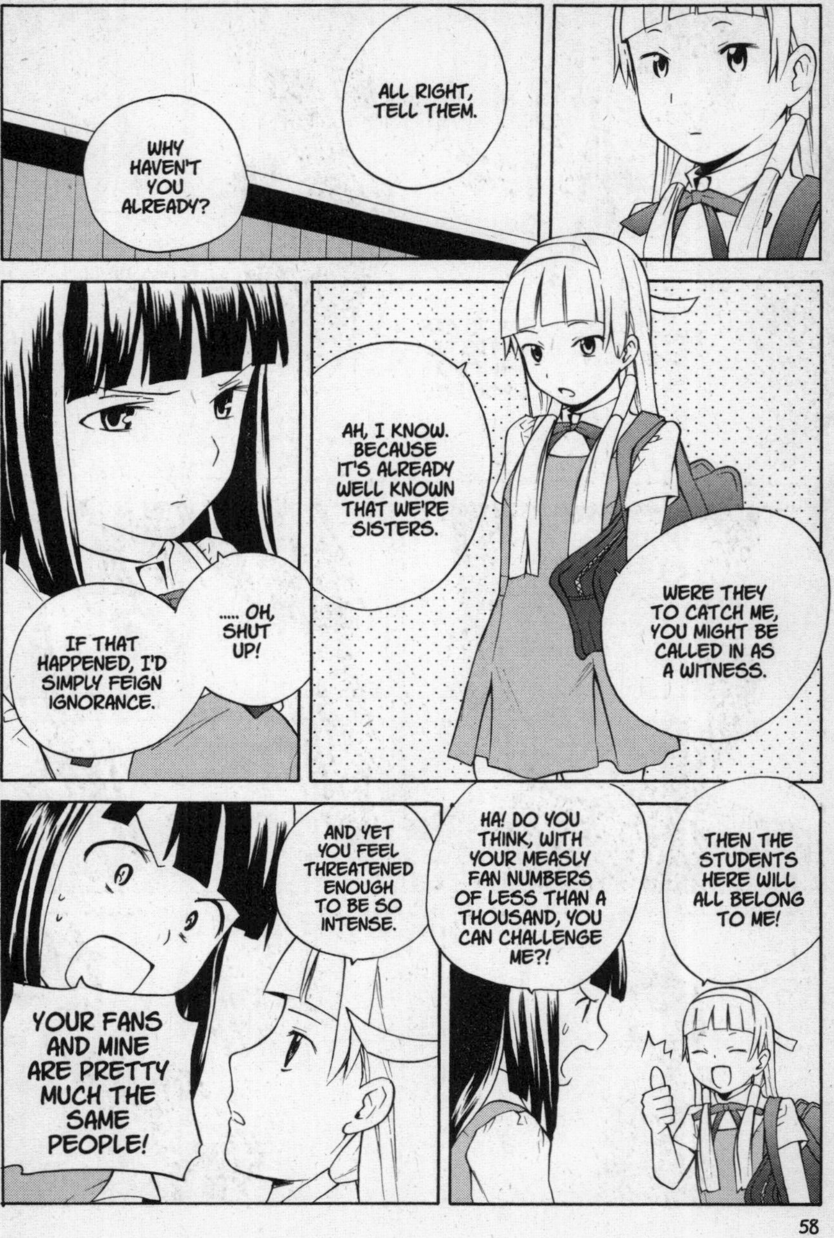
ALL RIGHT, TELL THEM.
WHY HAVEN'T YOU ALREADY?
AH, I KNOW. BECAUSE IT'S ALREADY WELL KNOWN THAT WE'RE SISTERS.
WERE THEY TO CATCH ME, YOU MIGHT BE CALLED IN AS A WITNESS.
..... OH, SHUT UP!
IF THAT HAPPENED, I'D SIMPLY FEIGN IGNORANCE.
THEN THE STUDENTS HERE WILL ALL BELONG TO ME!
HA! DO YOU THINK, WITH YOUR MEASLY FAN NUMBERS OF LESS THAN A THOUSAND, YOU CAN CHALLENGE ME?!
AND YET YOU FEEL THREATENED ENOUGH TO BE SO INTENSE.
YOUR FANS AND MINE ARE PRETTY MUCH THE SAME PEOPLE!

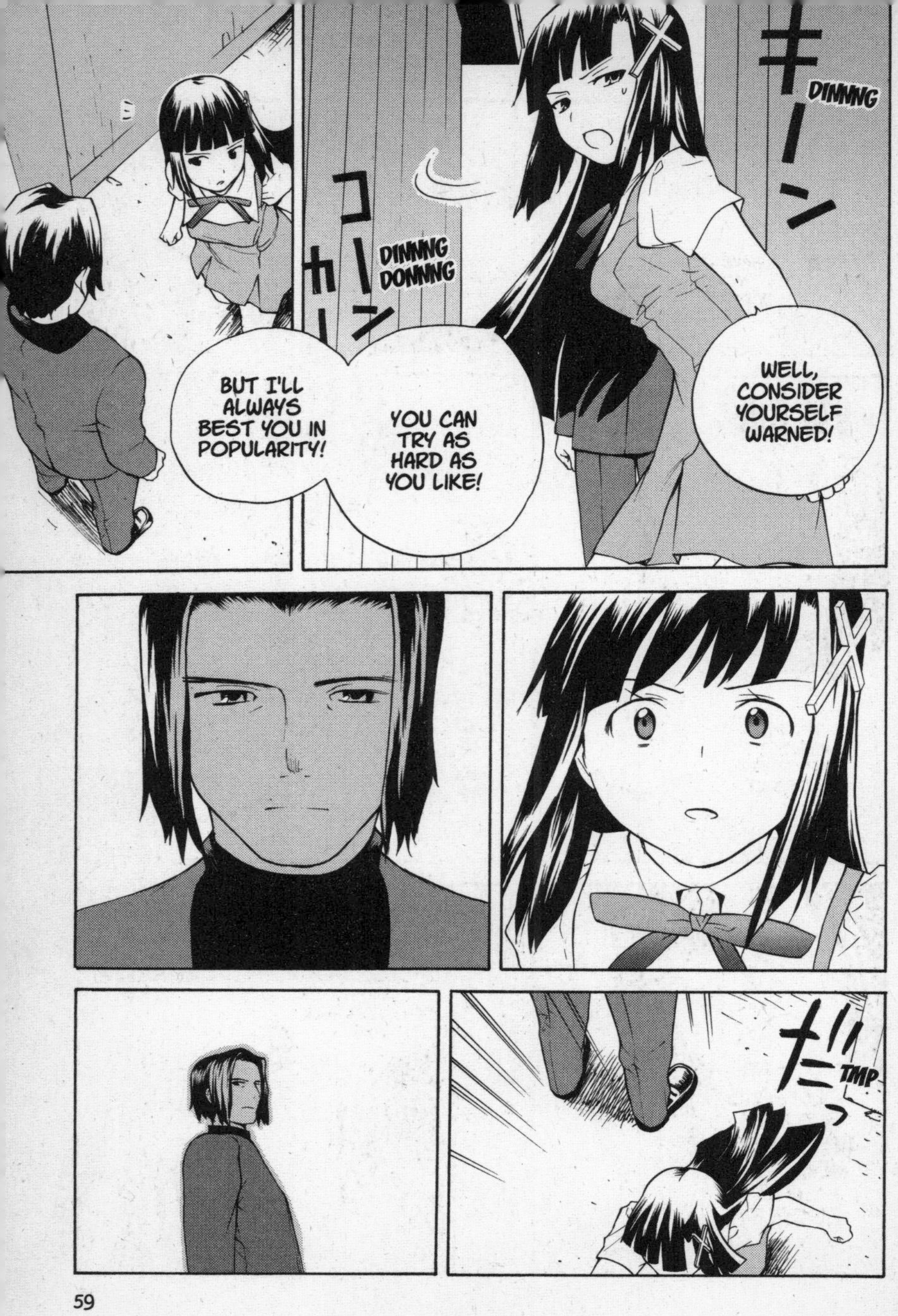

キーン
DINNNG
WELL, CONSIDER YOURSELF WARNED!
YOU CAN TRY AS HARD AS YOU LIKE!
BUT I'LL ALWAYS BEST YOU IN POPULARITY!
コーン カーン
DINNNG DONNNG
ダッ
TMP

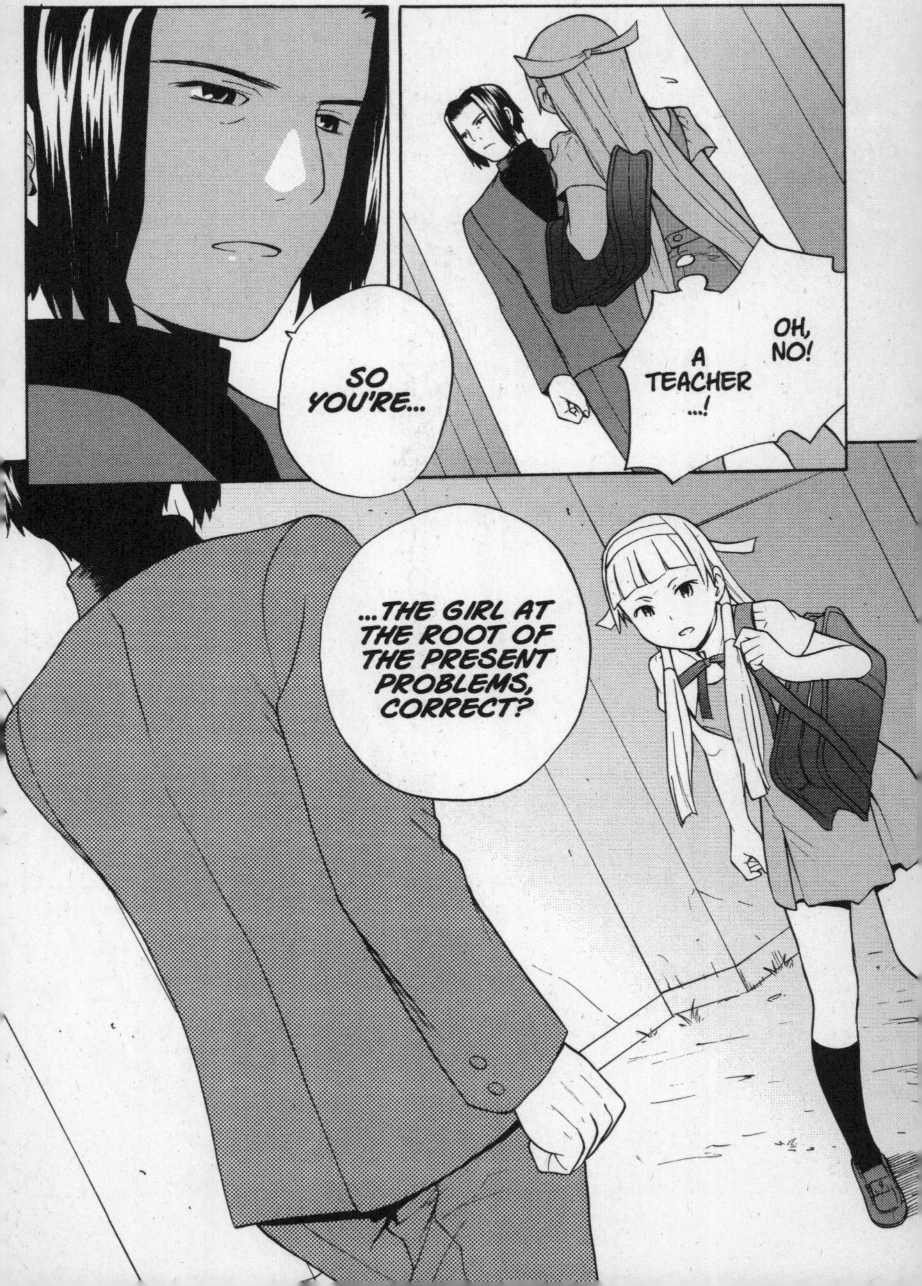
OH, NO! A TEACHER ...!
SO YOU'RE...
...THE GIRL AT THE ROOT OF THE PRESENT PROBLEMS, CORRECT?

K A N N A G I

THE MARATHON HAD TO BE TODAY, DIDN'T IT?!

PANT PANT

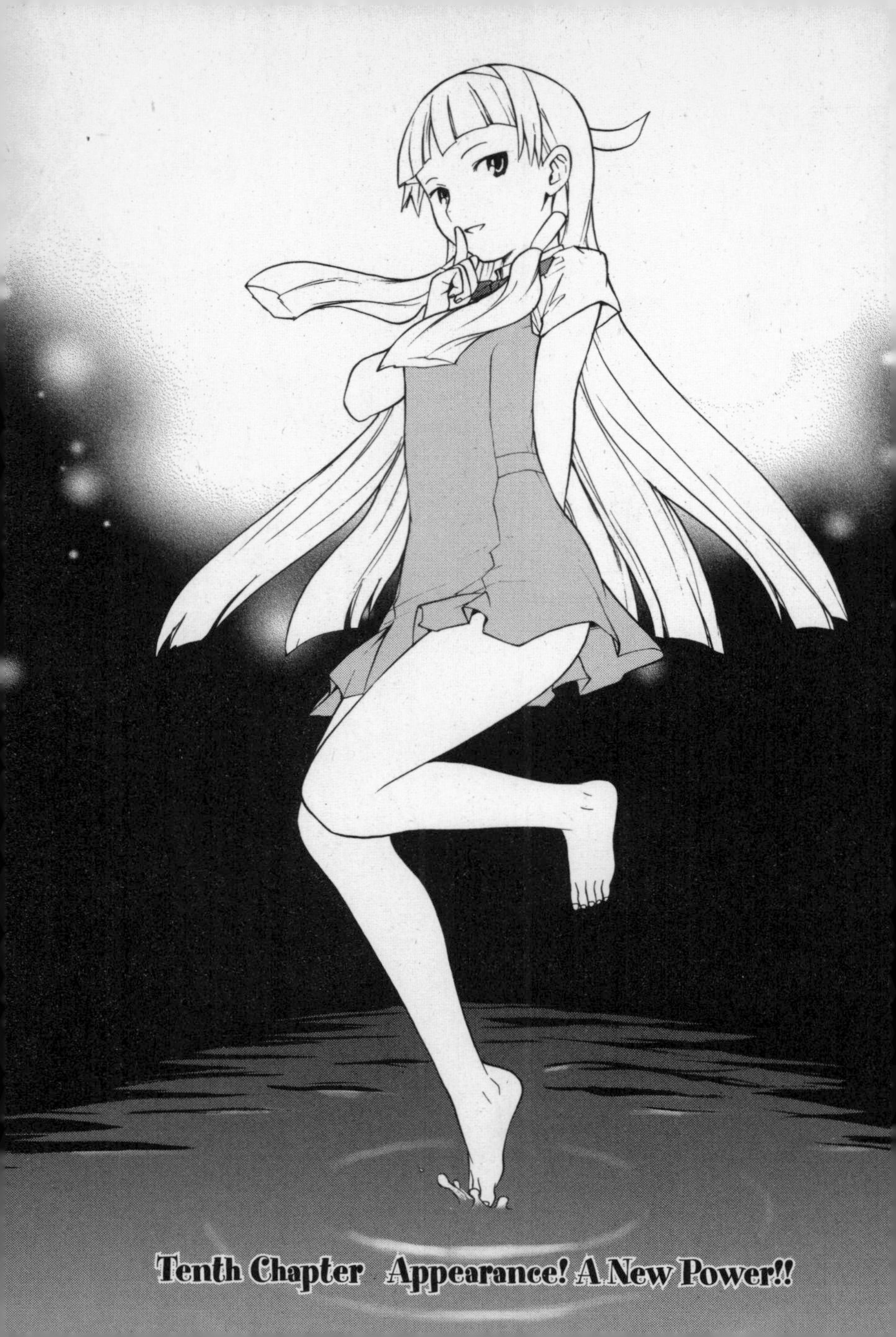

Tenth Chapter Appearance! A New Power!!

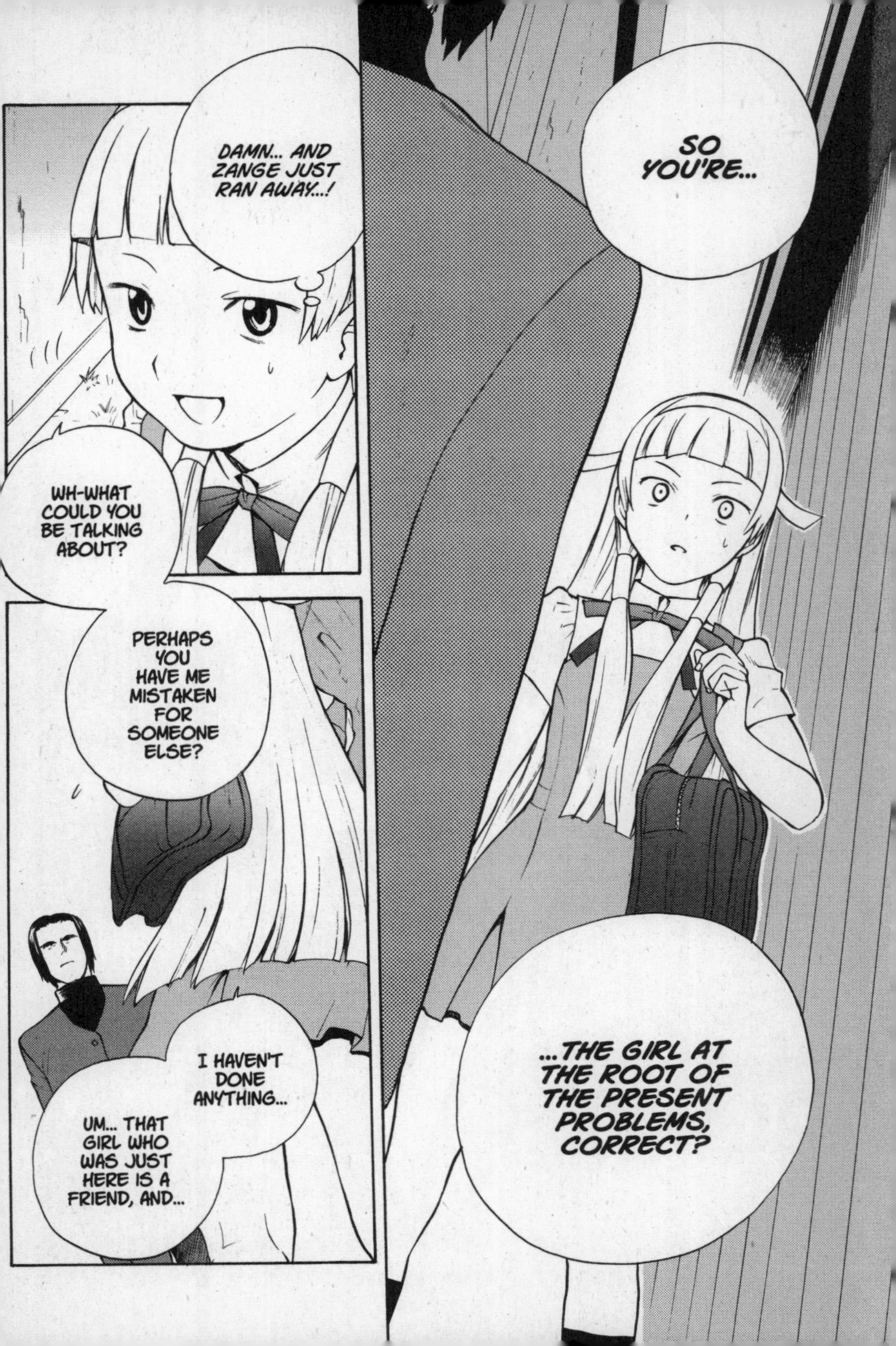
SO YOU'RE...
...THE GIRL AT THE ROOT OF THE PRESENT PROBLEMS, CORRECT?
DAMN... AND ZANGE JUST RAN AWAY...!
WH-WHAT COULD YOU BE TALKING ABOUT?
PERHAPS YOU HAVE ME MISTAKEN FOR SOMEONE ELSE?
I HAVEN'T DONE ANYTHING...
UM... THAT GIRL WHO WAS JUST HERE IS A FRIEND, AND...

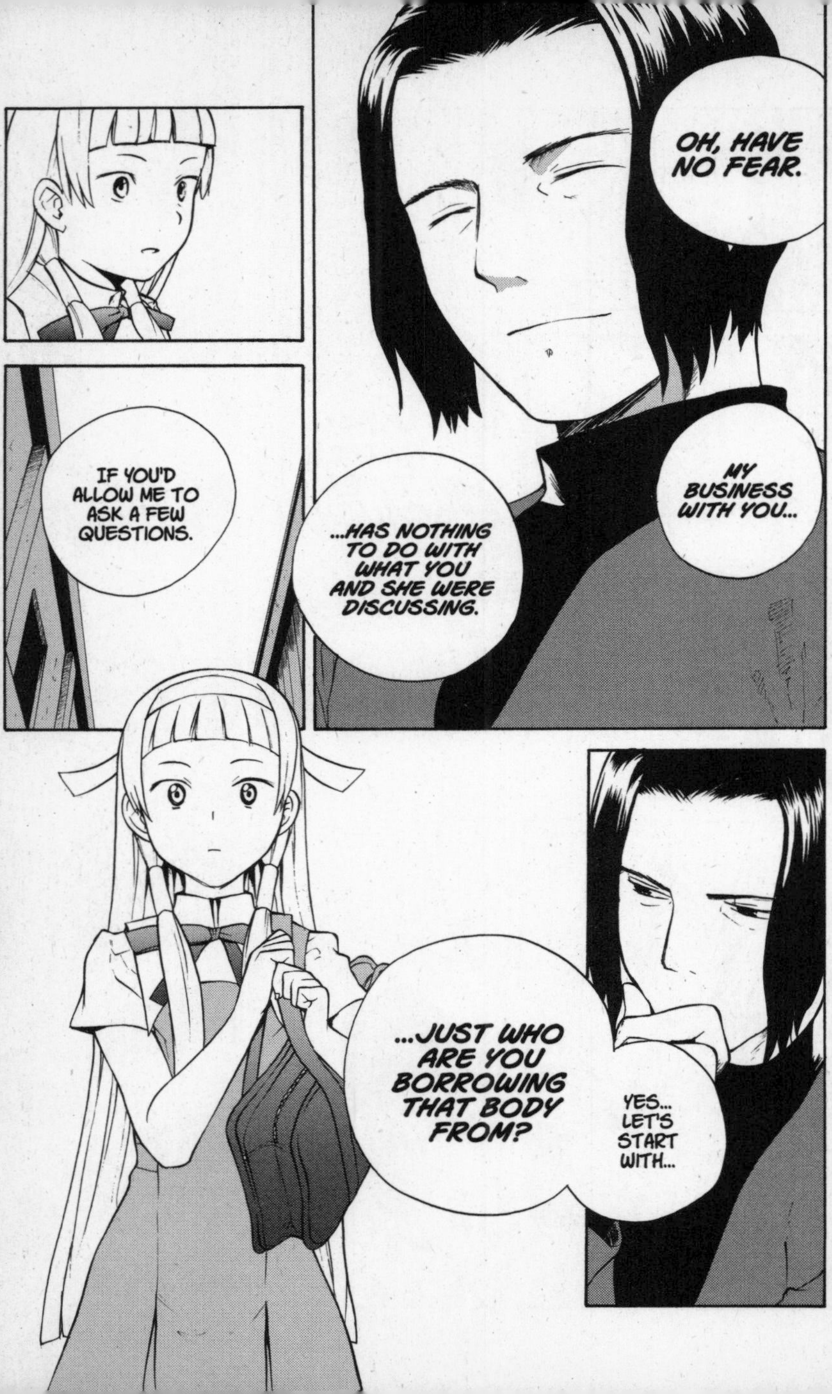
OH, HAVE NO FEAR.
MY BUSINESS WITH YOU...
...HAS NOTHING TO DO WITH WHAT YOU AND SHE WERE DISCUSSING.
IF YOU'D ALLOW ME TO ASK A FEW QUESTIONS.
YES... LET'S START WITH...
...JUST WHO ARE YOU BORROWING THAT BODY FROM?

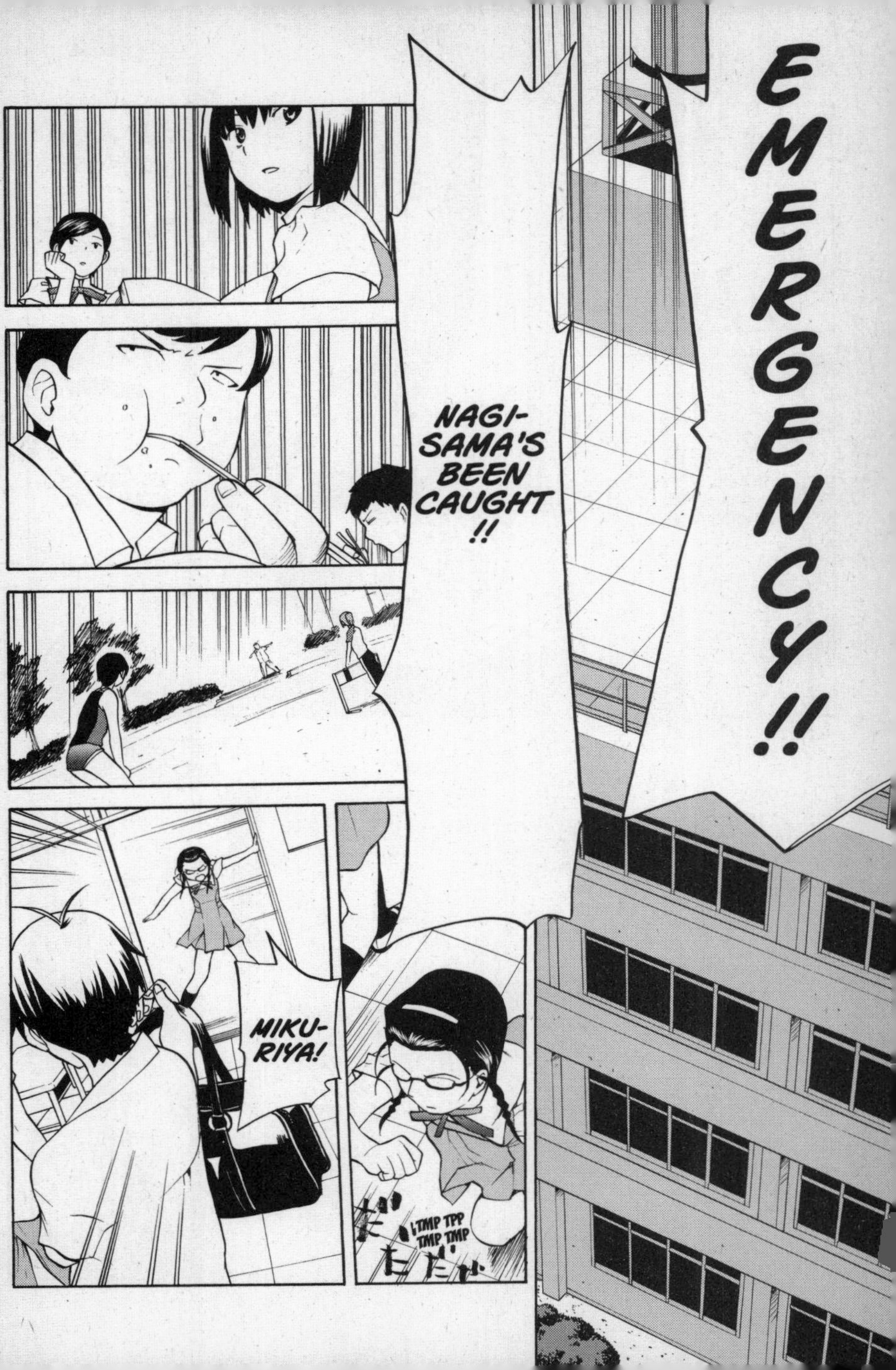
EMERGENCY!!
NAGI-SAMA'S BEEN CAUGHT!!
MIKU-RIYA!
TMP TPP TMP TMP

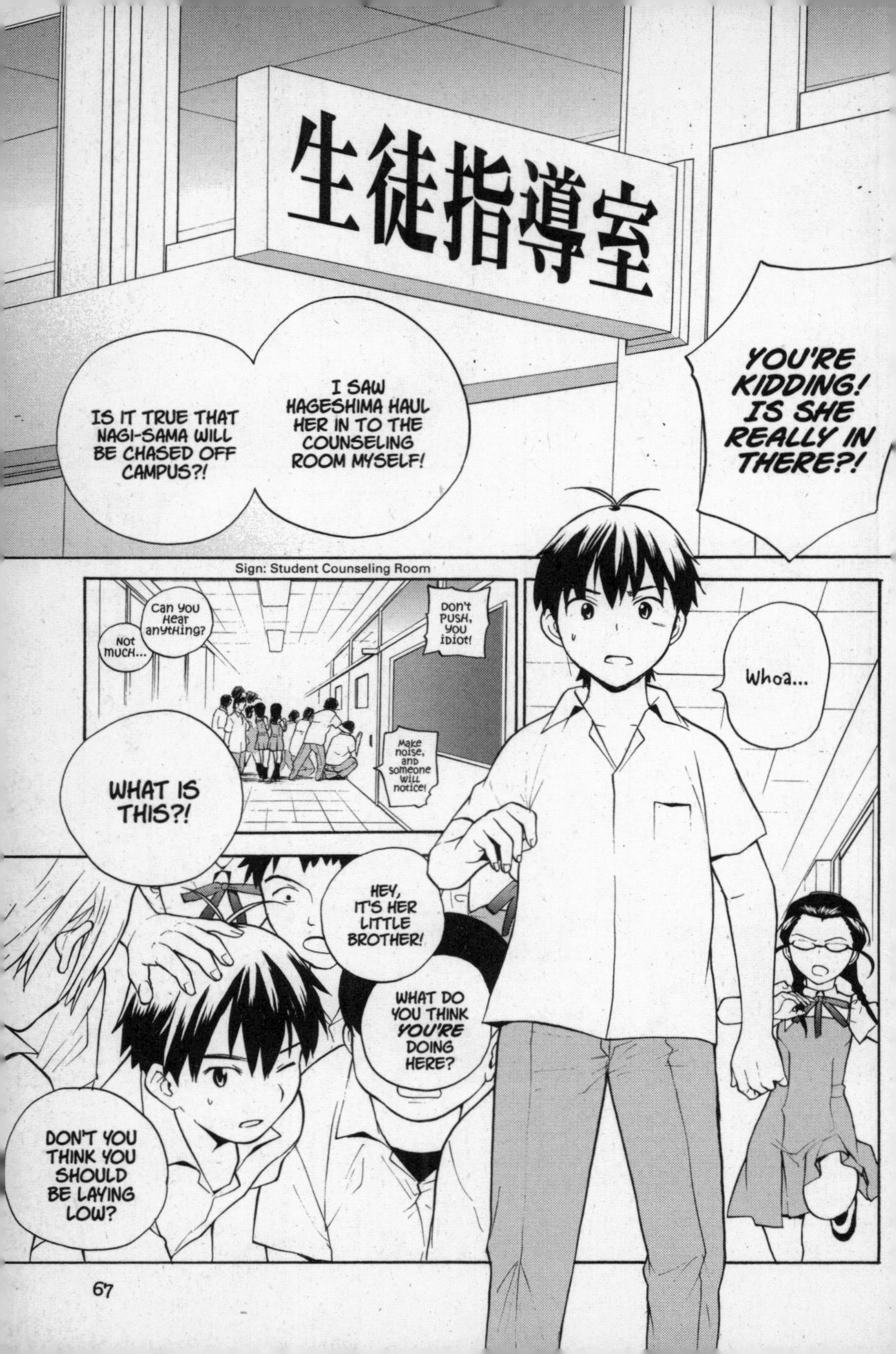

生徒指導室
YOU'RE KIDDING! IS SHE REALLY IN THERE?!
I SAW HAGESHIMA HAUL HER IN TO THE COUNSELING ROOM MYSELF!
IS IT TRUE THAT NAGI-SAMA WILL BE CHASED OFF CAMPUS?!
Whoa...
Don't push, you idiot!
Make noise, and someone will notice!
Can you hear anything?
Not much...
WHAT IS THIS?!
HEY, IT'S HER LITTLE BROTHER!
WHAT DO YOU THINK YOU'RE DOING HERE?
DON'T YOU THINK YOU SHOULD BE LAYING LOW?

Sign: Student Counseling Room

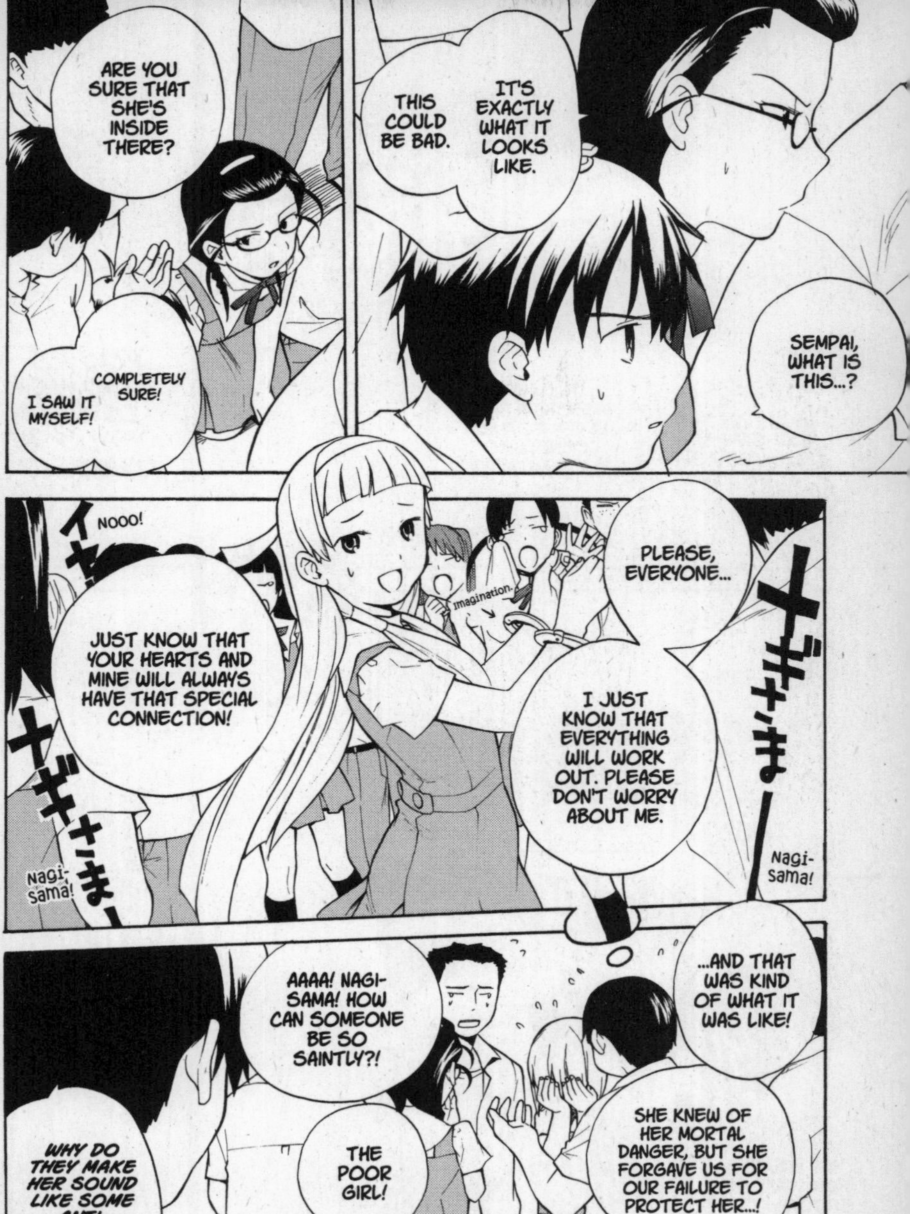
SEMPAI, WHAT IS THIS...?
IT'S EXACTLY WHAT IT LOOKS LIKE.
THIS COULD BE BAD.
ARE YOU SURE THAT SHE'S INSIDE THERE?
COMPLETELY SURE!
I SAW IT MYSELF!
PLEASE, EVERYONE...
I JUST KNOW THAT EVERYTHING WILL WORK OUT. PLEASE DON'T WORRY ABOUT ME.
ナギさまー
Nagi-sama!
Imagination.
JUST KNOW THAT YOUR HEARTS AND MINE WILL ALWAYS HAVE THAT SPECIAL CONNECTION!
NOOO!
ナギさまー
Nagi-sama!
...AND THAT WAS KIND OF WHAT IT WAS LIKE!
SHE KNEW OF HER MORTAL DANGER, BUT SHE FORGAVE US FOR OUR FAILURE TO PROTECT HER...!
AAAA! NAGI-SAMA! HOW CAN SOMEONE BE SO SAINTLY?!
THE POOR GIRL!
WHY DO THEY MAKE HER SOUND LIKE SOME ANTI-GOVERNMENT LEADER?

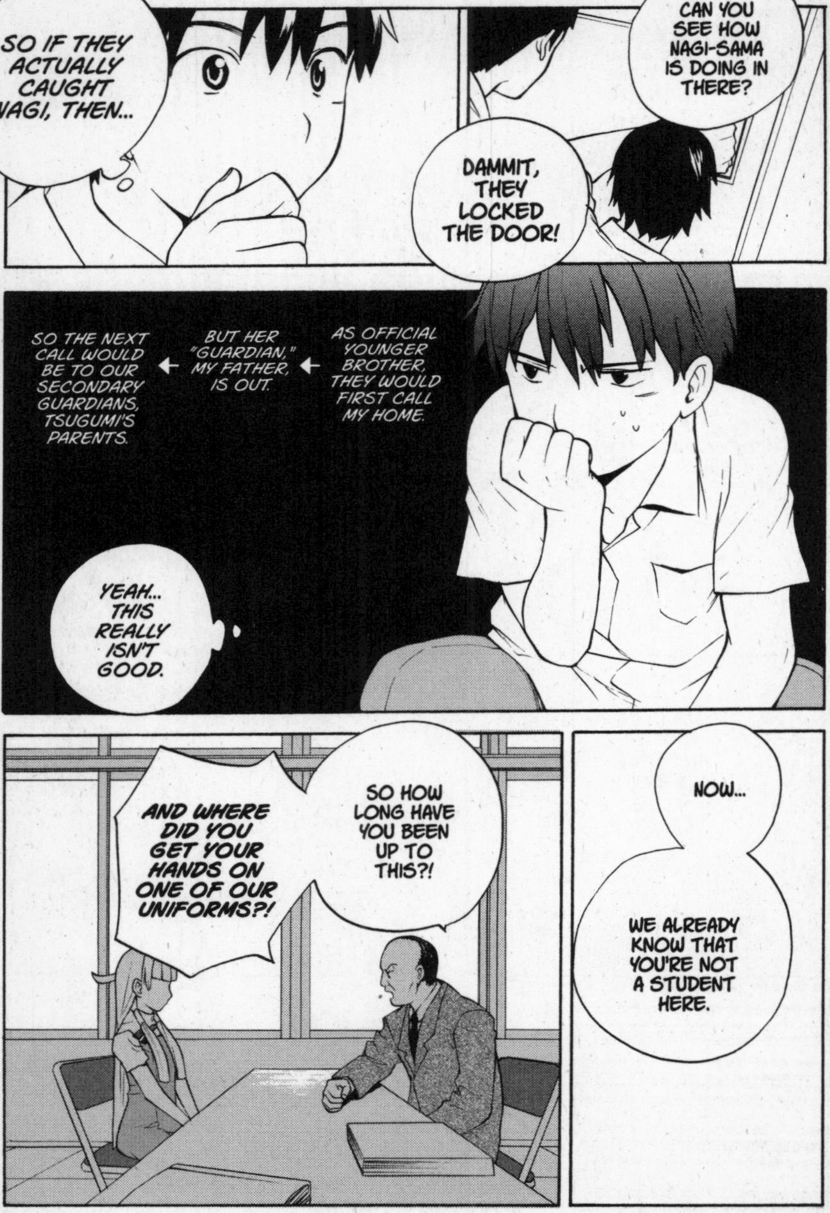
CAN YOU SEE HOW NAGI-SAMA IS DOING IN THERE?
DAMMIT, THEY LOCKED THE DOOR!
SO IF THEY ACTUALLY CAUGHT NAGI, THEN...
AS OFFICIAL YOUNGER BROTHER, THEY WOULD FIRST CALL MY HOME.
BUT HER "GUARDIAN," MY FATHER, IS OUT.
SO THE NEXT CALL WOULD BE TO OUR SECONDARY GUARDIANS, TSUGUMI'S PARENTS.
YEAH... THIS REALLY ISN'T GOOD.
NOW...
WE ALREADY KNOW THAT YOU'RE NOT A STUDENT HERE.
SO HOW LONG HAVE YOU BEEN UP TO THIS?!
AND WHERE DID YOU GET YOUR HANDS ON ONE OF OUR UNIFORMS?!

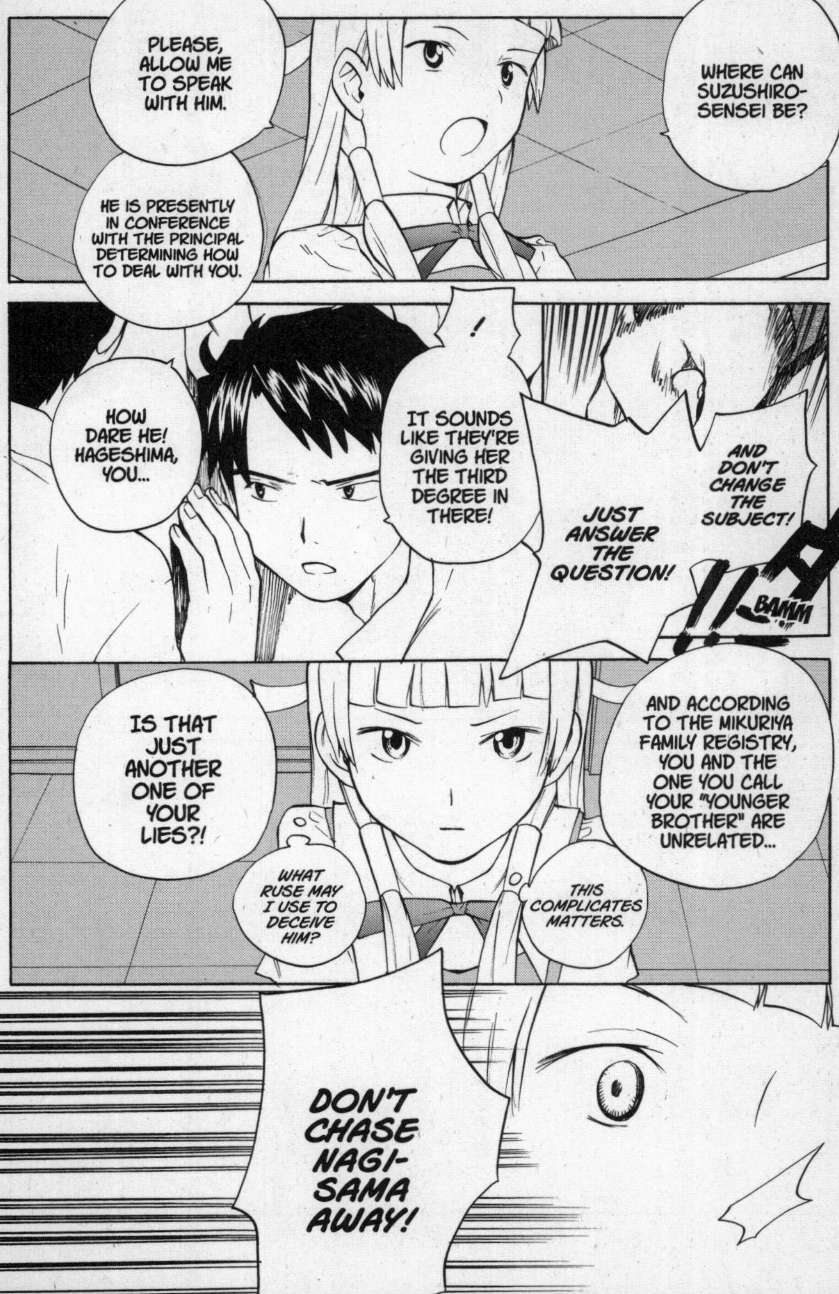
WHERE CAN SUZUSHIRO-SENSEI BE?
PLEASE, ALLOW ME TO SPEAK WITH HIM.
HE IS PRESENTLY IN CONFERENCE WITH THE PRINCIPAL DETERMINING HOW TO DEAL WITH YOU.
AND DON'T CHANGE THE SUBJECT!
JUST ANSWER THE QUESTION!
BAMM
!
IT SOUNDS LIKE THEY'RE GIVING HER THE THIRD DEGREE IN THERE!
HOW DARE HE! HAGESHIMA, YOU...
AND ACCORDING TO THE MIKURIYA FAMILY REGISTRY, YOU AND THE ONE YOU CALL YOUR "YOUNGER BROTHER" ARE UNRELATED...
IS THAT JUST ANOTHER ONE OF YOUR LIES?!
THIS COMPLICATES MATTERS.
WHAT RUSE MAY I USE TO DECEIVE HIM?
DON'T CHASE NAGI-SAMA AWAY!

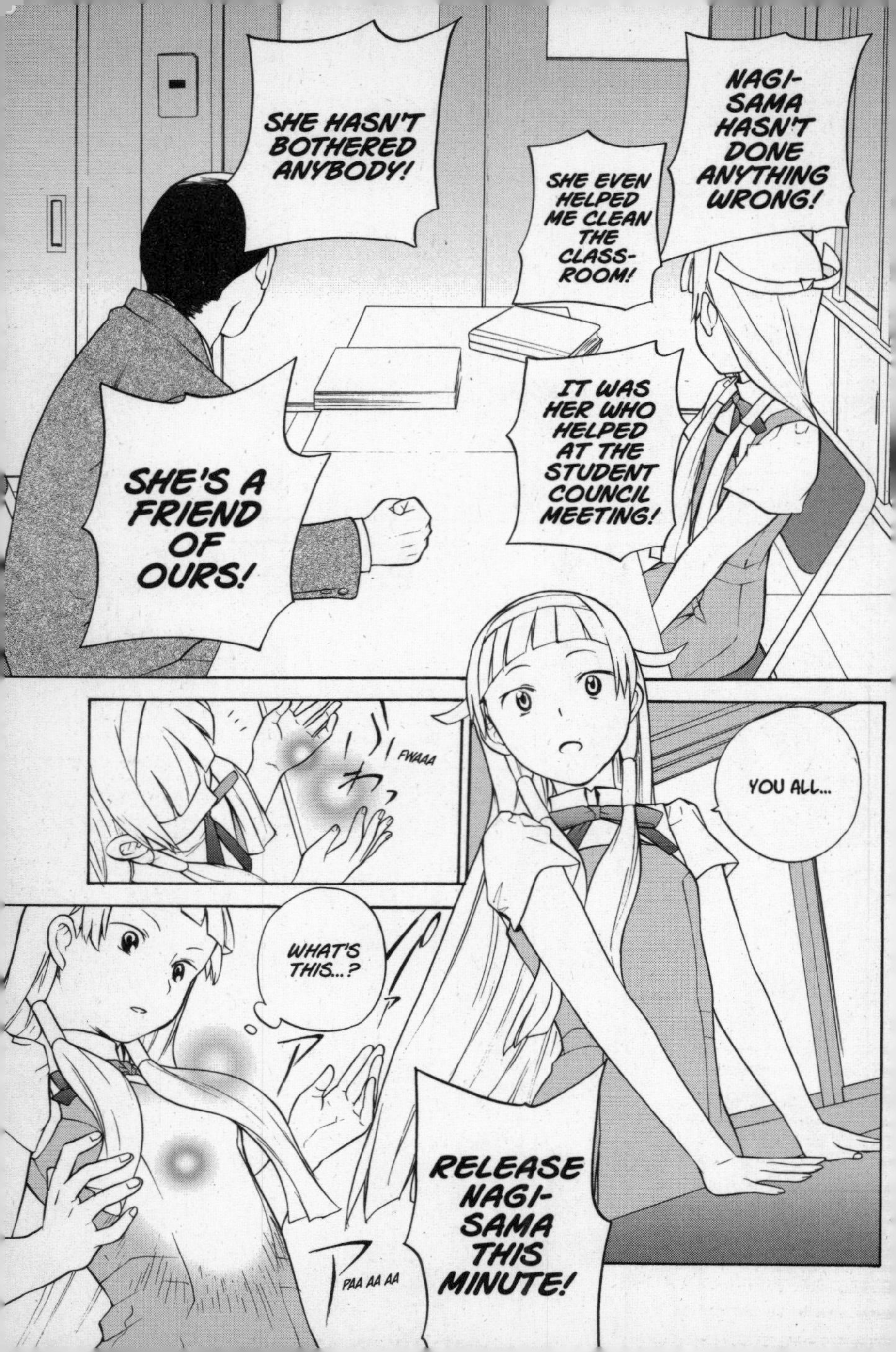

NAGI-SAMA HASN'T DONE ANYTHING WRONG!
SHE EVEN HELPED ME CLEAN THE CLASS-ROOM!
SHE HASN'T BOTHERED ANYBODY!
IT WAS HER WHO HELPED AT THE STUDENT COUNCIL MEETING!
SHE'S A FRIEND OF OURS!
YOU ALL...
FWAAA
WHAT'S THIS...?
PAA AA AA
RELEASE NAGI-SAMA THIS MINUTE!

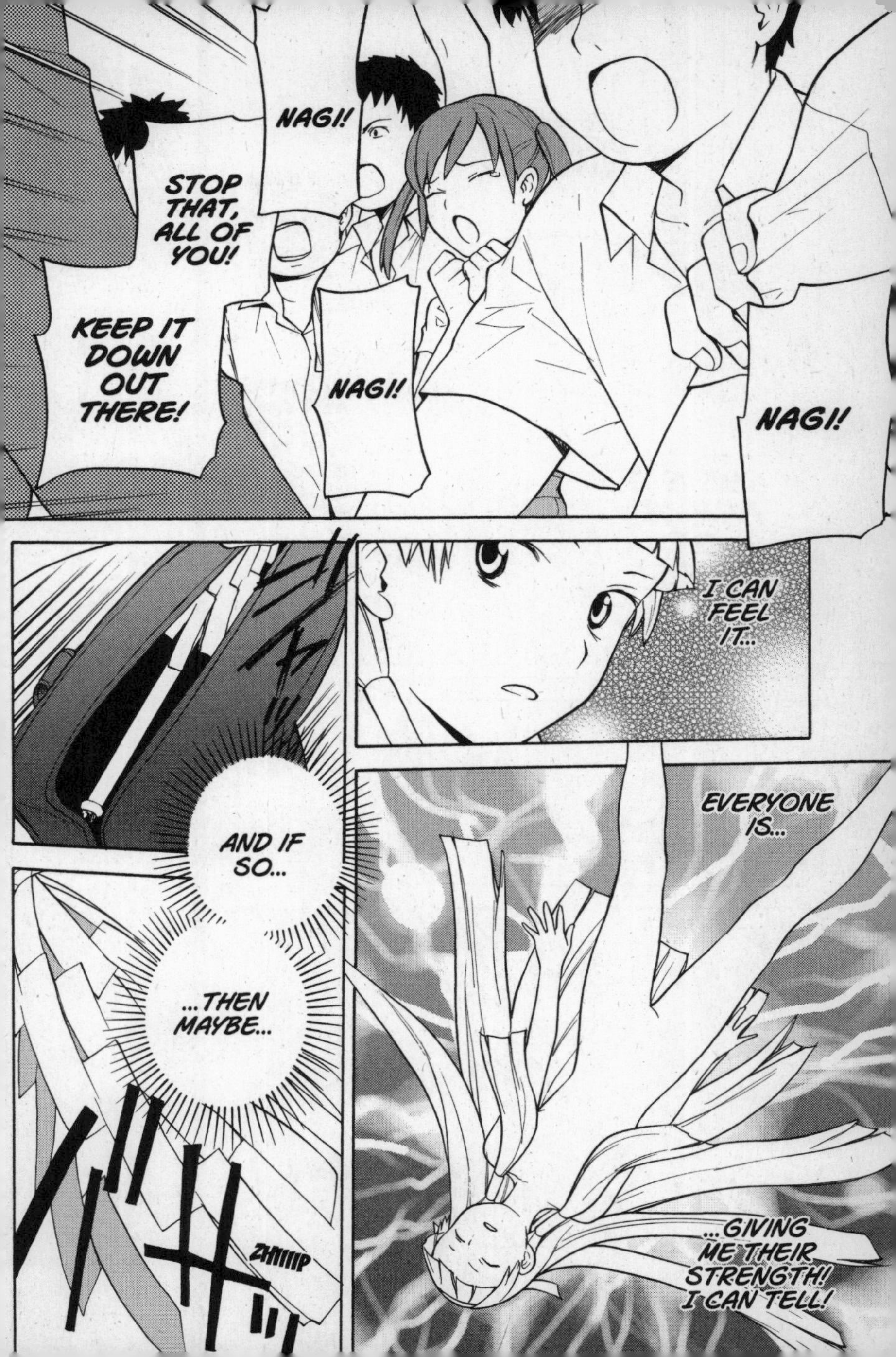

NAGI!
NAGI!
NAGI!
STOP THAT, ALL OF YOU!
KEEP IT DOWN OUT THERE!
I CAN FEEL IT...
EVERYONE IS...
...GIVING ME THEIR STRENGTH! I CAN TELL!
AND IF SO...
...THEN MAYBE...
ZHIIIIP

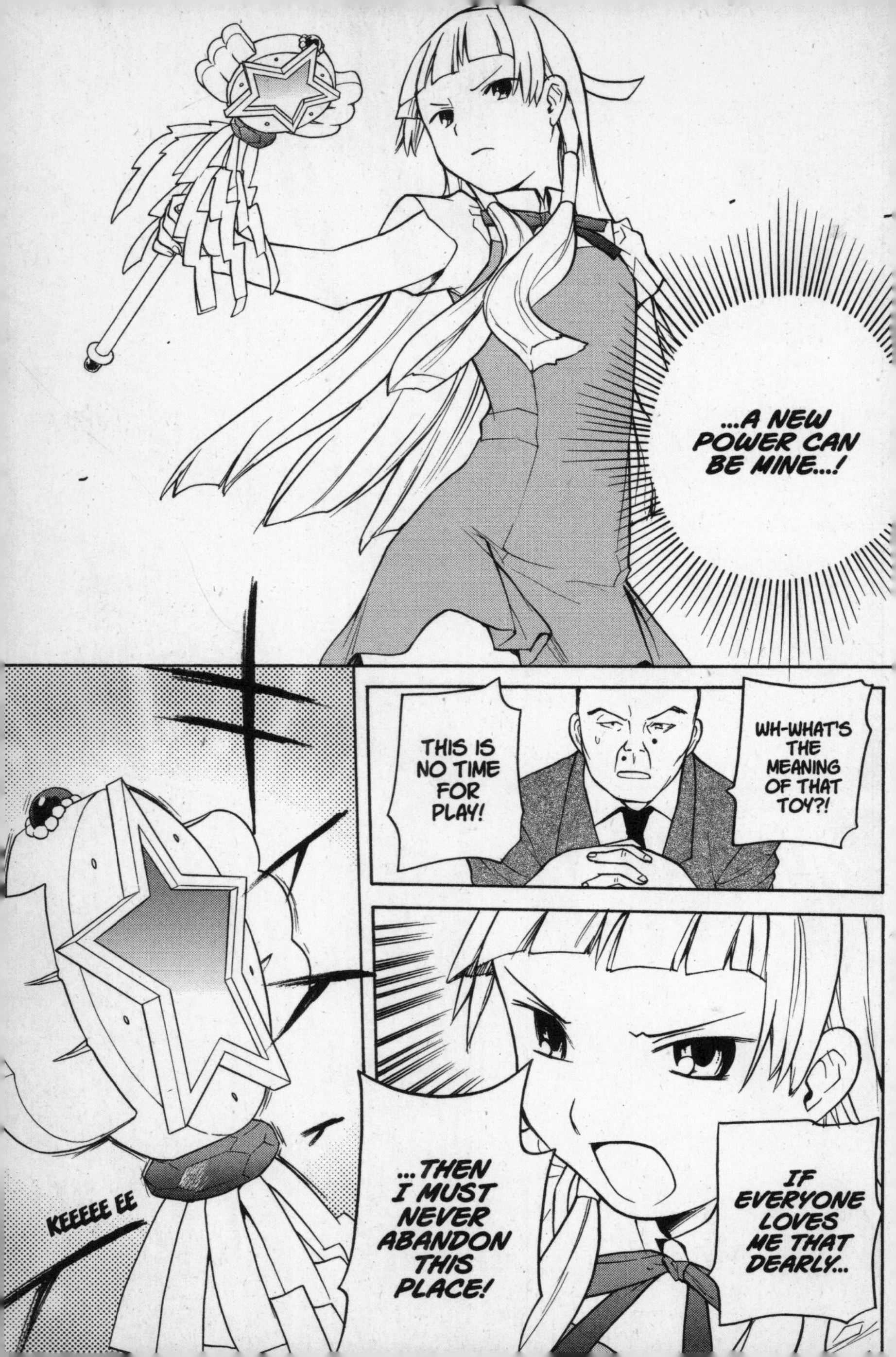
...A NEW POWER CAN BE MINE...!
WH-WHAT'S THE MEANING OF THAT TOY?!
THIS IS NO TIME FOR PLAY!
IF EVERYONE LOVES ME THAT DEARLY...
...THEN I MUST NEVER ABANDON THIS PLACE!
KEEEEE EE

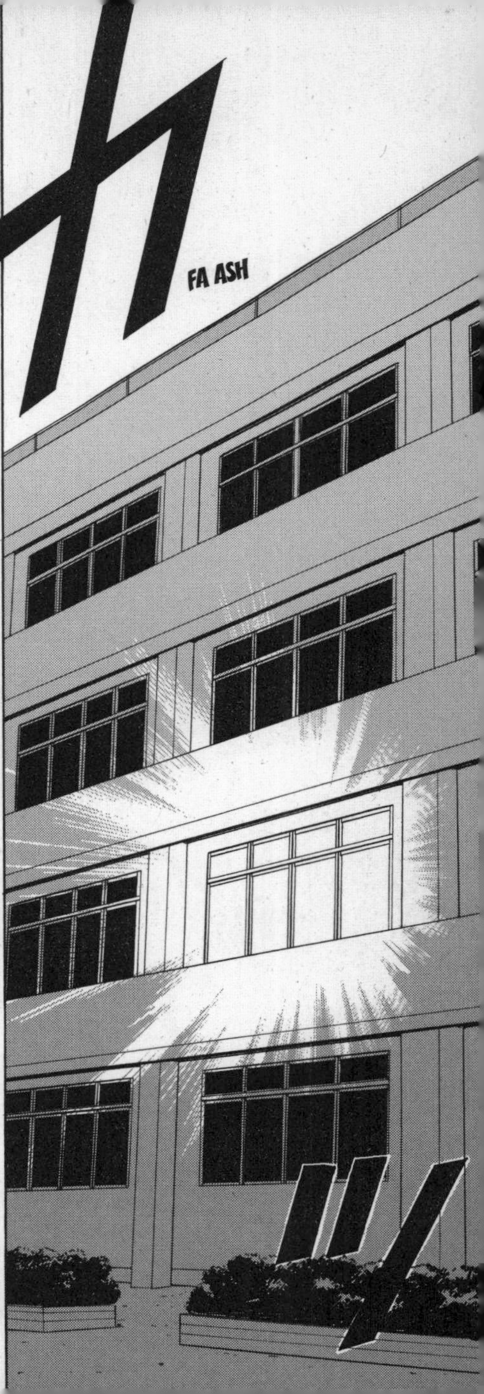
カ
FA ASH
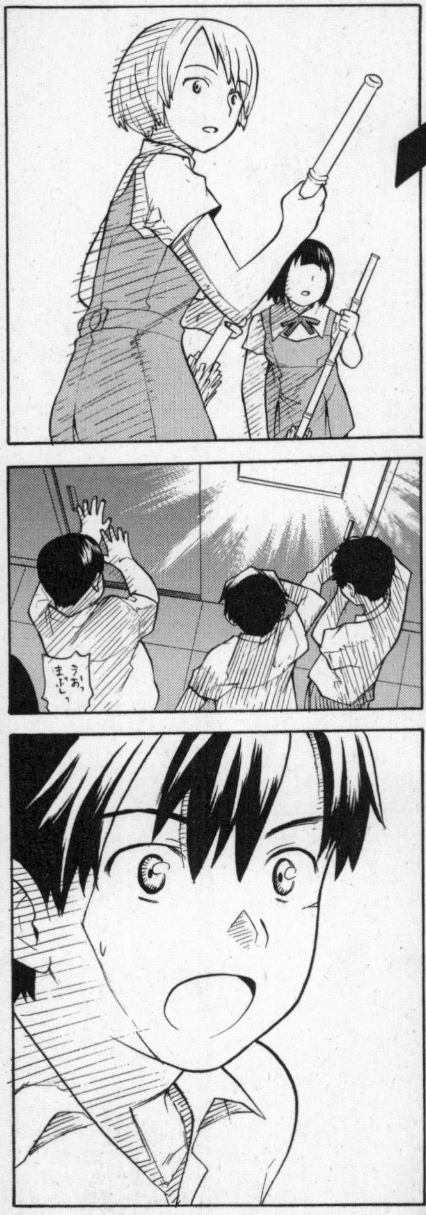
うおっ まぶしっ

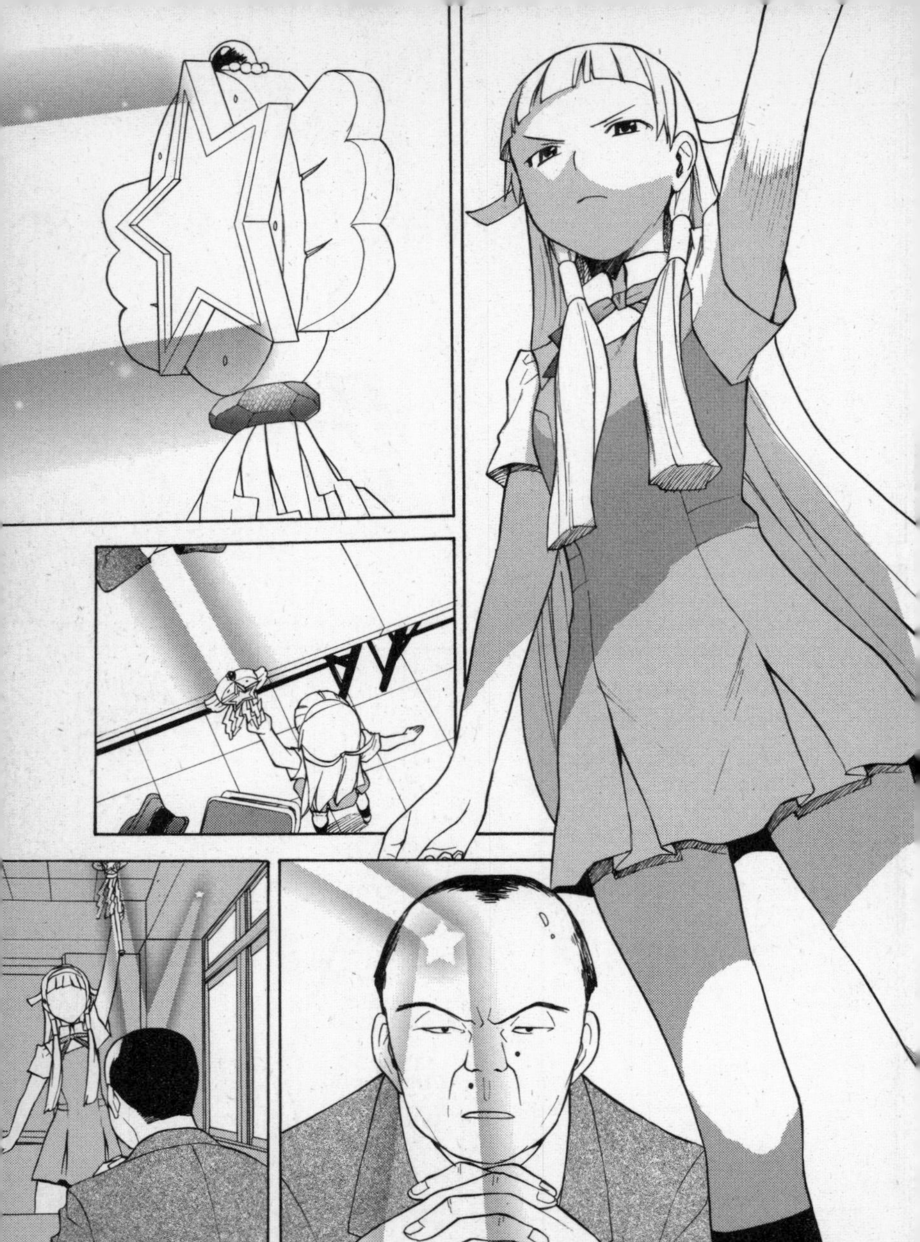

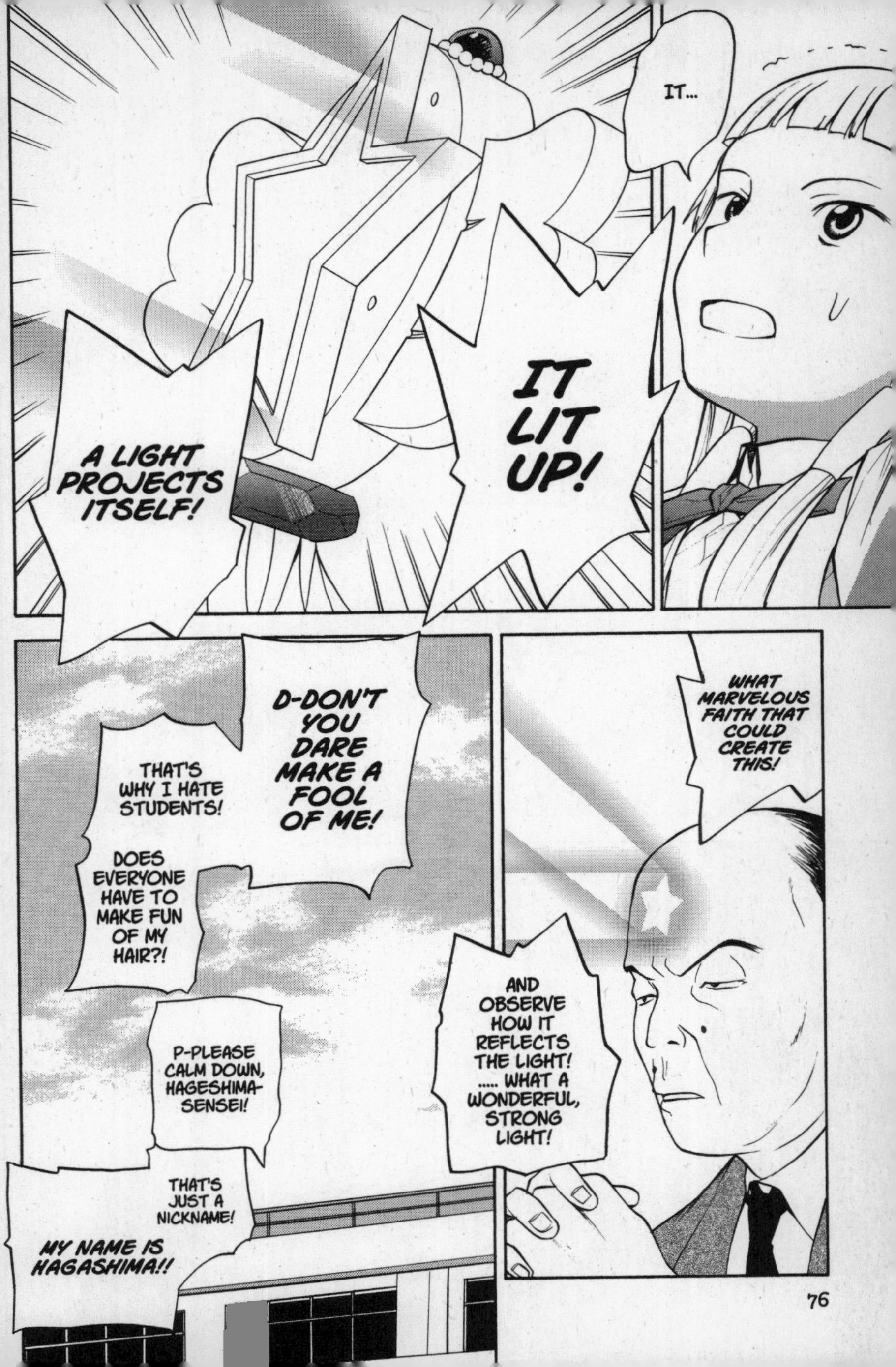
IT...
IT LIT UP!
A LIGHT PROJECTS ITSELF!
WHAT MARVELOUS FAITH THAT COULD CREATE THIS!
AND OBSERVE HOW IT REFLECTS THE LIGHT! ..... WHAT A WONDERFUL, STRONG LIGHT!
D-DON'T YOU DARE MAKE A FOOL OF ME!
THAT'S WHY I HATE STUDENTS!
DOES EVERYONE HAVE TO MAKE FUN OF MY HAIR?!
P-PLEASE CALM DOWN, HAGESHIMA-SENSEI!
THAT'S JUST A NICKNAME!
MY NAME IS HAGASHIMA!!

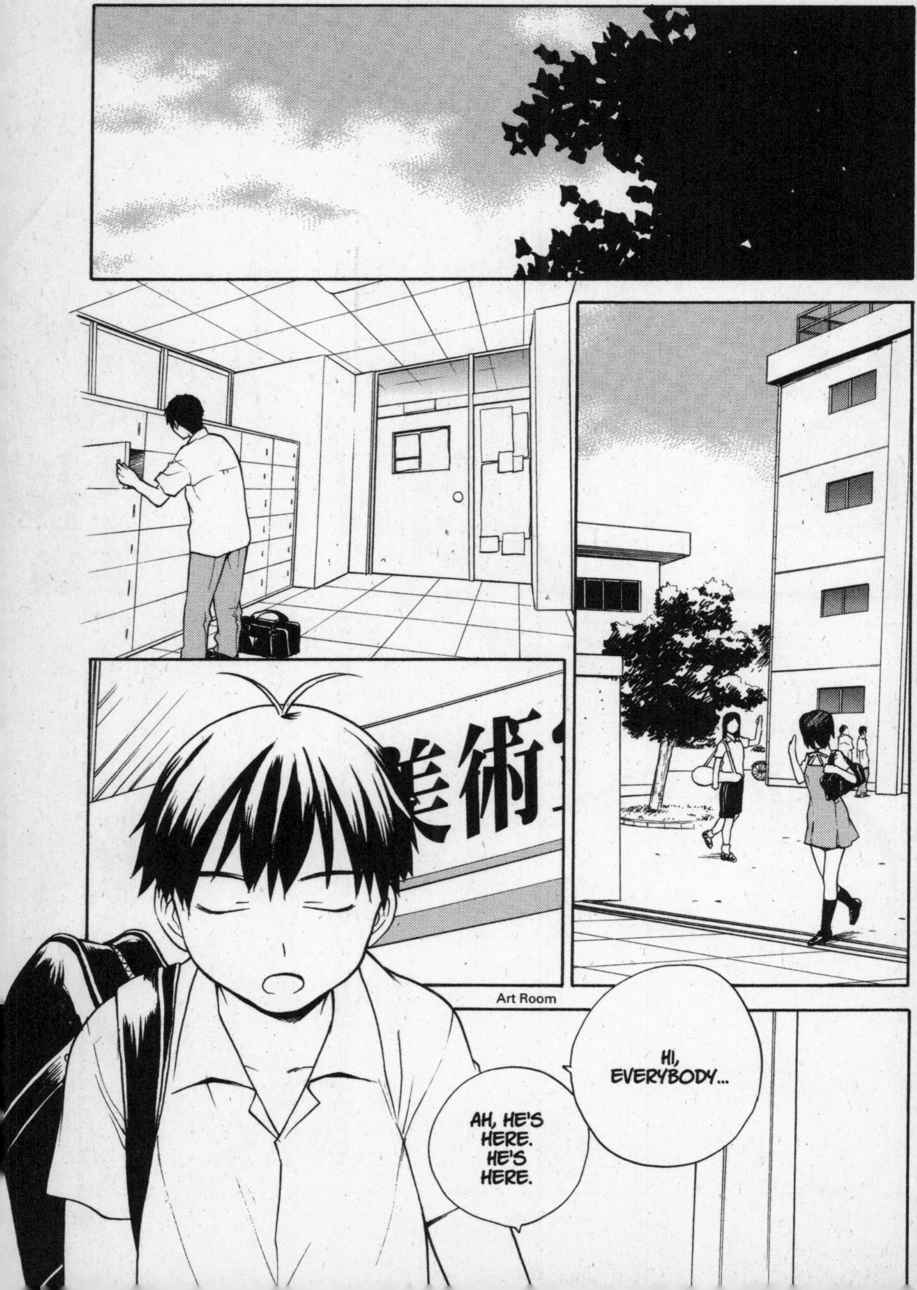
Art Room
HI, EVERYBODY...
AH, HE'S HERE. HE'S HERE.

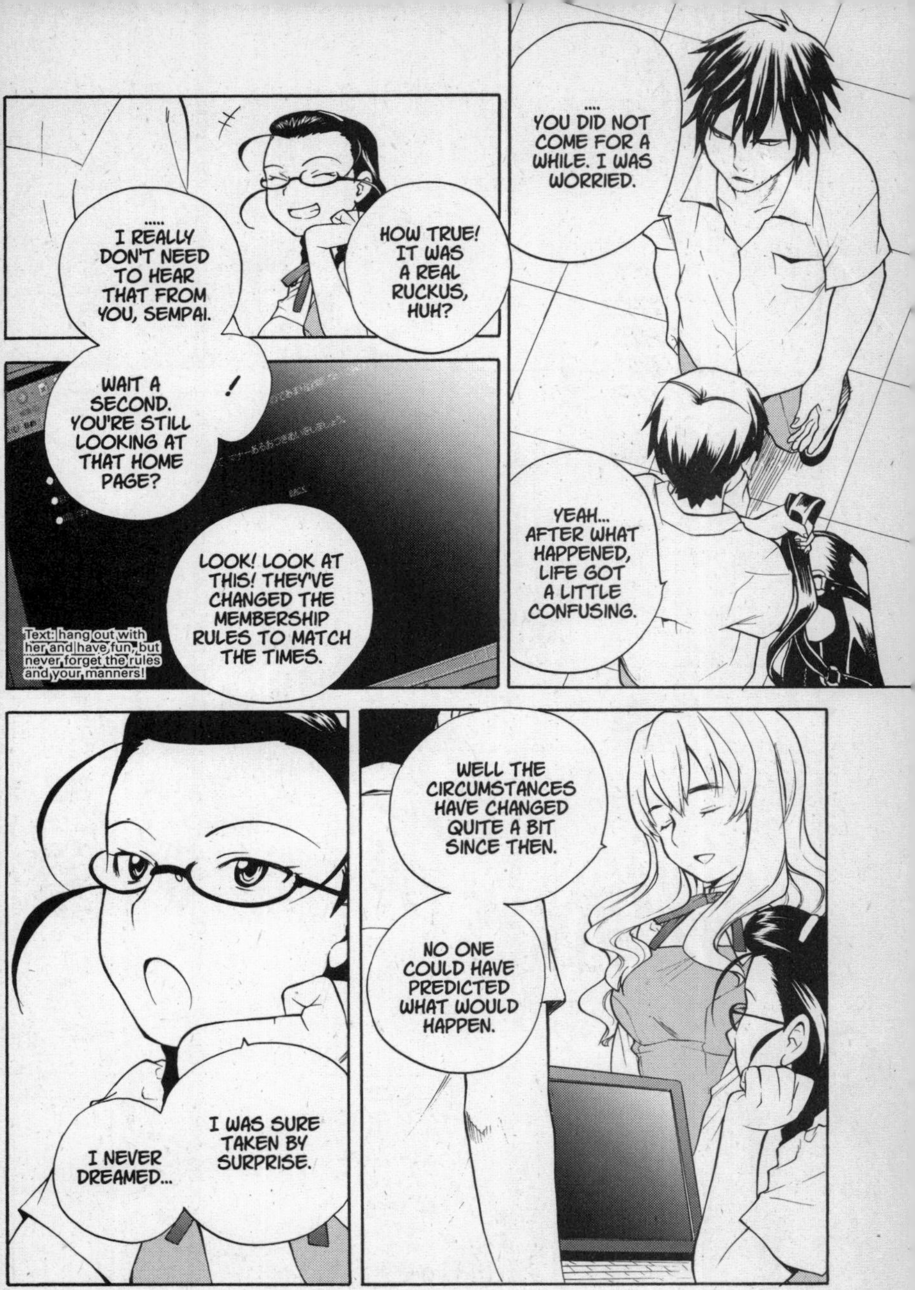

.... YOU DID NOT COME FOR A WHILE. I WAS WORRIED.
YEAH... AFTER WHAT HAPPENED, LIFE GOT A LITTLE CONFUSING.
HOW TRUE! IT WAS A REAL RUCKUS, HUH?
..... I REALLY DON'T NEED TO HEAR THAT FROM YOU, SEMPAI.
!
WAIT A SECOND. YOU'RE STILL LOOKING AT THAT HOME PAGE?
LOOK! LOOK AT THIS! THEY'VE CHANGED THE MEMBERSHIP RULES TO MATCH THE TIMES.
Text: hang out with her and have fun, but never forget the rules and your manners!
WELL THE CIRCUMSTANCES HAVE CHANGED QUITE A BIT SINCE THEN.
NO ONE COULD HAVE PREDICTED WHAT WOULD HAPPEN.
I WAS SURE TAKEN BY SURPRISE.
I NEVER DREAMED...

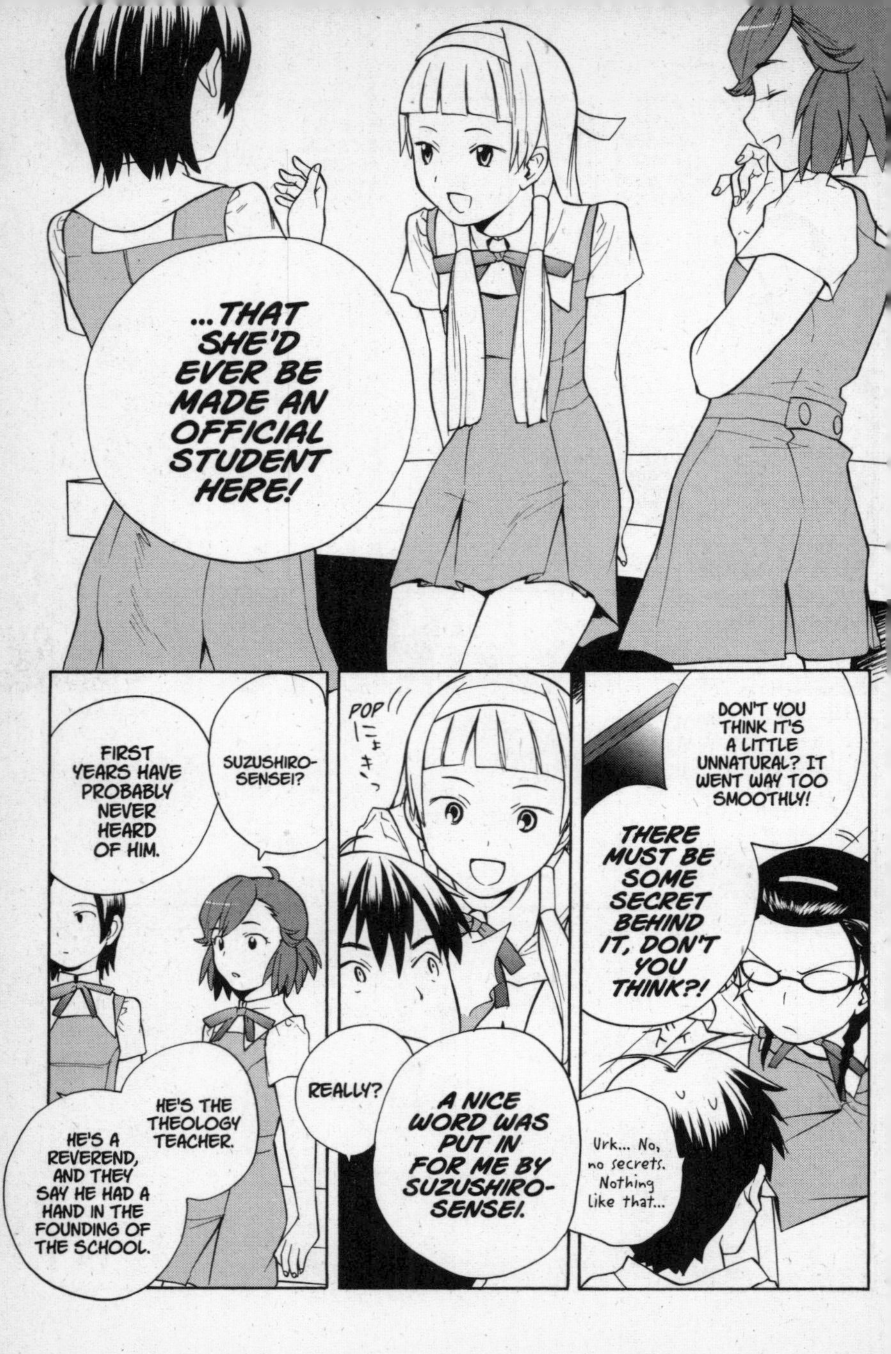
...THAT SHE'D EVER BE MADE AN OFFICIAL STUDENT HERE!
DON'T YOU THINK IT'S A LITTLE UNNATURAL? IT WENT WAY TOO SMOOTHLY!
THERE MUST BE SOME SECRET BEHIND IT, DON'T YOU THINK?!
Urk... No, no secrets. Nothing like that...
POP
にょきっ
A NICE WORD WAS PUT IN FOR ME BY SUZUSHIRO-SENSEI.
REALLY?
SUZUSHIRO-SENSEI?
FIRST YEARS HAVE PROBABLY NEVER HEARD OF HIM.
HE'S THE THEOLOGY TEACHER.
HE'S A REVEREND, AND THEY SAY HE HAD A HAND IN THE FOUNDING OF THE SCHOOL.

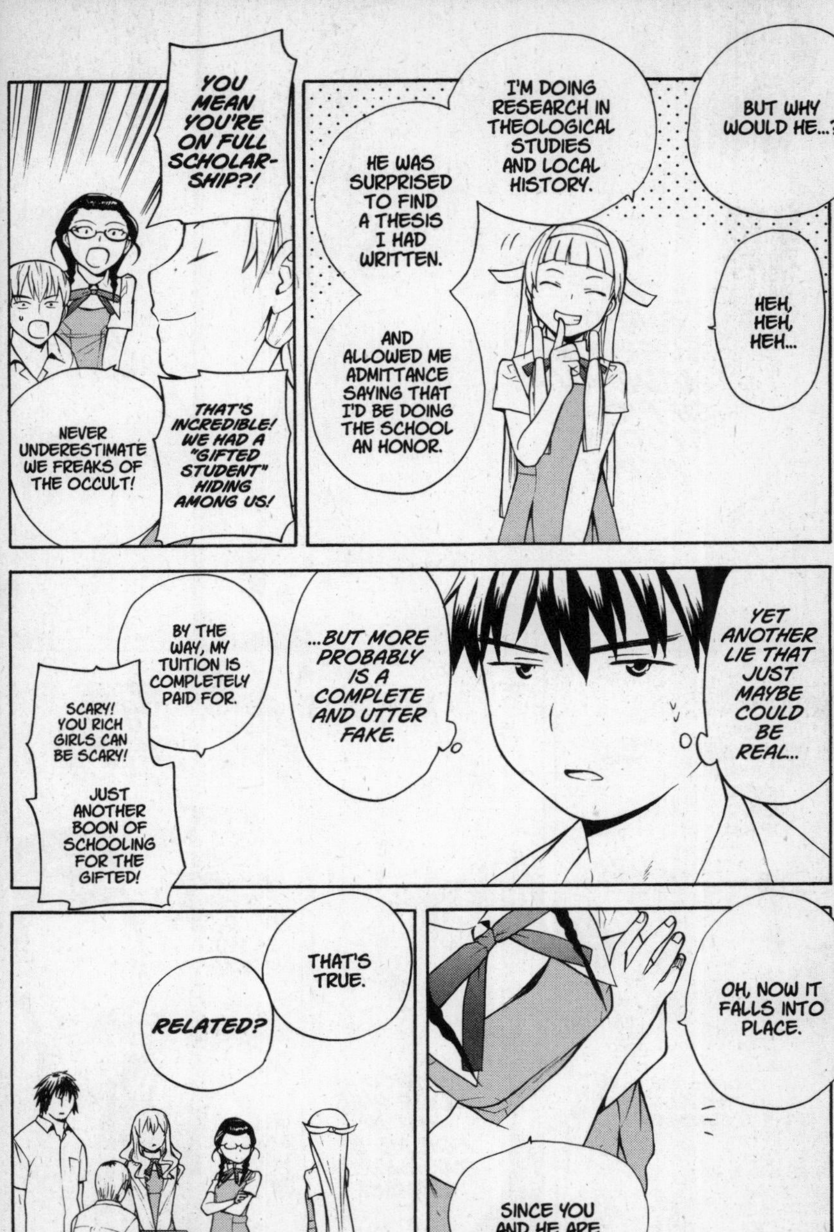
BUT WHY WOULD HE...?
HEH, HEH, HEH...
I'M DOING RESEARCH IN THEOLOGICAL STUDIES AND LOCAL HISTORY.
HE WAS SURPRISED TO FIND A THESIS I HAD WRITTEN.
AND ALLOWED ME ADMITTANCE SAYING THAT I'D BE DOING THE SCHOOL AN HONOR.
YOU MEAN YOU'RE ON FULL SCHOLAR-SHIP?!
THAT'S INCREDIBLE! WE HAD A "GIFTED STUDENT" HIDING AMONG US!
NEVER UNDERESTIMATE WE FREAKS OF THE OCCULT!
YET ANOTHER LIE THAT JUST MAYBE COULD BE REAL...
...BUT MORE PROBABLY IS A COMPLETE AND UTTER FAKE.
BY THE WAY, MY TUITION IS COMPLETELY PAID FOR.
SCARY! YOU RICH GIRLS CAN BE SCARY!
JUST ANOTHER BOON OF SCHOOLING FOR THE GIFTED!
OH, NOW IT FALLS INTO PLACE.
SINCE YOU AND HE ARE RELATED.
THAT'S TRUE.
RELATED?

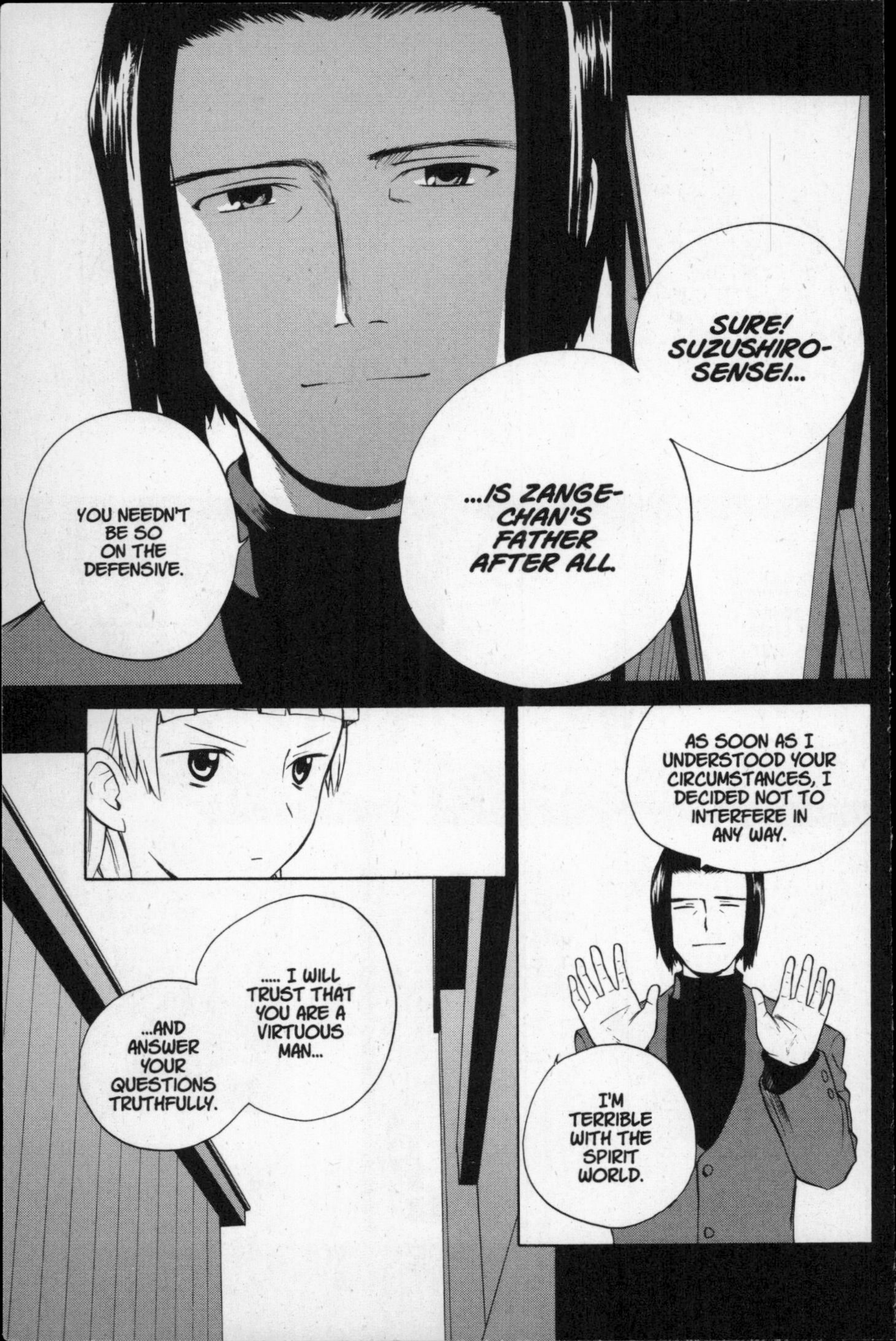
SURE! SUZUSHIRO-SENSEI...
...IS ZANGE-CHAN'S FATHER AFTER ALL.
YOU NEEDN'T BE SO ON THE DEFENSIVE.
AS SOON AS I UNDERSTOOD YOUR CIRCUMSTANCES, I DECIDED NOT TO INTERFERE IN ANY WAY.
I'M TERRIBLE WITH THE SPIRIT WORLD.
..... I WILL TRUST THAT YOU ARE A VIRTUOUS MAN...
...AND ANSWER YOUR QUESTIONS TRUTHFULLY.

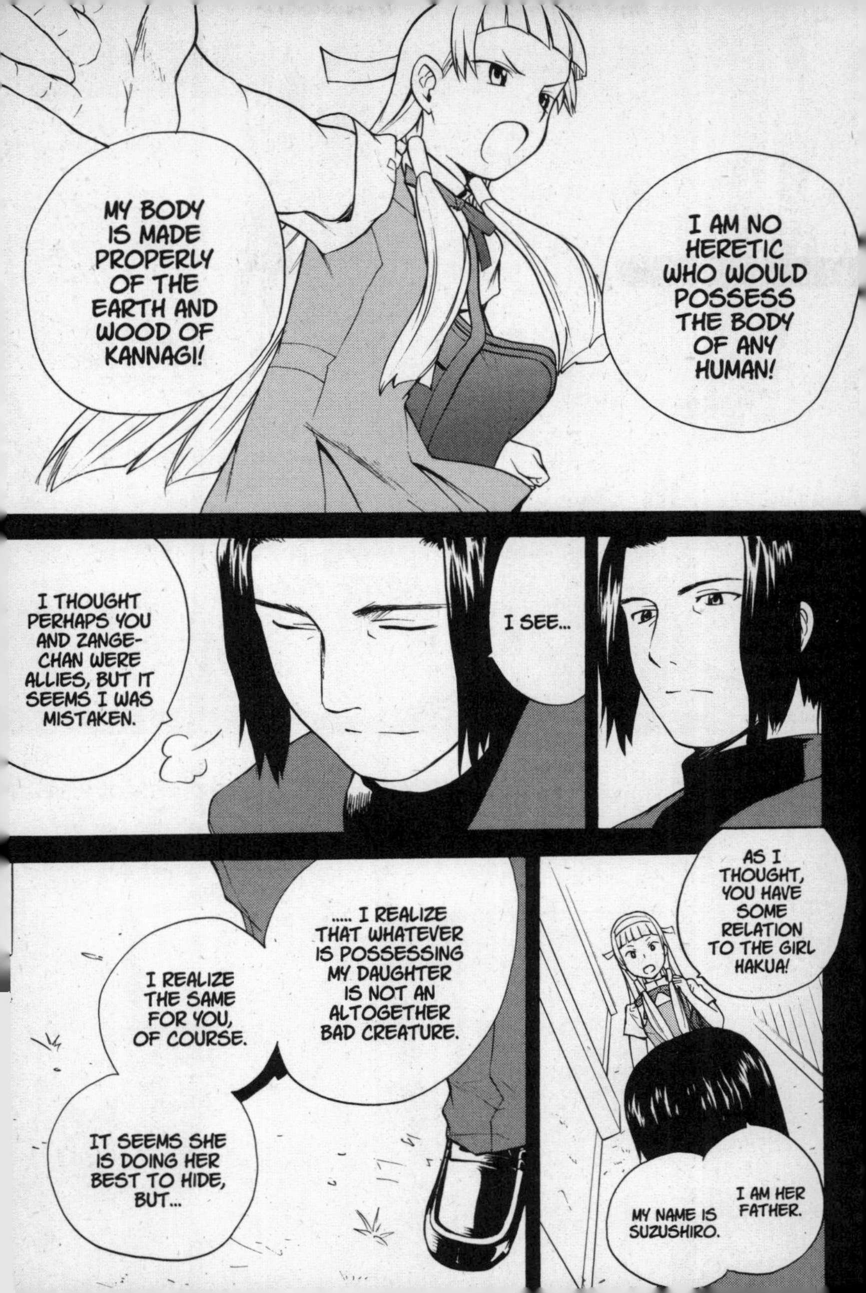
I AM NO HERETIC WHO WOULD POSSESS THE BODY OF ANY HUMAN!
MY BODY IS MADE PROPERLY OF THE EARTH AND WOOD OF KANNAGI!
I SEE...
I THOUGHT PERHAPS YOU AND ZANGE-CHAN WERE ALLIES, BUT IT SEEMS I WAS MISTAKEN.
AS I THOUGHT, YOU HAVE SOME RELATION TO THE GIRL HAKUA!
I AM HER FATHER.
MY NAME IS SUZUSHIRO.
..... I REALIZE THAT WHATEVER IS POSSESSING MY DAUGHTER IS NOT AN ALTOGETHER BAD CREATURE.
I REALIZE THE SAME FOR YOU, OF COURSE.
IT SEEMS SHE IS DOING HER BEST TO HIDE, BUT...

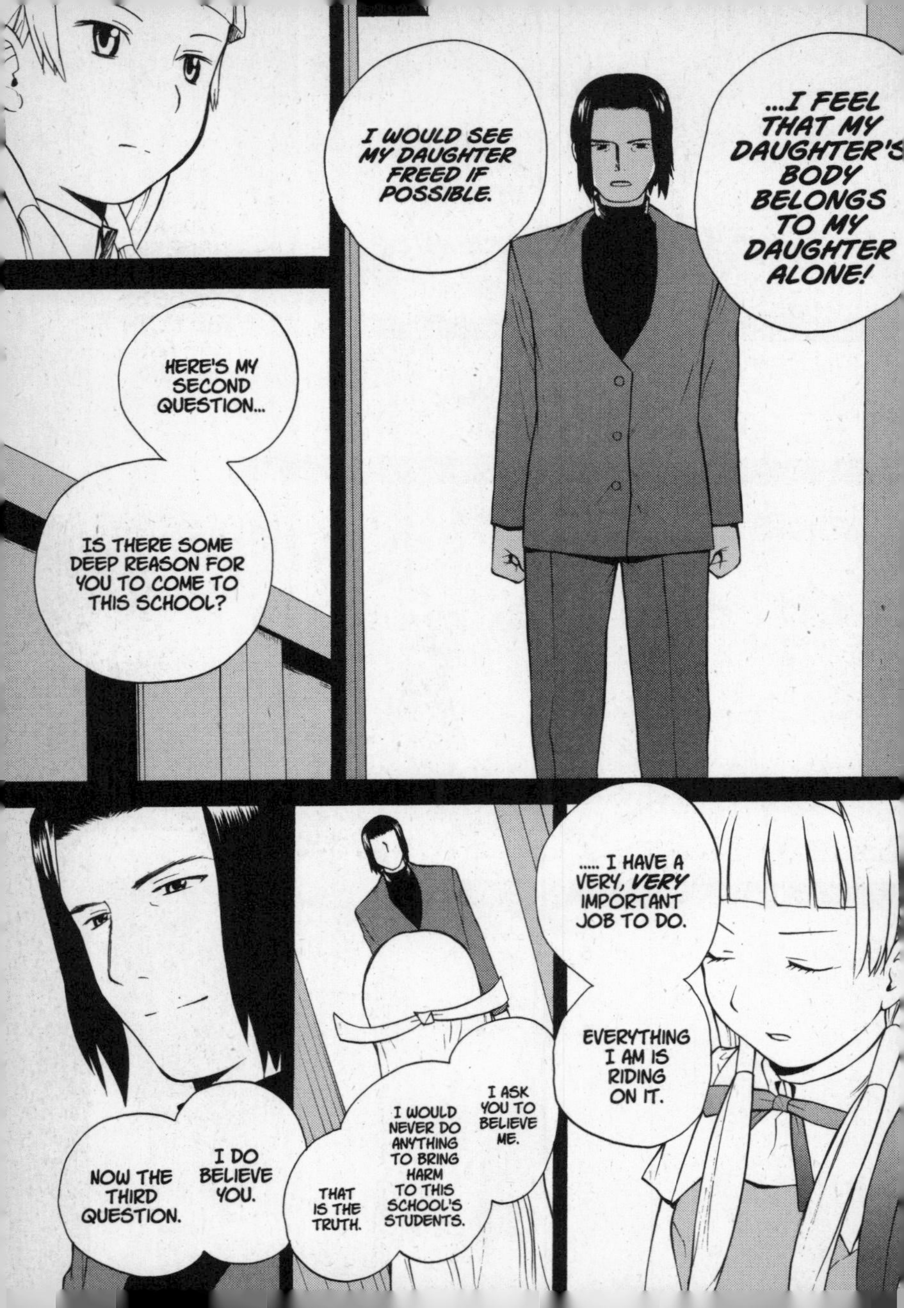
...I FEEL THAT MY DAUGHTER'S BODY BELONGS TO MY DAUGHTER ALONE!
I WOULD SEE MY DAUGHTER FREED IF POSSIBLE.
HERE'S MY SECOND QUESTION...
IS THERE SOME DEEP REASON FOR YOU TO COME TO THIS SCHOOL?
..... I HAVE A VERY, VERY IMPORTANT JOB TO DO.
EVERYTHING I AM IS RIDING ON IT.
I ASK YOU TO BELIEVE ME.
I WOULD NEVER DO ANYTHING TO BRING HARM TO THIS SCHOOL'S STUDENTS.
THAT IS THE TRUTH.
I DO BELIEVE YOU.
NOW THE THIRD QUESTION.

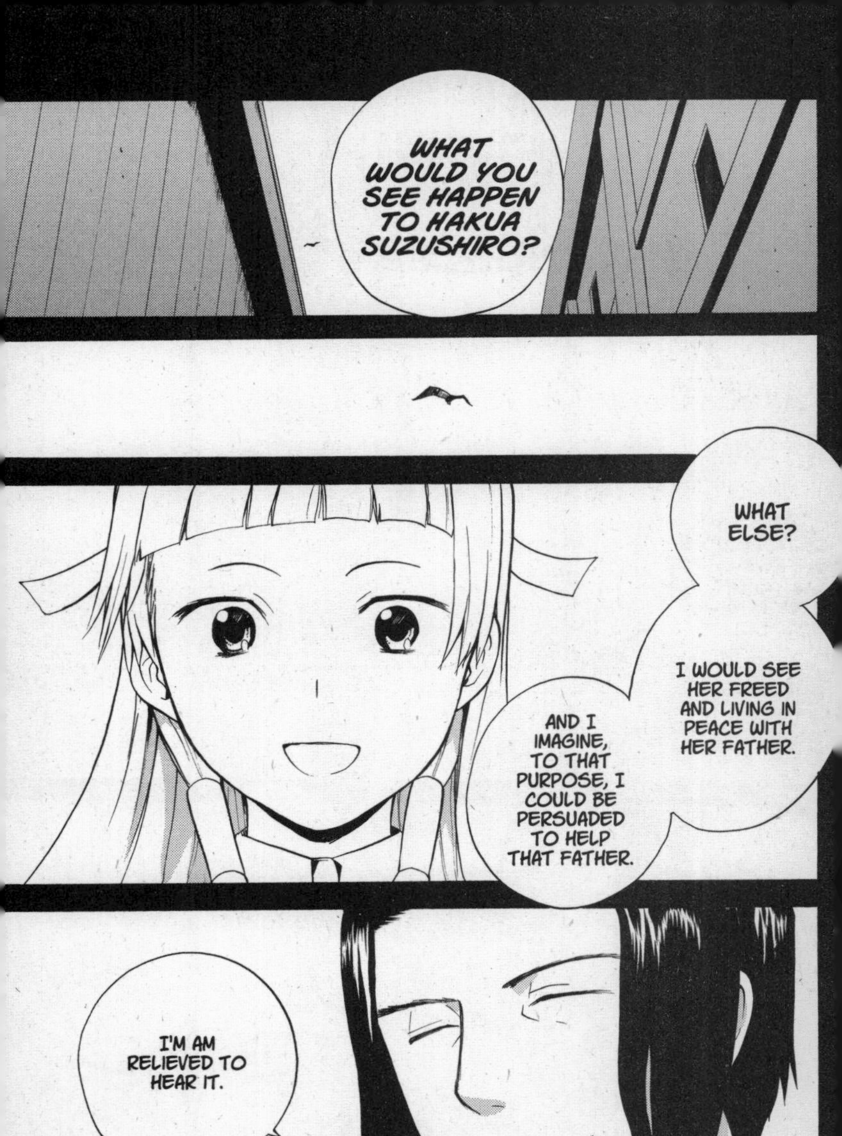
WHAT WOULD YOU SEE HAPPEN TO HAKUA SUZUSHIRO?
WHAT ELSE?
I WOULD SEE HER FREED AND LIVING IN PEACE WITH HER FATHER.
AND I IMAGINE, TO THAT PURPOSE, I COULD BE PERSUADED TO HELP THAT FATHER.
I'M AM RELIEVED TO HEAR IT.

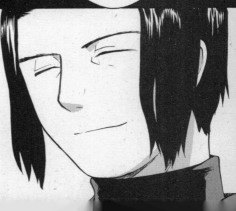

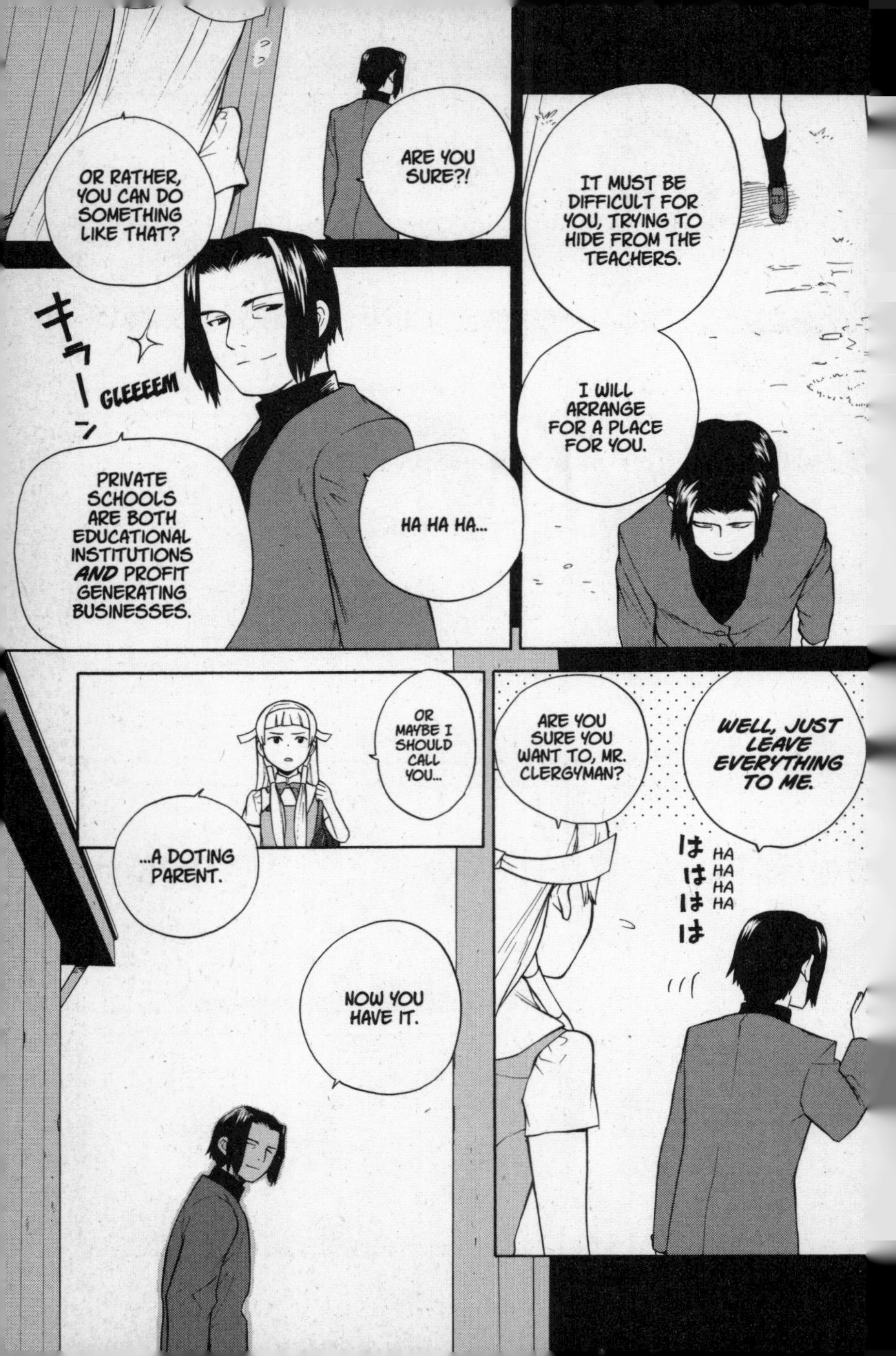

IT MUST BE DIFFICULT FOR YOU, TRYING TO HIDE FROM THE TEACHERS.
I WILL ARRANGE FOR A PLACE FOR YOU.
ARE YOU SURE?!
OR RATHER, YOU CAN DO SOMETHING LIKE THAT?
HA HA HA...
キラーン
GLEEEEM
PRIVATE SCHOOLS ARE BOTH EDUCATIONAL INSTITUTIONS AND PROFIT GENERATING BUSINESSES.
WELL, JUST LEAVE EVERYTHING TO ME.
ははははは
HA HA HA HA
ARE YOU SURE YOU WANT TO, MR. CLERGYMAN?
OR MAYBE I SHOULD CALL YOU...
...A DOTING PARENT.
NOW YOU HAVE IT.

Text: 2525 [line cut off], 2526 Kanno, Haruka, 2527 Suzushiro, Hakua,
2528 [cut off]no, Tetsuya, 2529 [cut off]ba, Kazushi, 2530 [cut off]no, Mai, 2531 [cut off]

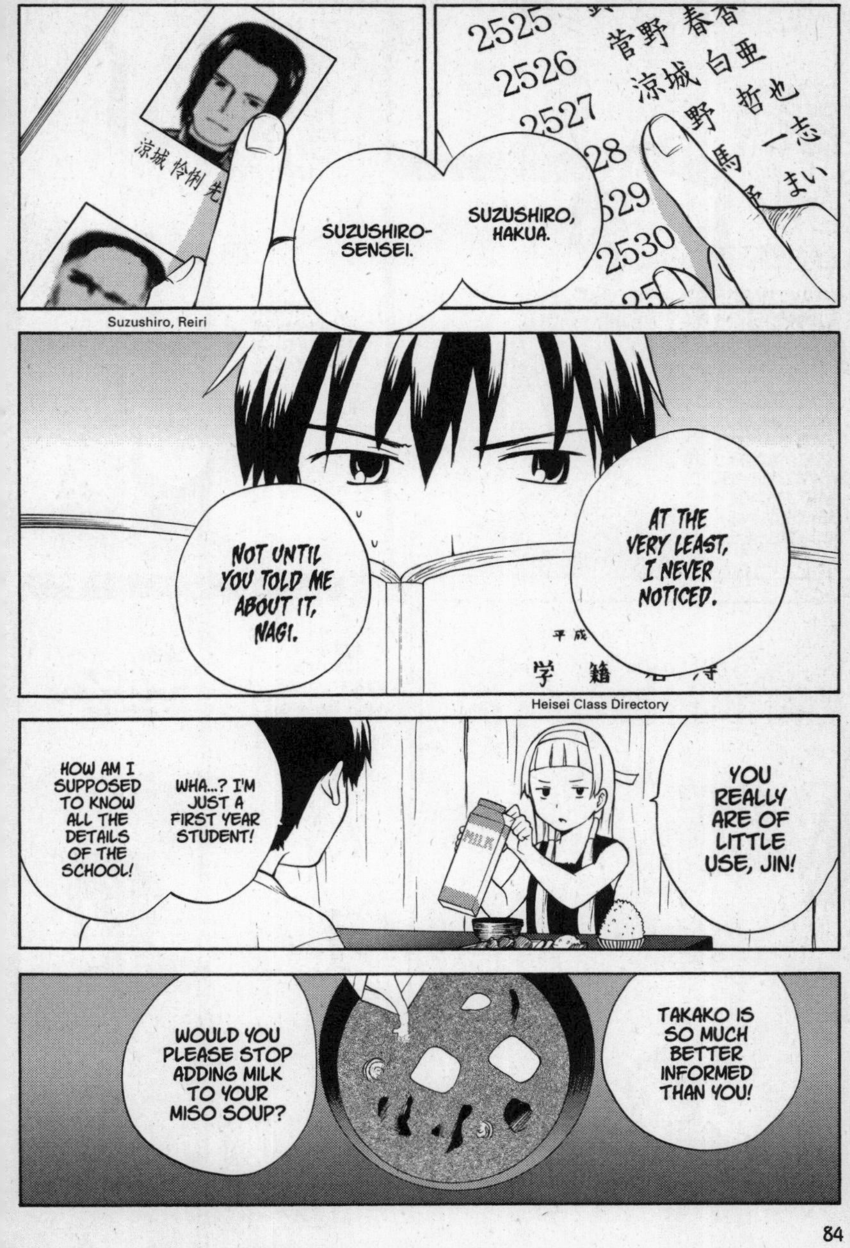
2525
2526 菅野 春香
2527 涼城 白亜
野 哲也
馬 一志
まい
2530
涼城 怜悧 先
SUZUSHIRO, HAKUA.
SUZUSHIRO-SENSEI.
AT THE VERY LEAST, I NEVER NOTICED.
NOT UNTIL YOU TOLD ME ABOUT IT, NAGI.
平成
YOU REALLY ARE OF LITTLE USE, JIN!
WHA...? I'M JUST A FIRST YEAR STUDENT!
HOW AM I SUPPOSED TO KNOW ALL THE DETAILS OF THE SCHOOL!
MILK
TAKAKO IS SO MUCH BETTER INFORMED THAN YOU!
WOULD YOU PLEASE STOP ADDING MILK TO YOUR MISO SOUP?

Suzushiro, Reiri

Heisei Class Directory

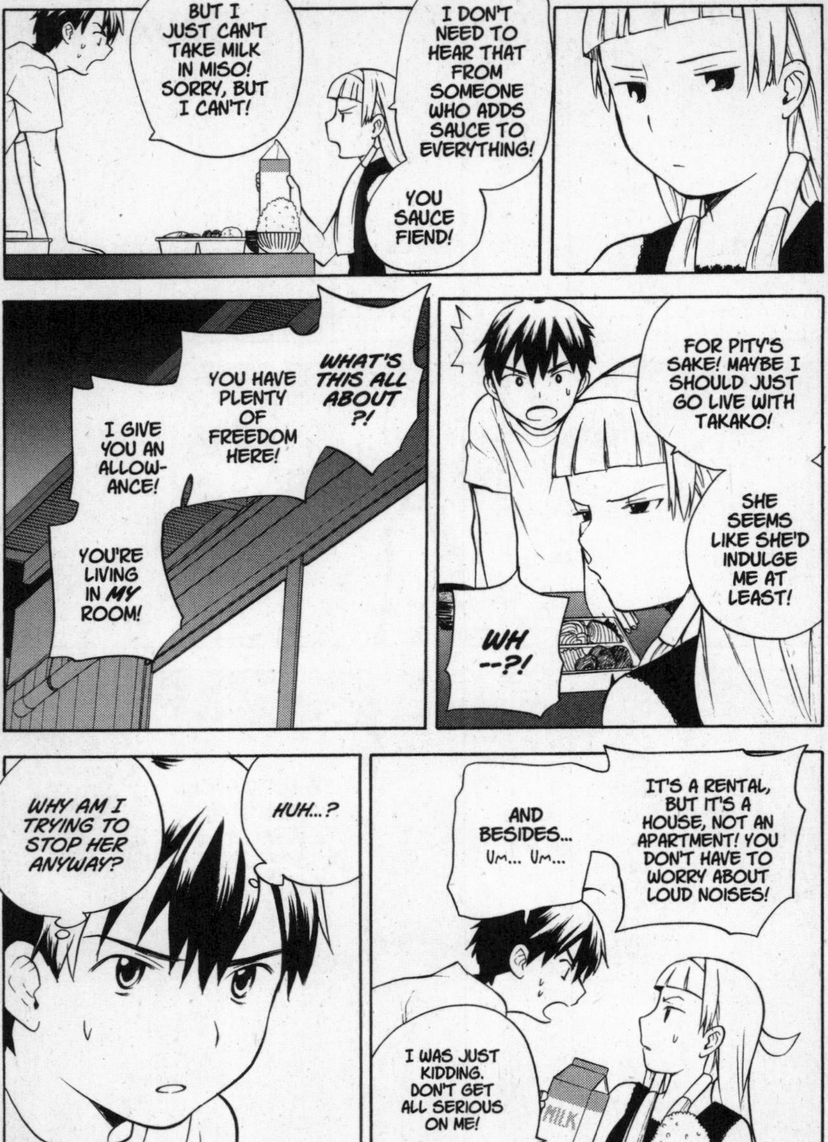
BUT I JUST CAN'T TAKE MILK IN MISO! SORRY, BUT I CAN'T!
I DON'T NEED TO HEAR THAT FROM SOMEONE WHO ADDS SAUCE TO EVERYTHING!
YOU SAUCE FIEND!
FOR PITY'S SAKE! MAYBE I SHOULD JUST GO LIVE WITH TAKAKO!
SHE SEEMS LIKE SHE'D INDULGE ME AT LEAST!
WH--?!
WHAT'S THIS ALL ABOUT?!
YOU HAVE PLENTY OF FREEDOM HERE!
I GIVE YOU AN ALLOW-ANCE!
YOU'RE LIVING IN MY ROOM!
IT'S A RENTAL, BUT IT'S A HOUSE, NOT AN APARTMENT! YOU DON'T HAVE TO WORRY ABOUT LOUD NOISES!
AND BESIDES...
Um... Um...
I WAS JUST KIDDING. DON'T GET ALL SERIOUS ON ME!
Don't make me spill my rice.
MILK
HUH...?
WHY AM I TRYING TO STOP HER ANYWAY?

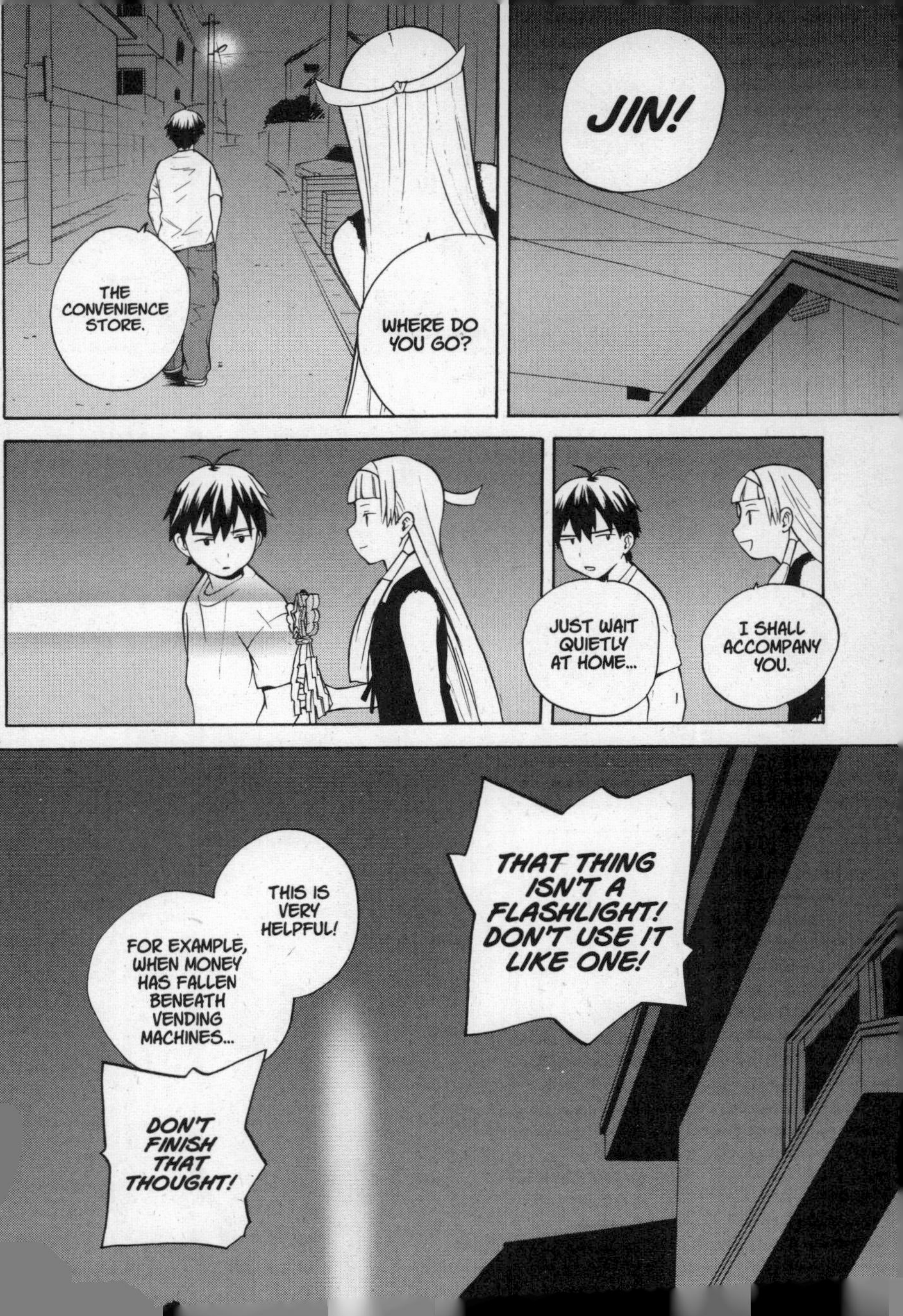
JIN!
WHERE DO YOU GO?
THE CONVENIENCE STORE.
I SHALL ACCOMPANY YOU.
JUST WAIT QUIETLY AT HOME...
THAT THING ISN'T A FLASHLIGHT! DON'T USE IT LIKE ONE!
THIS IS VERY HELPFUL!
FOR EXAMPLE, WHEN MONEY HAS FALLEN BENEATH VENDING MACHINES...
DON'T FINISH THAT THOUGHT!

K A N N A G I

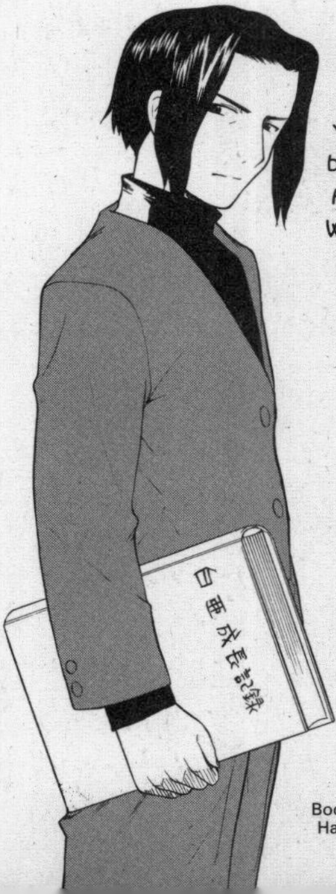
白亜成長記録

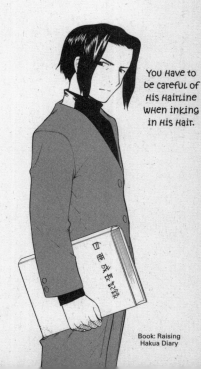

You Have to be careful of His Hairline when inking in His Hair.

Book: Raising Hakua Diary

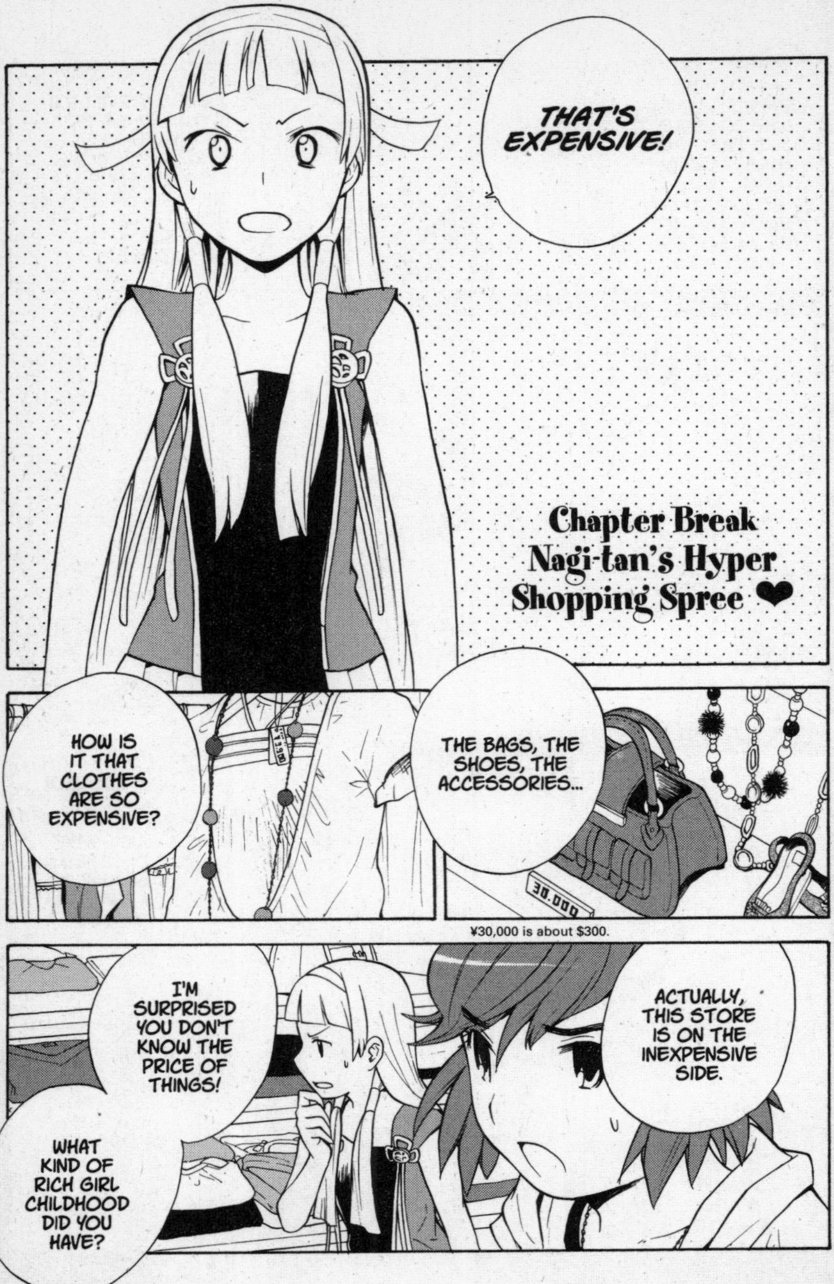
THAT'S EXPENSIVE!
Chapter Break Nagi-tan's Hyper Shopping Spree ❤
THE BAGS, THE SHOES, THE ACCESSORIES...
30,000
HOW IS IT THAT CLOTHES ARE SO EXPENSIVE?
ACTUALLY, THIS STORE IS ON THE INEXPENSIVE SIDE.
I'M SURPRISED YOU DON'T KNOW THE PRICE OF THINGS!
WHAT KIND OF RICH GIRL CHILDHOOD DID YOU HAVE?

¥30,000 is about $300.

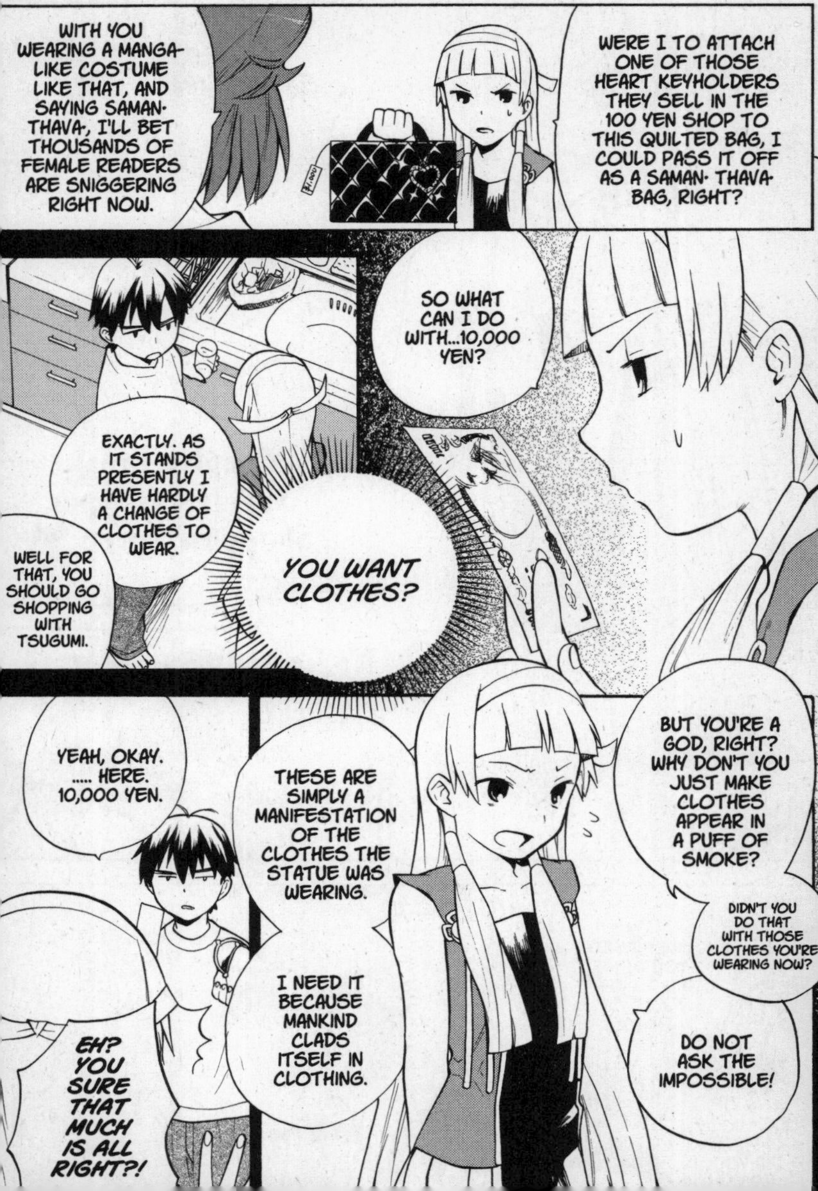
WERE I TO ATTACH ONE OF THOSE HEART KEYHOLDERS THEY SELL IN THE 100 YEN SHOP TO THIS QUILTED BAG, I COULD PASS IT OFF AS A SAMAN- THAVA- BAG, RIGHT?
WITH YOU WEARING A MANGA-LIKE COSTUME LIKE THAT, AND SAYING SAMAN-THAVA-, I'LL BET THOUSANDS OF FEMALE READERS ARE SNIGGERING RIGHT NOW.
SO WHAT CAN I DO WITH...10,000 YEN?
YOU WANT CLOTHES?
EXACTLY. AS IT STANDS PRESENTLY I HAVE HARDLY A CHANGE OF CLOTHES TO WEAR.
WELL FOR THAT, YOU SHOULD GO SHOPPING WITH TSUGUMI.
BUT YOU'RE A GOD, RIGHT? WHY DON'T YOU JUST MAKE CLOTHES APPEAR IN A PUFF OF SMOKE?
DIDN'T YOU DO THAT WITH THOSE CLOTHES YOU'RE WEARING NOW?
DO NOT ASK THE IMPOSSIBLE!
THESE ARE SIMPLY A MANIFESTATION OF THE CLOTHES THE STATUE WAS WEARING.
I NEED IT BECAUSE MANKIND CLADS ITSELF IN CLOTHING.
YEAH, OKAY. ..... HERE. 10,000 YEN.
EH? YOU SURE THAT MUCH IS ALL RIGHT?!

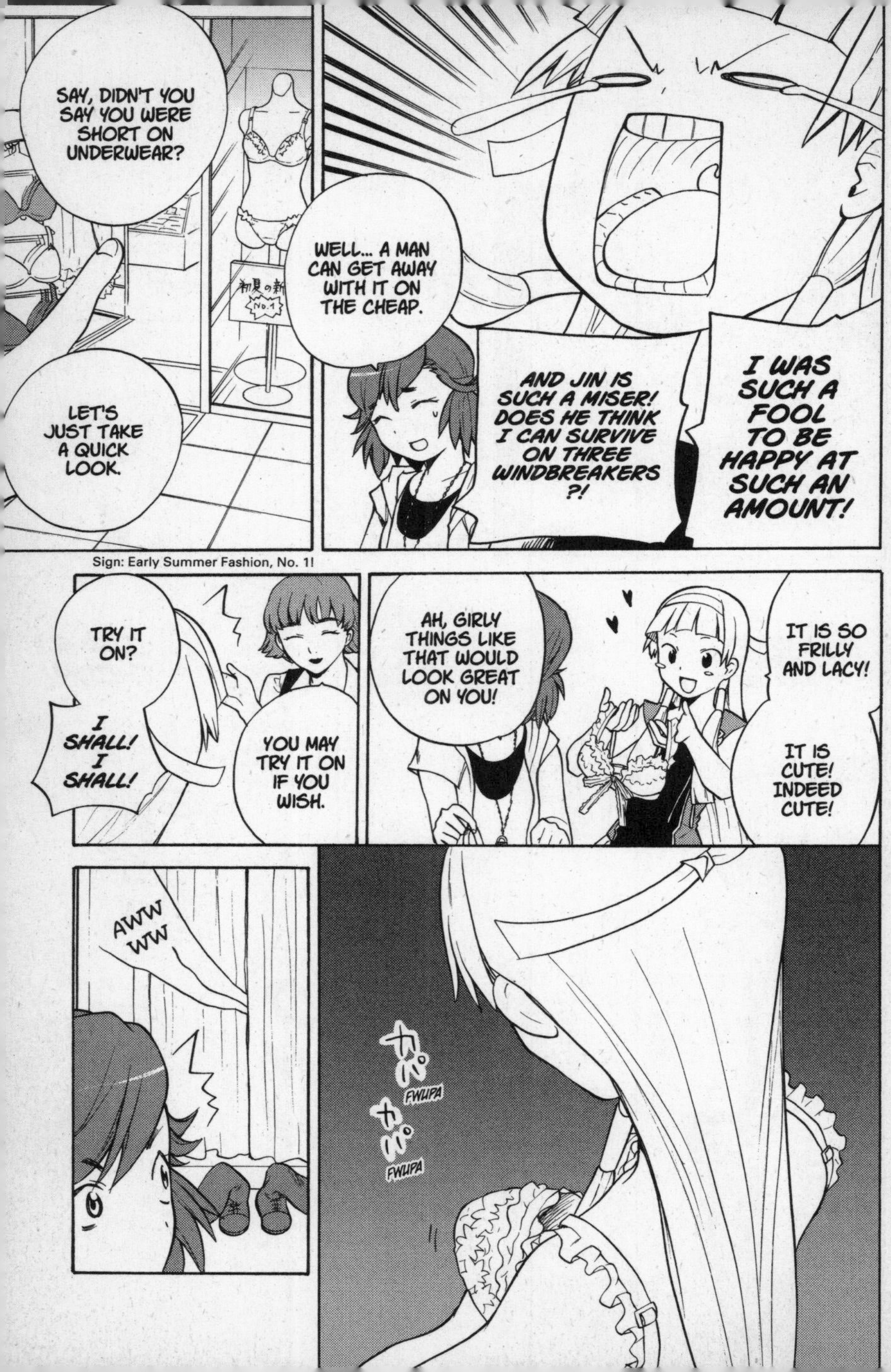
I WAS SUCH A FOOL TO BE HAPPY AT SUCH AN AMOUNT!
AND JIN IS SUCH A MISER! DOES HE THINK I CAN SURVIVE ON THREE WINDBREAKERS?!
WELL... A MAN CAN GET AWAY WITH IT ON THE CHEAP.
SAY, DIDN'T YOU SAY YOU WERE SHORT ON UNDERWEAR?
初夏の新
No.1
LET'S JUST TAKE A QUICK LOOK.
Sign: Early Summer Fashion, No. 1!
IT IS SO FRILLY AND LACY!
IT IS CUTE! INDEED CUTE!
AH, GIRLY THINGS LIKE THAT WOULD LOOK GREAT ON YOU!
YOU MAY TRY IT ON IF YOU WISH.
TRY IT ON?
I SHALL! I SHALL!
FWUPA
FWUPA
AWW WW

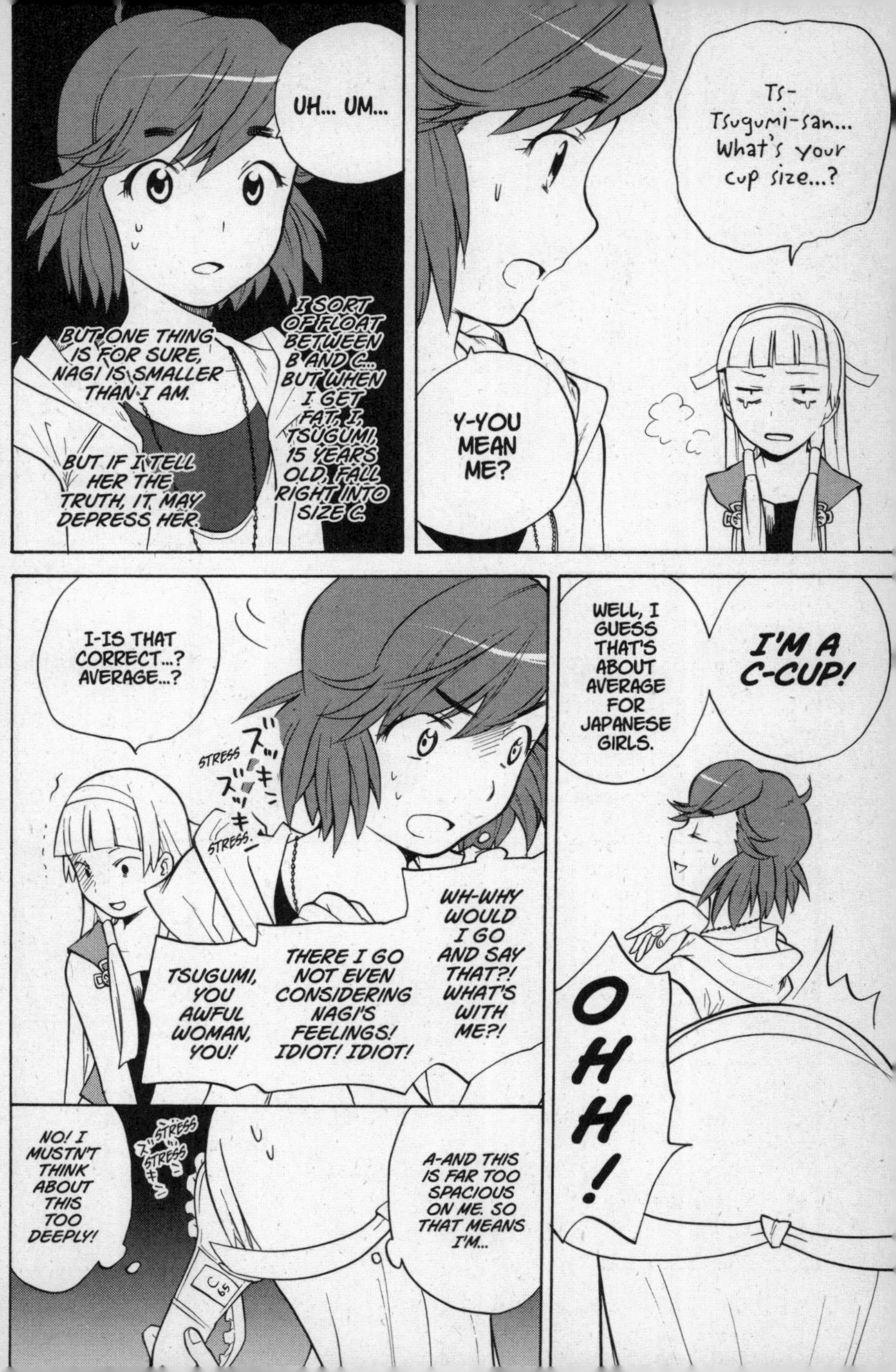
Ts-Tsugumi-san... What's your cup size...?
Y-YOU MEAN ME?
UH... UM...
I SORT OF FLOAT BETWEEN B AND C... BUT WHEN I GET FAT, I, TSUGUMI, 15 YEARS OLD, FALL RIGHT INTO SIZE C.
BUT ONE THING IS FOR SURE, NAGI IS SMALLER THAN I AM.
BUT IF I TELL HER THE TRUTH, IT MAY DEPRESS HER.
I'M A C-CUP!
WELL, I GUESS THAT'S ABOUT AVERAGE FOR JAPANESE GIRLS.
OHH!
I-IS THAT CORRECT...? AVERAGE...?
STRESS
STRESS
WH-WHY WOULD I GO AND SAY THAT?! WHAT'S WITH ME?!
THERE I GO NOT EVEN CONSIDERING NAGI'S FEELINGS! IDIOT! IDIOT!
TSUGUMI, YOU AWFUL WOMAN, YOU!
A-AND THIS IS FAR TOO SPACIOUS ON ME. SO THAT MEANS I'M...
STRESS
STRESS
NO! I MUSTN'T THINK ABOUT THIS TOO DEEPLY!

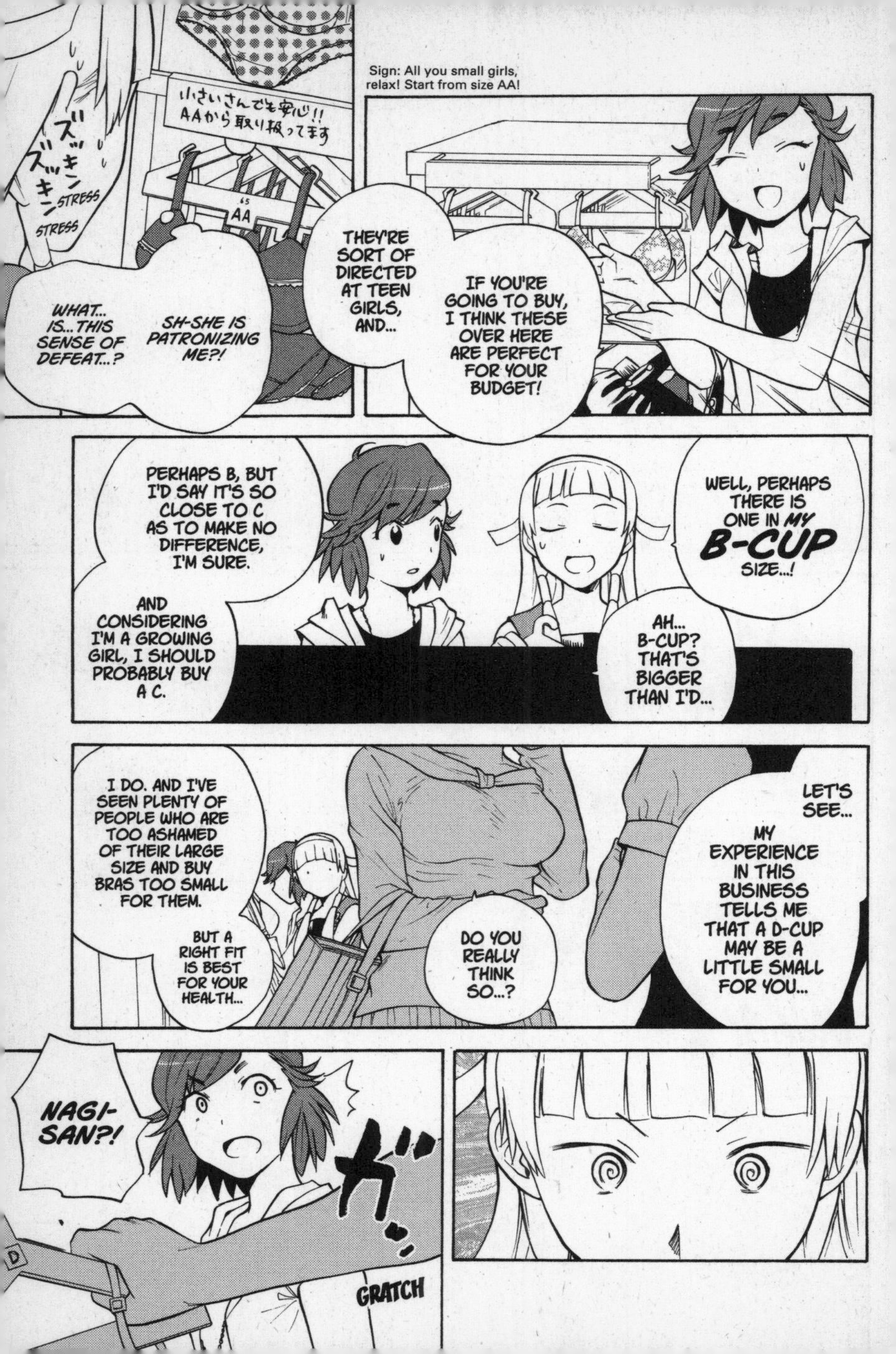
Sign: All you small girls, relax! Start from size AA!
IF YOU'RE GOING TO BUY, I THINK THESE OVER HERE ARE PERFECT FOR YOUR BUDGET!
THEY'RE SORT OF DIRECTED AT TEEN GIRLS, AND...
小さいさんでも安心!! AAから取り扱ってます
65 AA
ズッキン ズッキン STRESS STRESS
SH-SHE IS PATRONIZING ME?!
WHAT... IS...THIS SENSE OF DEFEAT...?
WELL, PERHAPS THERE IS ONE IN MY B-CUP SIZE...!
AH... B-CUP? THAT'S BIGGER THAN I'D...
PERHAPS B, BUT I'D SAY IT'S SO CLOSE TO C AS TO MAKE NO DIFFERENCE, I'M SURE.
AND CONSIDERING I'M A GROWING GIRL, I SHOULD PROBABLY BUY A C.
LET'S SEE...
MY EXPERIENCE IN THIS BUSINESS TELLS ME THAT A D-CUP MAY BE A LITTLE SMALL FOR YOU...
DO YOU REALLY THINK SO...?
I DO. AND I'VE SEEN PLENTY OF PEOPLE WHO ARE TOO ASHAMED OF THEIR LARGE SIZE AND BUY BRAS TOO SMALL FOR THEM.
BUT A RIGHT FIT IS BEST FOR YOUR HEALTH...
NAGI-SAN?!
ガッ
GRATCH
D

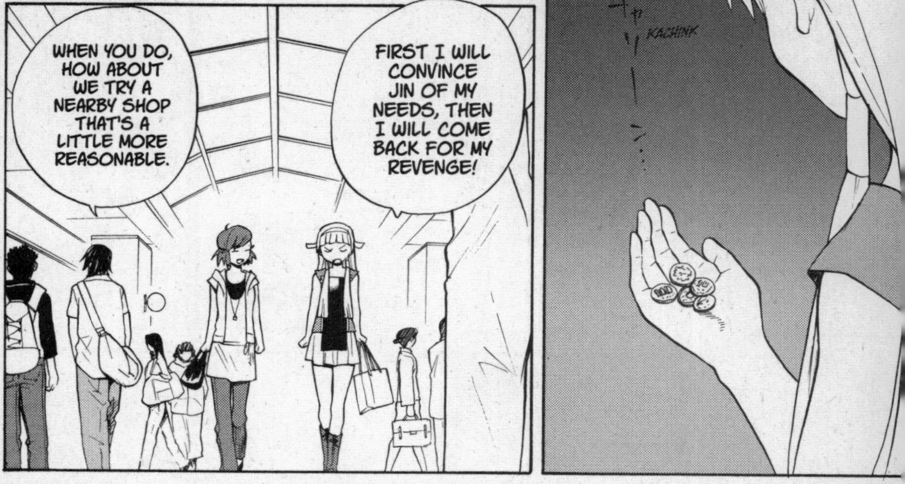
KACHINK
FIRST I WILL CONVINCE JIN OF MY NEEDS, THEN I WILL COME BACK FOR MY REVENGE!
WHEN YOU DO, HOW ABOUT WE TRY A NEARBY SHOP THAT'S A LITTLE MORE REASONABLE.

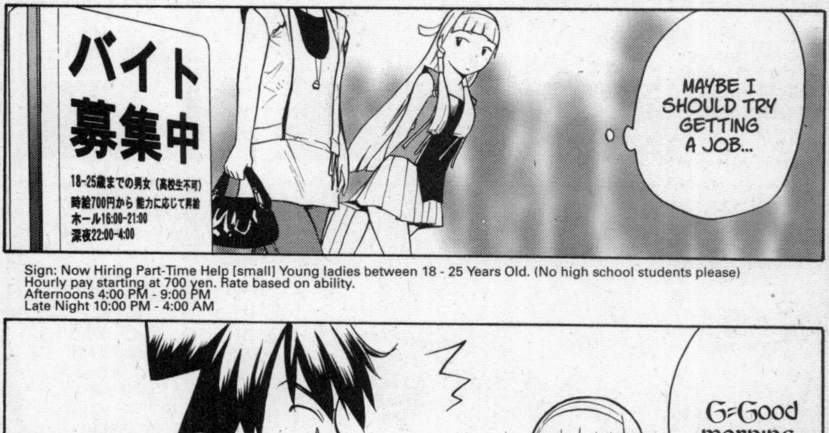
MAYBE I SHOULD TRY GETTING A JOB...
バイト
募集中
18-25歳までの男女（高校生不可）
時給700円から 能力に応じて昇給
ホール16:00-21:00
深夜22:00-4:00

Sign: Now Hiring Part-Time Help [small] Young ladies between 18 - 25 Years Old. (No high school students please)
Hourly pay starting at 700 yen. Rate based on ability.
Afternoons 4:00 PM - 9:00 PM
Late Night 10:00 PM - 4:00 AM

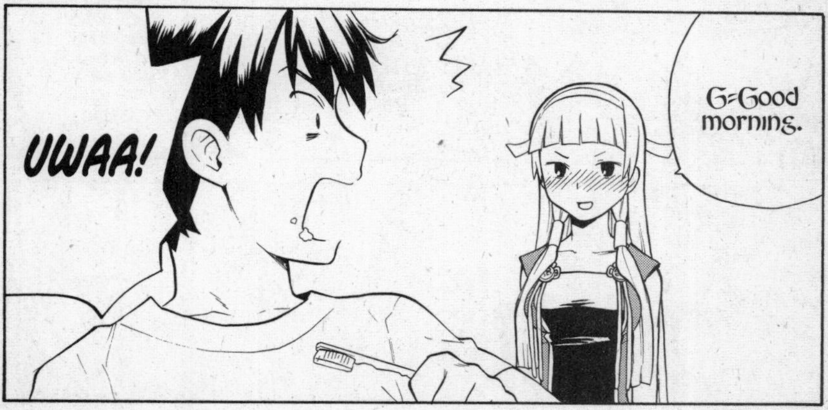
G-Good morning.
UWAA!

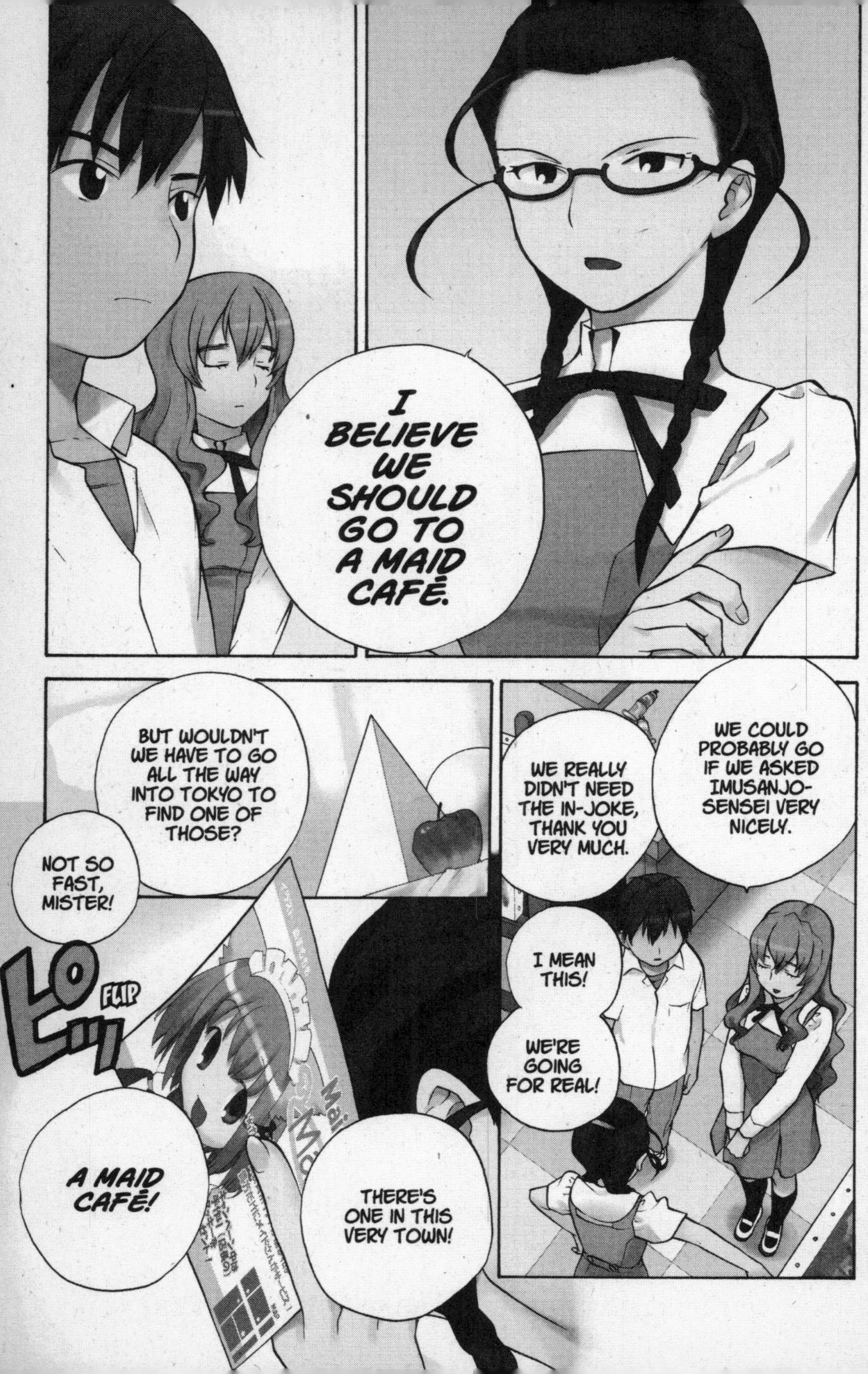

I BELIEVE WE SHOULD GO TO A MAID CAFÉ.
WE COULD PROBABLY GO IF WE ASKED IMUSANJO-SENSEI VERY NICELY.
WE REALLY DIDN'T NEED THE IN-JOKE, THANK YOU VERY MUCH.
I MEAN THIS!
WE'RE GOING FOR REAL!
BUT WOULDN'T WE HAVE TO GO ALL THE WAY INTO TOKYO TO FIND ONE OF THOSE?
NOT SO FAST, MISTER!
FLIP
THERE'S ONE IN THIS VERY TOWN!
A MAID CAFÉ!

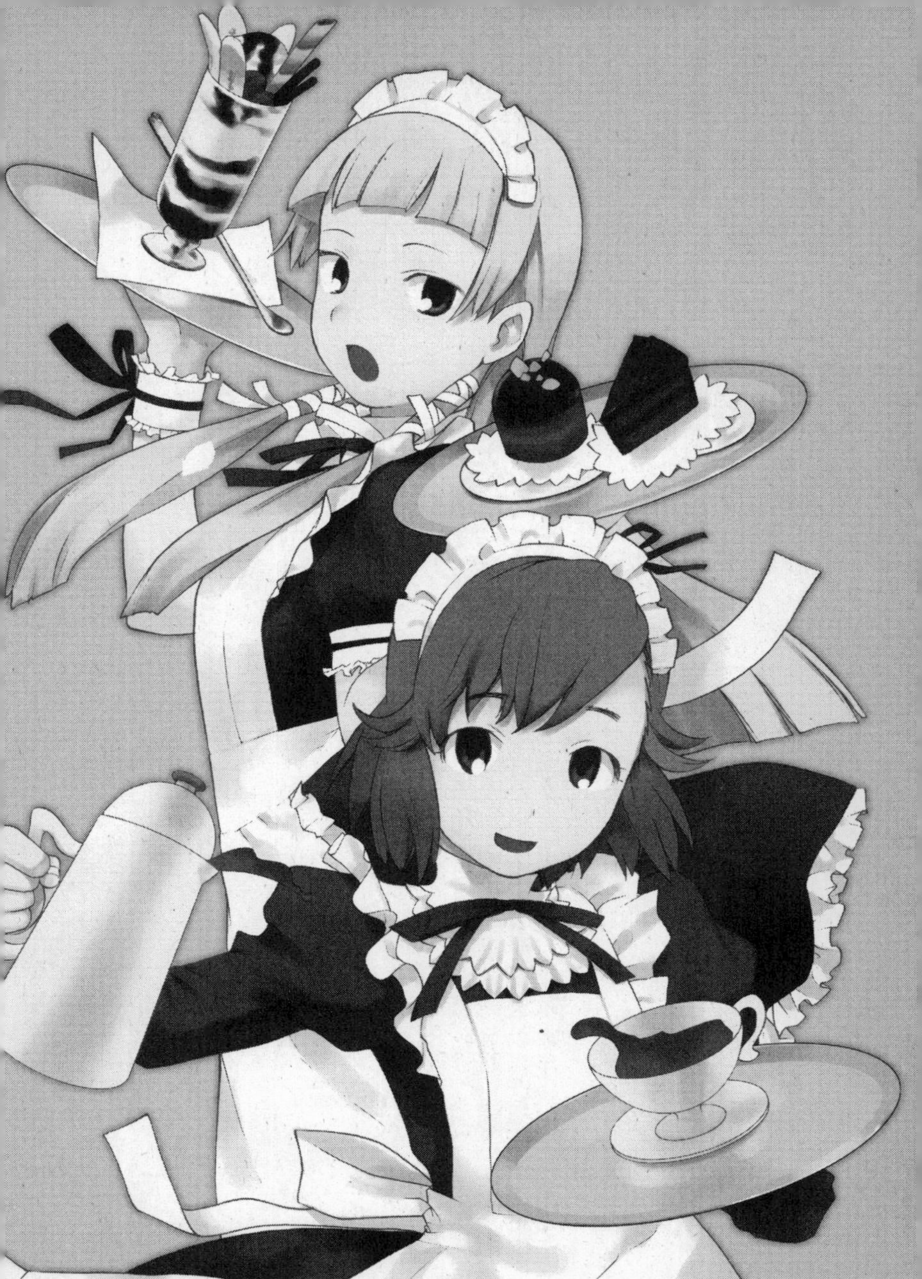

Eleventh Chapter Those Girls Are Crazy

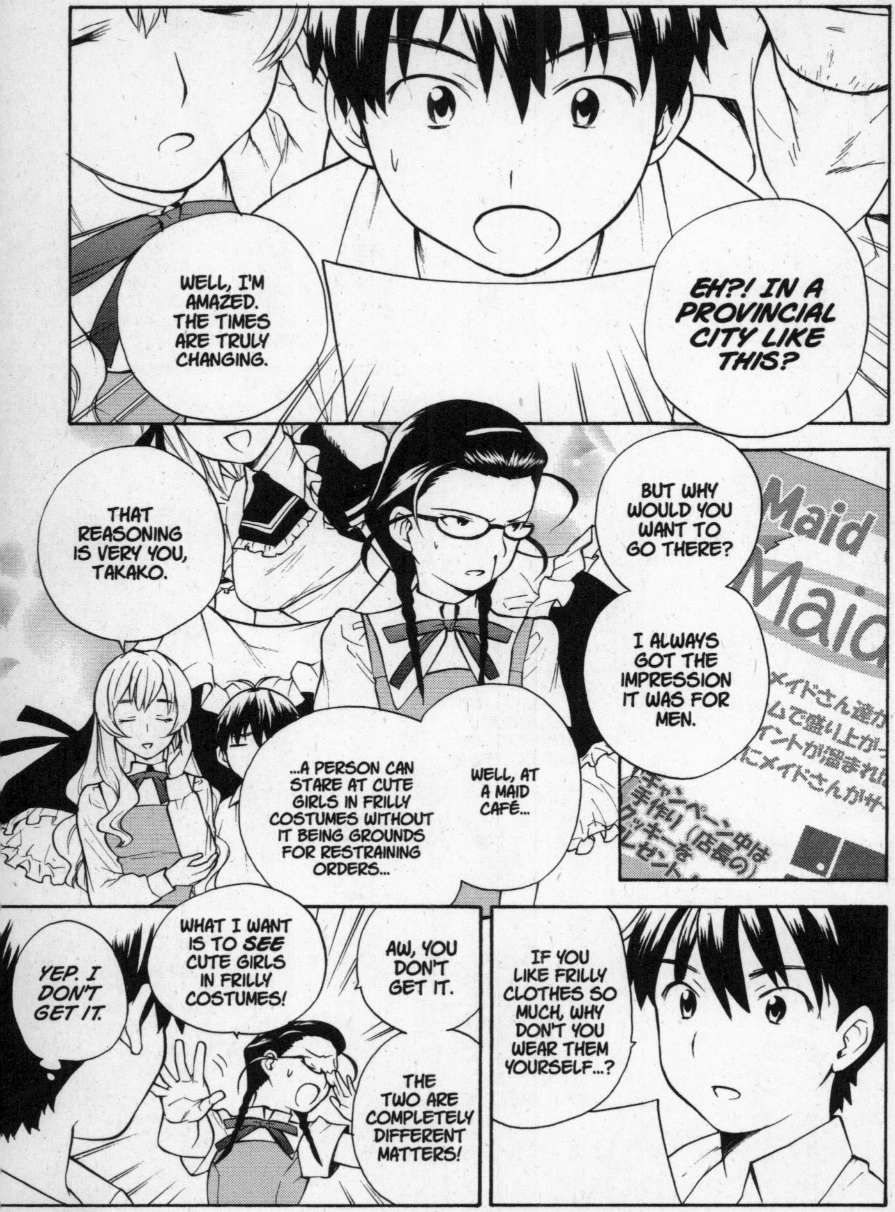
EH?! IN A PROVINCIAL CITY LIKE THIS?
WELL, I'M AMAZED. THE TIMES ARE TRULY CHANGING.
Maid
Maid
BUT WHY WOULD YOU WANT TO GO THERE?
I ALWAYS GOT THE IMPRESSION IT WAS FOR MEN.
THAT REASONING IS VERY YOU, TAKAKO.
WELL, AT A MAID CAFÉ...
...A PERSON CAN STARE AT CUTE GIRLS IN FRILLY COSTUMES WITHOUT IT BEING GROUNDS FOR RESTRAINING ORDERS...
IF YOU LIKE FRILLY CLOTHES SO MUCH, WHY DON'T YOU WEAR THEM YOURSELF...?
AW, YOU DON'T GET IT.
WHAT I WANT IS TO *SEE* CUTE GIRLS IN FRILLY COSTUMES!
THE TWO ARE COMPLETELY DIFFERENT MATTERS!
YEP. I DON'T GET IT.

Flyer: Our maids will [cut off] Sings Karaoke, Plays games with enthusiasm and [cut off]
Registered members can earn points to [cut off] as your maid does [cut off]
Special offer! Receive homemade cookies (made by the head manager) as a free gift to you!

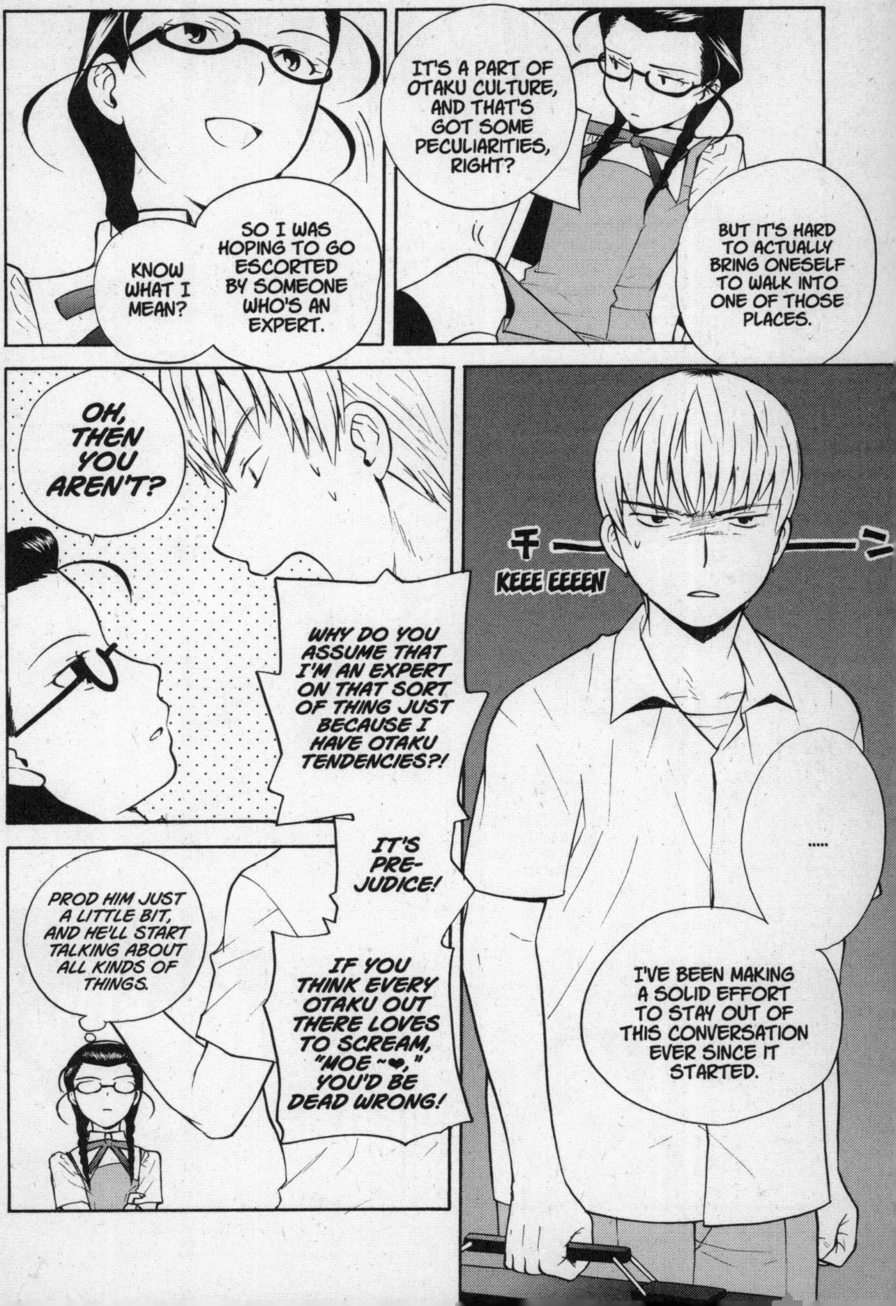
IT'S A PART OF OTAKU CULTURE, AND THAT'S GOT SOME PECULIARITIES, RIGHT?
BUT IT'S HARD TO ACTUALLY BRING ONESELF TO WALK INTO ONE OF THOSE PLACES.
SO I WAS HOPING TO GO ESCORTED BY SOMEONE WHO'S AN EXPERT.
KNOW WHAT I MEAN?
KEEE EEEEN
.....
I'VE BEEN MAKING A SOLID EFFORT TO STAY OUT OF THIS CONVERSATION EVER SINCE IT STARTED.
OH, THEN YOU AREN'T?
WHY DO YOU ASSUME THAT I'M AN EXPERT ON THAT SORT OF THING JUST BECAUSE I HAVE OTAKU TENDENCIES?!
IT'S PRE-JUDICE!
IF YOU THINK EVERY OTAKU OUT THERE LOVES TO SCREAM, "MOE ~❤," YOU'D BE DEAD WRONG!
PROD HIM JUST A LITTLE BIT, AND HE'LL START TALKING ABOUT ALL KINDS OF THINGS.

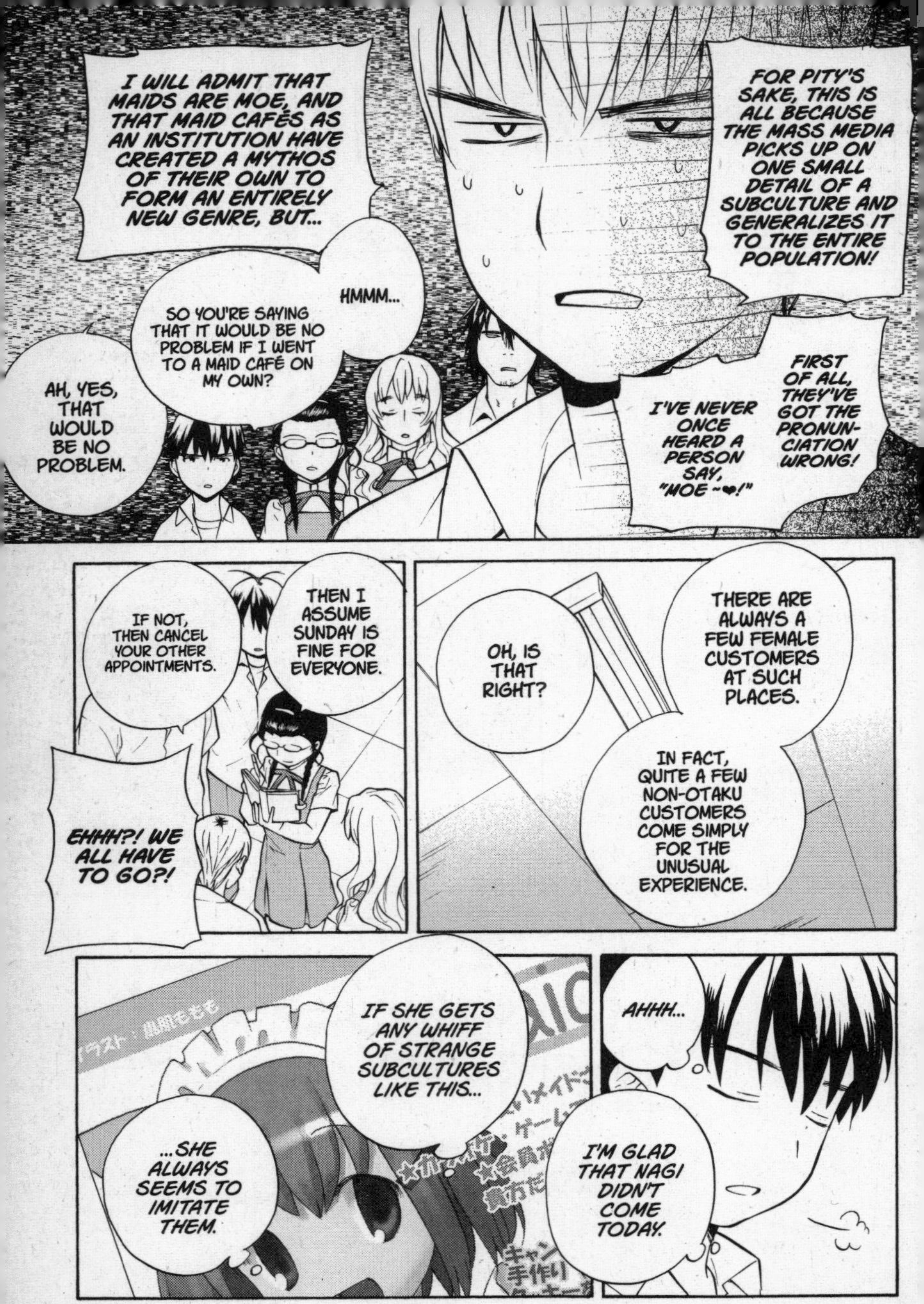
FOR PITY'S SAKE, THIS IS ALL BECAUSE THE MASS MEDIA PICKS UP ON ONE SMALL DETAIL OF A SUBCULTURE AND GENERALIZES IT TO THE ENTIRE POPULATION!
I WILL ADMIT THAT MAIDS ARE MOE, AND THAT MAID CAFÉS AS AN INSTITUTION HAVE CREATED A MYTHOS OF THEIR OWN TO FORM AN ENTIRELY NEW GENRE, BUT...
FIRST OF ALL, THEY'VE GOT THE PRONUNCIATION WRONG!
I'VE NEVER ONCE HEARD A PERSON SAY, "MOE ~♥!"
HMMM...
SO YOU'RE SAYING THAT IT WOULD BE NO PROBLEM IF I WENT TO A MAID CAFÉ ON MY OWN?
AH, YES, THAT WOULD BE NO PROBLEM.
THERE ARE ALWAYS A FEW FEMALE CUSTOMERS AT SUCH PLACES.
OH, IS THAT RIGHT?
IN FACT, QUITE A FEW NON-OTAKU CUSTOMERS COME SIMPLY FOR THE UNUSUAL EXPERIENCE.
THEN I ASSUME SUNDAY IS FINE FOR EVERYONE.
IF NOT, THEN CANCEL YOUR OTHER APPOINTMENTS.
EHHH?! WE ALL HAVE TO GO?!
AHHH...
I'M GLAD THAT NAGI DIDN'T COME TODAY.
IF SHE GETS ANY WHIFF OF STRANGE SUBCULTURES LIKE THIS...
...SHE ALWAYS SEEMS TO IMITATE THEM.

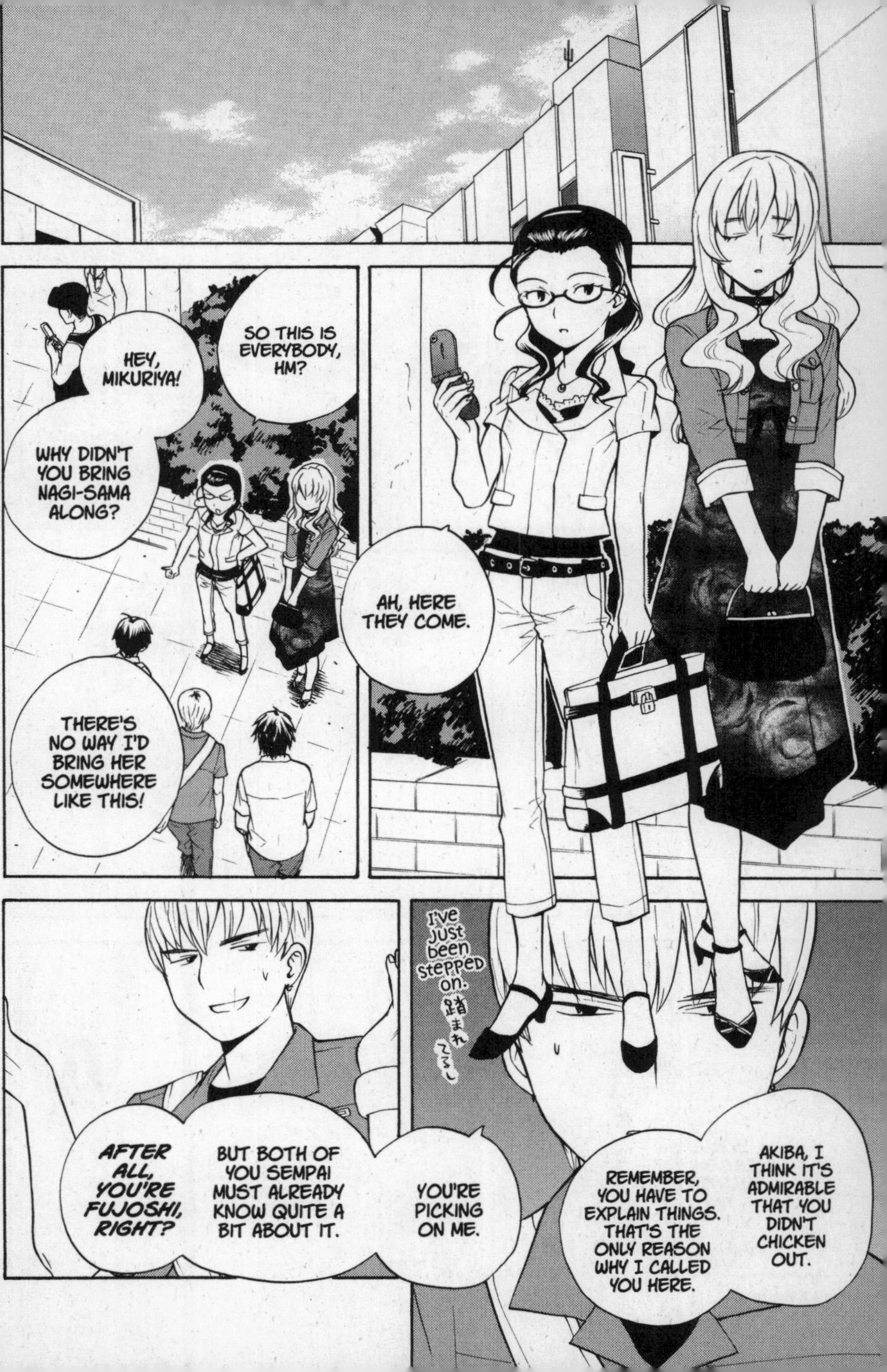
AH, HERE THEY COME.
SO THIS IS EVERYBODY, HM?
HEY, MIKURIYA!
WHY DIDN'T YOU BRING NAGI-SAMA ALONG?
THERE'S NO WAY I'D BRING HER SOMEWHERE LIKE THIS!
I've just been stepped on.
踏まれてるし
AKIBA, I THINK IT'S ADMIRABLE THAT YOU DIDN'T CHICKEN OUT.
REMEMBER, YOU HAVE TO EXPLAIN THINGS. THAT'S THE ONLY REASON WHY I CALLED YOU HERE.
YOU'RE PICKING ON ME.
BUT BOTH OF YOU SEMPAI MUST ALREADY KNOW QUITE A BIT ABOUT IT.
AFTER ALL, YOU'RE FUJOSHI, RIGHT?

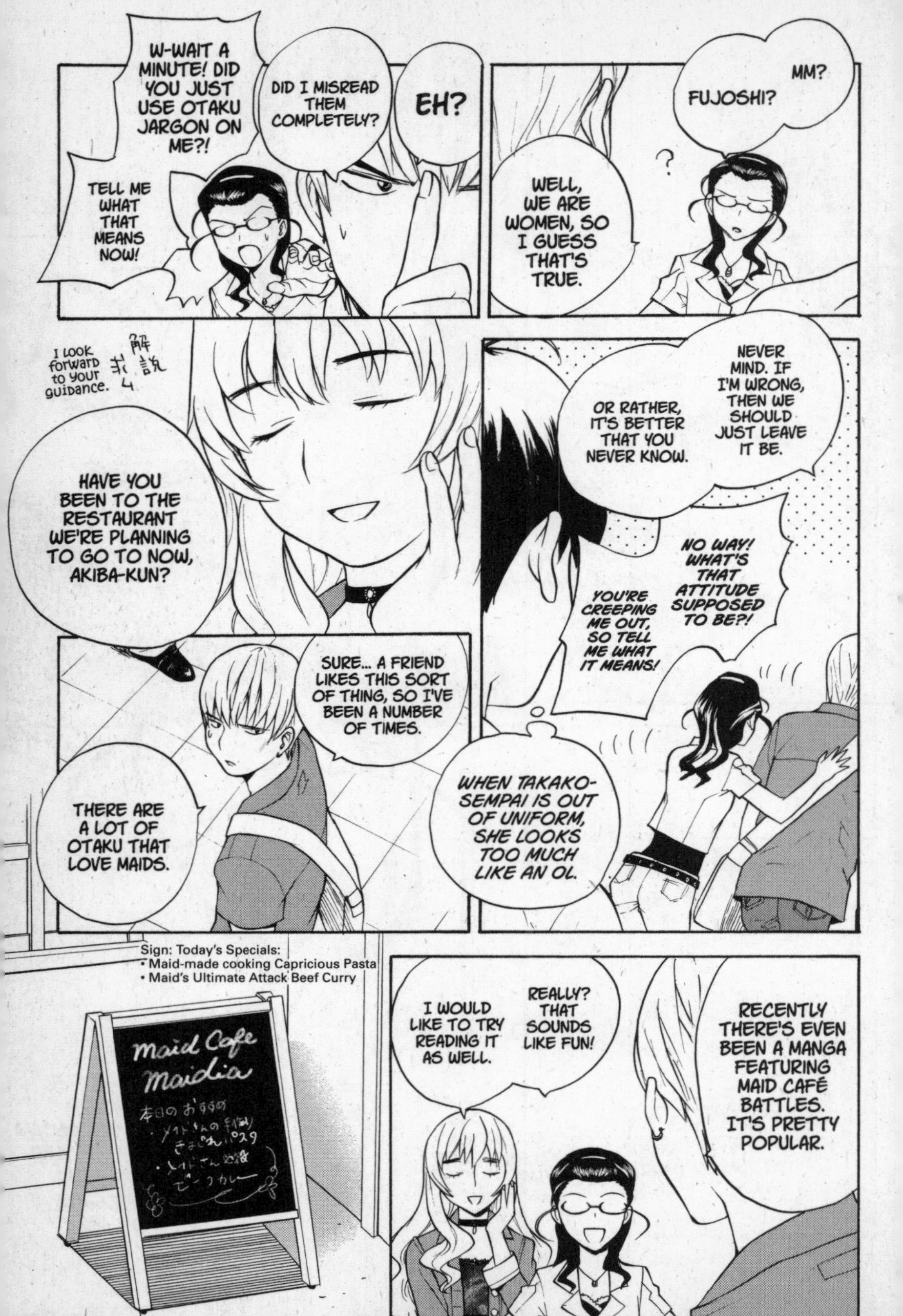
MM?
FUJOSHI?
WELL, WE ARE WOMEN, SO I GUESS THAT'S TRUE.
EH?
DID I MISREAD THEM COMPLETELY?
W-WAIT A MINUTE! DID YOU JUST USE OTAKU JARGON ON ME?!
TELL ME WHAT THAT MEANS NOW!
NEVER MIND. IF I'M WRONG, THEN WE SHOULD JUST LEAVE IT BE.
OR RATHER, IT'S BETTER THAT YOU NEVER KNOW.
NO WAY! WHAT'S THAT ATTITUDE SUPPOSED TO BE?!
YOU'RE CREEPING ME OUT, SO TELL ME WHAT IT MEANS!
WHEN TAKAKO-SEMPAI IS OUT OF UNIFORM, SHE LOOKS TOO MUCH LIKE AN OL.
解説求む
I LOOK forward to your guidance.
HAVE YOU BEEN TO THE RESTAURANT WE'RE PLANNING TO GO TO NOW, AKIBA-KUN?
SURE... A FRIEND LIKES THIS SORT OF THING, SO I'VE BEEN A NUMBER OF TIMES.
THERE ARE A LOT OF OTAKU THAT LOVE MAIDS.
RECENTLY THERE'S EVEN BEEN A MANGA FEATURING MAID CAFÉ BATTLES. IT'S PRETTY POPULAR.
REALLY? THAT SOUNDS LIKE FUN!
I WOULD LIKE TO TRY READING IT AS WELL.
maid Cafe
maidia
Sign: Today's Specials:
• Maid-made cooking Capricious Pasta
• Maid's Ultimate Attack Beef Curry

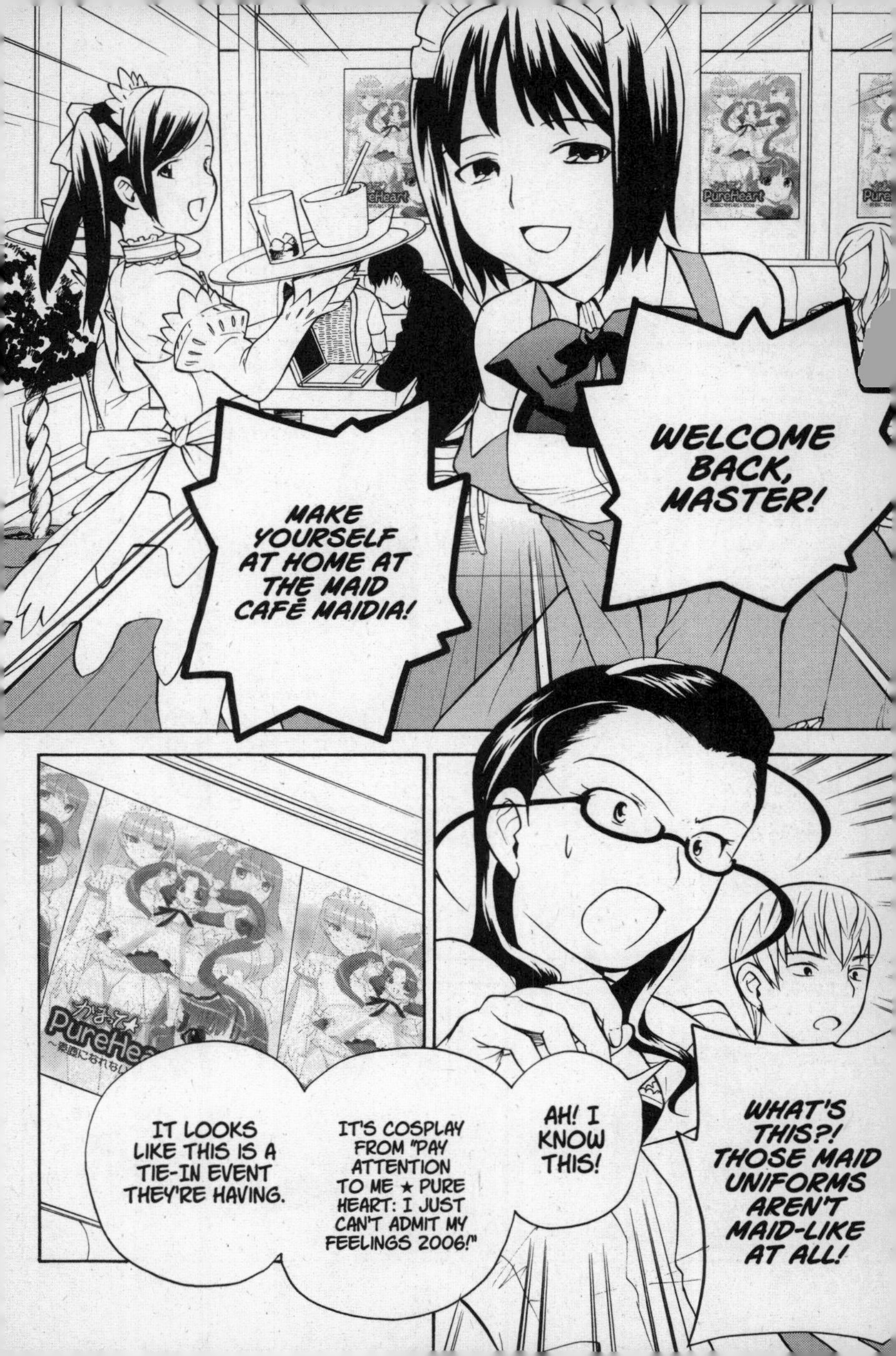
WELCOME BACK, MASTER!
MAKE YOURSELF AT HOME AT THE MAID CAFÉ MAIDIA!
WHAT'S THIS?! THOSE MAID UNIFORMS AREN'T MAID-LIKE AT ALL!
AH! I KNOW THIS!
IT'S COSPLAY FROM "PAY ATTENTION TO ME ★ PURE HEART: I JUST CAN'T ADMIT MY FEELINGS 2006!"
IT LOOKS LIKE THIS IS A TIE-IN EVENT THEY'RE HAVING.

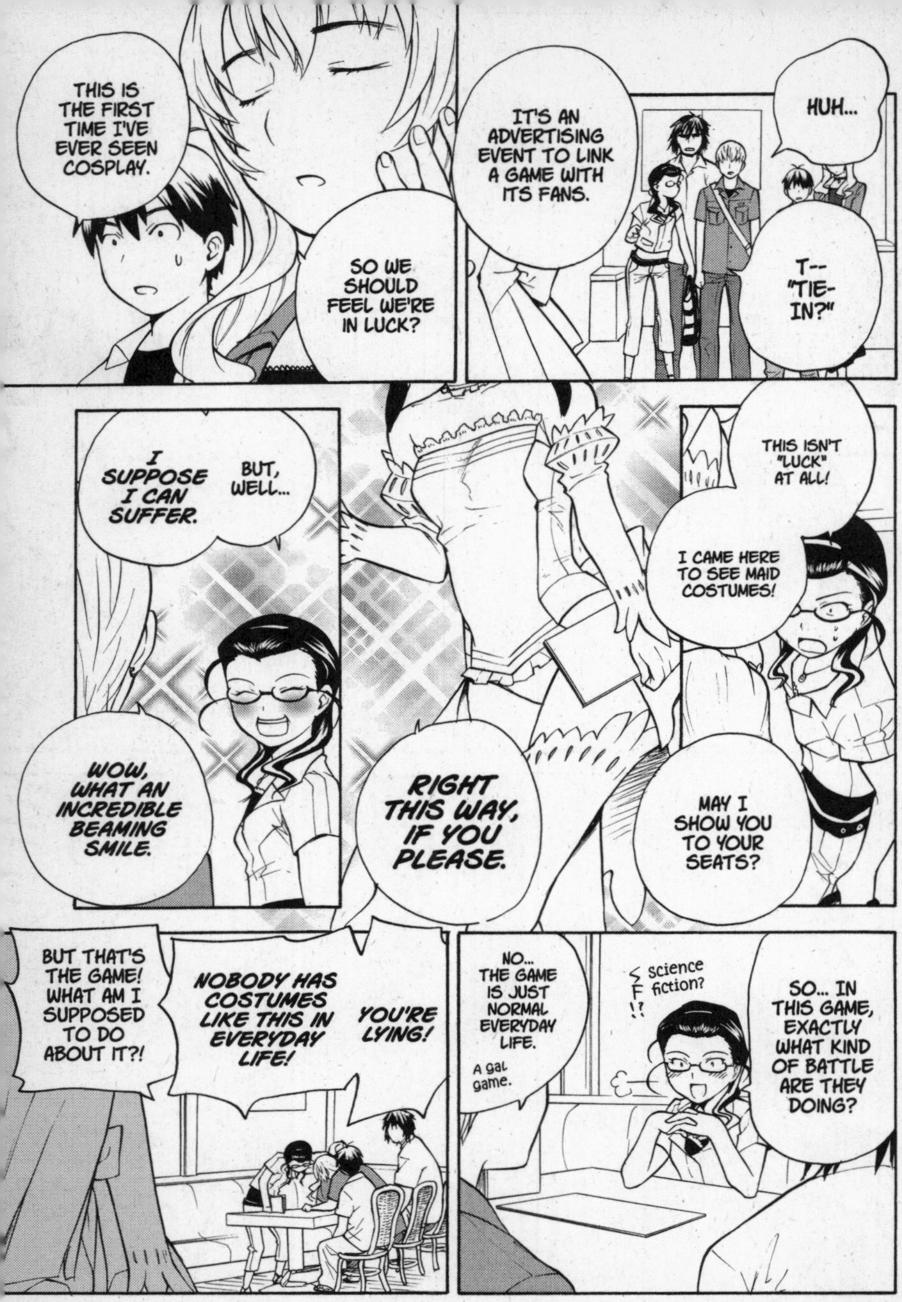
HUH...
IT'S AN ADVERTISING EVENT TO LINK A GAME WITH ITS FANS.
T-- "TIE-IN?"
THIS IS THE FIRST TIME I'VE EVER SEEN COSPLAY.
SO WE SHOULD FEEL WE'RE IN LUCK?
THIS ISN'T "LUCK" AT ALL!
I CAME HERE TO SEE MAID COSTUMES!
MAY I SHOW YOU TO YOUR SEATS?
RIGHT THIS WAY, IF YOU PLEASE.
BUT, WELL...
I SUPPOSE I CAN SUFFER.
WOW, WHAT AN INCREDIBLE BEAMING SMILE.
SO... IN THIS GAME, EXACTLY WHAT KIND OF BATTLE ARE THEY DOING?
SF!?
science fiction?
NO... THE GAME IS JUST NORMAL EVERYDAY LIFE.
A gal game.
YOU'RE LYING!
NOBODY HAS COSTUMES LIKE THIS IN EVERYDAY LIFE!
BUT THAT'S THE GAME! WHAT AM I SUPPOSED TO DO ABOUT IT?!

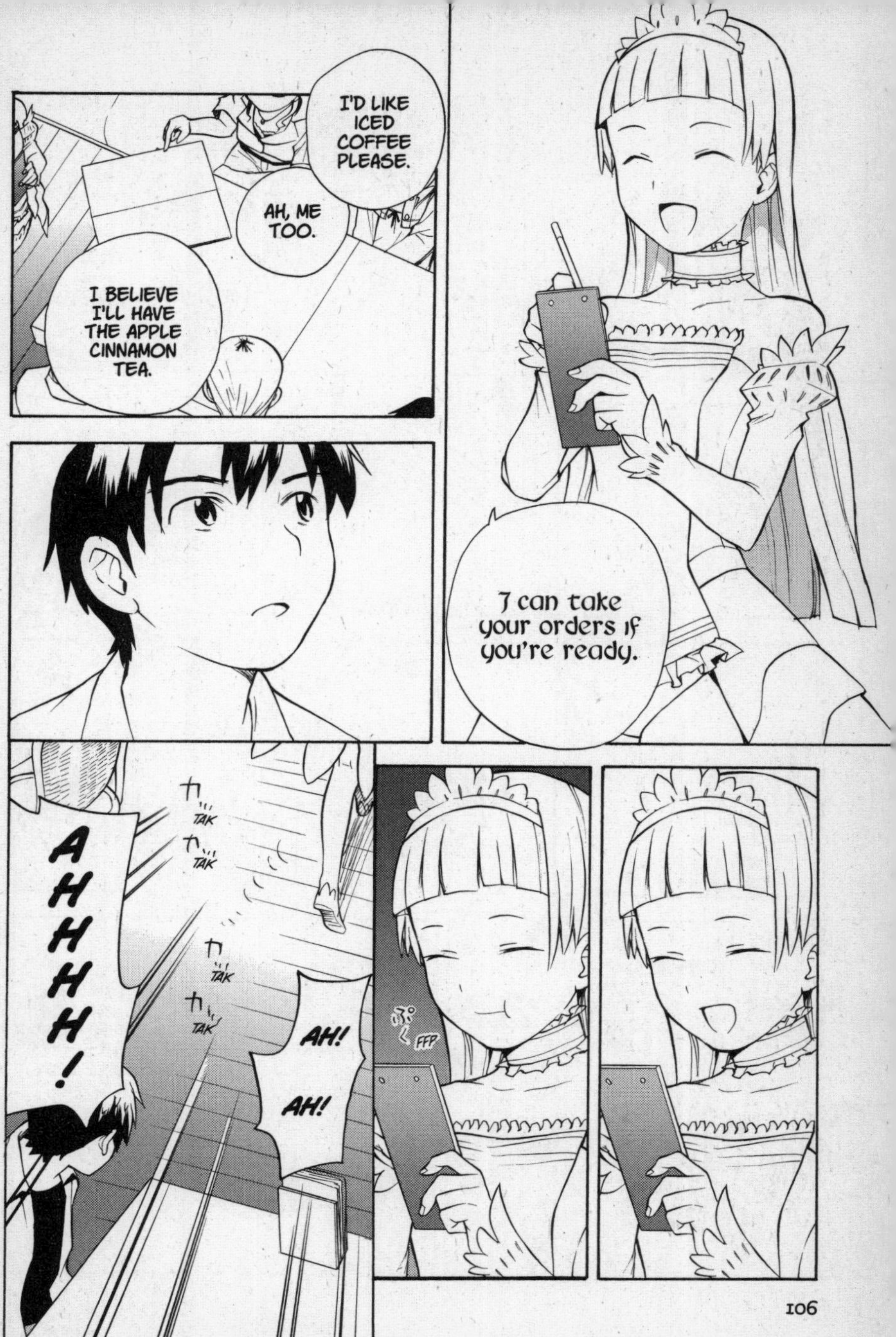
I can take your orders if you're ready.
I'D LIKE ICED COFFEE PLEASE.
AH, ME TOO.
I BELIEVE I'LL HAVE THE APPLE CINNAMON TEA.
ぷく FFP
TAK
TAK
TAK
TAK
AH!
AH!
AHHHHH!

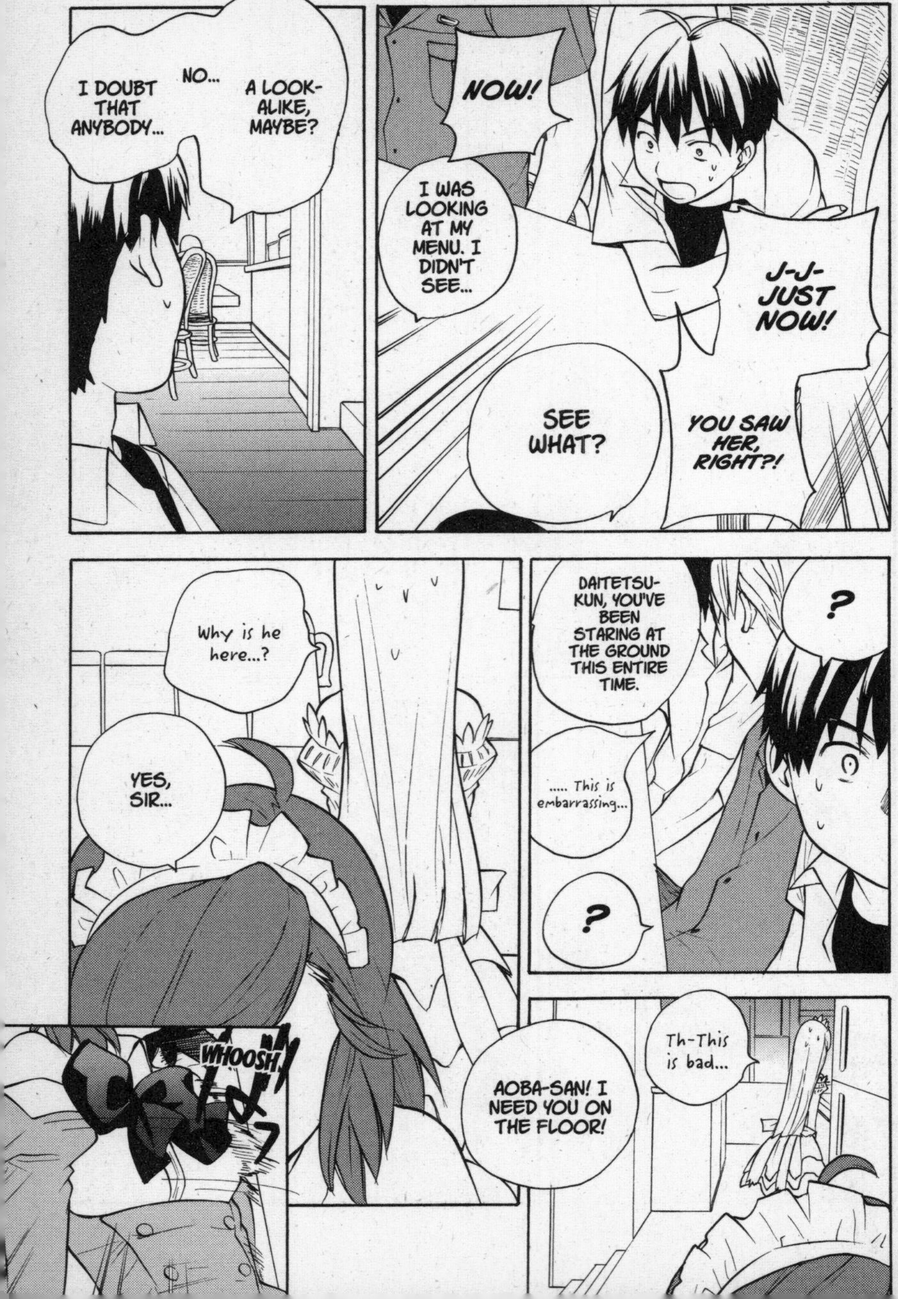
NOW!
J-J- JUST NOW!
YOU SAW HER, RIGHT?!
SEE WHAT?
I WAS LOOKING AT MY MENU. I DIDN'T SEE...
A LOOK-ALIKE, MAYBE?
NO...
I DOUBT THAT ANYBODY...
?
DAITETSU-KUN, YOU'VE BEEN STARING AT THE GROUND THIS ENTIRE TIME.
..... This is embarrassing...
?
Why is he here...?
YES, SIR...
Th-This is bad...
AOBA-SAN! I NEED YOU ON THE FLOOR!
WHOOSH

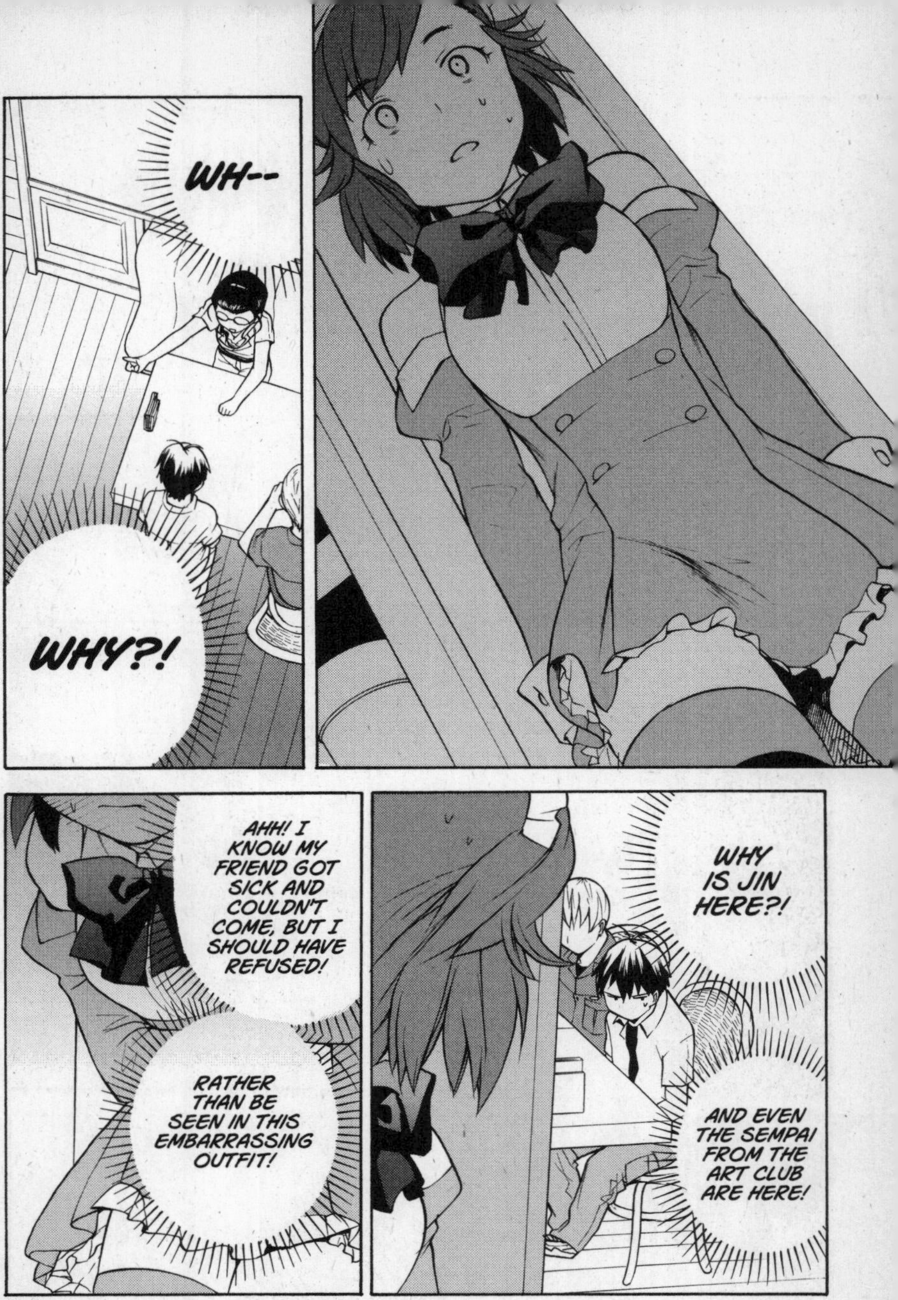
WH--
WHY?!
WHY IS JIN HERE?!
AND EVEN THE SEMPAI FROM THE ART CLUB ARE HERE!
AHH! I KNOW MY FRIEND GOT SICK AND COULDN'T COME, BUT I SHOULD HAVE REFUSED!
RATHER THAN BE SEEN IN THIS EMBARRASSING OUTFIT!

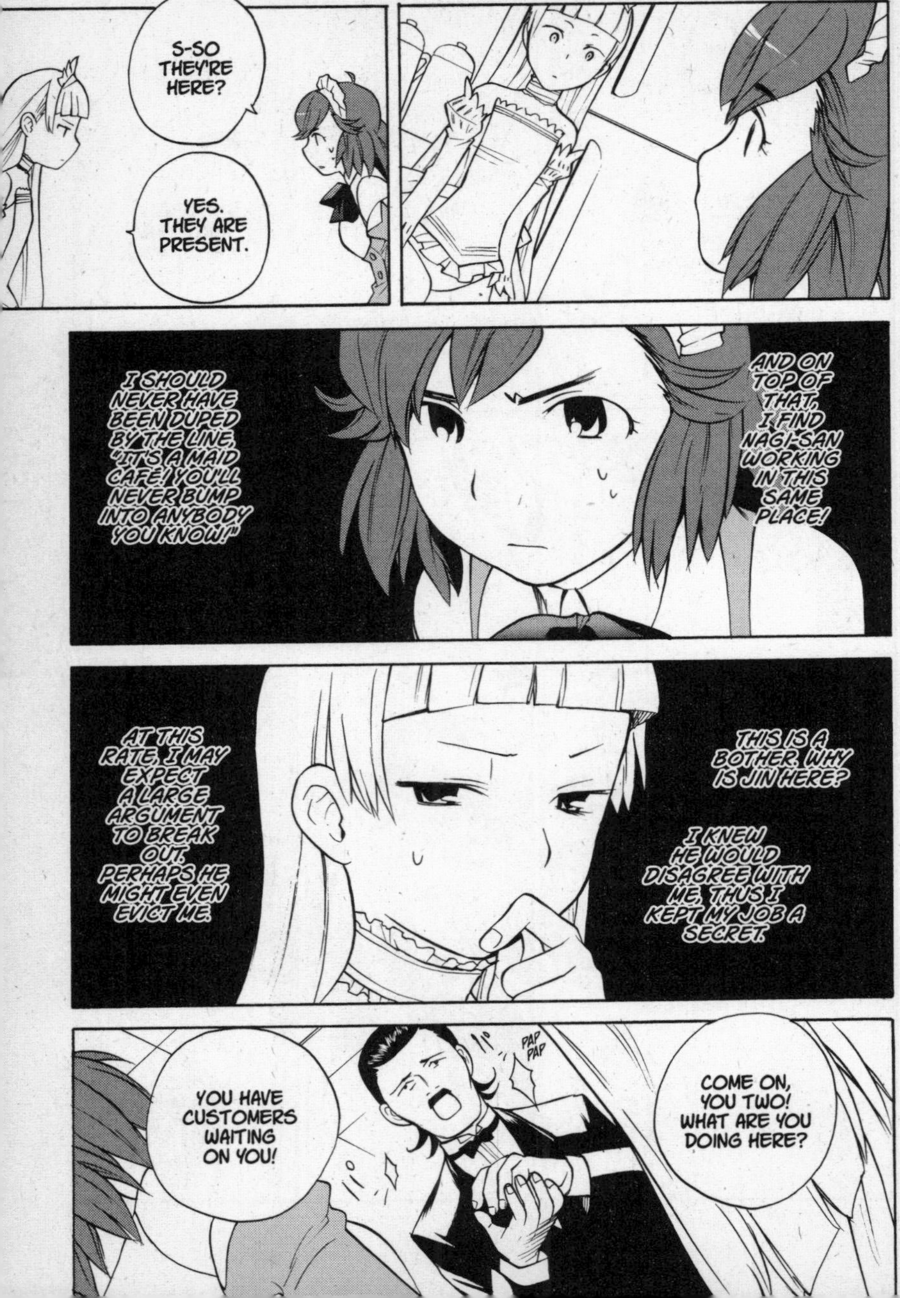
S-SO THEY'RE HERE?
YES. THEY ARE PRESENT.
AND ON TOP OF THAT, I FIND NAGI-SAN WORKING IN THIS SAME PLACE!
I SHOULD NEVER HAVE BEEN DUPED BY THE LINE, "IT'S A MAID CAFÉ! YOU'LL NEVER BUMP INTO ANYBODY YOU KNOW!"
THIS IS A BOTHER. WHY IS JIN HERE?
I KNEW HE WOULD DISAGREE WITH ME, THUS I KEPT MY JOB A SECRET.
AT THIS RATE, I MAY EXPECT A LARGE ARGUMENT TO BREAK OUT. PERHAPS HE MIGHT EVEN EVICT ME.
COME ON, YOU TWO! WHAT ARE YOU DOING HERE?
PAP PAP
YOU HAVE CUSTOMERS WAITING ON YOU!

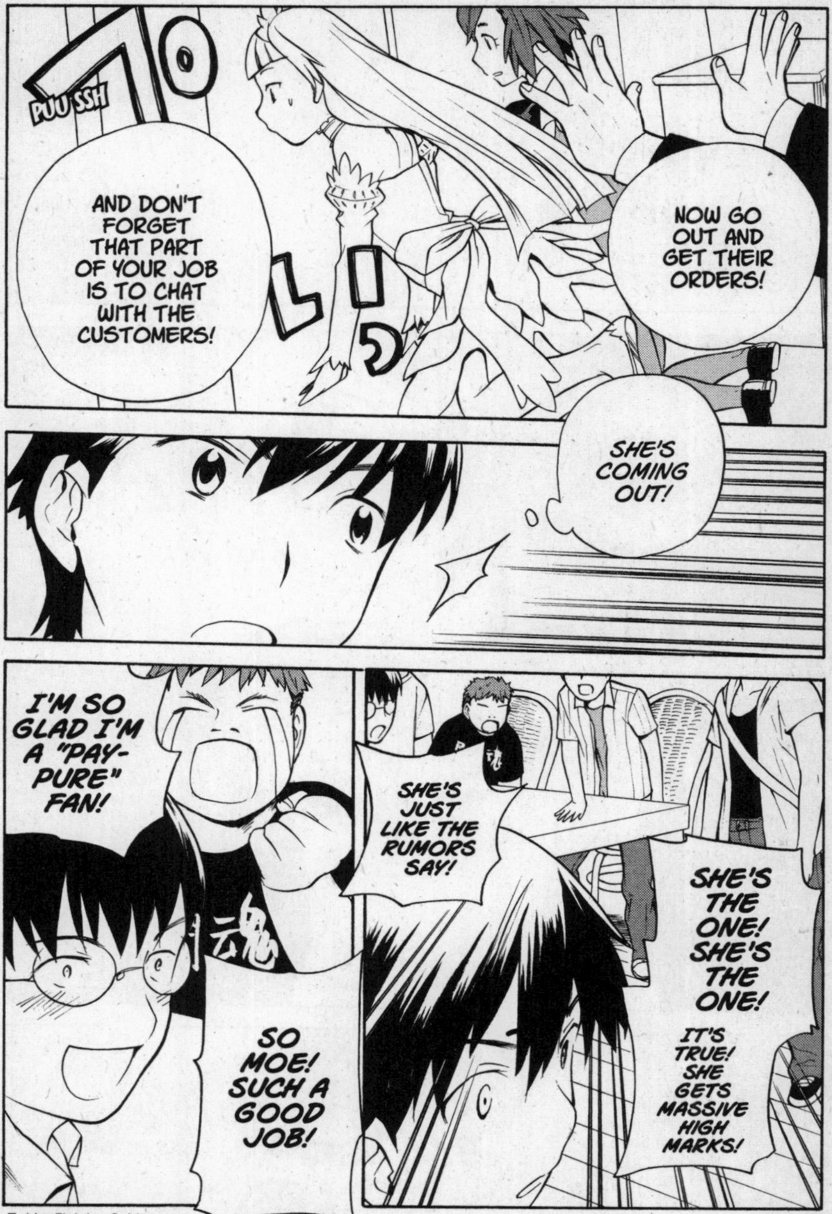
PUU SSH
NOW GO OUT AND GET THEIR ORDERS!
AND DON'T FORGET THAT PART OF YOUR JOB IS TO CHAT WITH THE CUSTOMERS!
SHE'S COMING OUT!
SHE'S JUST LIKE THE RUMORS SAY!
SHE'S THE ONE! SHE'S THE ONE!
IT'S TRUE! SHE GETS MASSIVE HIGH MARKS!
I'M SO GLAD I'M A "PAY-PURE" FAN!
SO MOE! SUCH A GOOD JOB!

T-shirt: Fighting Spirit

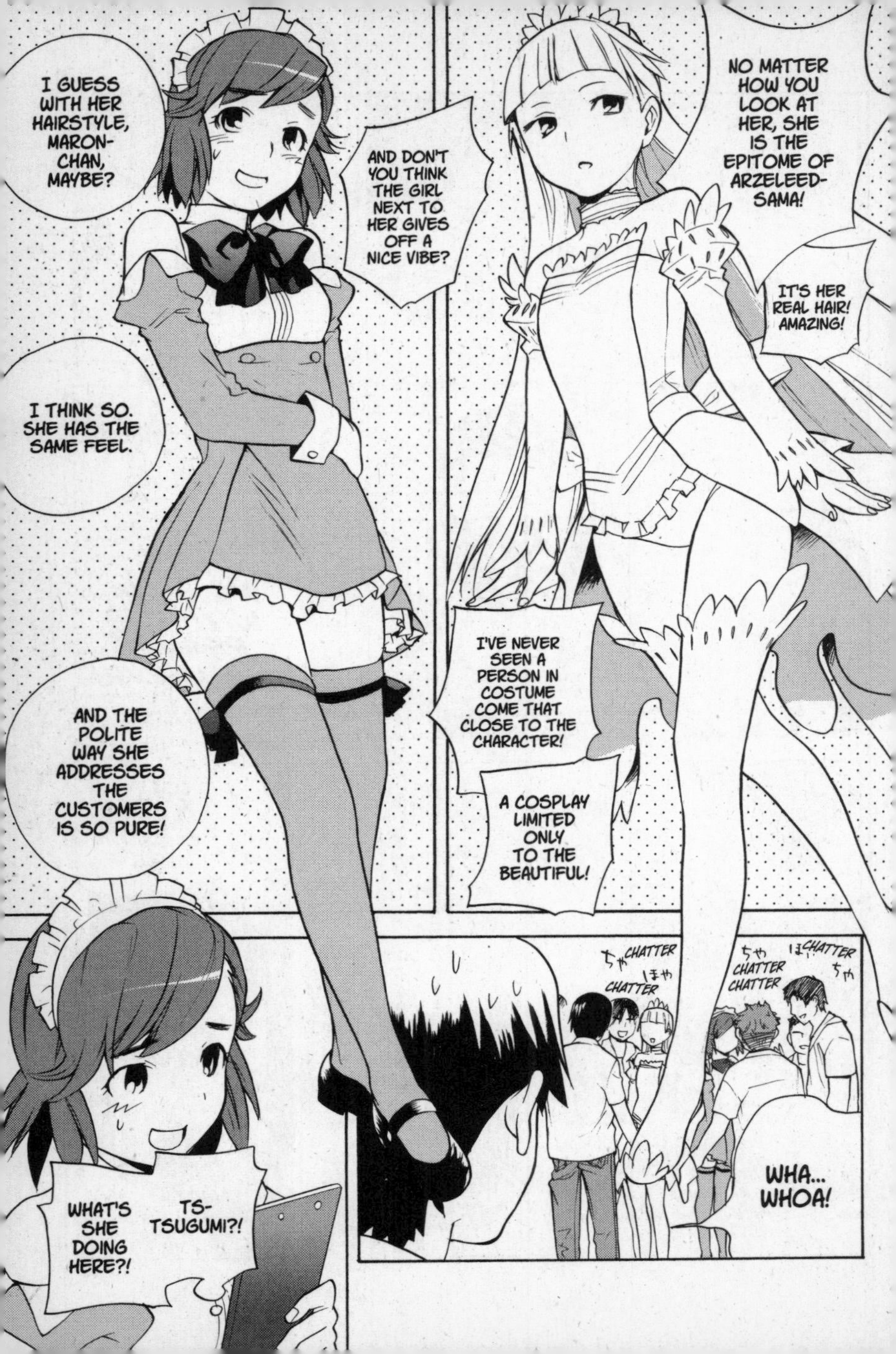
NO MATTER HOW YOU LOOK AT HER, SHE IS THE EPITOME OF ARZELEED-SAMA!
IT'S HER REAL HAIR! AMAZING!
I'VE NEVER SEEN A PERSON IN COSTUME COME THAT CLOSE TO THE CHARACTER!
A COSPLAY LIMITED ONLY TO THE BEAUTIFUL!
AND DON'T YOU THINK THE GIRL NEXT TO HER GIVES OFF A NICE VIBE?
I GUESS WITH HER HAIRSTYLE, MARON-CHAN, MAYBE?
I THINK SO. SHE HAS THE SAME FEEL.
AND THE POLITE WAY SHE ADDRESSES THE CUSTOMERS IS SO PURE!
CHATTER
CHATTER CHATTER
CHATTER
CHATTER
WHA... WHOA!
TS-TSUGUMI?!
WHAT'S SHE DOING HERE?!

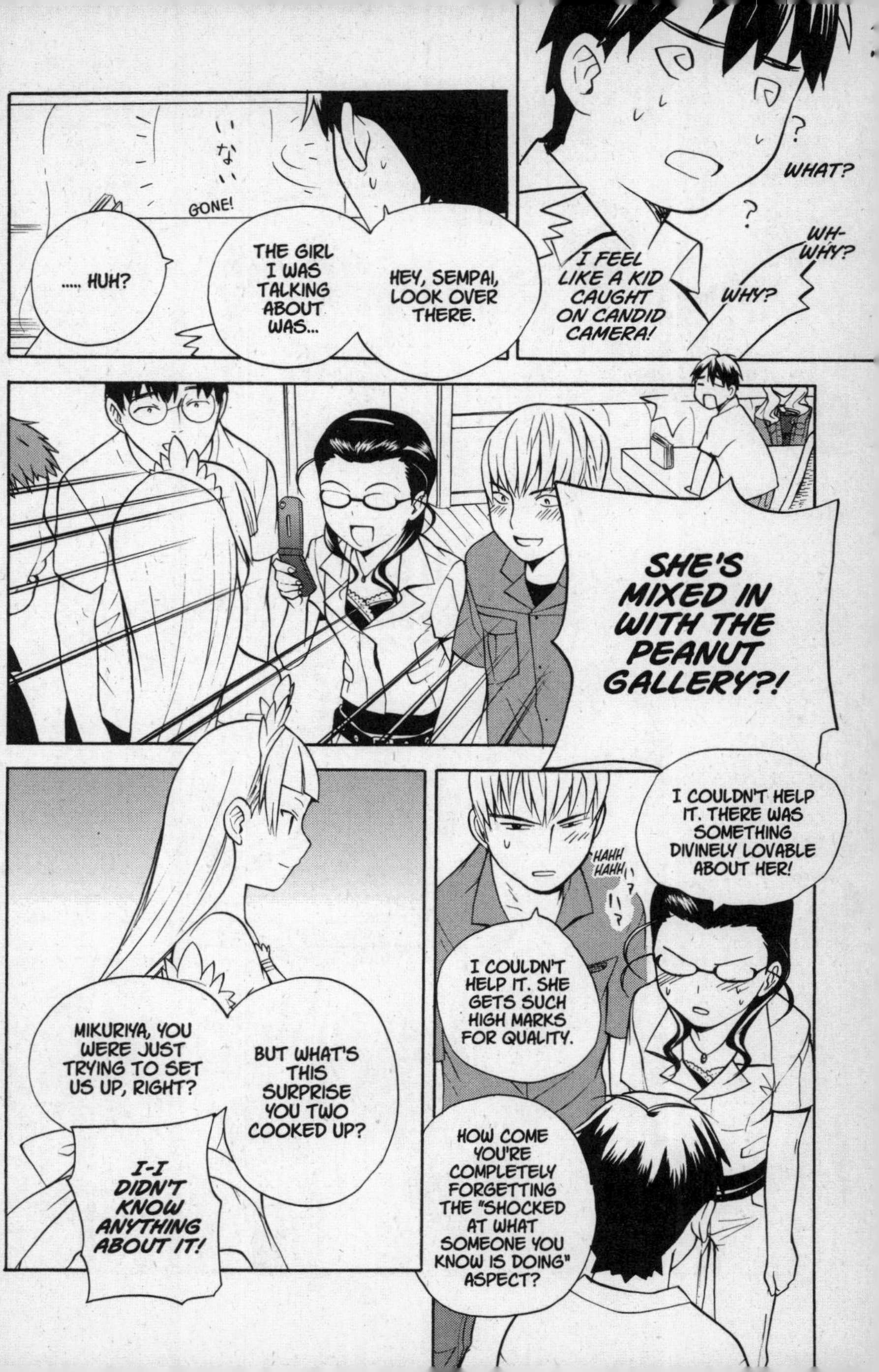
WHAT?
WH-WHY?
I FEEL LIKE A KID CAUGHT ON CANDID CAMERA!
WHY?
いない
GONE!
HEY, SEMPAI, LOOK OVER THERE.
THE GIRL I WAS TALKING ABOUT WAS...
..... HUH?
SHE'S MIXED IN WITH THE PEANUT GALLERY?!
I COULDN'T HELP IT. THERE WAS SOMETHING DIVINELY LOVABLE ABOUT HER!
HAHH HAHH
I COULDN'T HELP IT. SHE GETS SUCH HIGH MARKS FOR QUALITY.
HOW COME YOU'RE COMPLETELY FORGETTING THE "SHOCKED AT WHAT SOMEONE YOU KNOW IS DOING" ASPECT?
BUT WHAT'S THIS SURPRISE YOU TWO COOKED UP?
MIKURIYA, YOU WERE JUST TRYING TO SET US UP, RIGHT?
I-I DIDN'T KNOW ANYTHING ABOUT IT!

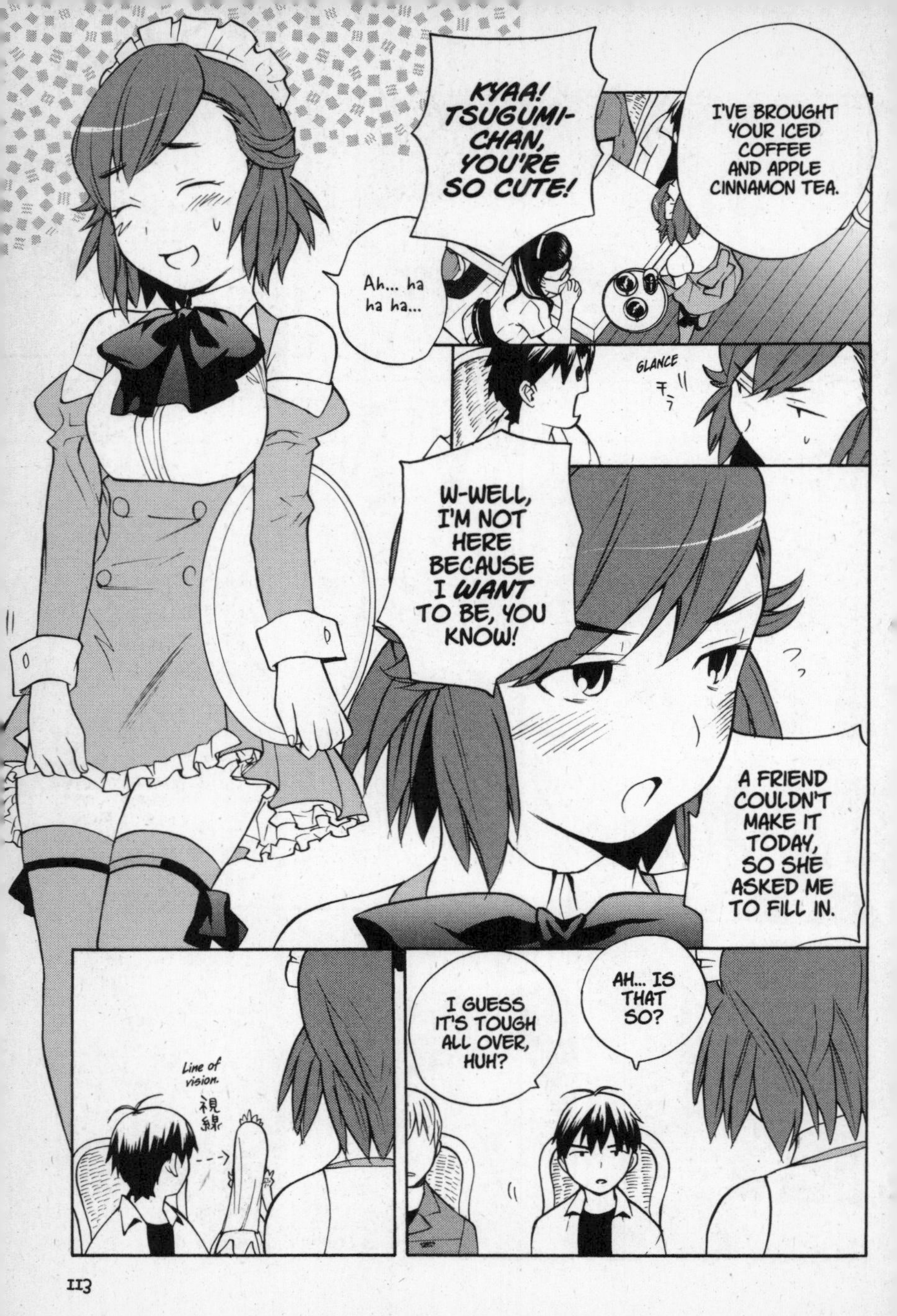
I'VE BROUGHT YOUR ICED COFFEE AND APPLE CINNAMON TEA.
KYAA! TSUGUMI-CHAN, YOU'RE SO CUTE!
Ah... ha ha ha...
GLANCE
W-WELL, I'M NOT HERE BECAUSE I WANT TO BE, YOU KNOW!
A FRIEND COULDN'T MAKE IT TODAY, SO SHE ASKED ME TO FILL IN.
AH... IS THAT SO?
I GUESS IT'S TOUGH ALL OVER, HUH?
Line of vision.
視線

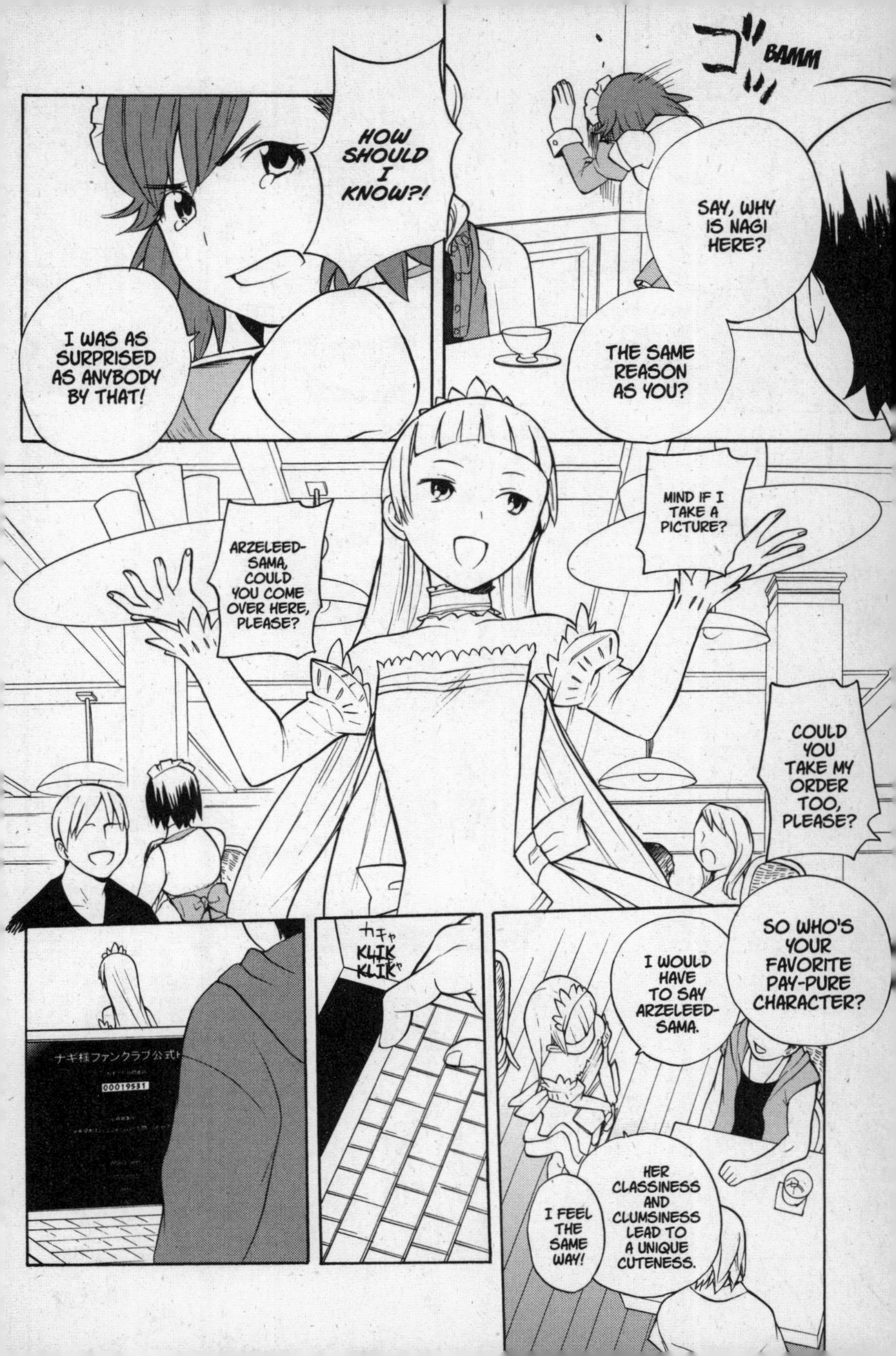
ゴッ
BAMM
SAY, WHY IS NAGI HERE?
THE SAME REASON AS YOU?
HOW SHOULD I KNOW?!
I WAS AS SURPRISED AS ANYBODY BY THAT!
MIND IF I TAKE A PICTURE?
ARZELEED-SAMA, COULD YOU COME OVER HERE, PLEASE?
COULD YOU TAKE MY ORDER TOO, PLEASE?
SO WHO'S YOUR FAVORITE PAY-PURE CHARACTER?
I WOULD HAVE TO SAY ARZELEED-SAMA.
HER CLASSINESS AND CLUMSINESS LEAD TO A UNIQUE CUTENESS.
I FEEL THE SAME WAY!
カチャ
KLIK KLIK
ナギ様ファンクラブ公式
00019531

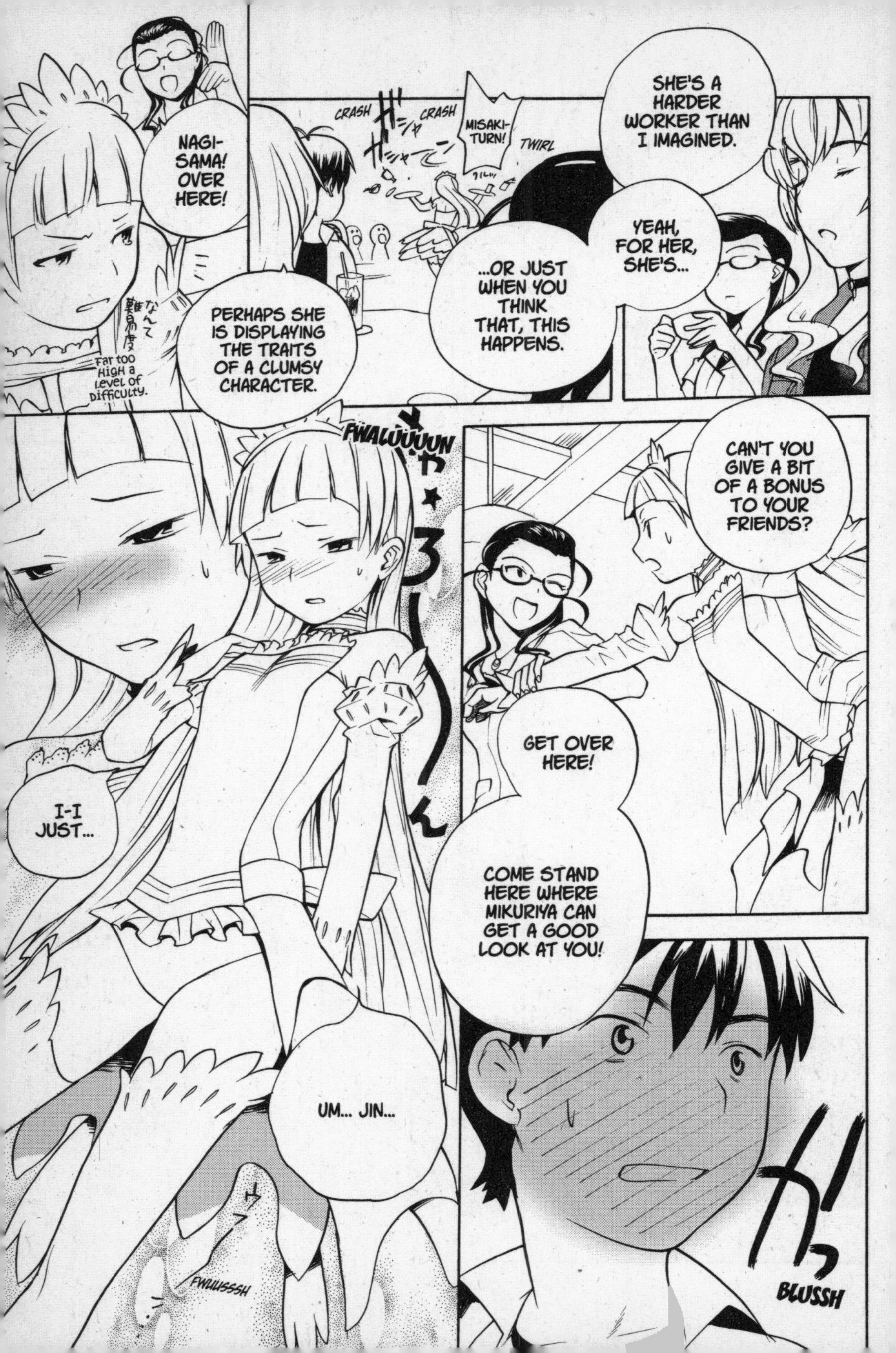
SHE'S A HARDER WORKER THAN I IMAGINED.
YEAH, FOR HER, SHE'S...
CRASH
CRASH
MISAKI-TURN!
TWIRL
...OR JUST WHEN YOU THINK THAT, THIS HAPPENS.
NAGI-SAMA! OVER HERE!
PERHAPS SHE IS DISPLAYING THE TRAITS OF A CLUMSY CHARACTER.
なんて難易度
Far too High a level of difficulty.
CAN'T YOU GIVE A BIT OF A BONUS TO YOUR FRIENDS?
GET OVER HERE!
COME STAND HERE WHERE MIKURIYA CAN GET A GOOD LOOK AT YOU!
BLUSSH
FWALUUUUN
I-I JUST...
UM... JIN...
FWUUSSSH

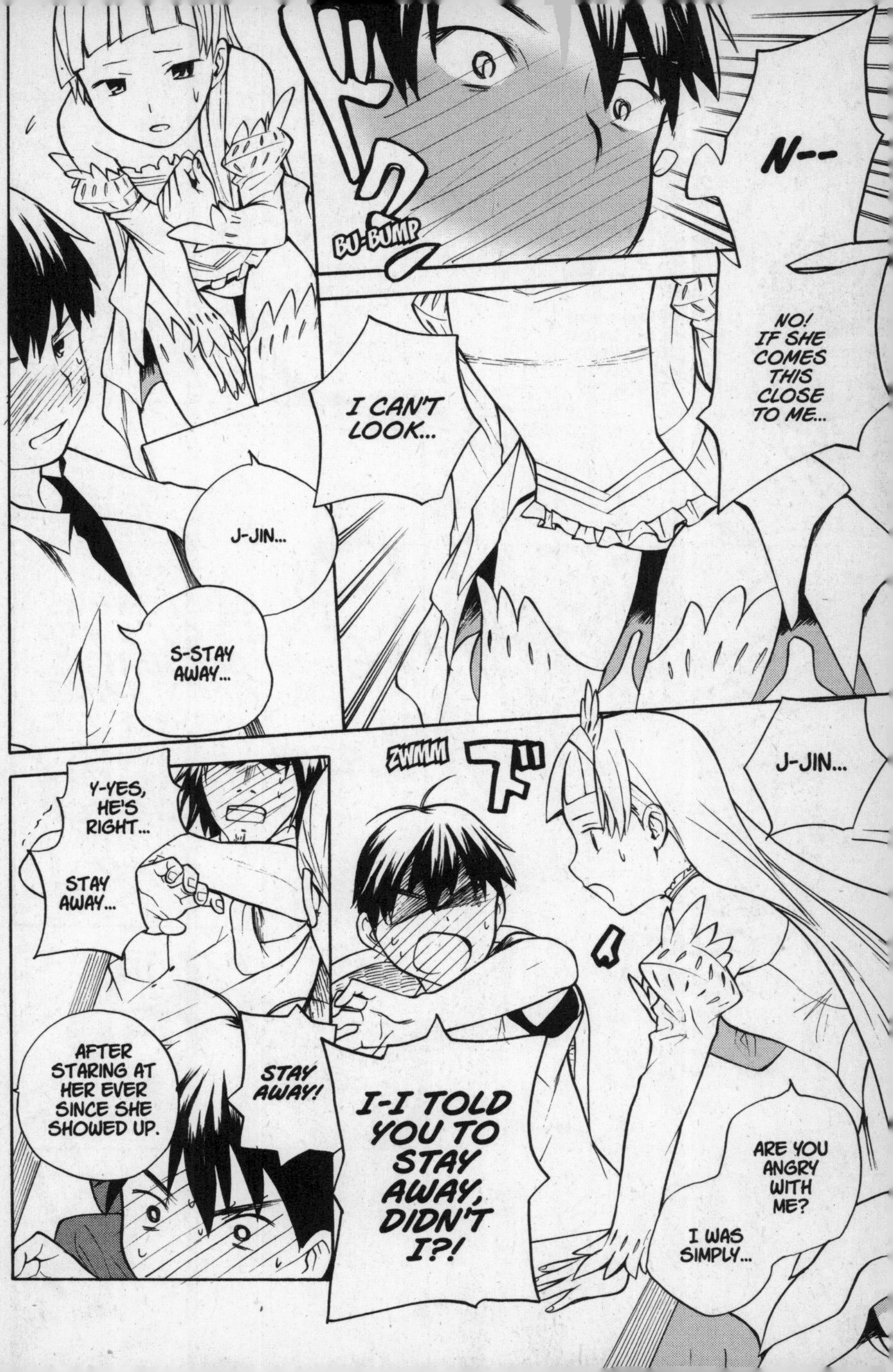

N--
BU-BUMP
NO! IF SHE COMES THIS CLOSE TO ME...
I CAN'T LOOK...
J-JIN...
S-STAY AWAY...
J-JIN...
ZWMM
I-I TOLD YOU TO STAY AWAY, DIDN'T I?!
ARE YOU ANGRY WITH ME?
I WAS SIMPLY...
Y-YES, HE'S RIGHT...
STAY AWAY...
STAY AWAY!
AFTER STARING AT HER EVER SINCE SHE SHOWED UP.

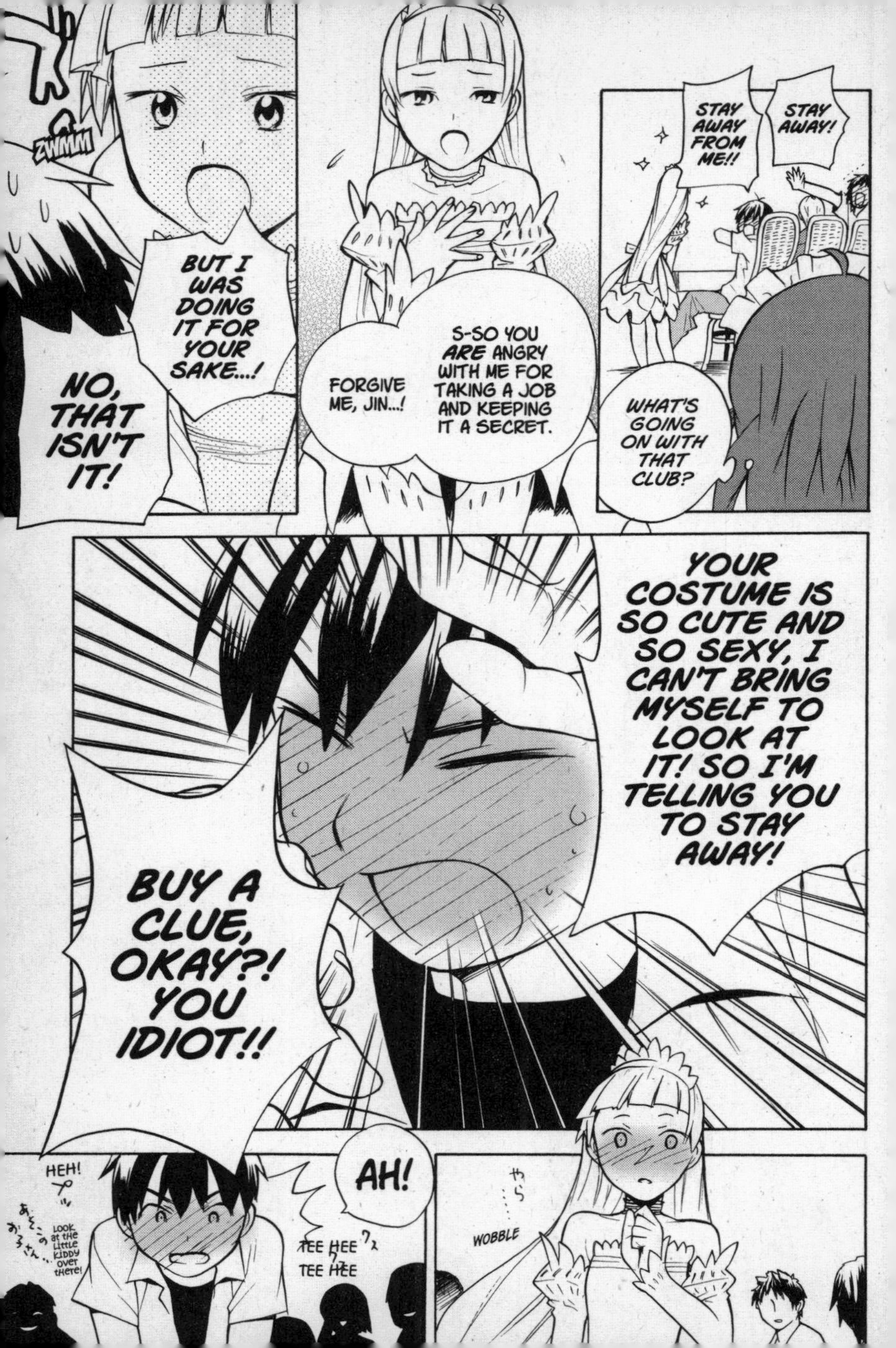

STAY AWAY!
STAY AWAY FROM ME!!
WHAT'S GOING ON WITH THAT CLUB?
S-SO YOU *ARE* ANGRY WITH ME FOR TAKING A JOB AND KEEPING IT A SECRET.
FORGIVE ME, JIN...!
ZWMMM
BUT I WAS DOING IT FOR YOUR SAKE...!
NO, THAT ISN'T IT!
YOUR COSTUME IS SO CUTE AND SO SEXY, I CAN'T BRING MYSELF TO LOOK AT IT! SO I'M TELLING YOU TO STAY AWAY!
BUY A CLUE, OKAY?! YOU IDIOT!!
WOBBLE
AH!
HEH!
LOOK at the little kiddy over there!
TEE HEE
TEE HEE

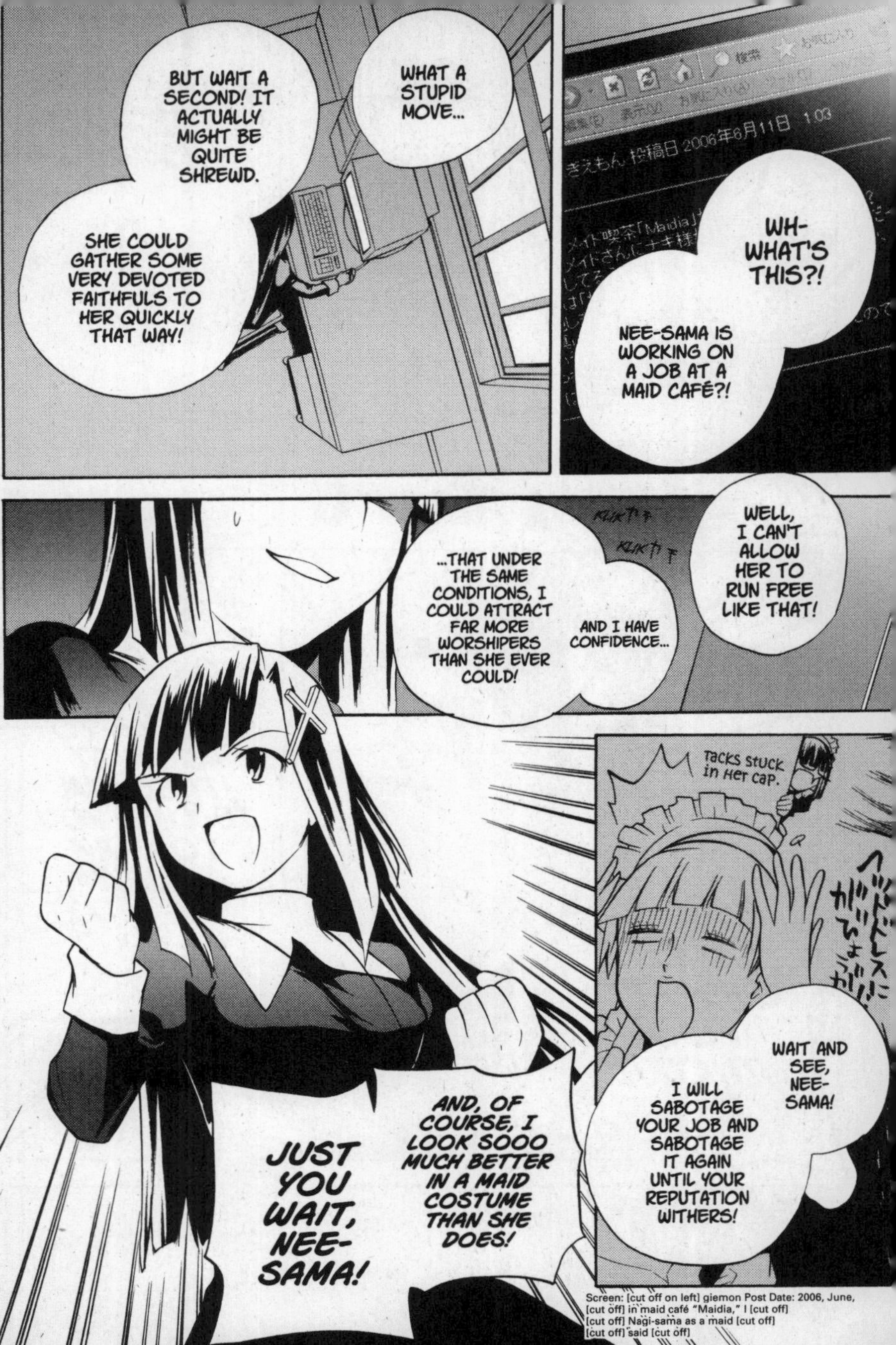
WH- WHAT'S THIS?!
NEE-SAMA IS WORKING ON A JOB AT A MAID CAFÉ?!
WHAT A STUPID MOVE...
BUT WAIT A SECOND! IT ACTUALLY MIGHT BE QUITE SHREWD.
SHE COULD GATHER SOME VERY DEVOTED FAITHFULS TO HER QUICKLY THAT WAY!
WELL, I CAN'T ALLOW HER TO RUN FREE LIKE THAT!
KLIK
KLIK
AND I HAVE CONFIDENCE...
...THAT UNDER THE SAME CONDITIONS, I COULD ATTRACT FAR MORE WORSHIPERS THAN SHE EVER COULD!
Tacks stuck in her cap.
WAIT AND SEE, NEE-SAMA!
I WILL SABOTAGE YOUR JOB AND SABOTAGE IT AGAIN UNTIL YOUR REPUTATION WITHERS!
AND, OF COURSE, I LOOK SOOO MUCH BETTER IN A MAID COSTUME THAN SHE DOES!
JUST YOU WAIT, NEE-SAMA!

Screen: [cut off on left] giemon Post Date: 2006, June, [cut off] in maid café "Maidia," I [cut off] [cut off] Nagi-sama as a maid [cut off] [cut off] said [cut off]

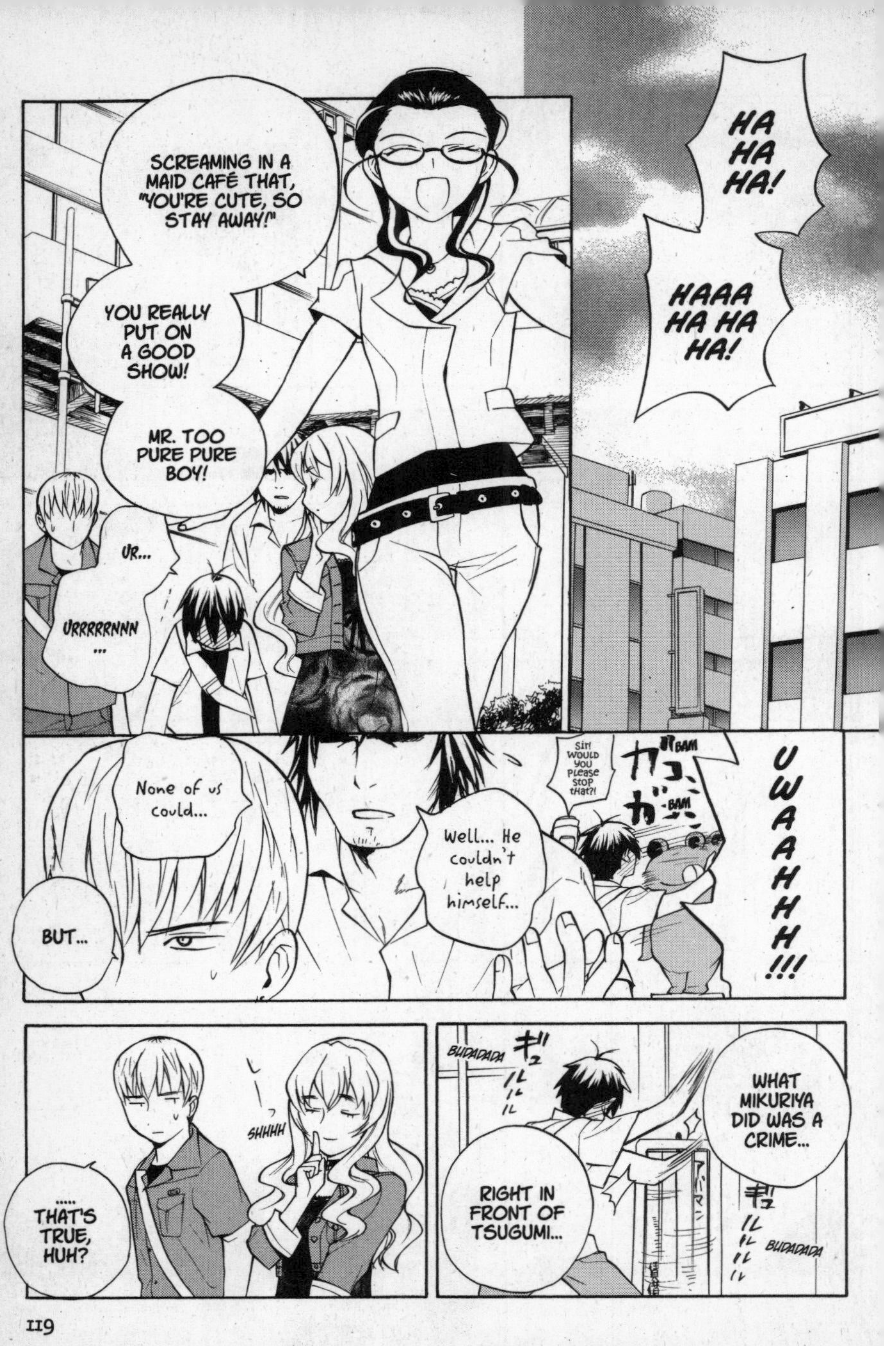
HA HA HA!
HAAA HA HA HA!
SCREAMING IN A MAID CAFÉ THAT, "YOU'RE CUTE, SO STAY AWAY!"
YOU REALLY PUT ON A GOOD SHOW!
MR. TOO PURE PURE BOY!
UR...
URRRRRNNN ...
UWAAHHH!!!
Sir! Would you please stop that?!
BAM
BAM
Well... He couldn't help himself...
None of us could...
BUT...
BUDADADA
WHAT MIKURIYA DID WAS A CRIME...
RIGHT IN FRONT OF TSUGUMI...
BUDADADA
SHHHH
..... THAT'S TRUE, HUH?

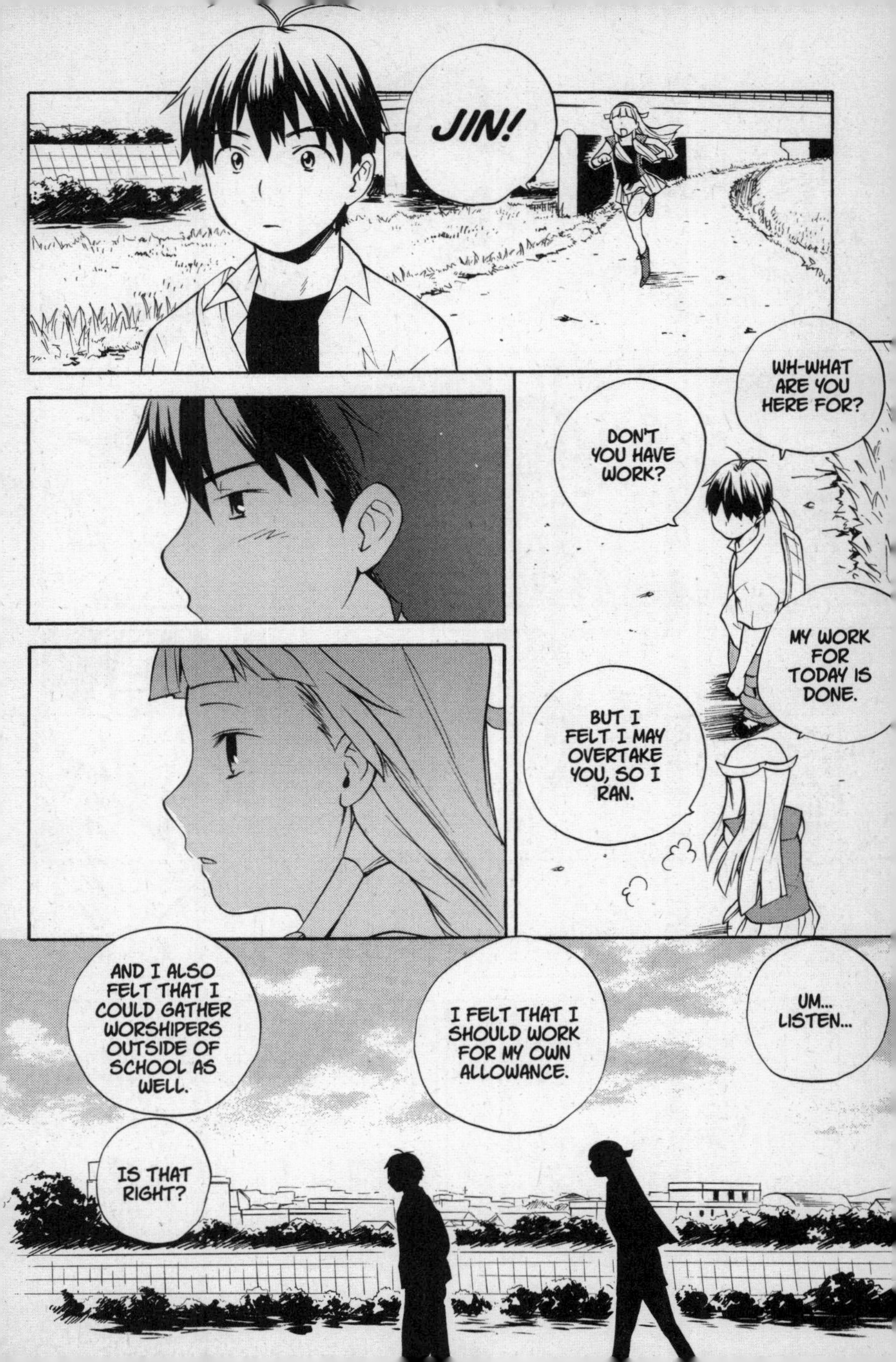
JIN!
WH-WHAT ARE YOU HERE FOR?
DON'T YOU HAVE WORK?
MY WORK FOR TODAY IS DONE.
BUT I FELT I MAY OVERTAKE YOU, SO I RAN.
UM... LISTEN...
I FELT THAT I SHOULD WORK FOR MY OWN ALLOWANCE.
AND I ALSO FELT THAT I COULD GATHER WORSHIPERS OUTSIDE OF SCHOOL AS WELL.
IS THAT RIGHT?

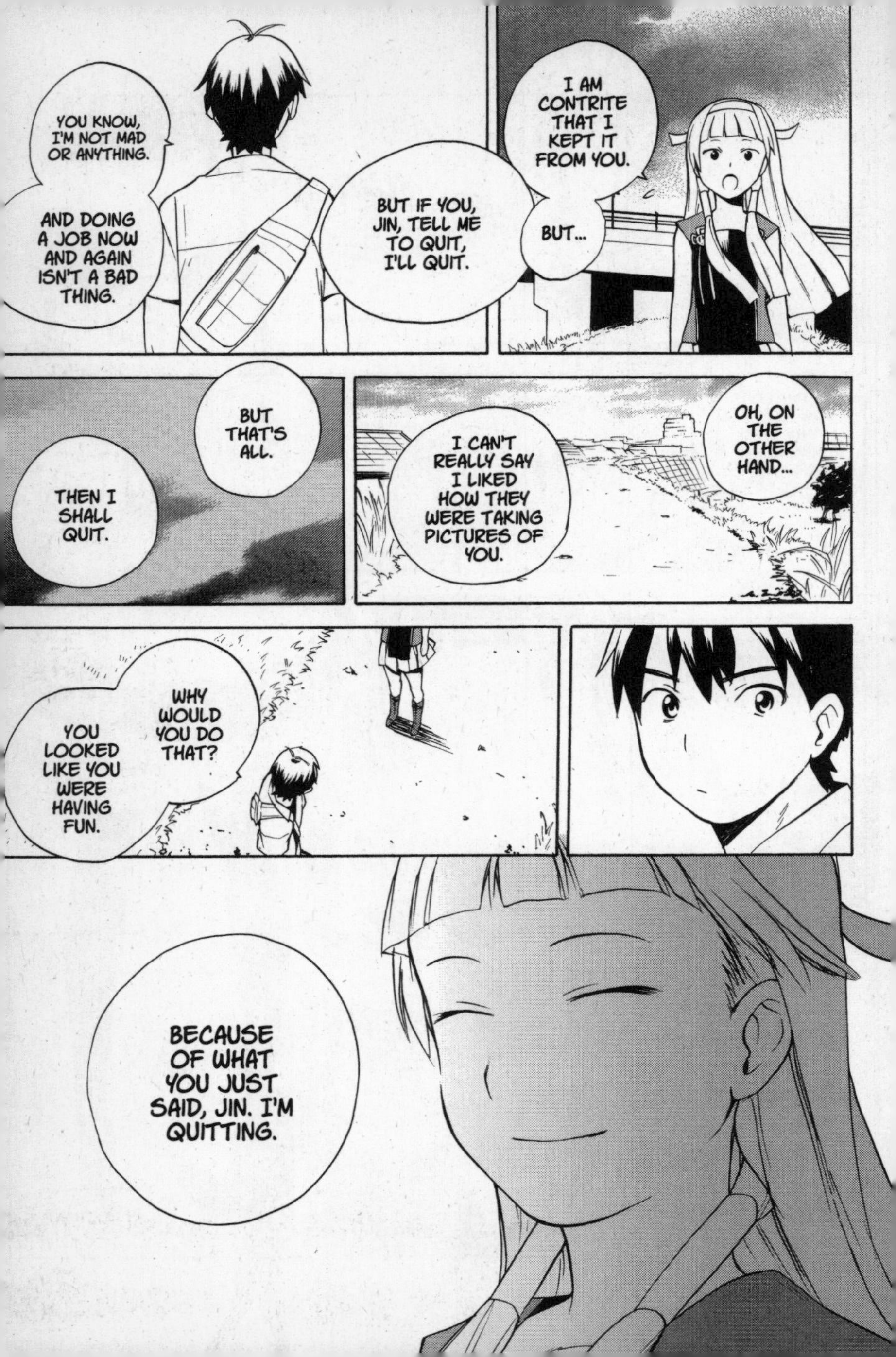
I AM CONTRITE THAT I KEPT IT FROM YOU.
BUT...
BUT IF YOU, JIN, TELL ME TO QUIT, I'LL QUIT.
YOU KNOW, I'M NOT MAD OR ANYTHING.
AND DOING A JOB NOW AND AGAIN ISN'T A BAD THING.
OH, ON THE OTHER HAND...
I CAN'T REALLY SAY I LIKED HOW THEY WERE TAKING PICTURES OF YOU.
BUT THAT'S ALL.
THEN I SHALL QUIT.
WHY WOULD YOU DO THAT?
YOU LOOKED LIKE YOU WERE HAVING FUN.
BECAUSE OF WHAT YOU JUST SAID, JIN. I'M QUITTING.

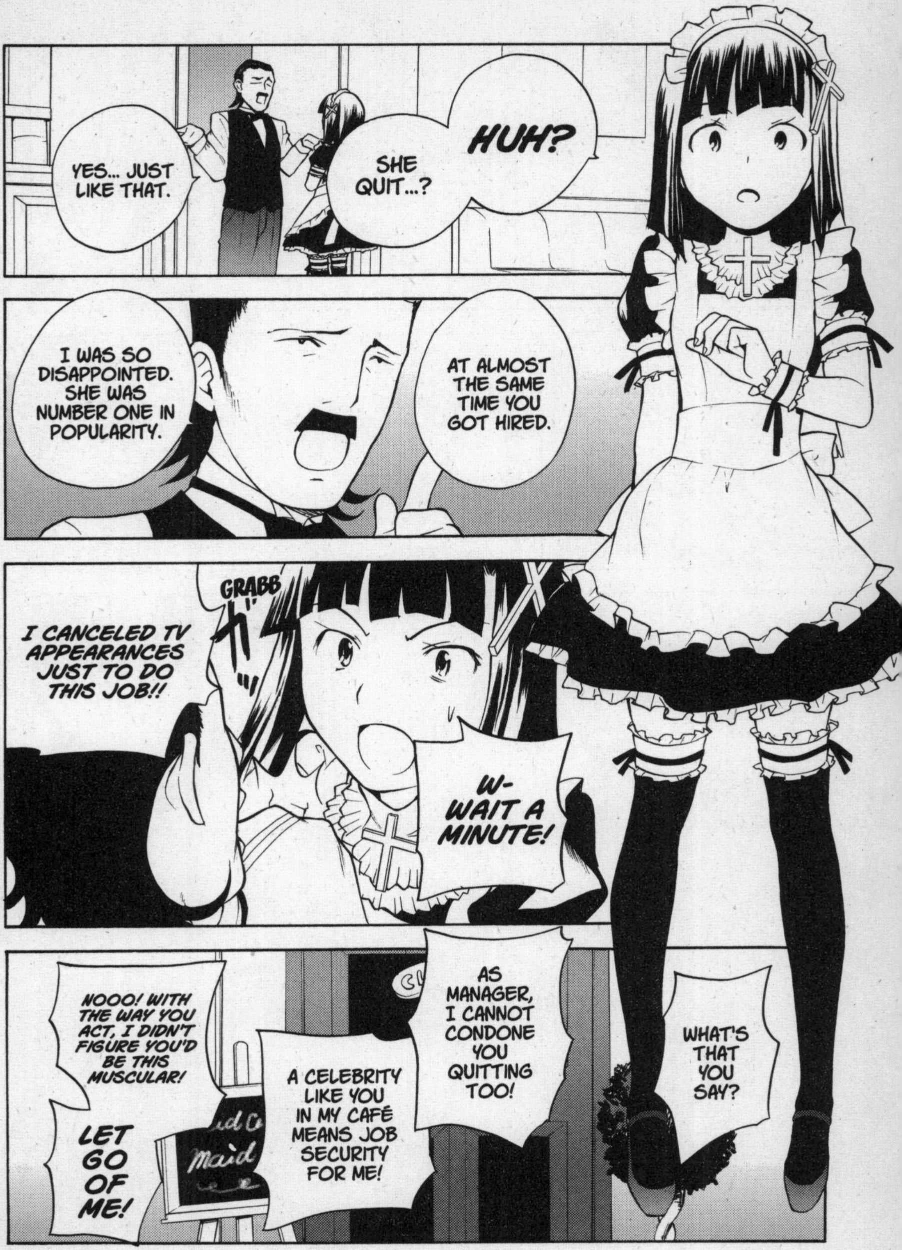
HUH?
SHE QUIT...?
YES... JUST LIKE THAT.
AT ALMOST THE SAME TIME YOU GOT HIRED.
I WAS SO DISAPPOINTED. SHE WAS NUMBER ONE IN POPULARITY.
GRABB
W-WAIT A MINUTE!
I CANCELED TV APPEARANCES JUST TO DO THIS JOB!!
WHAT'S THAT YOU SAY?
AS MANAGER, I CANNOT CONDONE YOU QUITTING TOO!
A CELEBRITY LIKE YOU IN MY CAFÉ MEANS JOB SECURITY FOR ME!
NOOO! WITH THE WAY YOU ACT, I DIDN'T FIGURE YOU'D BE THIS MUSCULAR!
LET GO OF ME!

K A N N A G I

WH-WHat DO YOU tHink?

See, I can PULL tHis off too... I'm So... Aren't I?

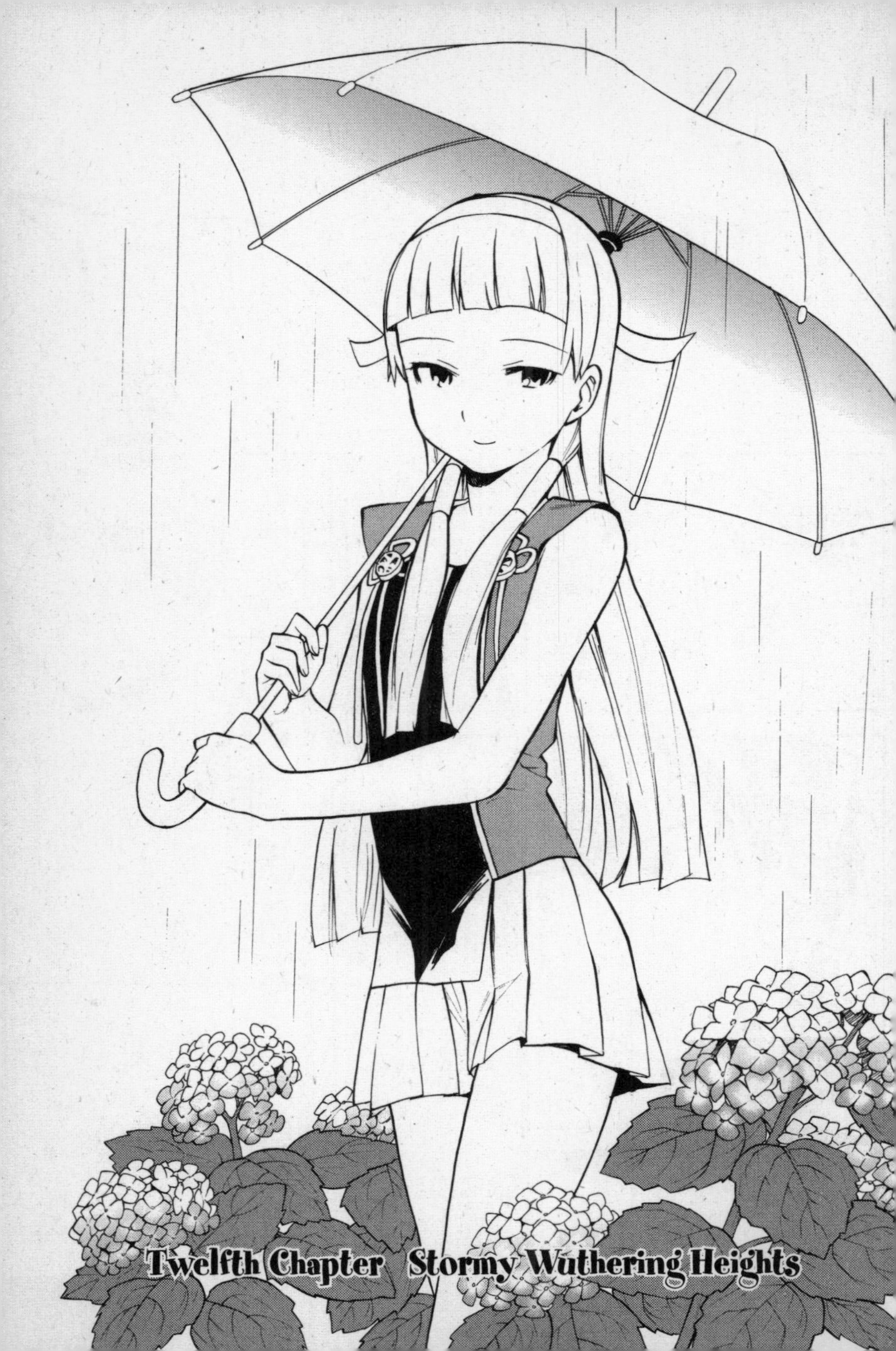

Twelfth Chapter Stormy Wuthering Heights

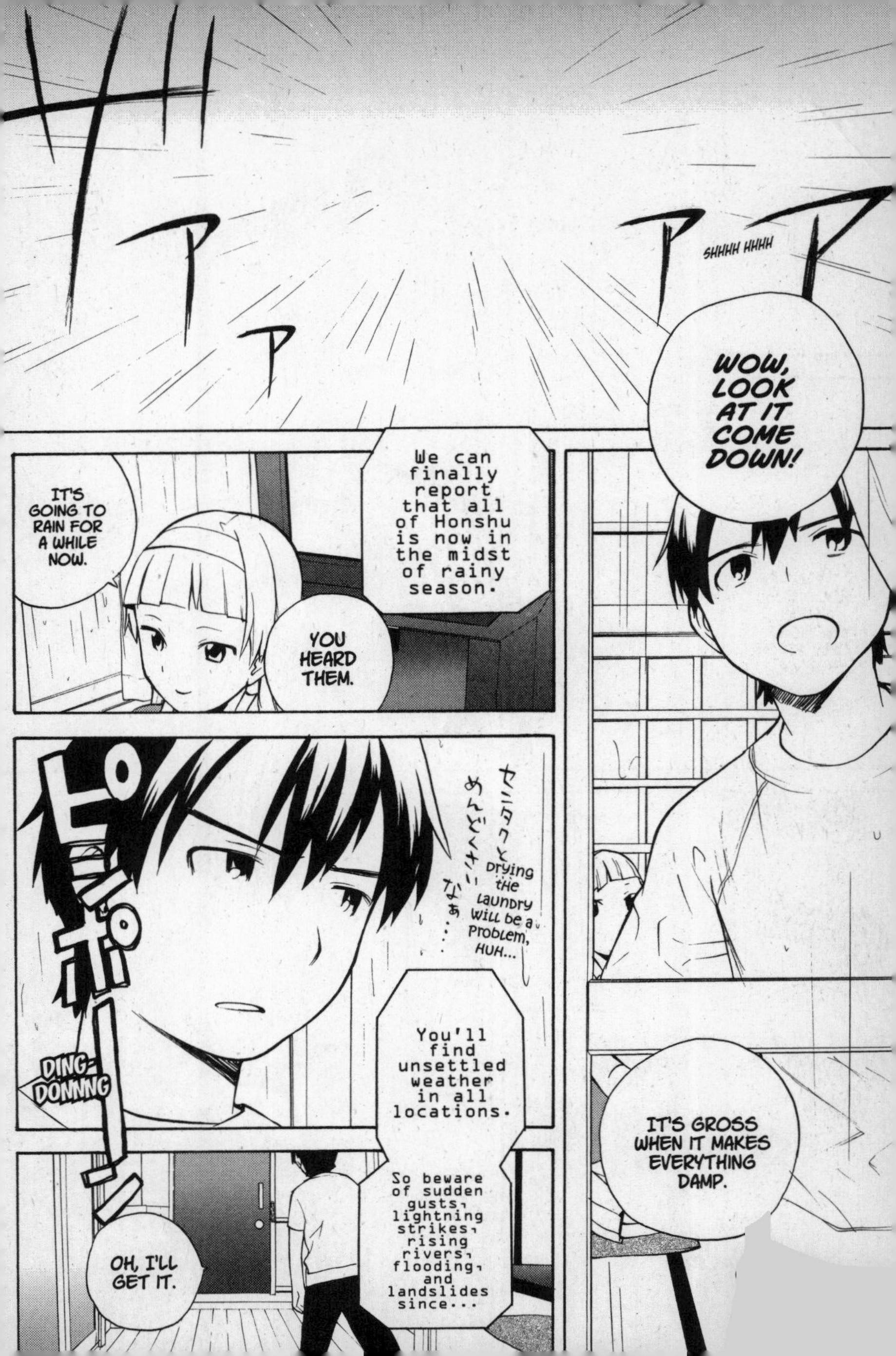
SHHHH HHHH
WOW, LOOK AT IT COME DOWN!
IT'S GROSS WHEN IT MAKES EVERYTHING DAMP.
We can finally report that all of Honshu is now in the midst of rainy season.
IT'S GOING TO RAIN FOR A WHILE NOW.
YOU HEARD THEM.
センタクと めんどくさいなぁ…
Drying the laundry will be a problem, huh...
DING-DONNNG
You'll find unsettled weather in all locations.
So beware of sudden gusts, lightning strikes, rising rivers, flooding, and landslides since...
OH, I'LL GET IT.

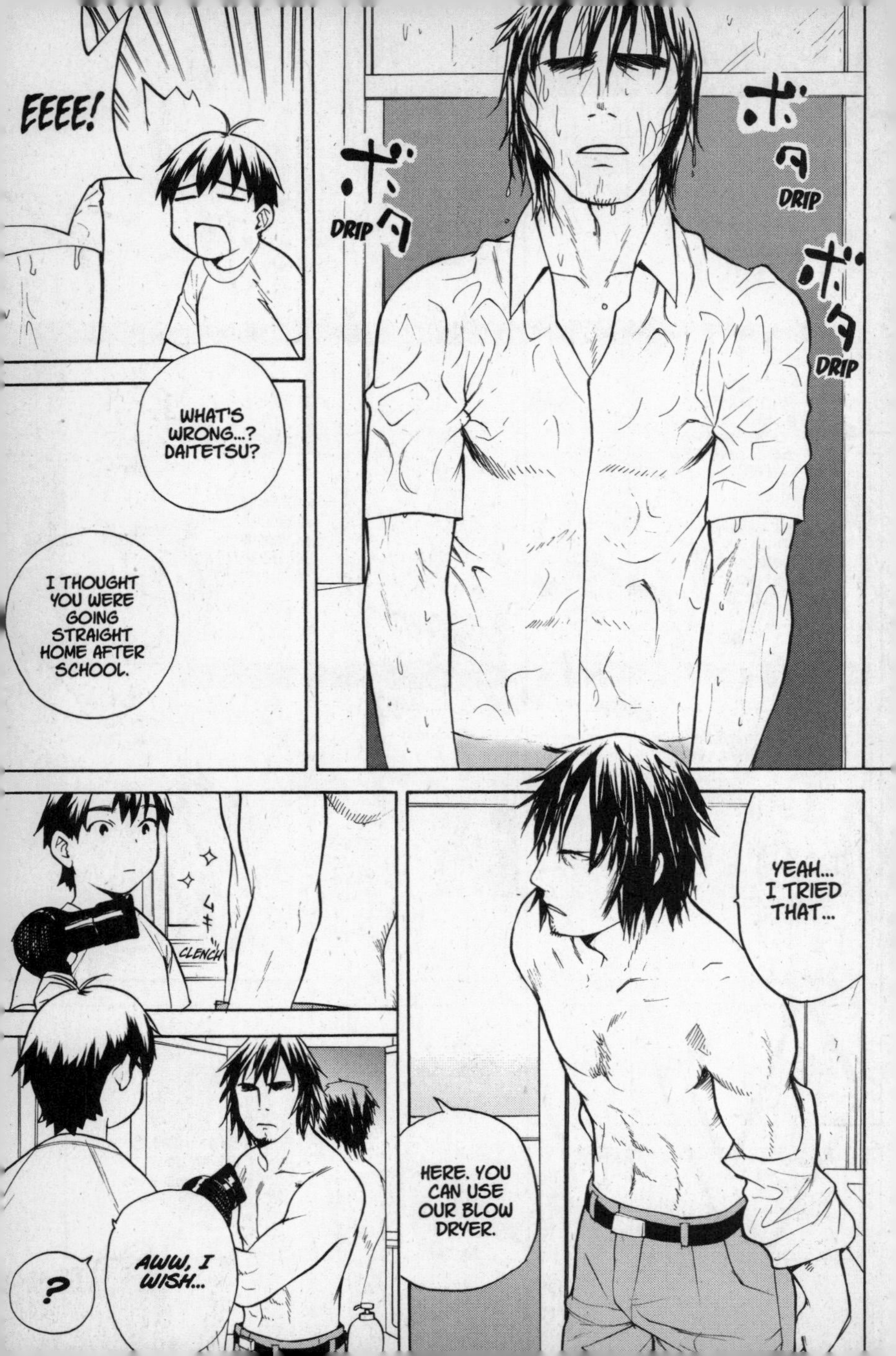
ボタ
DRIP
ボタ
DRIP
ボタ
DRIP
EEEE!
WHAT'S WRONG...? DAITETSU?
I THOUGHT YOU WERE GOING STRAIGHT HOME AFTER SCHOOL.
YEAH... I TRIED THAT...
ムキ
CLENCH
HERE. YOU CAN USE OUR BLOW DRYER.
AWW, I WISH...
?

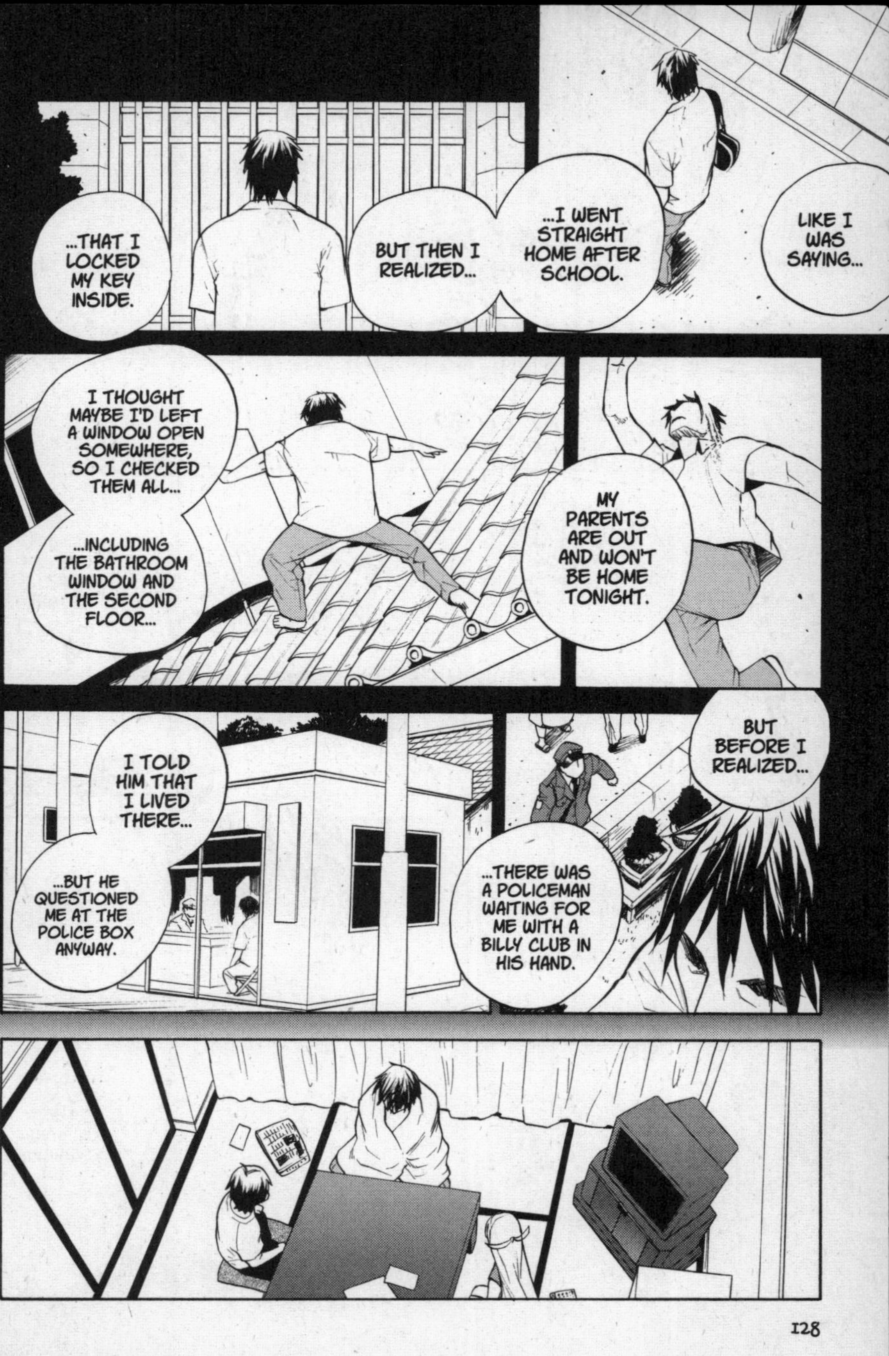
LIKE I WAS SAYING...
...I WENT STRAIGHT HOME AFTER SCHOOL.
BUT THEN I REALIZED...
...THAT I LOCKED MY KEY INSIDE.
MY PARENTS ARE OUT AND WON'T BE HOME TONIGHT.
I THOUGHT MAYBE I'D LEFT A WINDOW OPEN SOMEWHERE, SO I CHECKED THEM ALL...
...INCLUDING THE BATHROOM WINDOW AND THE SECOND FLOOR...
BUT BEFORE I REALIZED...
...THERE WAS A POLICEMAN WAITING FOR ME WITH A BILLY CLUB IN HIS HAND.
I TOLD HIM THAT I LIVED THERE...
...BUT HE QUESTIONED ME AT THE POLICE BOX ANYWAY.

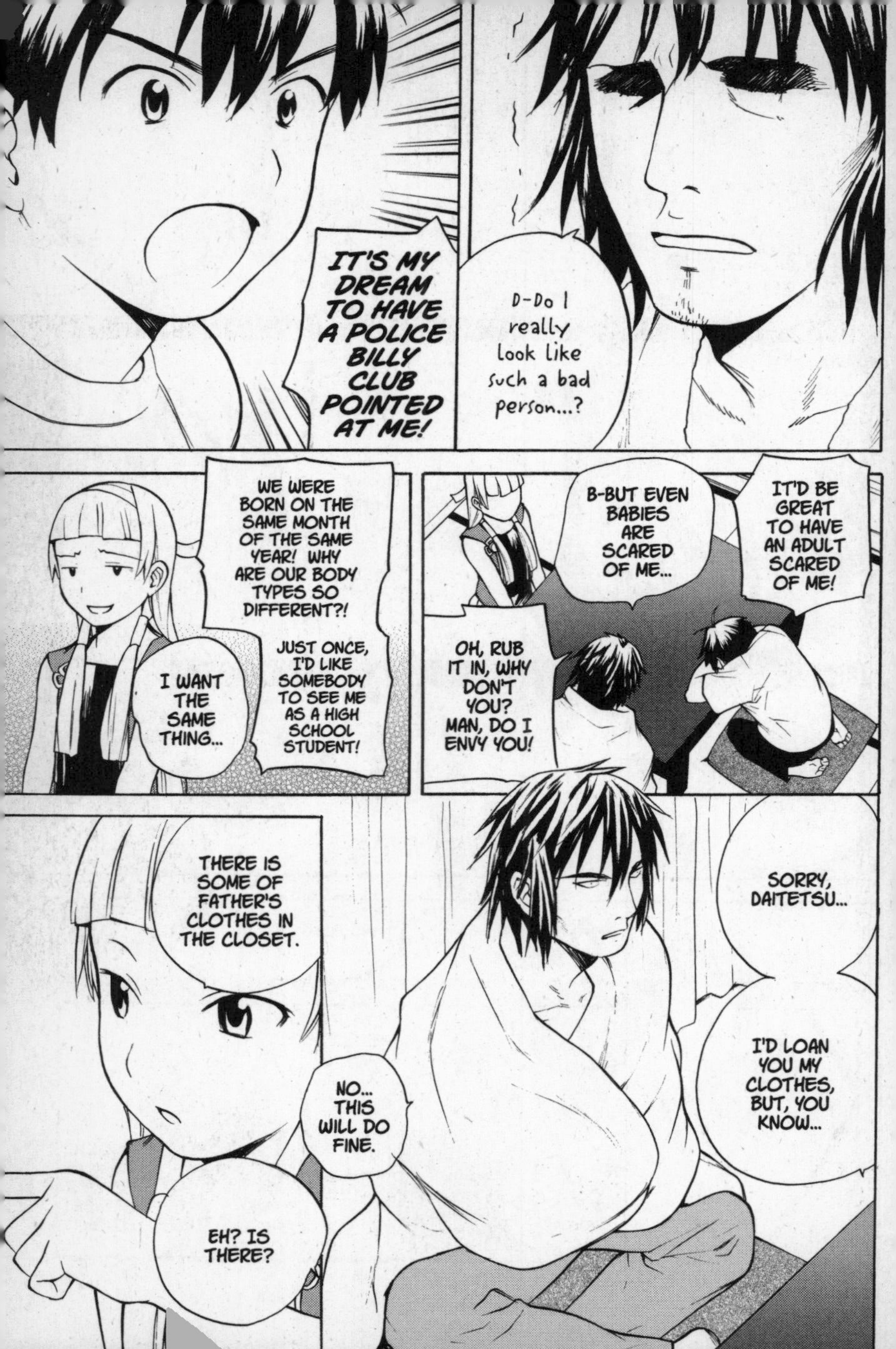
D-Do I really look like such a bad person...?
IT'S MY DREAM TO HAVE A POLICE BILLY CLUB POINTED AT ME!
IT'D BE GREAT TO HAVE AN ADULT SCARED OF ME!
B-BUT EVEN BABIES ARE SCARED OF ME...
OH, RUB IT IN, WHY DON'T YOU? MAN, DO I ENVY YOU!
WE WERE BORN ON THE SAME MONTH OF THE SAME YEAR! WHY ARE OUR BODY TYPES SO DIFFERENT?!
JUST ONCE, I'D LIKE SOMEBODY TO SEE ME AS A HIGH SCHOOL STUDENT!
I WANT THE SAME THING...
SORRY, DAITETSU...
I'D LOAN YOU MY CLOTHES, BUT, YOU KNOW...
NO... THIS WILL DO FINE.
THERE IS SOME OF FATHER'S CLOTHES IN THE CLOSET.
EH? IS THERE?

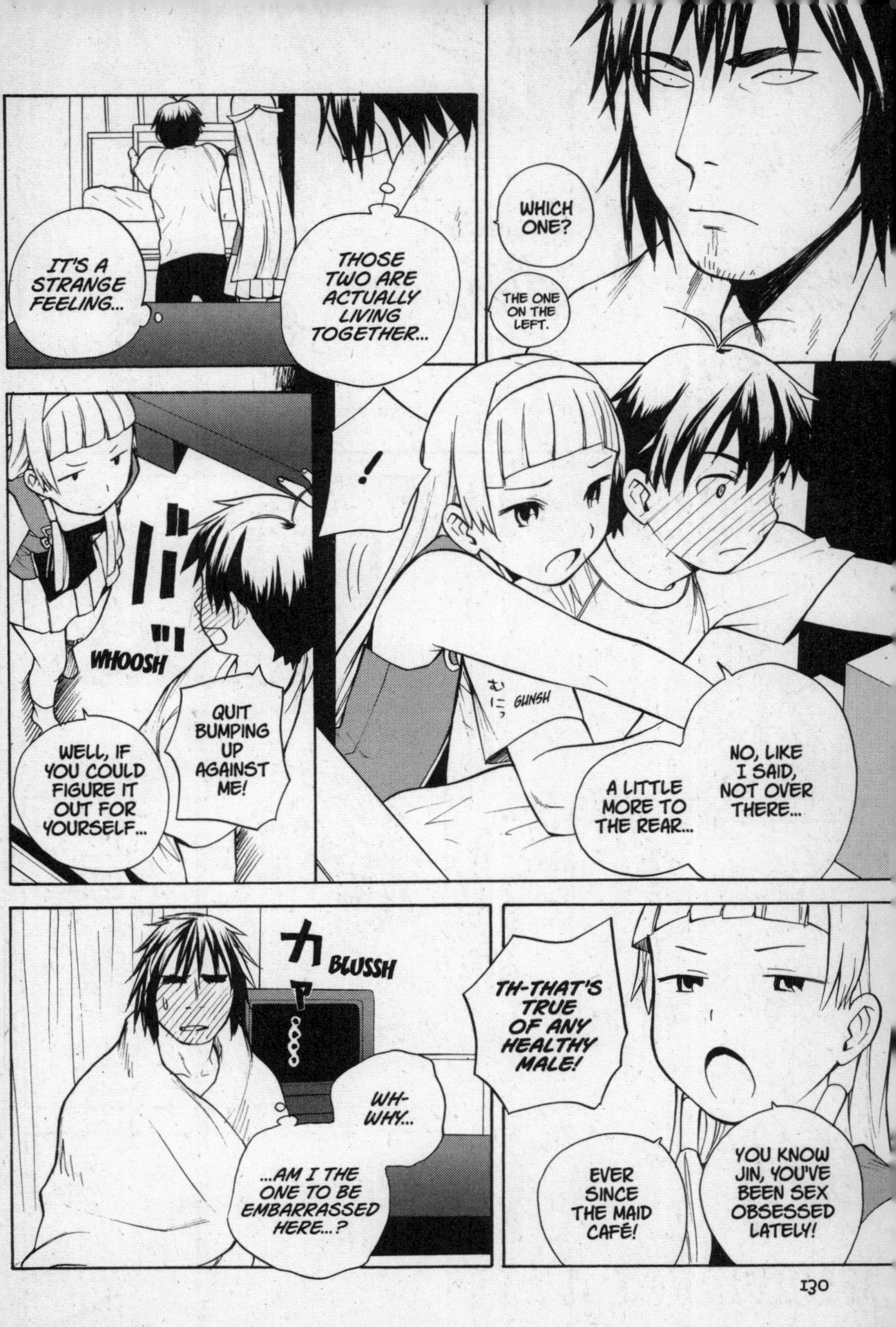
WHICH ONE?
THE ONE ON THE LEFT.
THOSE TWO ARE ACTUALLY LIVING TOGETHER...
IT'S A STRANGE FEELING...
!
GUNSH
NO, LIKE I SAID, NOT OVER THERE...
A LITTLE MORE TO THE REAR...
WHOOSH
QUIT BUMPING UP AGAINST ME!
WELL, IF YOU COULD FIGURE IT OUT FOR YOURSELF...
YOU KNOW JIN, YOU'VE BEEN SEX OBSESSED LATELY!
EVER SINCE THE MAID CAFÉ!
TH-THAT'S TRUE OF ANY HEALTHY MALE!
BLUSSH
WH-WHY...
...AM I THE ONE TO BE EMBARRASSED HERE...?

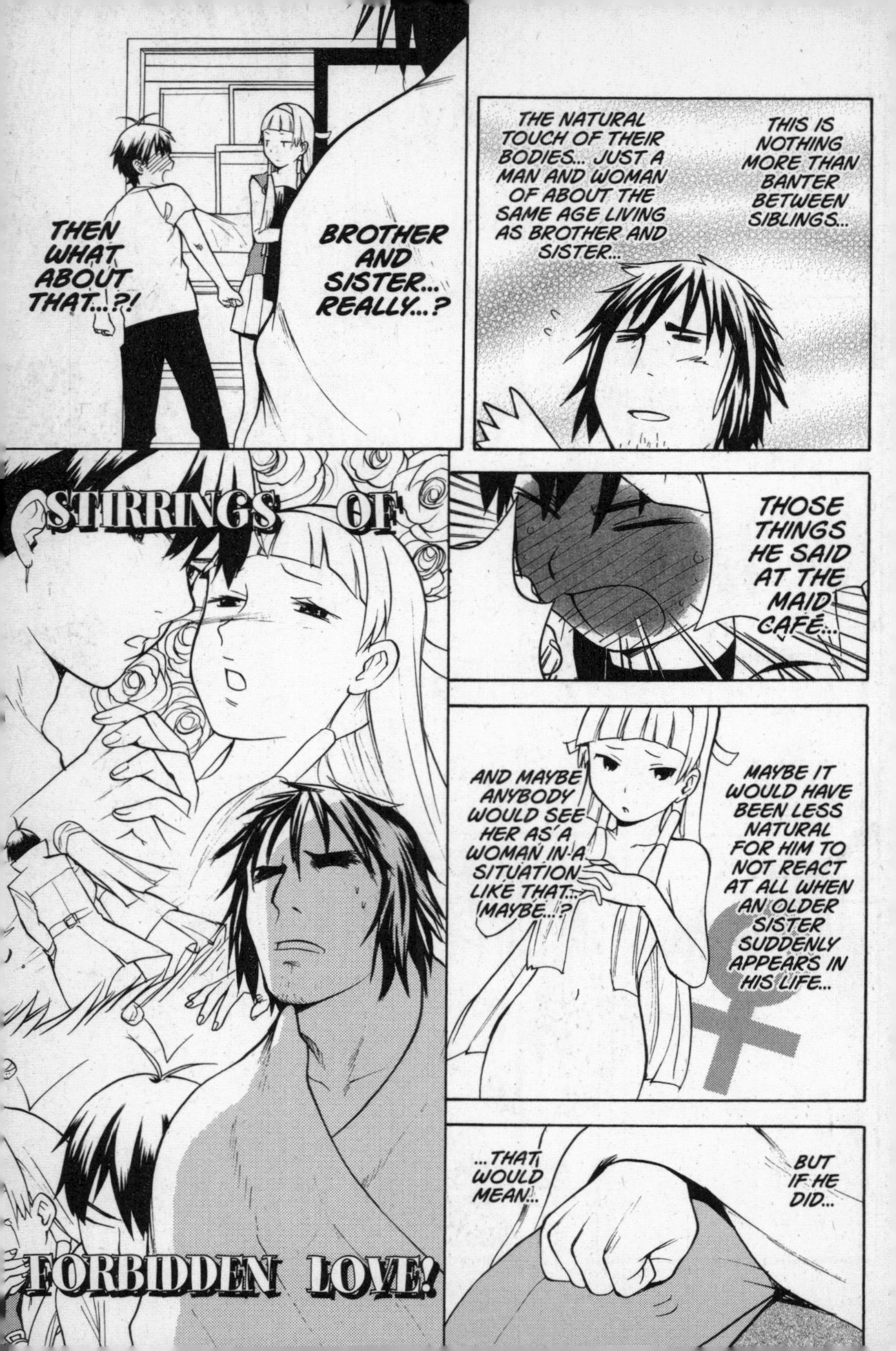
THIS IS NOTHING MORE THAN BANTER BETWEEN SIBLINGS...
THE NATURAL TOUCH OF THEIR BODIES... JUST A MAN AND WOMAN OF ABOUT THE SAME AGE LIVING AS BROTHER AND SISTER...
BROTHER AND SISTER... REALLY...?
THEN WHAT ABOUT THAT...?!
THOSE THINGS HE SAID AT THE MAID CAFÉ...
MAYBE IT WOULD HAVE BEEN LESS NATURAL FOR HIM TO NOT REACT AT ALL WHEN AN OLDER SISTER SUDDENLY APPEARS IN HIS LIFE...
AND MAYBE ANYBODY WOULD SEE HER AS A WOMAN IN A SITUATION LIKE THAT... MAYBE...?
BUT IF HE DID...
...THAT WOULD MEAN...
STIRRINGS OF
FORBIDDEN LOVE!

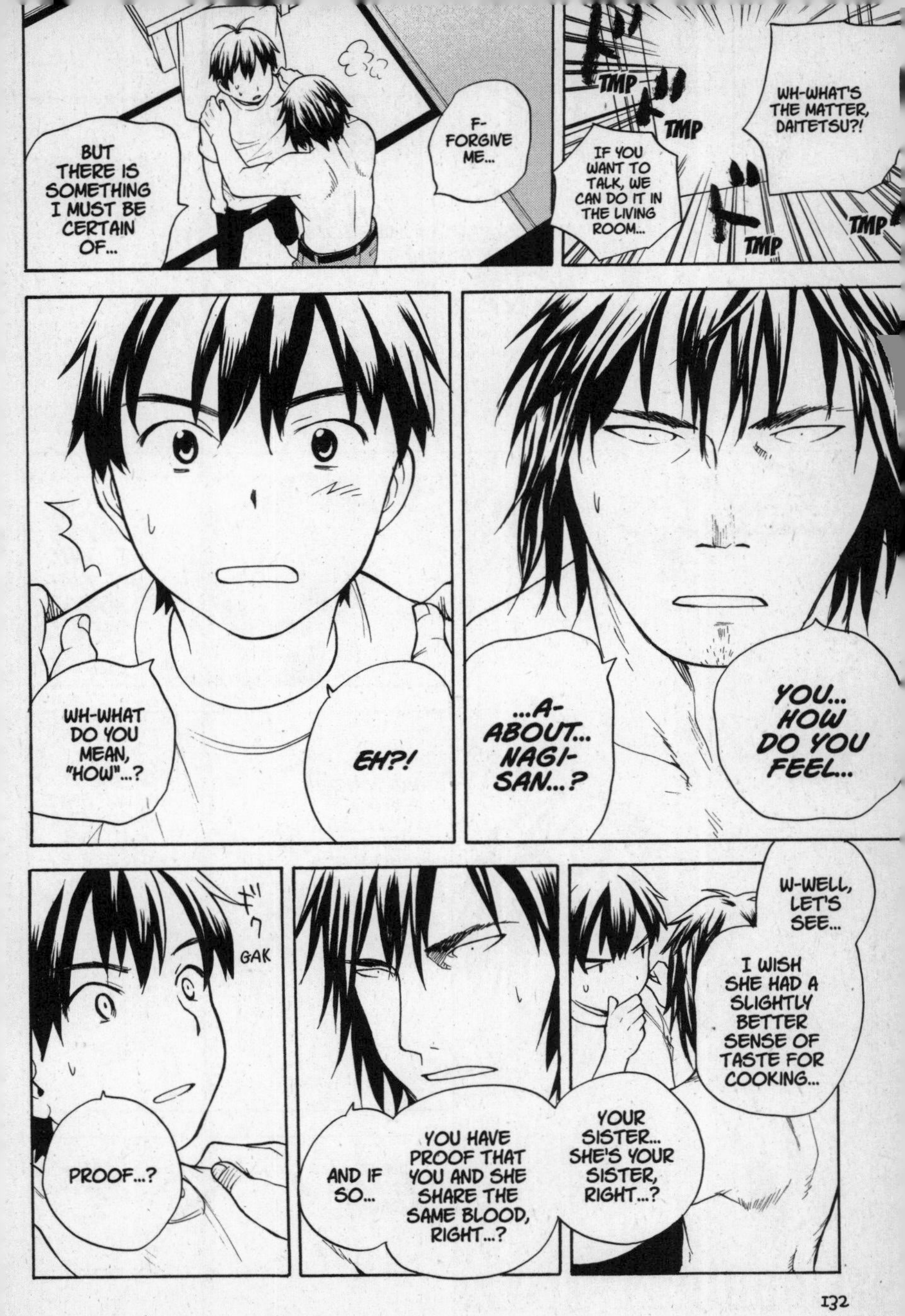
WH-WHAT'S THE MATTER, DAITETSU?!
TMP
TMP
TMP
TMP
IF YOU WANT TO TALK, WE CAN DO IT IN THE LIVING ROOM...
F-FORGIVE ME...
BUT THERE IS SOMETHING I MUST BE CERTAIN OF...
YOU... HOW DO YOU FEEL...
...A-ABOUT... NAGI-SAN...?
EH?!
WH-WHAT DO YOU MEAN, "HOW"...?
W-WELL, LET'S SEE...
I WISH SHE HAD A SLIGHTLY BETTER SENSE OF TASTE FOR COOKING...
YOUR SISTER... SHE'S YOUR SISTER, RIGHT...?
YOU HAVE PROOF THAT YOU AND SHE SHARE THE SAME BLOOD, RIGHT...?
AND IF SO...
GAK
PROOF...?

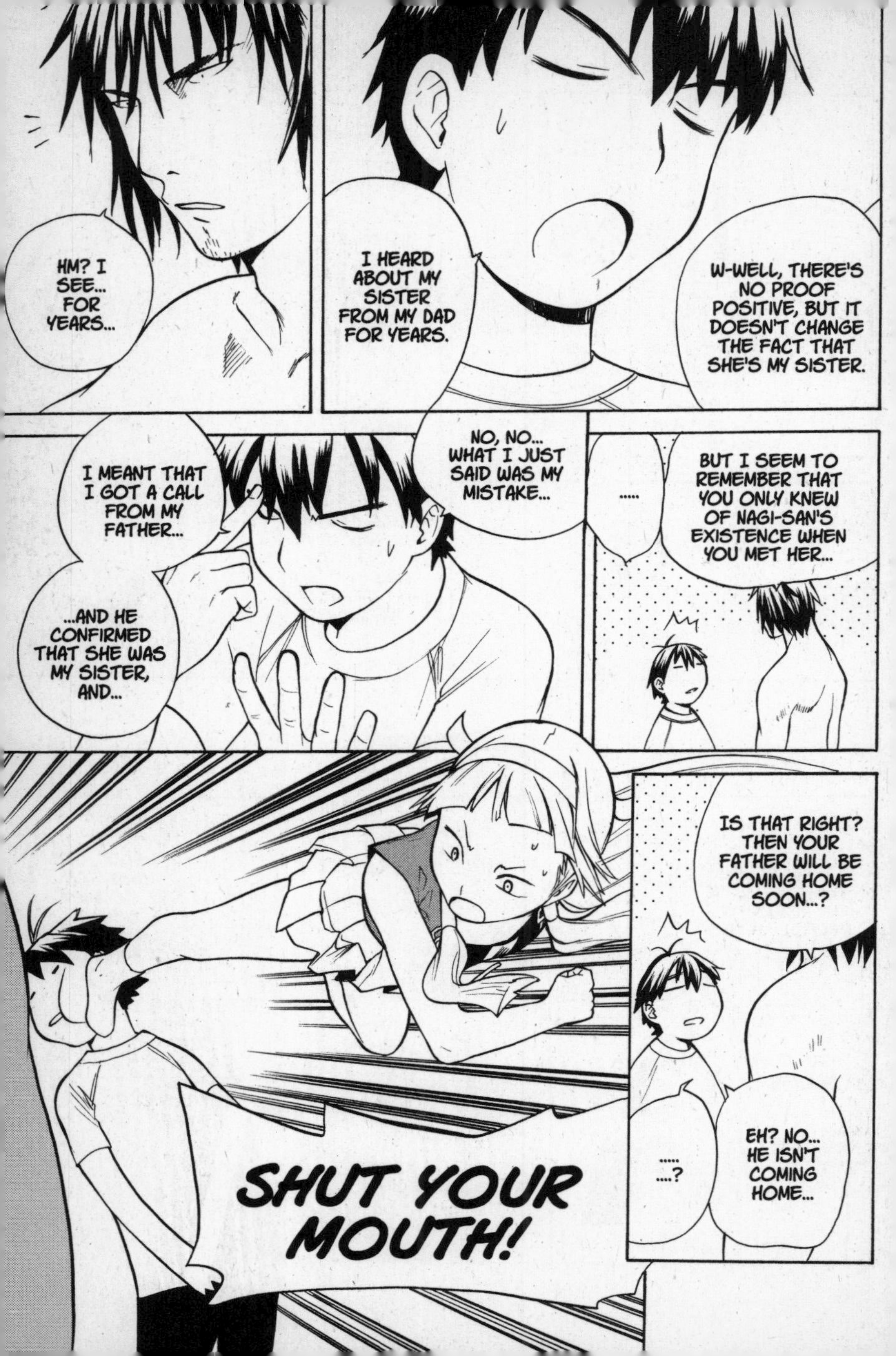
W-WELL, THERE'S NO PROOF POSITIVE, BUT IT DOESN'T CHANGE THE FACT THAT SHE'S MY SISTER.
I HEARD ABOUT MY SISTER FROM MY DAD FOR YEARS.
HM? I SEE... FOR YEARS...
BUT I SEEM TO REMEMBER THAT YOU ONLY KNEW OF NAGI-SAN'S EXISTENCE WHEN YOU MET HER...
.....
NO, NO... WHAT I JUST SAID WAS MY MISTAKE...
I MEANT THAT I GOT A CALL FROM MY FATHER...
...AND HE CONFIRMED THAT SHE WAS MY SISTER, AND...
IS THAT RIGHT? THEN YOUR FATHER WILL BE COMING HOME SOON...?
EH? NO... HE ISN'T COMING HOME...
....?
SHUT YOUR MOUTH!

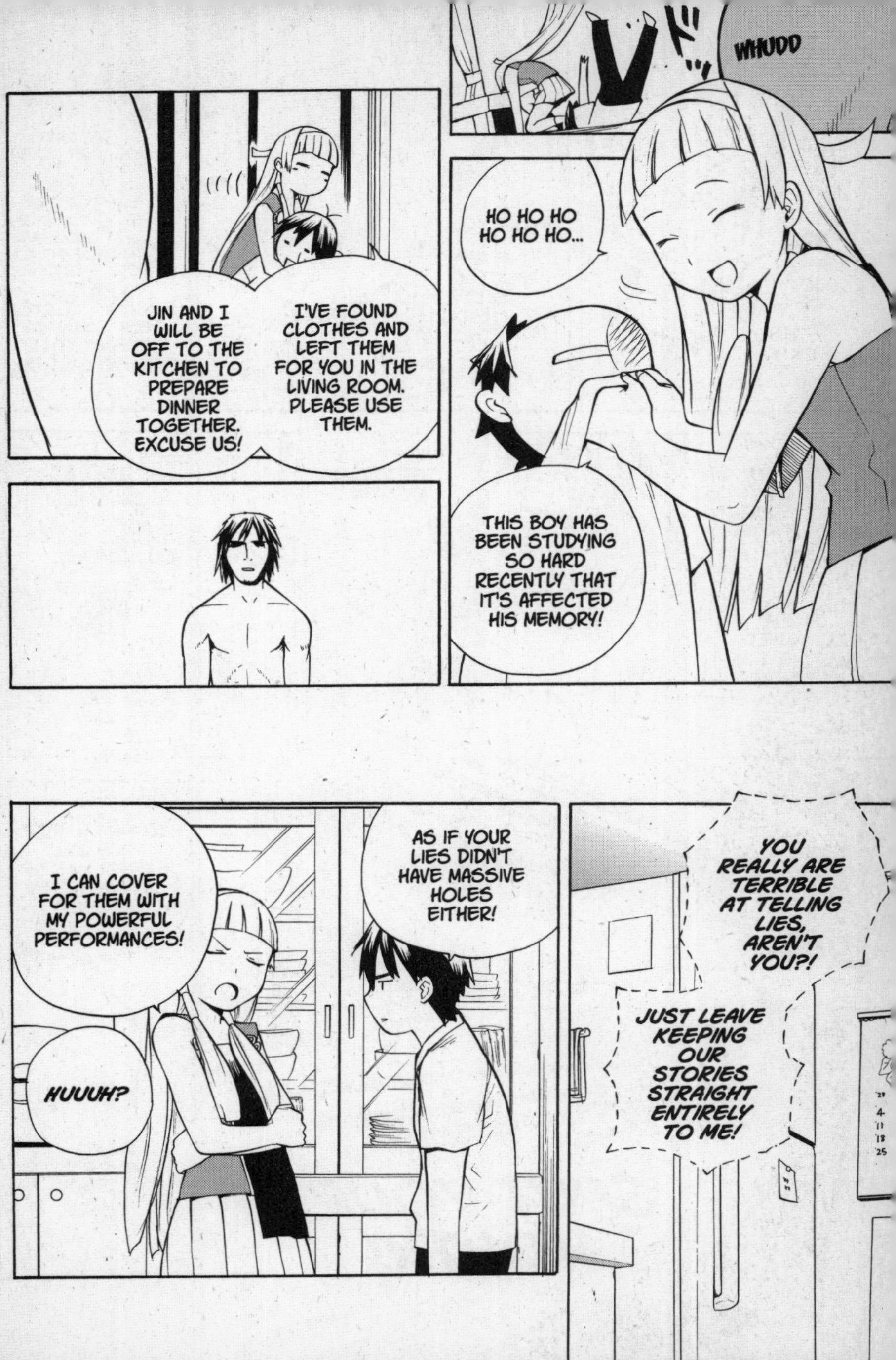
WHUDD
ド
HO HO HO HO HO HO...
THIS BOY HAS BEEN STUDYING SO HARD RECENTLY THAT IT'S AFFECTED HIS MEMORY!
I'VE FOUND CLOTHES AND LEFT THEM FOR YOU IN THE LIVING ROOM. PLEASE USE THEM.
JIN AND I WILL BE OFF TO THE KITCHEN TO PREPARE DINNER TOGETHER. EXCUSE US!
YOU REALLY ARE TERRIBLE AT TELLING LIES, AREN'T YOU?!
JUST LEAVE KEEPING OUR STORIES STRAIGHT ENTIRELY TO ME!
AS IF YOUR LIES DIDN'T HAVE MASSIVE HOLES EITHER!
I CAN COVER FOR THEM WITH MY POWERFUL PERFORMANCES!
HUUUH?

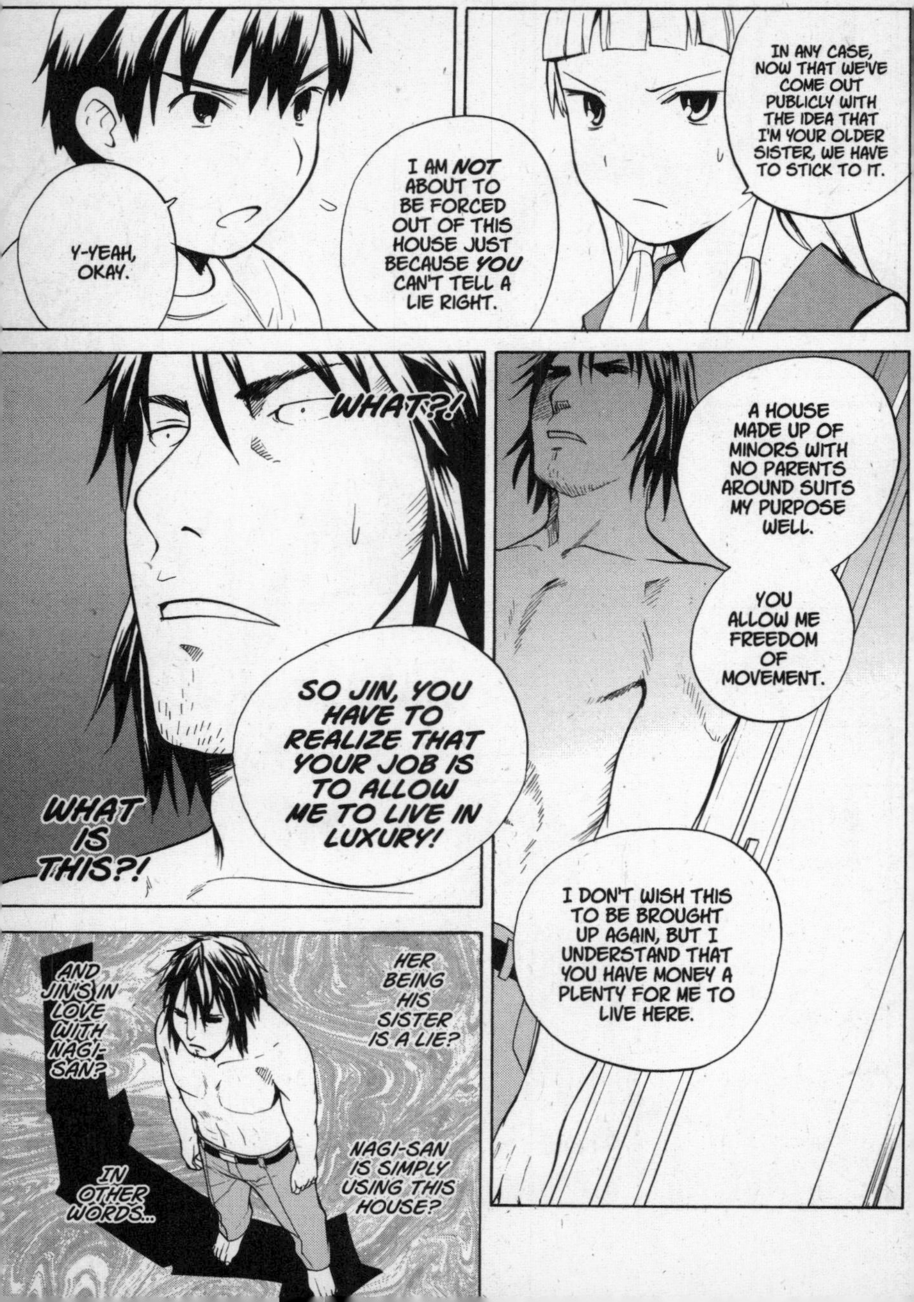
IN ANY CASE, NOW THAT WE'VE COME OUT PUBLICLY WITH THE IDEA THAT I'M YOUR OLDER SISTER, WE HAVE TO STICK TO IT.
I AM *NOT* ABOUT TO BE FORCED OUT OF THIS HOUSE JUST BECAUSE *YOU* CAN'T TELL A LIE RIGHT.
Y-YEAH, OKAY.
A HOUSE MADE UP OF MINORS WITH NO PARENTS AROUND SUITS MY PURPOSE WELL.
YOU ALLOW ME FREEDOM OF MOVEMENT.
I DON'T WISH THIS TO BE BROUGHT UP AGAIN, BUT I UNDERSTAND THAT YOU HAVE MONEY A PLENTY FOR ME TO LIVE HERE.
WHAT?!
SO JIN, YOU HAVE TO REALIZE THAT YOUR JOB IS TO ALLOW ME TO LIVE IN LUXURY!
WHAT IS THIS?!
HER BEING HIS SISTER IS A LIE?
AND JIN'S IN LOVE WITH NAGI-SAN?
NAGI-SAN IS SIMPLY USING THIS HOUSE?
IN OTHER WORDS...

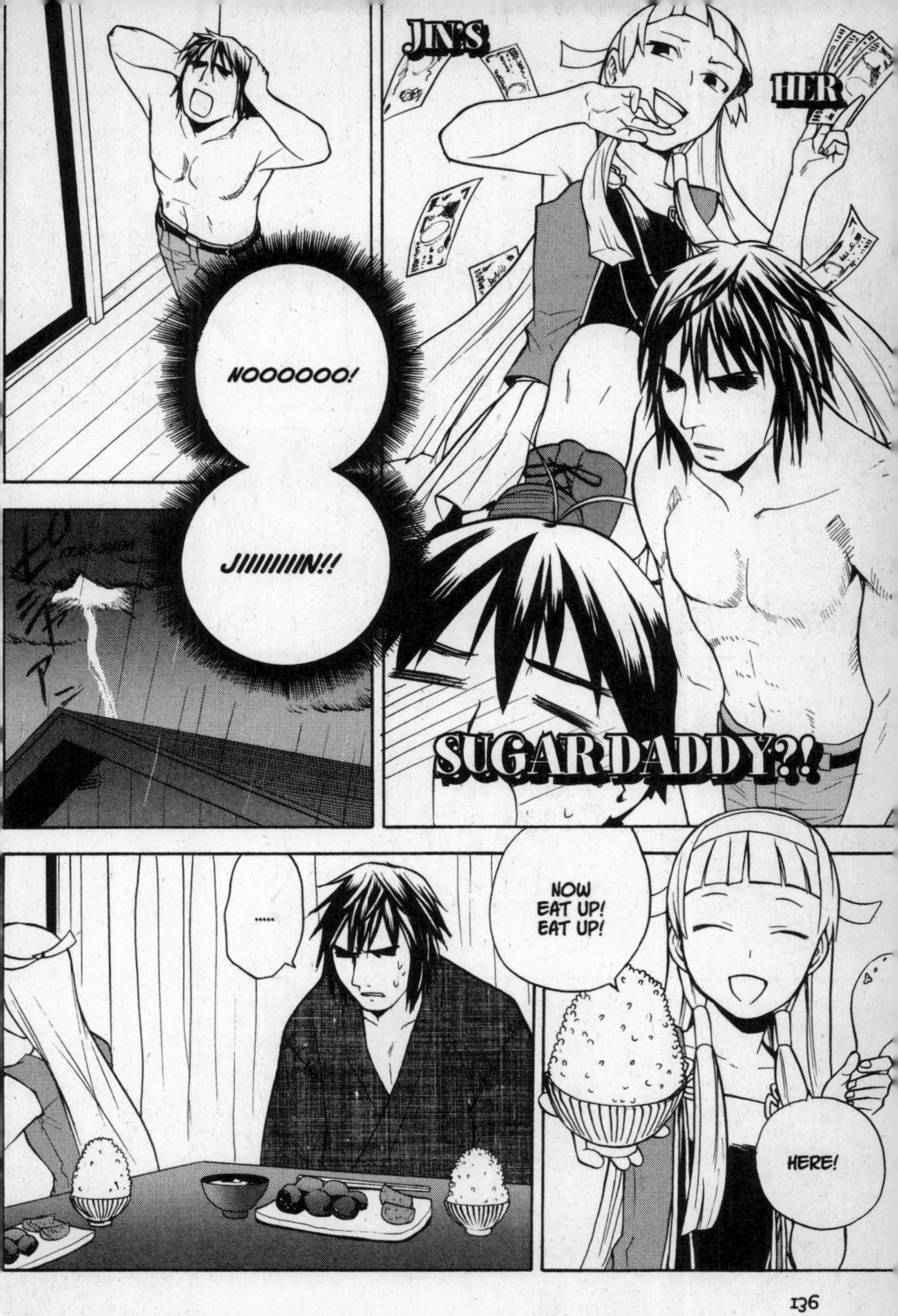
JIN'S
HER
SUGAR DADDY?!
NOOOOOO!
JIIIIIIIN!!
NOW EAT UP! EAT UP!
HERE!
.....

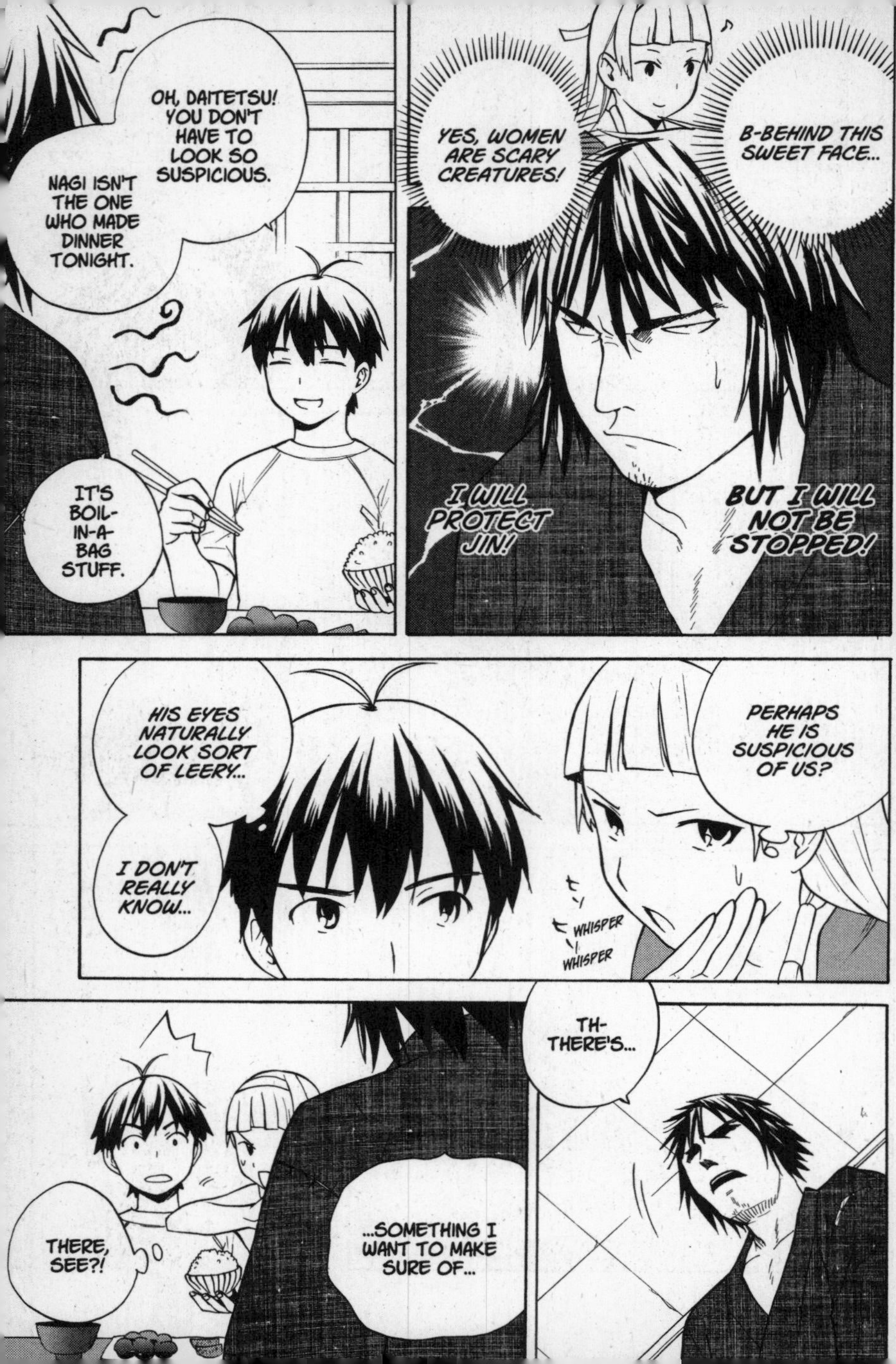
B-BEHIND THIS SWEET FACE...
YES, WOMEN ARE SCARY CREATURES!
BUT I WILL NOT BE STOPPED!
I WILL PROTECT JIN!
OH, DAITETSU! YOU DON'T HAVE TO LOOK SO SUSPICIOUS.
NAGI ISN'T THE ONE WHO MADE DINNER TONIGHT.
IT'S BOIL-IN-A-BAG STUFF.
PERHAPS HE IS SUSPICIOUS OF US?
WHISPER
WHISPER
HIS EYES NATURALLY LOOK SORT OF LEERY...
I DON'T REALLY KNOW...
TH-THERE'S...
...SOMETHING I WANT TO MAKE SURE OF...
THERE, SEE?!

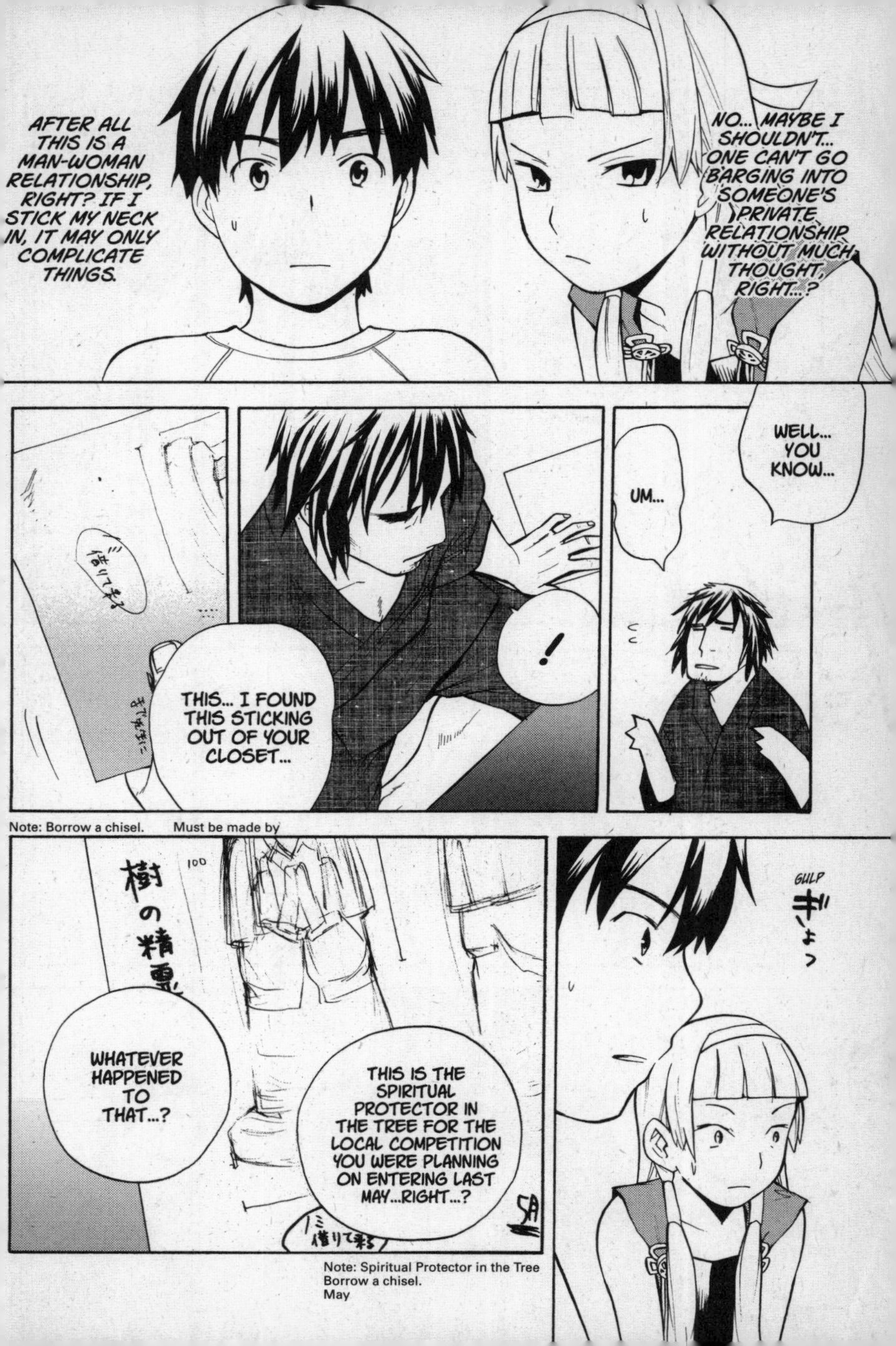
NO... MAYBE I SHOULDN'T... ONE CAN'T GO BARGING INTO SOMEONE'S PRIVATE RELATIONSHIP WITHOUT MUCH THOUGHT, RIGHT...?
AFTER ALL THIS IS A MAN-WOMAN RELATIONSHIP, RIGHT? IF I STICK MY NECK IN, IT MAY ONLY COMPLICATE THINGS.
WELL... YOU KNOW...
UM...
!
THIS... I FOUND THIS STICKING OUT OF YOUR CLOSET...
GULP
ぎょっ
樹の精霊
THIS IS THE SPIRITUAL PROTECTOR IN THE TREE FOR THE LOCAL COMPETITION YOU WERE PLANNING ON ENTERING LAST MAY...RIGHT...?
WHATEVER HAPPENED TO THAT...?

Note: Borrow a chisel. Must be made by

Note: Spiritual Protector in the Tree
Borrow a chisel.
May

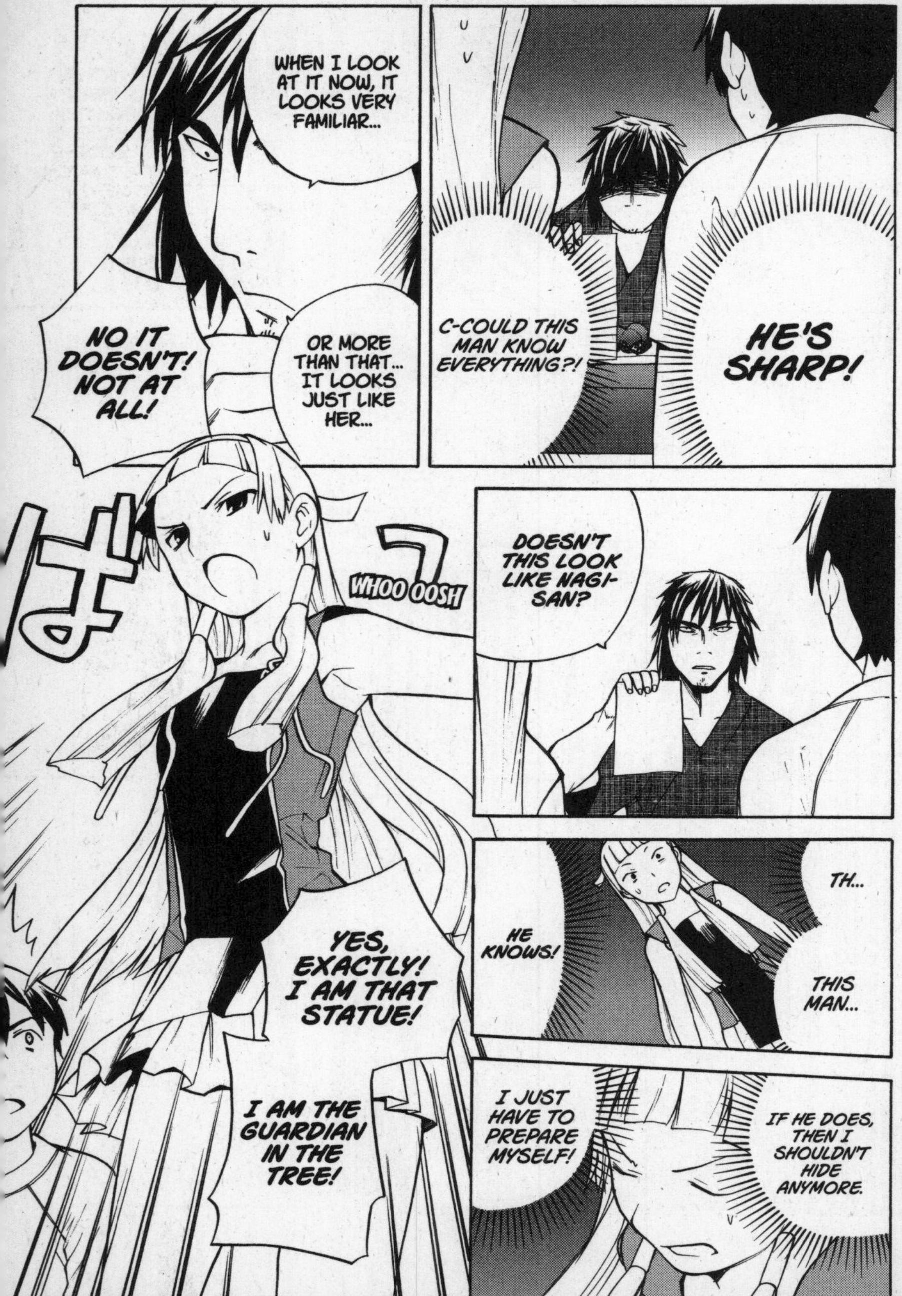
HE'S SHARP!
C-COULD THIS MAN KNOW EVERYTHING?!
WHEN I LOOK AT IT NOW, IT LOOKS VERY FAMILIAR...
OR MORE THAN THAT... IT LOOKS JUST LIKE HER...
DOESN'T THIS LOOK LIKE NAGI-SAN?
TH...
THIS MAN...
HE KNOWS!
IF HE DOES, THEN I SHOULDN'T HIDE ANYMORE.
I JUST HAVE TO PREPARE MYSELF!
NO IT DOESN'T! NOT AT ALL!
WHOO OOSH
ば
YES, EXACTLY! I AM THAT STATUE!
I AM THE GUARDIAN IN THE TREE!

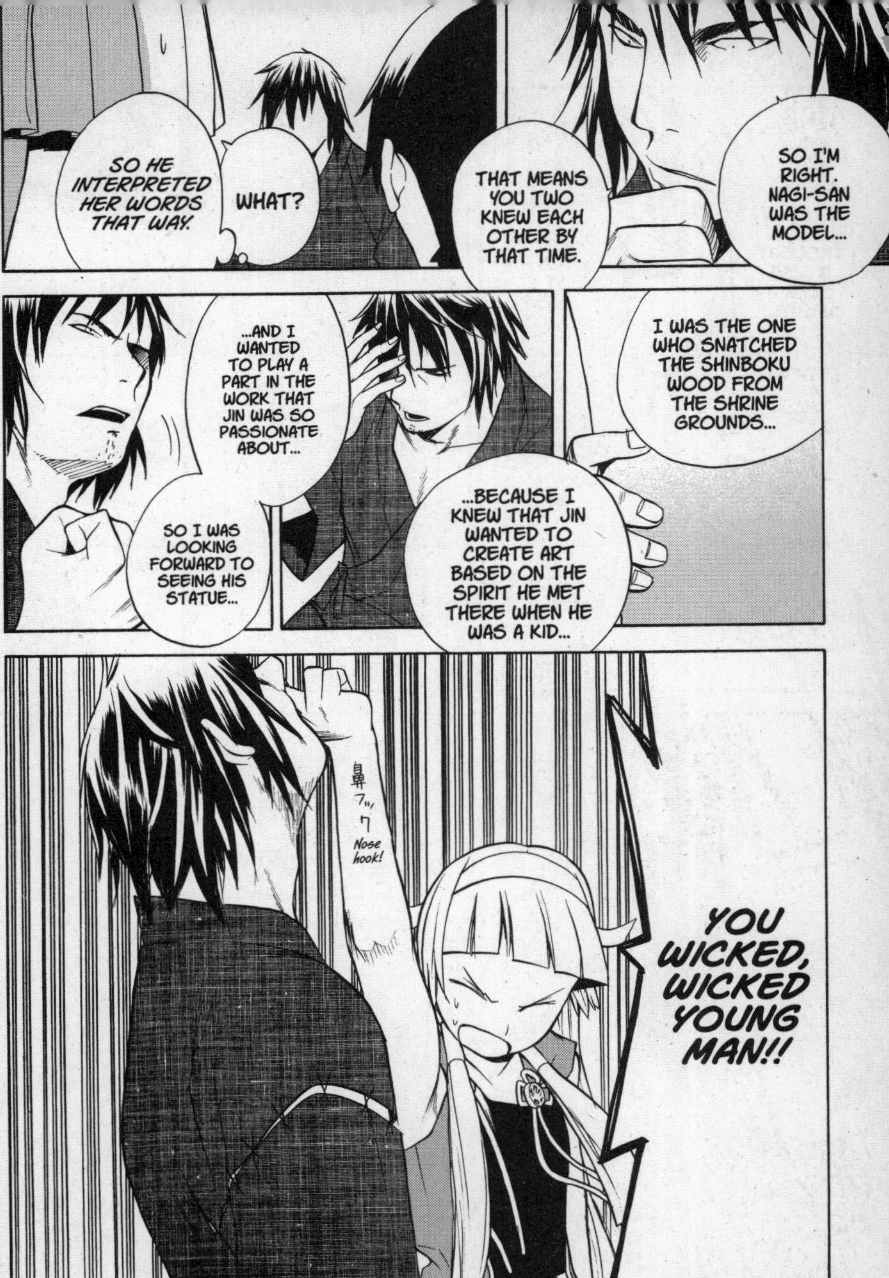
SO I'M RIGHT. NAGI-SAN WAS THE MODEL...
THAT MEANS YOU TWO KNEW EACH OTHER BY THAT TIME.
WHAT?
SO HE INTERPRETED HER WORDS THAT WAY.
I WAS THE ONE WHO SNATCHED THE SHINBOKU WOOD FROM THE SHRINE GROUNDS...
...BECAUSE I KNEW THAT JIN WANTED TO CREATE ART BASED ON THE SPIRIT HE MET THERE WHEN HE WAS A KID...
...AND I WANTED TO PLAY A PART IN THE WORK THAT JIN WAS SO PASSIONATE ABOUT...
SO I WAS LOOKING FORWARD TO SEEING HIS STATUE...
YOU WICKED, WICKED YOUNG MAN!!
鼻フック
Nose hook!

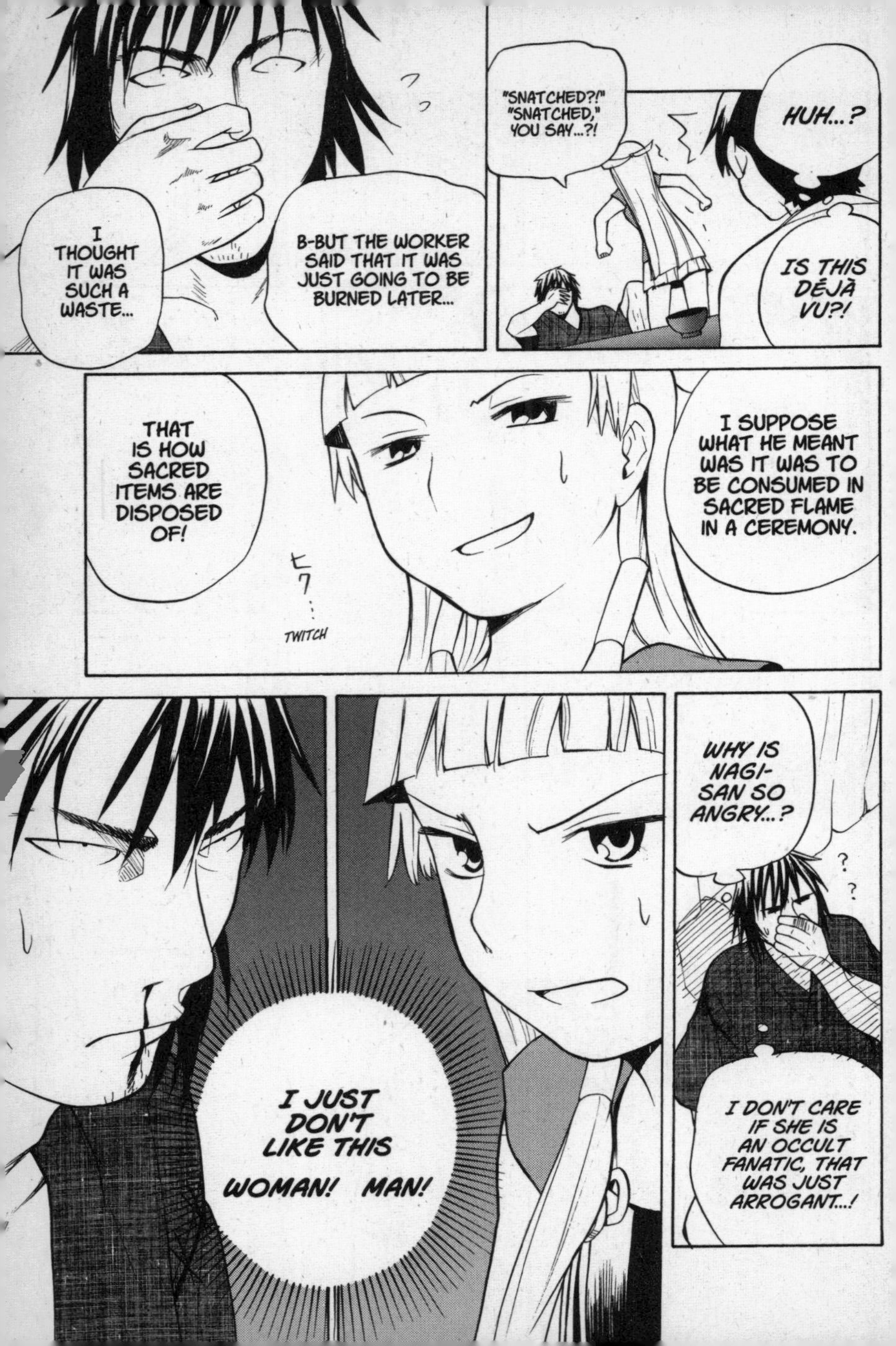
HUH...?
"SNATCHED?!" "SNATCHED," YOU SAY...?!
IS THIS DÉJÀ VU?!
B-BUT THE WORKER SAID THAT IT WAS JUST GOING TO BE BURNED LATER...
I THOUGHT IT WAS SUCH A WASTE...
I SUPPOSE WHAT HE MEANT WAS IT WAS TO BE CONSUMED IN SACRED FLAME IN A CEREMONY.
THAT IS HOW SACRED ITEMS ARE DISPOSED OF!
ヒク
TWITCH
WHY IS NAGI-SAN SO ANGRY...?
I DON'T CARE IF SHE IS AN OCCULT FANATIC, THAT WAS JUST ARROGANT...!
I JUST DON'T LIKE THIS
WOMAN! MAN!

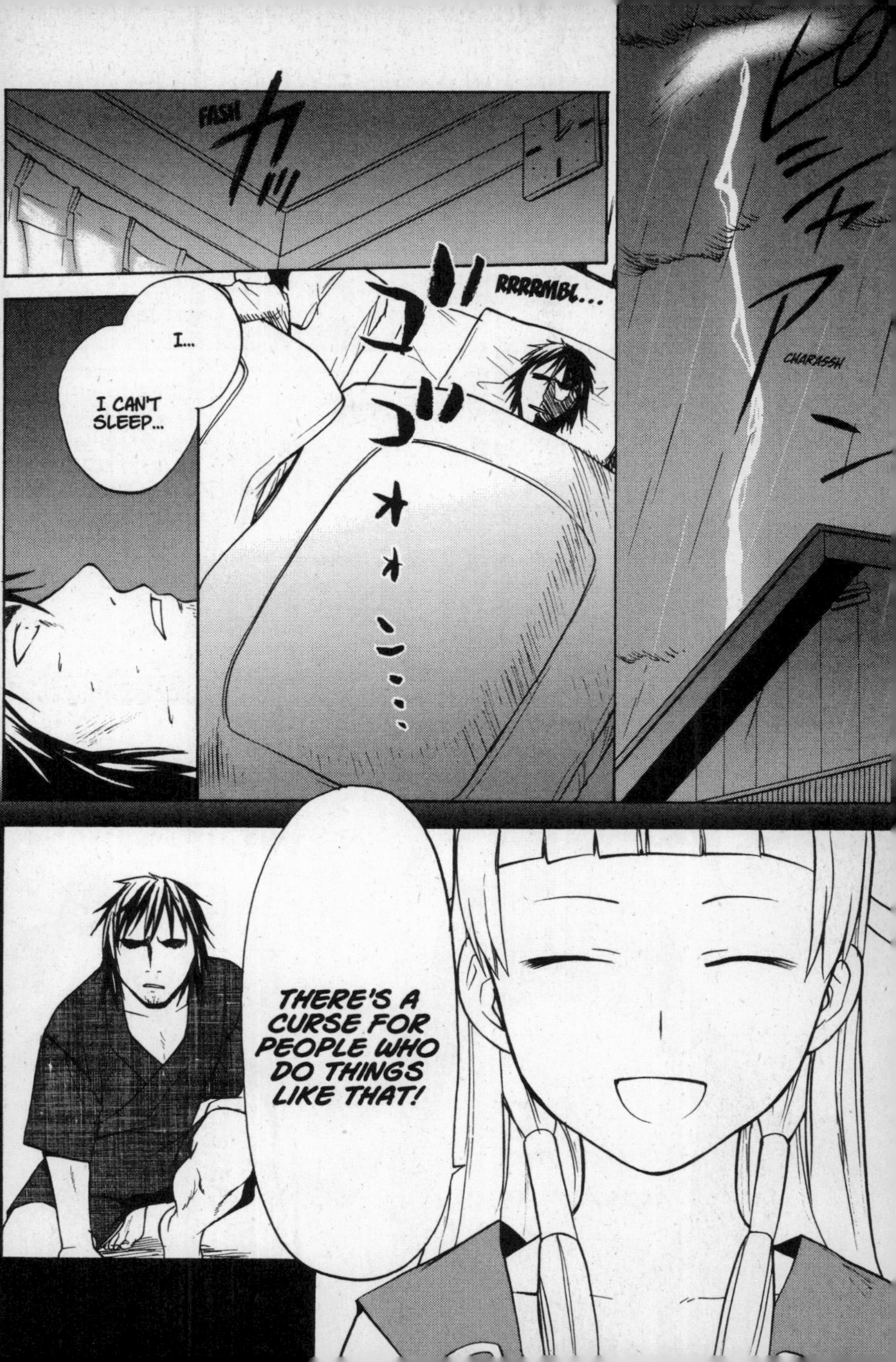
CHARASSH
FASH
RRRRMBL...
I...
I CAN'T SLEEP...
THERE'S A CURSE FOR PEOPLE WHO DO THINGS LIKE THAT!

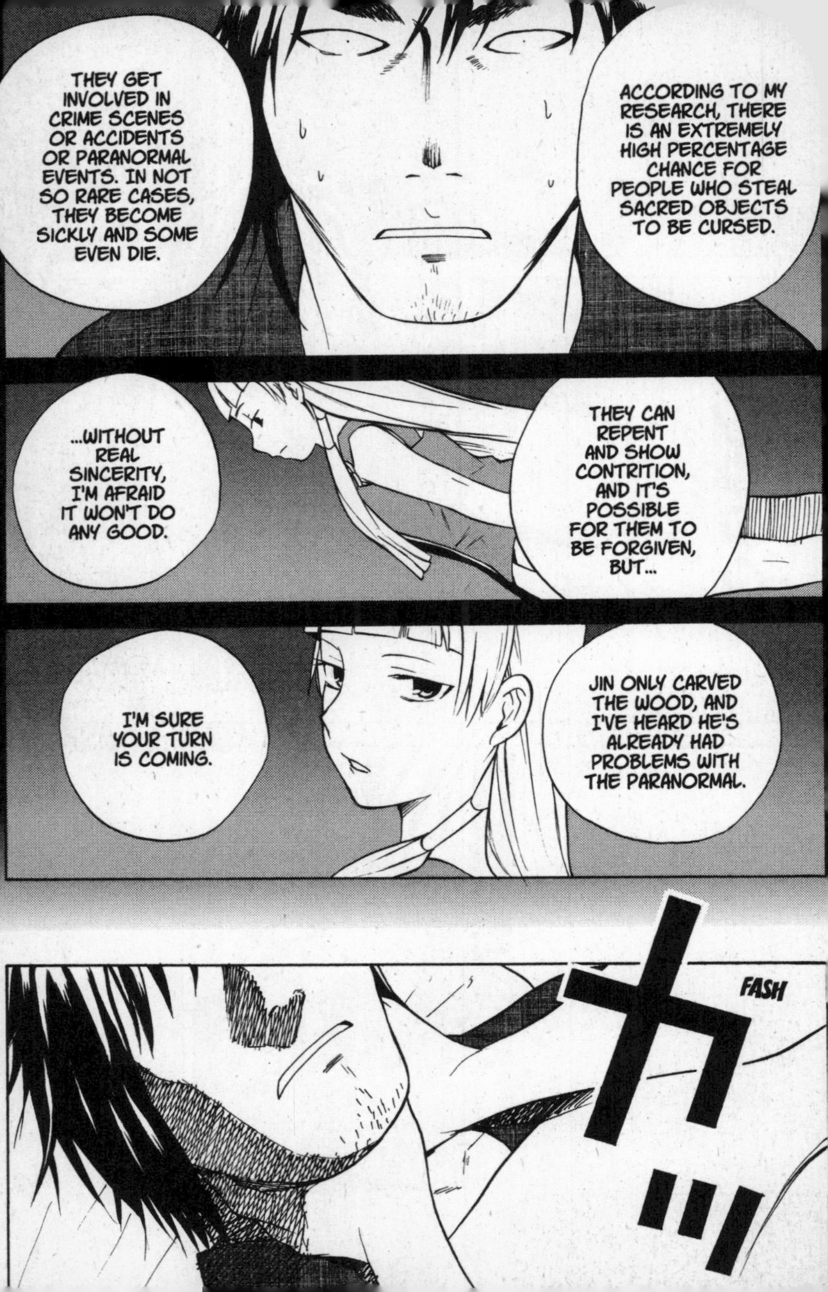
ACCORDING TO MY RESEARCH, THERE IS AN EXTREMELY HIGH PERCENTAGE CHANCE FOR PEOPLE WHO STEAL SACRED OBJECTS TO BE CURSED.
THEY GET INVOLVED IN CRIME SCENES OR ACCIDENTS OR PARANORMAL EVENTS. IN NOT SO RARE CASES, THEY BECOME SICKLY AND SOME EVEN DIE.
THEY CAN REPENT AND SHOW CONTRITION, AND IT'S POSSIBLE FOR THEM TO BE FORGIVEN, BUT...
...WITHOUT REAL SINCERITY, I'M AFRAID IT WON'T DO ANY GOOD.
JIN ONLY CARVED THE WOOD, AND I'VE HEARD HE'S ALREADY HAD PROBLEMS WITH THE PARANORMAL.
I'M SURE YOUR TURN IS COMING.
FASH

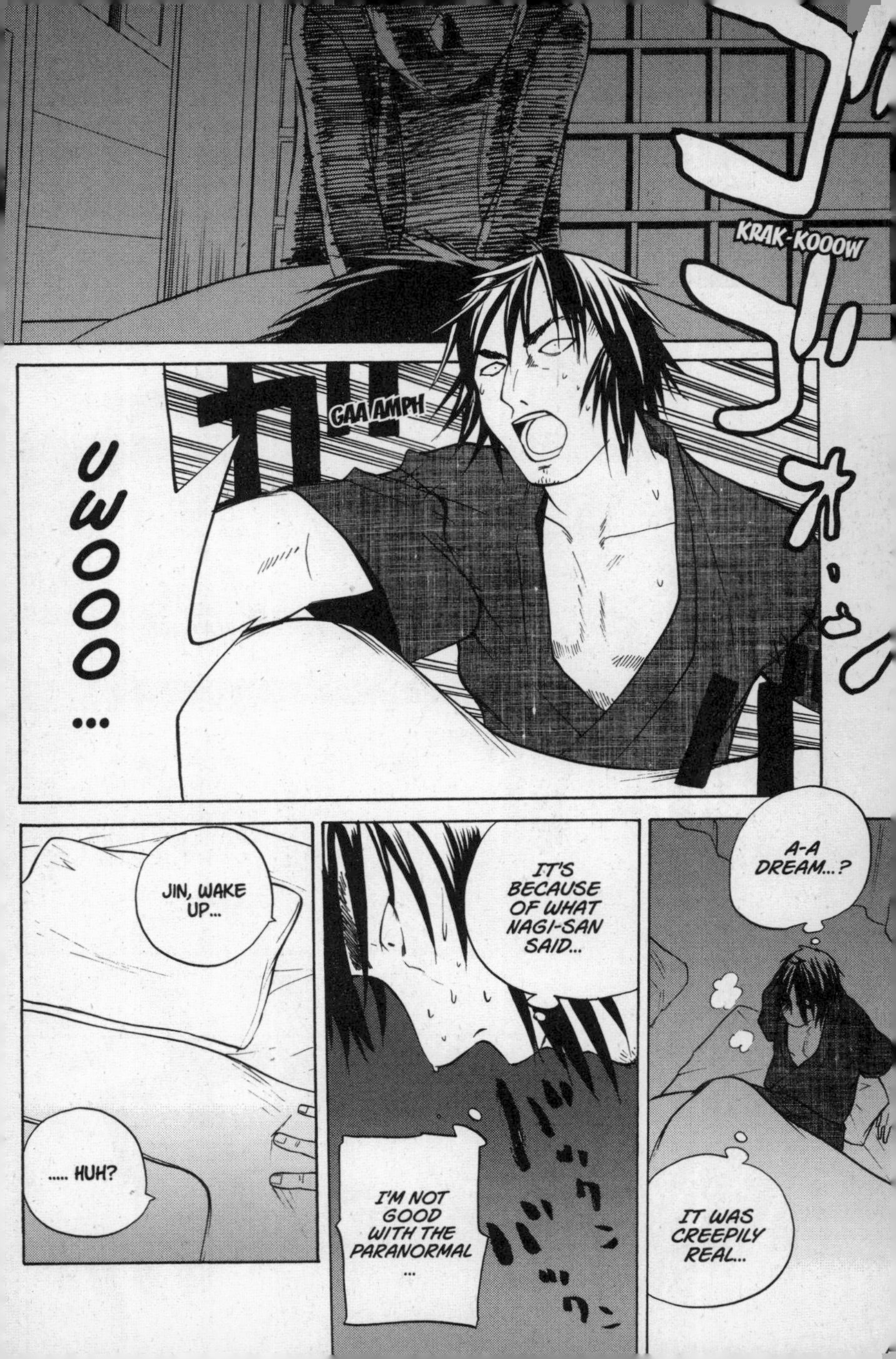
KRAK-KOOOW
GAA AMPH
UWOOOO...
A-A DREAM...?
IT WAS CREEPILY REAL...
IT'S BECAUSE OF WHAT NAGI-SAN SAID...
I'M NOT GOOD WITH THE PARANORMAL...
JIN, WAKE UP...
..... HUH?

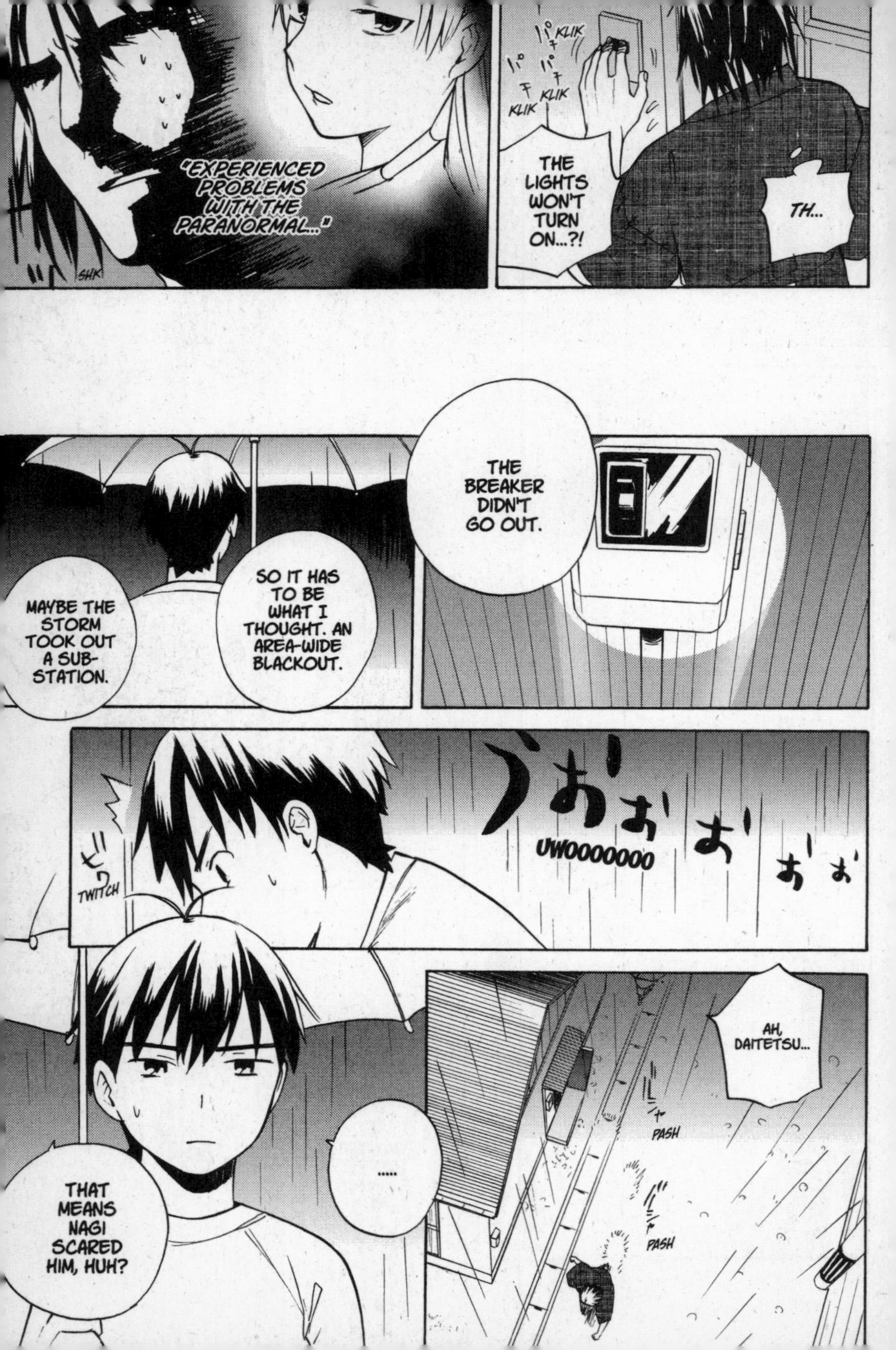
KLIK
KLIK
KLIK
THE LIGHTS WON'T TURN ON...?!
TH...
"EXPERIENCED PROBLEMS WITH THE PARANORMAL..."
SHK
THE BREAKER DIDN'T GO OUT.
SO IT HAS TO BE WHAT I THOUGHT. AN AREA-WIDE BLACKOUT.
MAYBE THE STORM TOOK OUT A SUB-STATION.
UWOOOOOOO
TWITCH
AH, DAITETSU...
PASH
PASH
.....
THAT MEANS NAGI SCARED HIM, HUH?

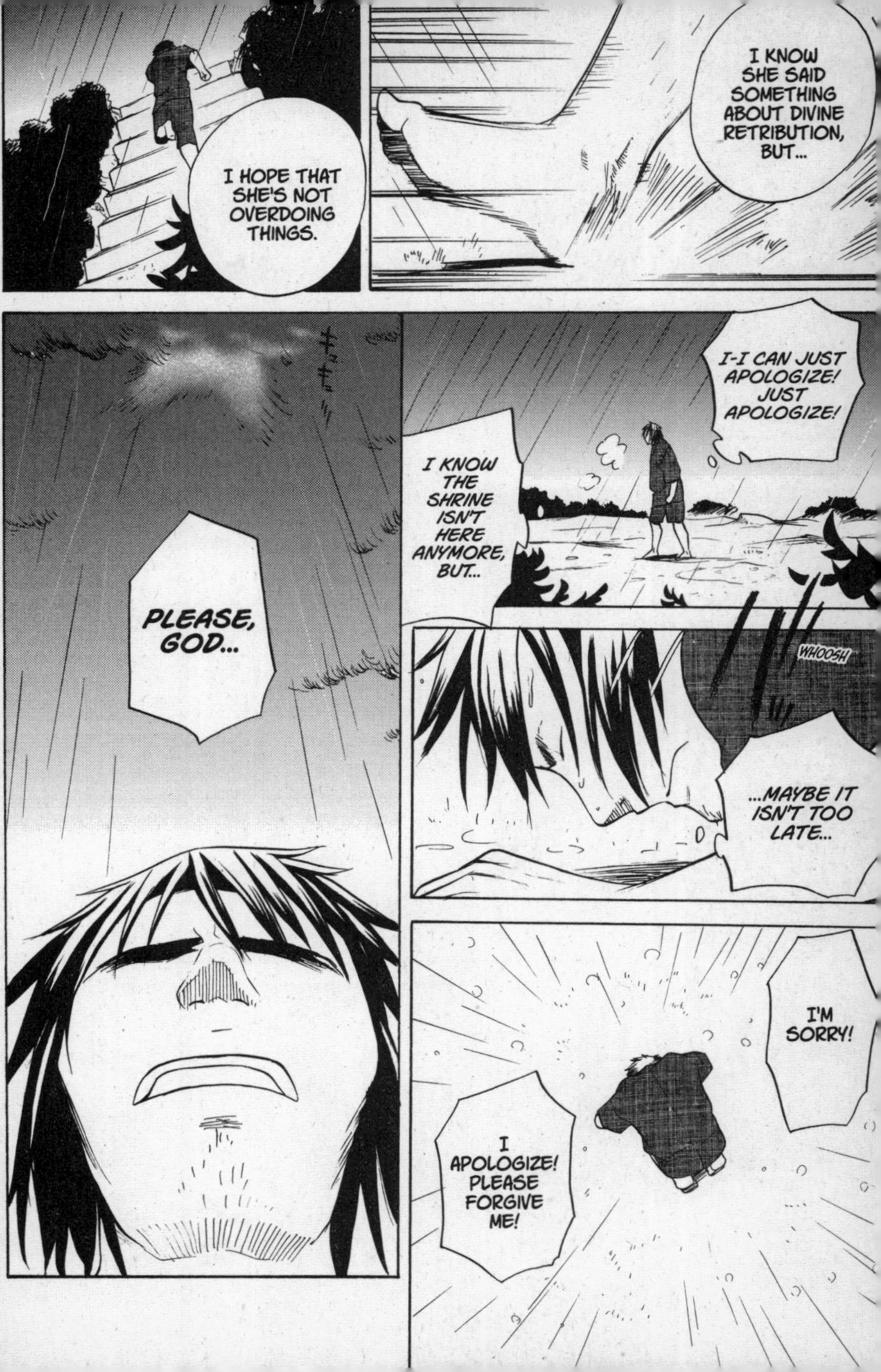
I KNOW SHE SAID SOMETHING ABOUT DIVINE RETRIBUTION, BUT...
I HOPE THAT SHE'S NOT OVERDOING THINGS.
I-I CAN JUST APOLOGIZE! JUST APOLOGIZE!
I KNOW THE SHRINE ISN'T HERE ANYMORE, BUT...
WHOOSH
...MAYBE IT ISN'T TOO LATE...
I'M SORRY!
I APOLOGIZE! PLEASE FORGIVE ME!
PLEASE, GOD...

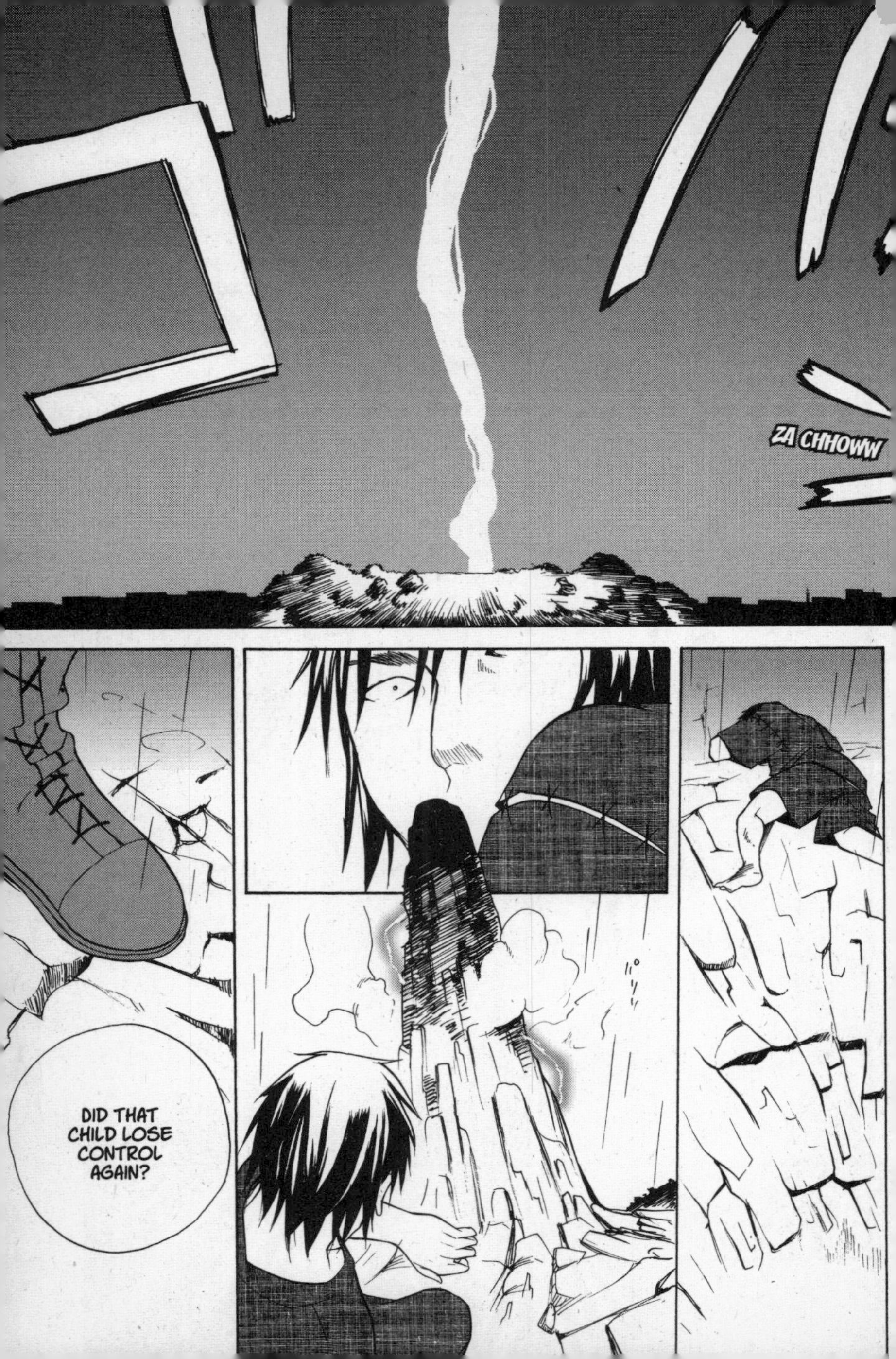
ZA CHHOWW
DID THAT CHILD LOSE CONTROL AGAIN?

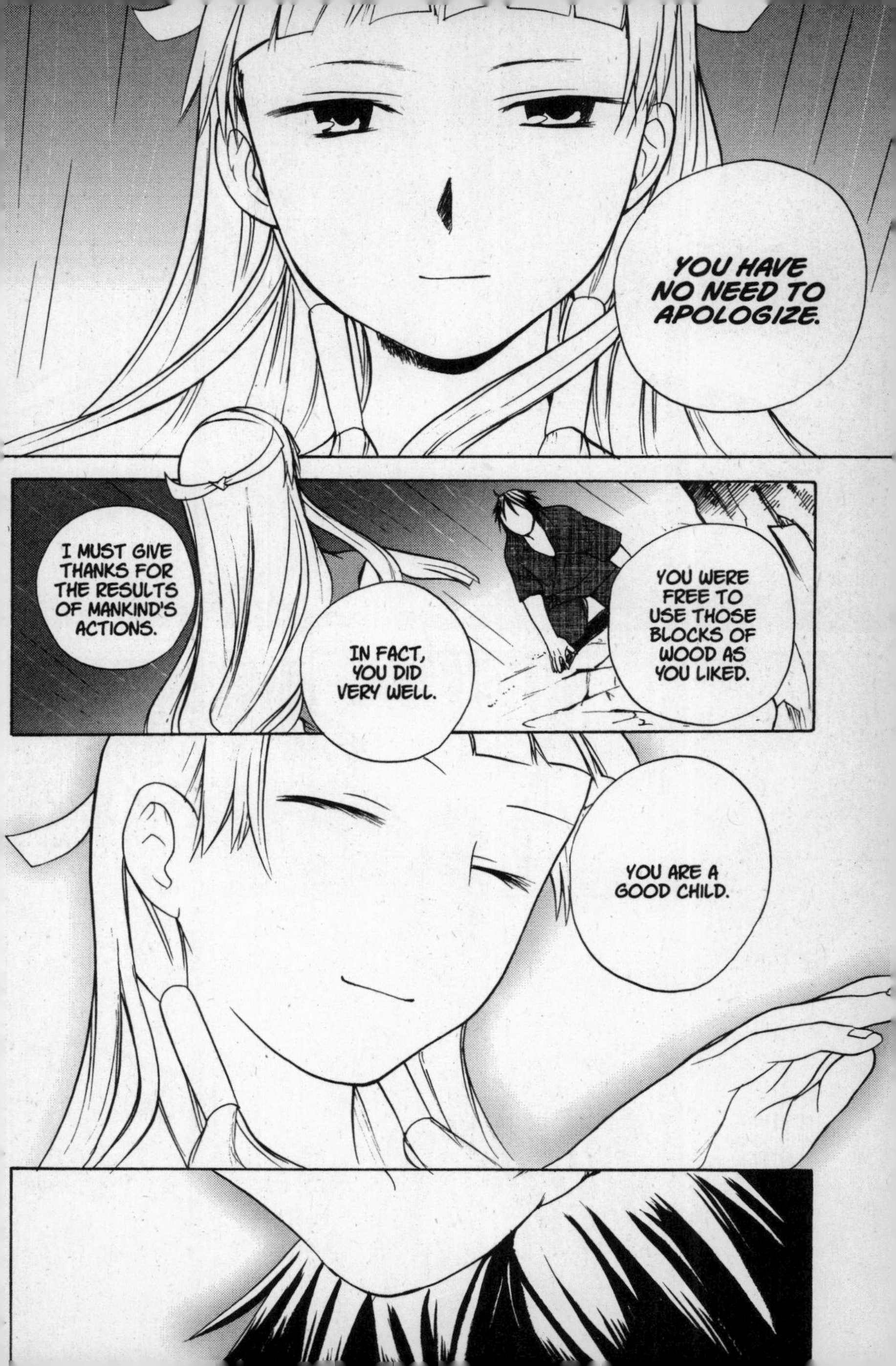
YOU HAVE NO NEED TO APOLOGIZE.
YOU WERE FREE TO USE THOSE BLOCKS OF WOOD AS YOU LIKED.
IN FACT, YOU DID VERY WELL.
I MUST GIVE THANKS FOR THE RESULTS OF MANKIND'S ACTIONS.
YOU ARE A GOOD CHILD.

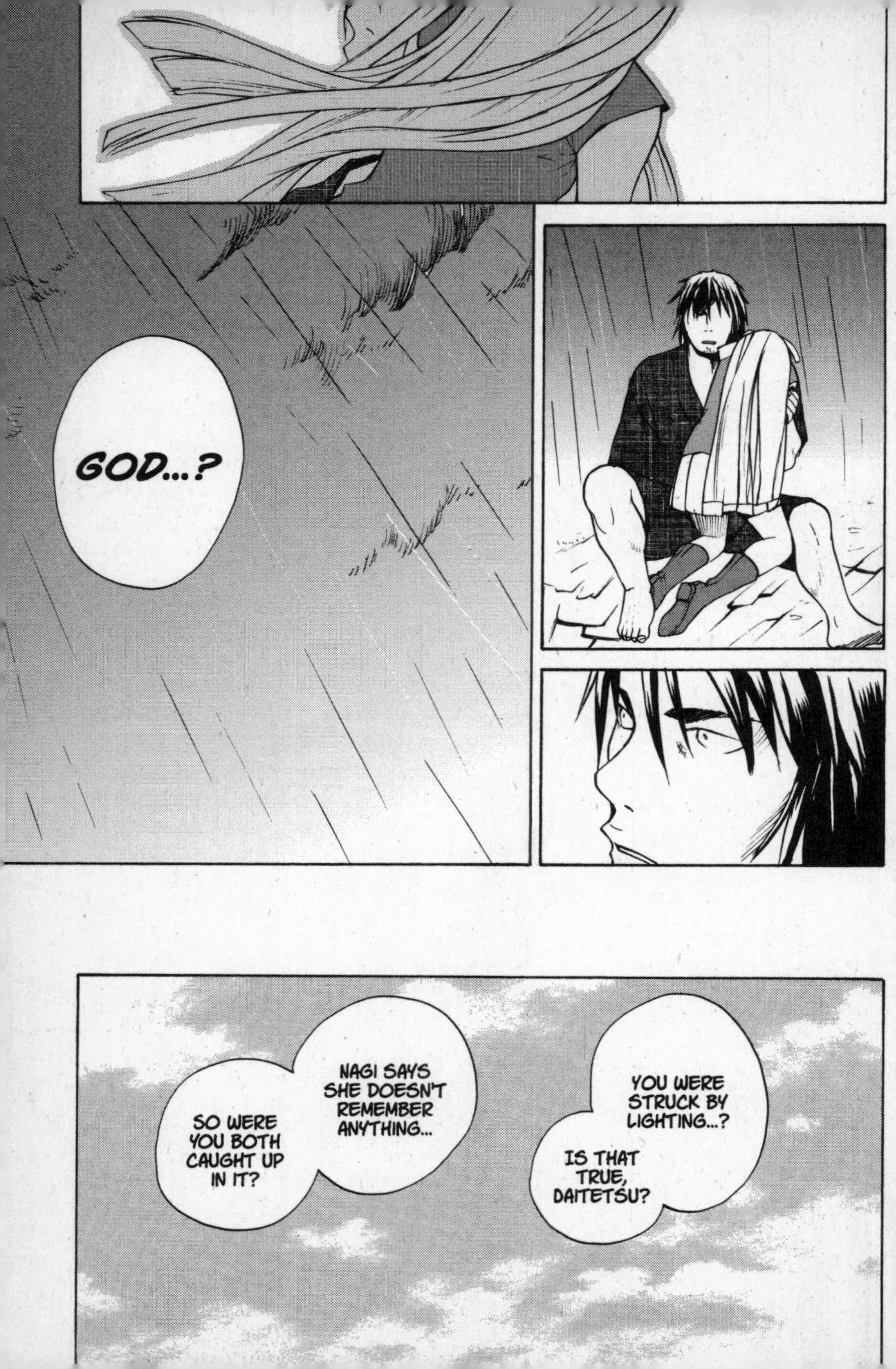
GOD...?
YOU WERE STRUCK BY LIGHTING...?
IS THAT TRUE, DAITETSU?
NAGI SAYS SHE DOESN'T REMEMBER ANYTHING...
SO WERE YOU BOTH CAUGHT UP IN IT?

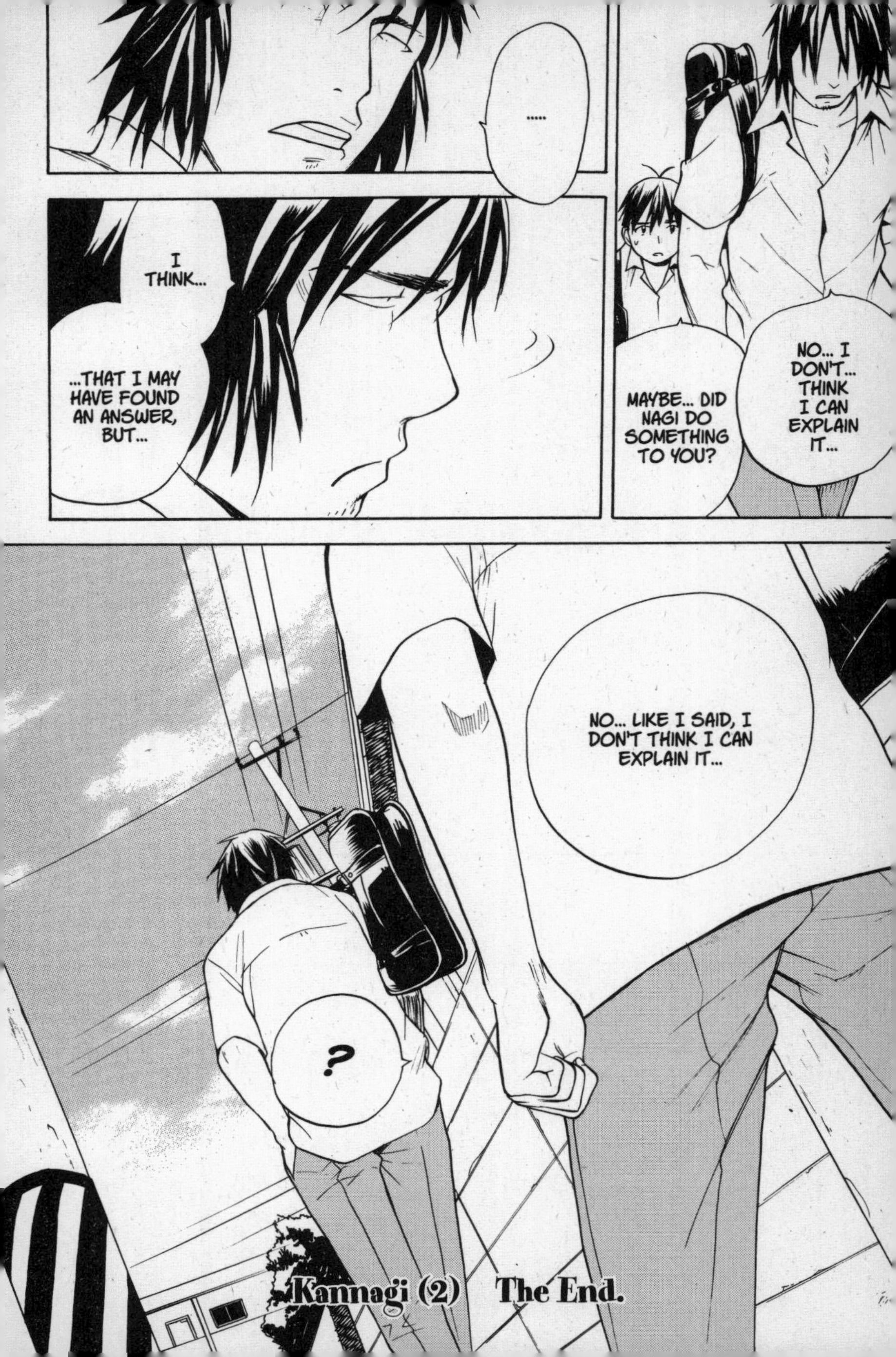

MAYBE... DID NAGI DO SOMETHING TO YOU?
NO... I DON'T... THINK I CAN EXPLAIN IT...
.....
I THINK...
...THAT I MAY HAVE FOUND AN ANSWER, BUT...
NO... LIKE I SAID, I DON'T THINK I CAN EXPLAIN IT...
?
Kannagi (2) The End.

o m a k e

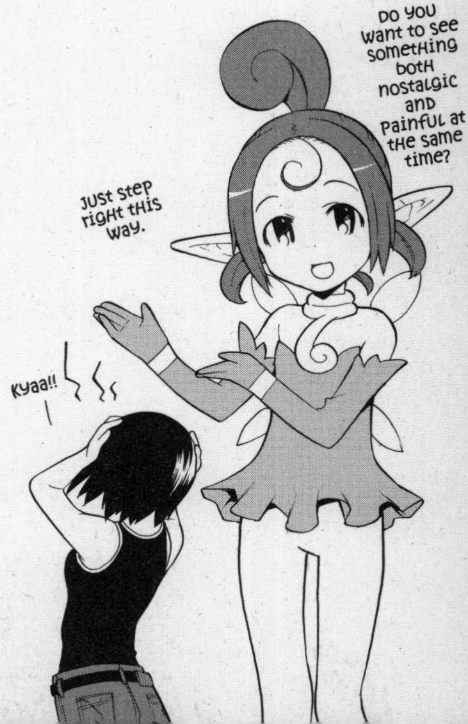

DO YOU want to see something both nostalgic and painful at the same time?
JUST step right this way.
Kyaa!!

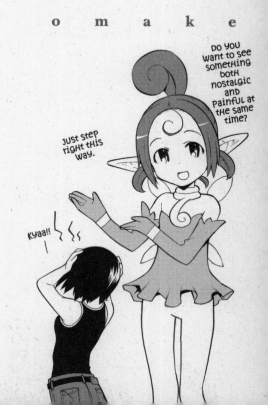

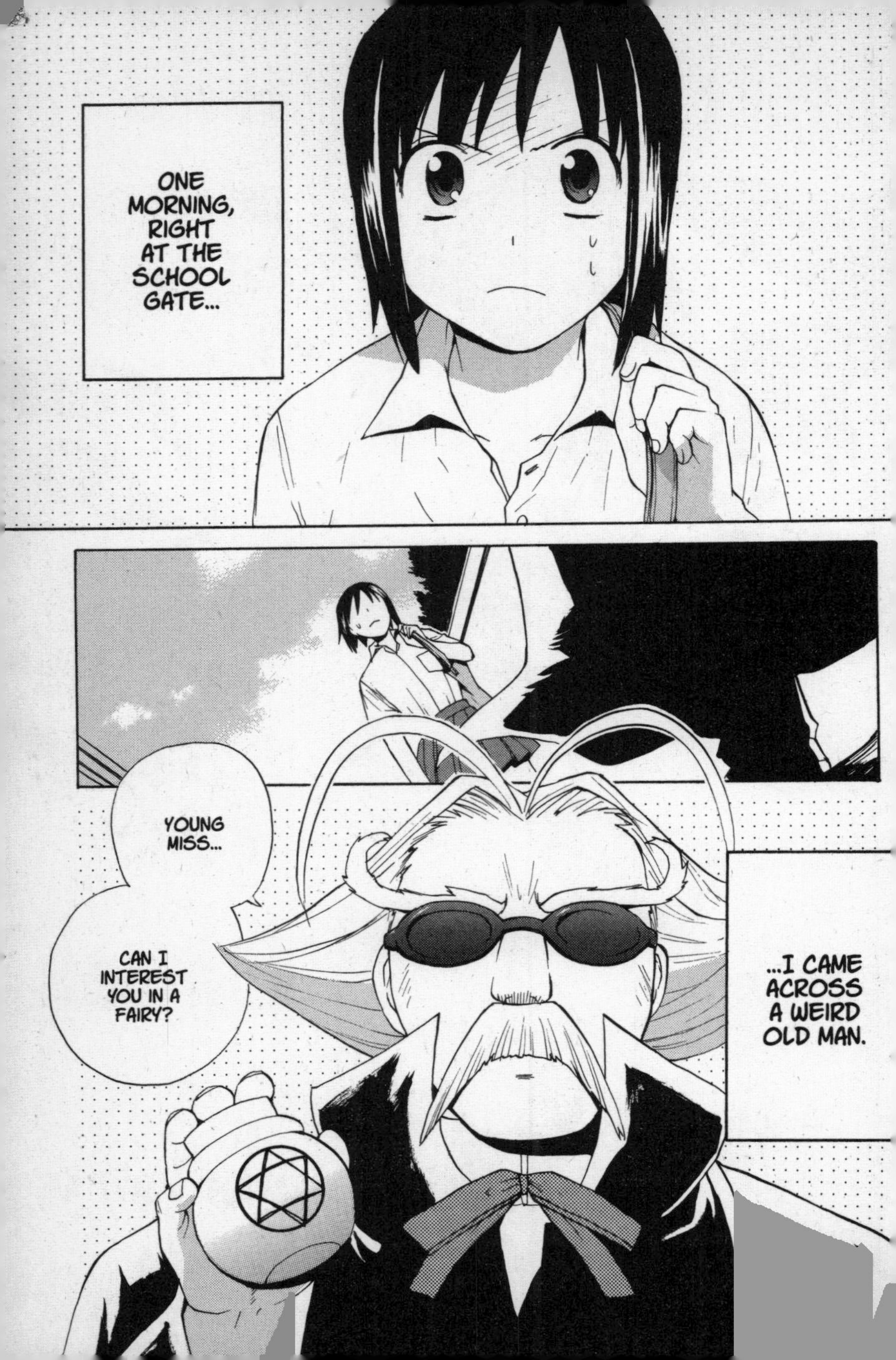
ONE MORNING, RIGHT AT THE SCHOOL GATE...
...I CAME ACROSS A WEIRD OLD MAN.
YOUNG MISS...
CAN I INTEREST YOU IN A FAIRY?

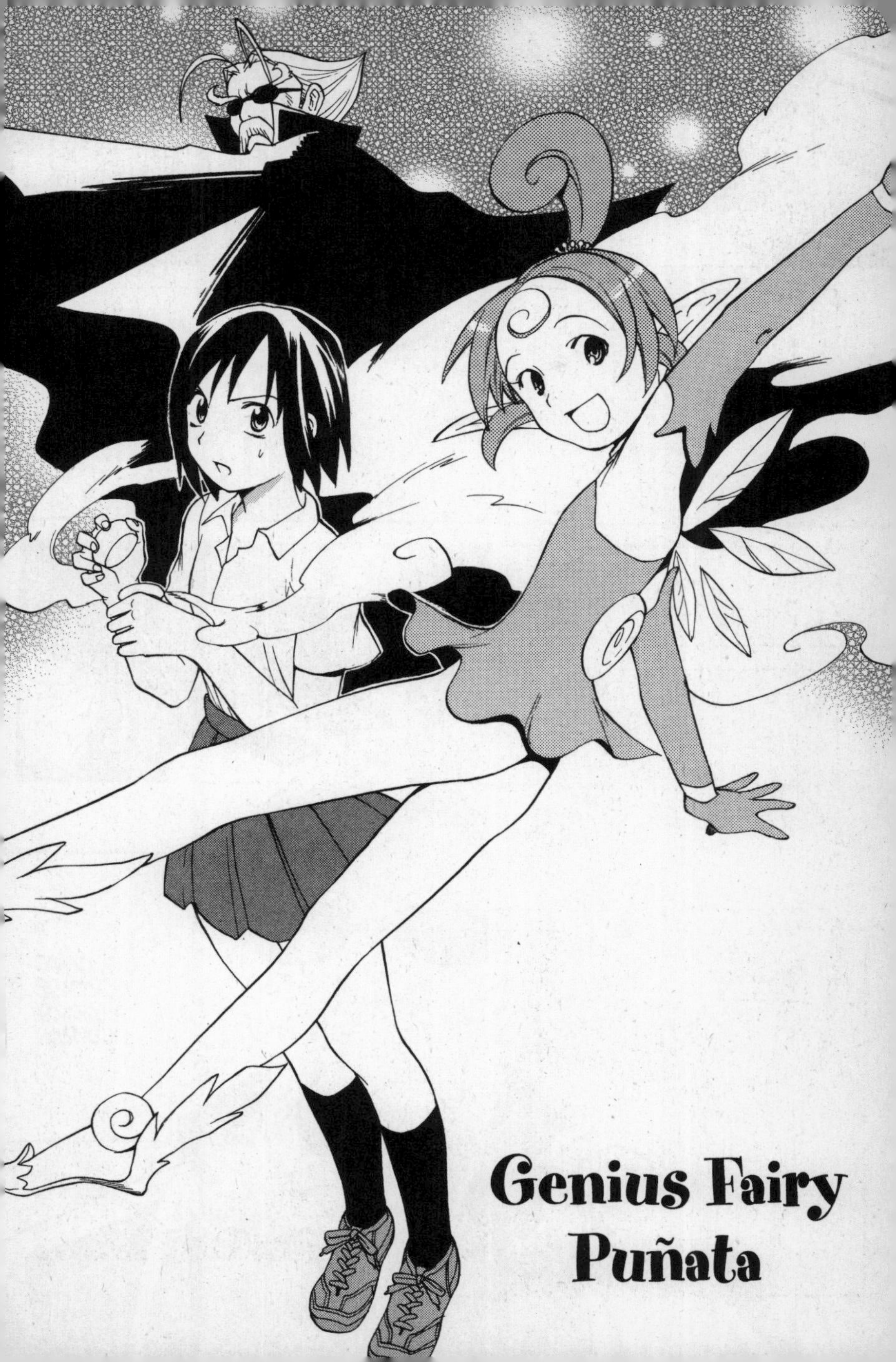
Genius Fairy
Puñata

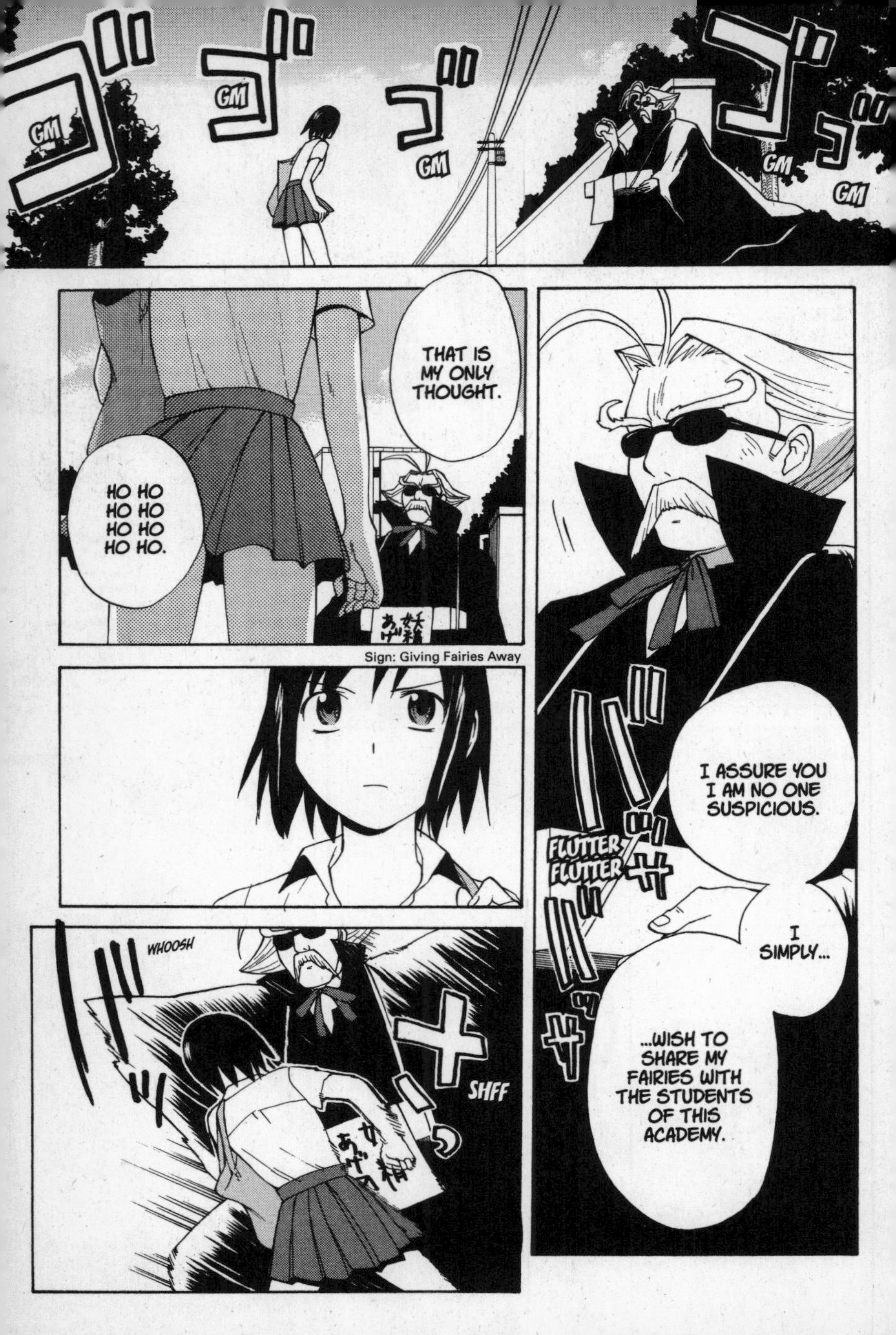

GM
GM
GM
GM
GM
I ASSURE YOU I AM NO ONE SUSPICIOUS.
FLUTTER FLUTTER
I SIMPLY...
...WISH TO SHARE MY FAIRIES WITH THE STUDENTS OF THIS ACADEMY.
THAT IS MY ONLY THOUGHT.
HO HO HO HO HO HO HO HO.
Sign: Giving Fairies Away
WHOOSH
SHFF

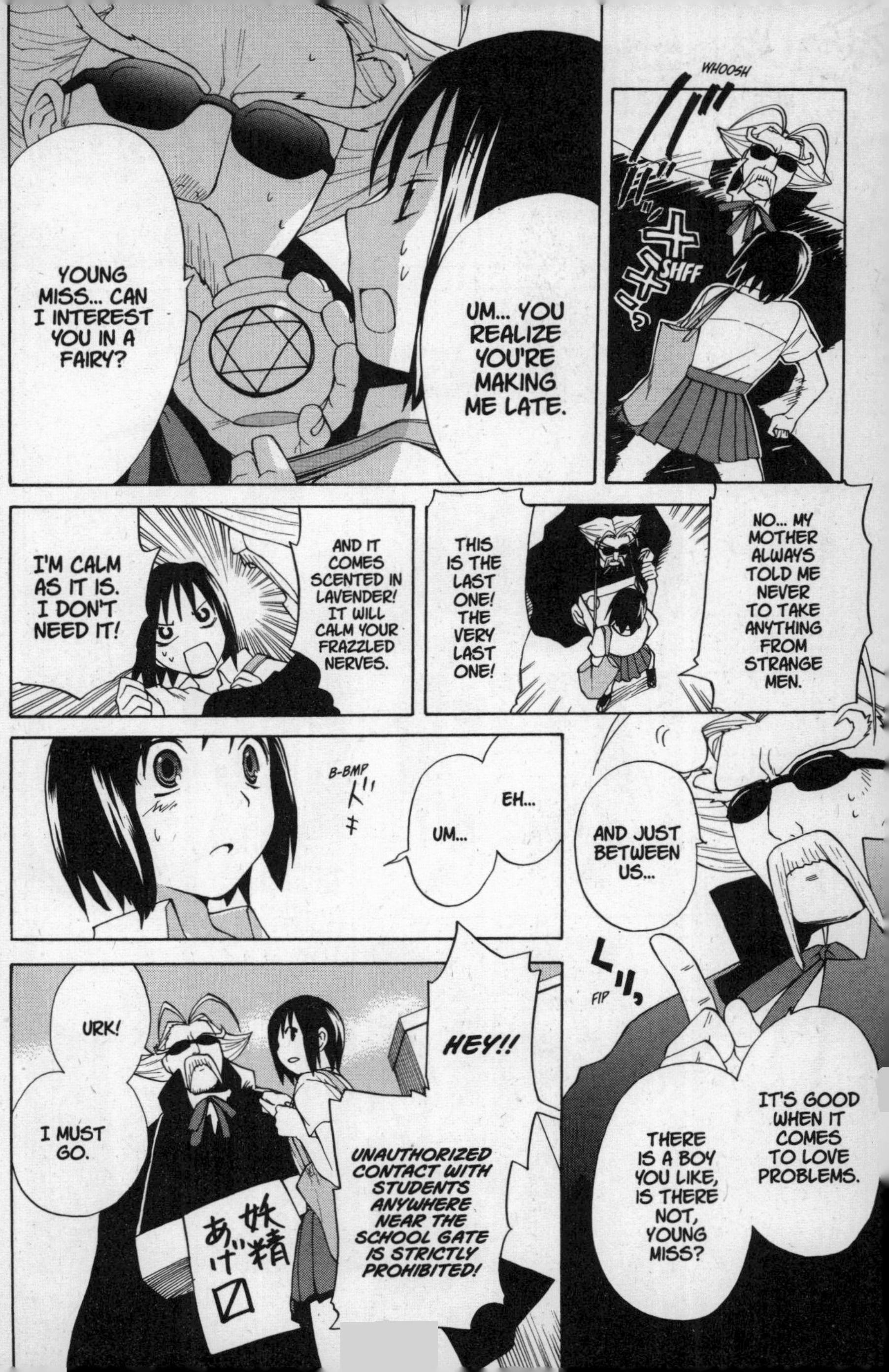
WHOOSH
SHFF
YOUNG MISS... CAN I INTEREST YOU IN A FAIRY?
UM... YOU REALIZE YOU'RE MAKING ME LATE.
NO... MY MOTHER ALWAYS TOLD ME NEVER TO TAKE ANYTHING FROM STRANGE MEN.
THIS IS THE LAST ONE! THE VERY LAST ONE!
AND IT COMES SCENTED IN LAVENDER! IT WILL CALM YOUR FRAZZLED NERVES.
I'M CALM AS IT IS. I DON'T NEED IT!
AND JUST BETWEEN US...
FIP
IT'S GOOD WHEN IT COMES TO LOVE PROBLEMS.
THERE IS A BOY YOU LIKE, IS THERE NOT, YOUNG MISS?
B-BMP
EH...
UM...
HEY!!
UNAUTHORIZED CONTACT WITH STUDENTS ANYWHERE NEAR THE SCHOOL GATE IS STRICTLY PROHIBITED!
URK!
I MUST GO.
妖精あげ

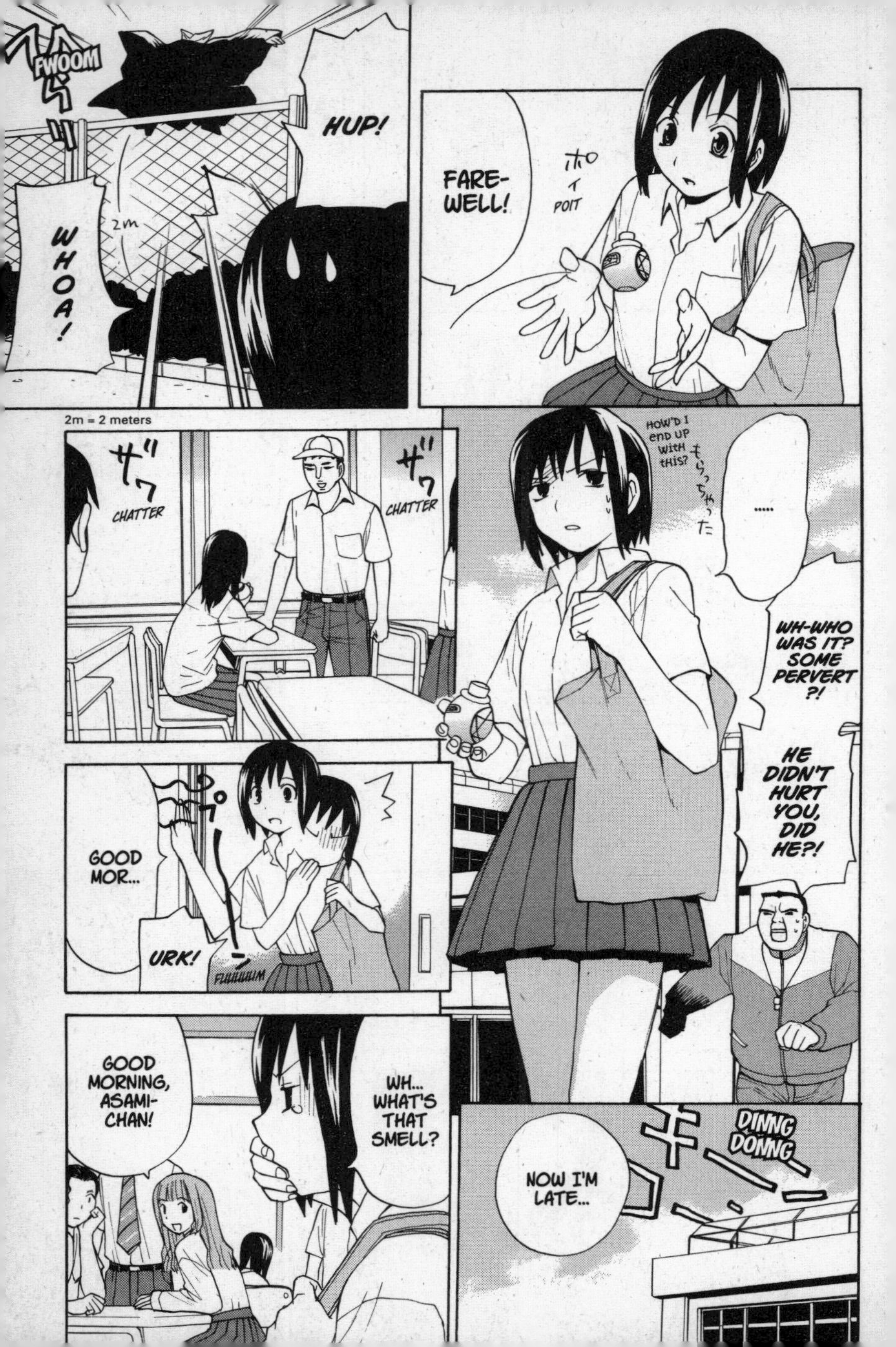

FARE-WELL!
ポイ
POIT
FWOOM
HUP!
2m
WHOA!
HOW'D I END UP WITH THIS?
もらっちゃった
.....
WH-WHO WAS IT? SOME PERVERT?!
HE DIDN'T HURT YOU, DID HE?!
NOW I'M LATE...
DINNG DONNG
ザワ
CHATTER
ザワ
CHATTER
GOOD MOR...
URK!
FUUUUUM
WH... WHAT'S THAT SMELL?
GOOD MORNING, ASAMI-CHAN!

2m = 2 meters

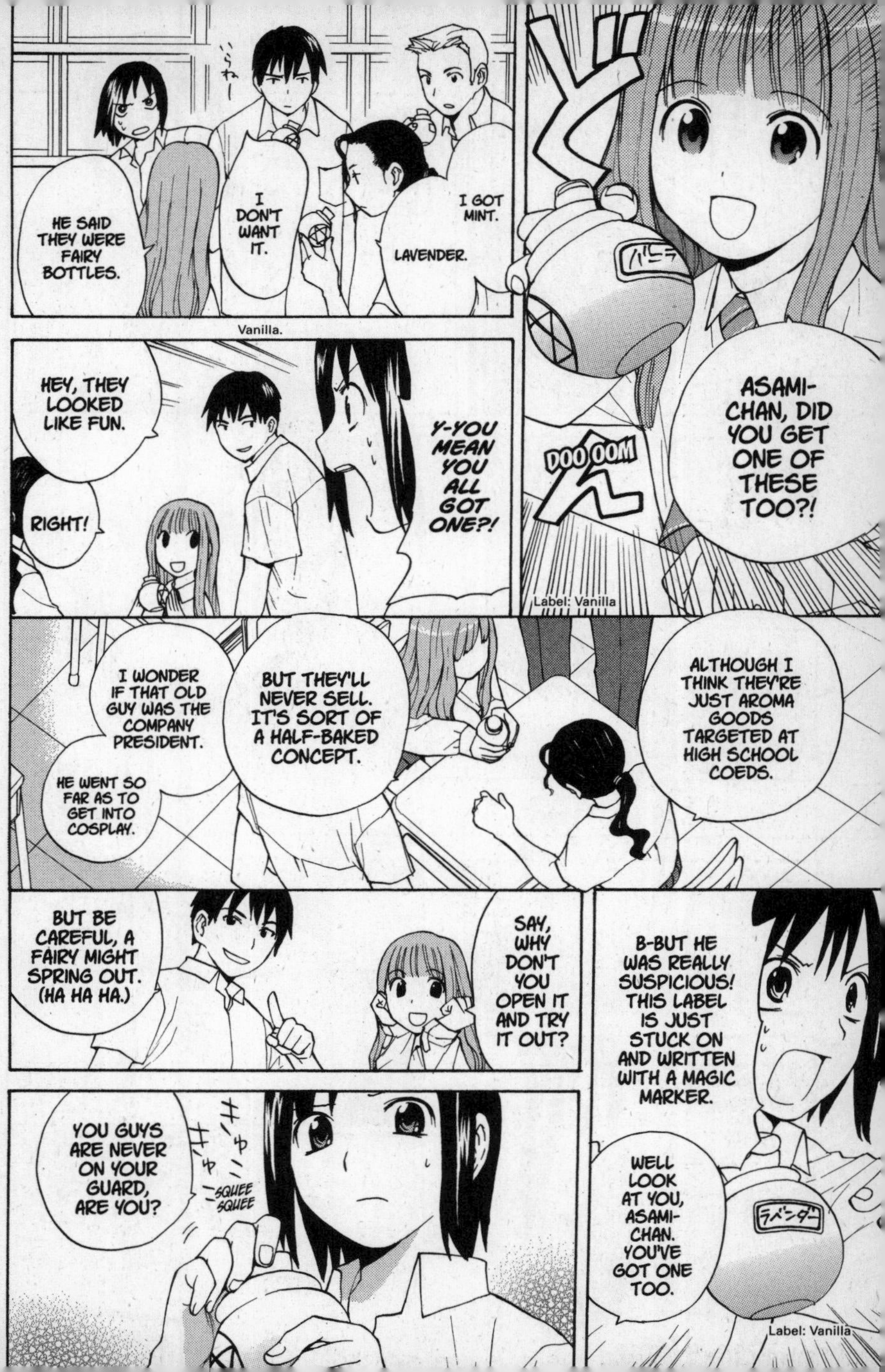
バニラ
ASAMI-CHAN, DID YOU GET ONE OF THESE TOO?!
DOO OOM
Label: Vanilla
いらねー
I GOT MINT.
LAVENDER.
I DON'T WANT IT.
HE SAID THEY WERE FAIRY BOTTLES.
Vanilla.
Y-YOU MEAN YOU ALL GOT ONE?!
HEY, THEY LOOKED LIKE FUN.
RIGHT!
ALTHOUGH I THINK THEY'RE JUST AROMA GOODS TARGETED AT HIGH SCHOOL COEDS.
BUT THEY'LL NEVER SELL. IT'S SORT OF A HALF-BAKED CONCEPT.
I WONDER IF THAT OLD GUY WAS THE COMPANY PRESIDENT.
HE WENT SO FAR AS TO GET INTO COSPLAY.
B-BUT HE WAS REALLY SUSPICIOUS! THIS LABEL IS JUST STUCK ON AND WRITTEN WITH A MAGIC MARKER.
WELL LOOK AT YOU, ASAMI-CHAN. YOU'VE GOT ONE TOO.
ラベンダー
Label: Vanilla
SAY, WHY DON'T YOU OPEN IT AND TRY IT OUT?
BUT BE CAREFUL, A FAIRY MIGHT SPRING OUT. (HA HA HA.)
YOU GUYS ARE NEVER ON YOUR GUARD, ARE YOU?
キュ キュ
SQUEE SQUEE

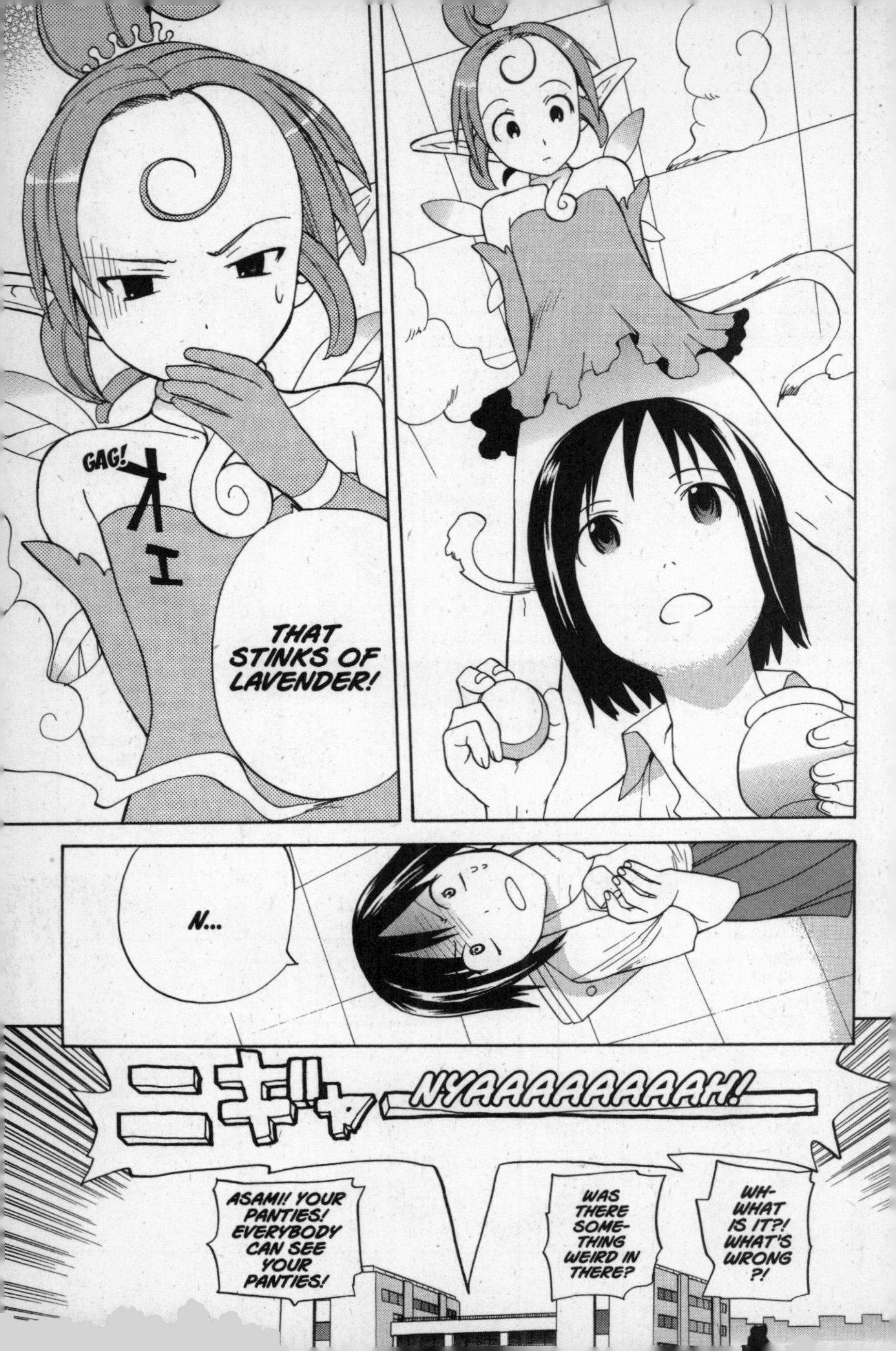

GAG!
オエ
THAT STINKS OF LAVENDER!
N...
ニギャ
NYAAAAAAAAAH!
WH-WHAT IS IT?! WHAT'S WRONG?!
WAS THERE SOMETHING WEIRD IN THERE?
ASAMI! YOUR PANTIES! EVERYBODY CAN SEE YOUR PANTIES!

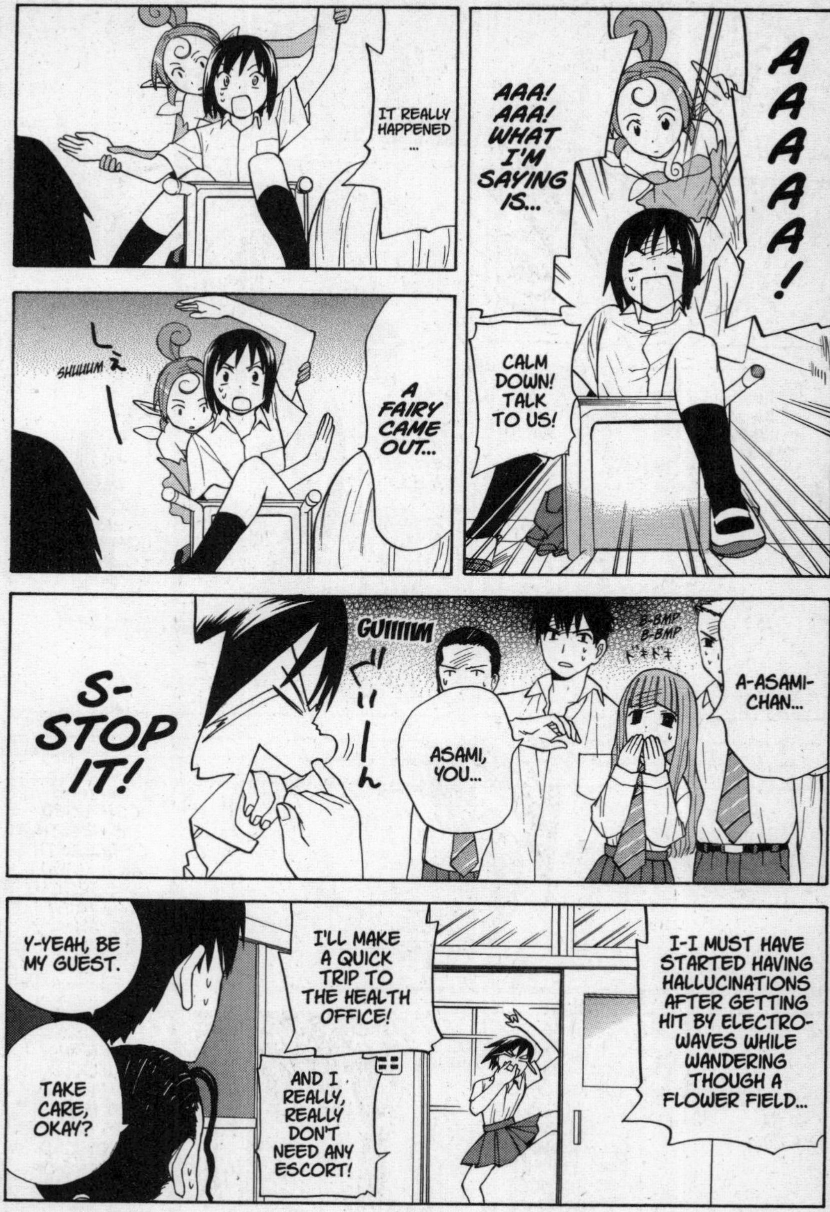
AAAAAA!
AAA! AAA! WHAT I'M SAYING IS...
CALM DOWN! TALK TO US!
IT REALLY HAPPENED...
A FAIRY CAME OUT...
SHUUUM
A-ASAMI-CHAN...
B-BMP B-BMP
ドキドキ
ASAMI, YOU...
GUIIIIM
ぐいーん
S-STOP IT!
I-I MUST HAVE STARTED HAVING HALLUCINATIONS AFTER GETTING HIT BY ELECTRO-WAVES WHILE WANDERING THOUGH A FLOWER FIELD...
AND I REALLY, REALLY DON'T NEED ANY ESCORT!
I'LL MAKE A QUICK TRIP TO THE HEALTH OFFICE!
Y-YEAH, BE MY GUEST.
TAKE CARE, OKAY?

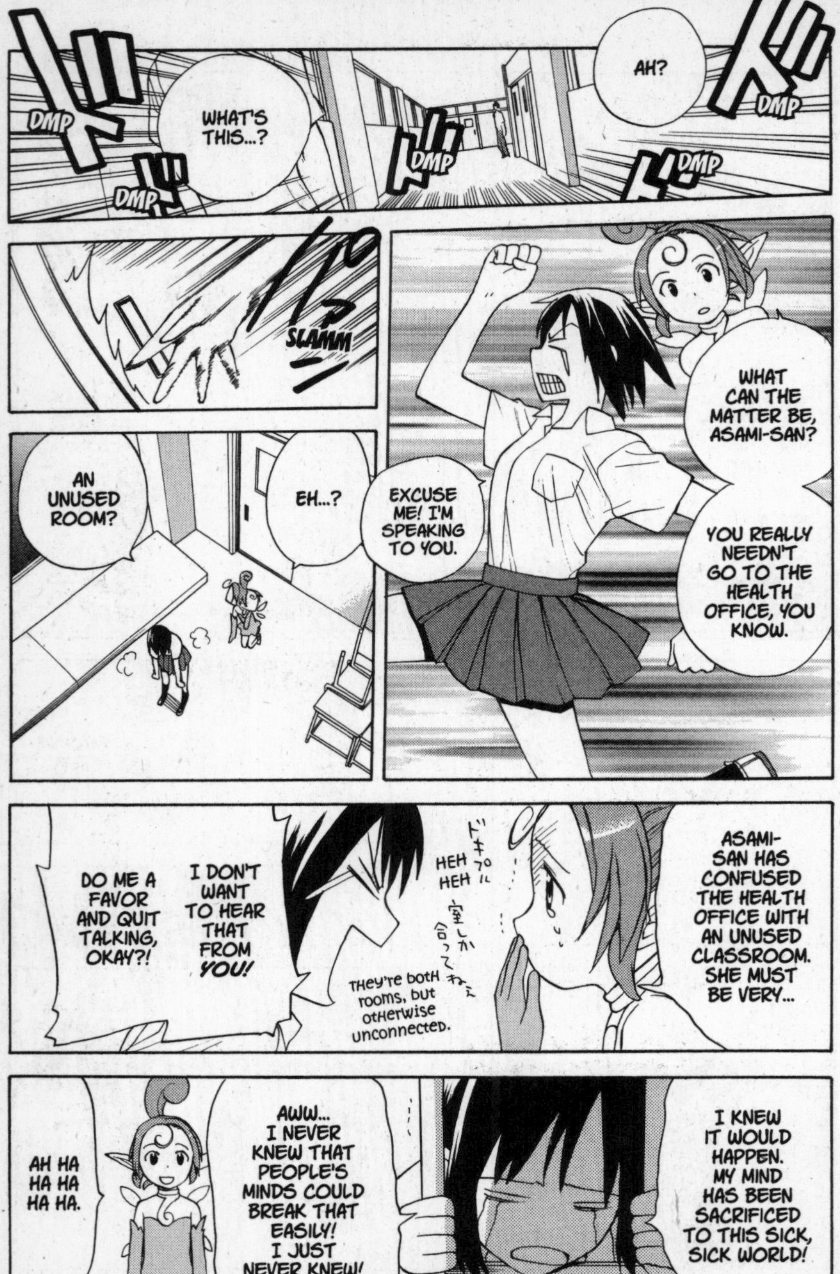
DMP
DMP
AH?
DMP
WHAT'S THIS...?
DMP
DMP
WHAT CAN THE MATTER BE, ASAMI-SAN?
YOU REALLY NEEDN'T GO TO THE HEALTH OFFICE, YOU KNOW.
EXCUSE ME! I'M SPEAKING TO YOU.
SLAMM
EH...?
AN UNUSED ROOM?
ASAMI-SAN HAS CONFUSED THE HEALTH OFFICE WITH AN UNUSED CLASSROOM. SHE MUST BE VERY...
HEH HEH
They're both rooms, but otherwise unconnected.
I DON'T WANT TO HEAR THAT FROM YOU!
DO ME A FAVOR AND QUIT TALKING, OKAY?!
I KNEW IT WOULD HAPPEN. MY MIND HAS BEEN SACRIFICED TO THIS SICK, SICK WORLD!
Chair
AWW... I NEVER KNEW THAT PEOPLE'S MINDS COULD BREAK THAT EASILY! I JUST NEVER KNEW!
AH HA HA HA HA HA.

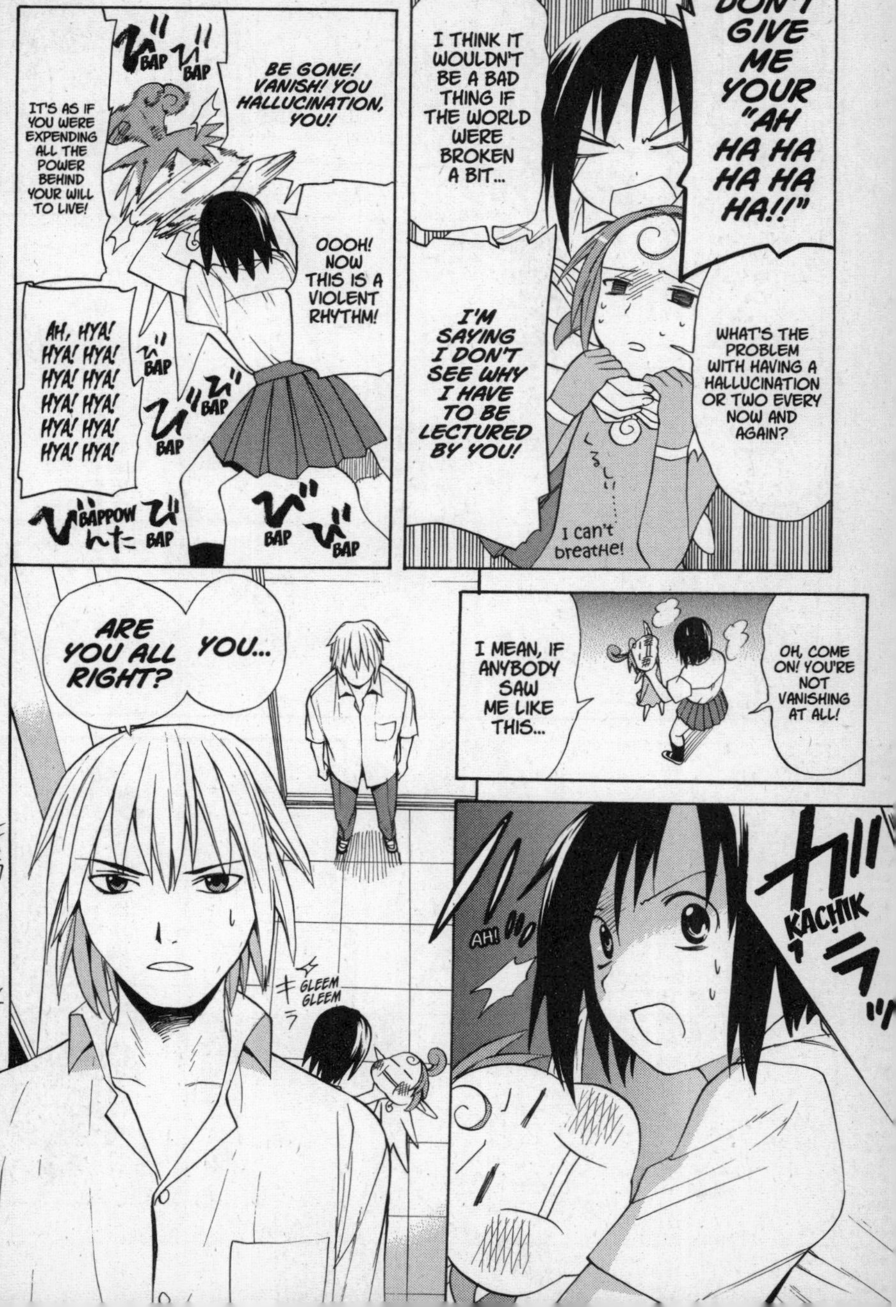
DON'T GIVE ME YOUR "AH HA HA HA HA HA!!"
I THINK IT WOULDN'T BE A BAD THING IF THE WORLD WERE BROKEN A BIT...
WHAT'S THE PROBLEM WITH HAVING A HALLUCINATION OR TWO EVERY NOW AND AGAIN?
I'M SAYING I DON'T SEE WHY I HAVE TO BE LECTURED BY YOU!
I can't breathe!
BAP BAP
BE GONE! VANISH! YOU HALLUCINATION, YOU!
IT'S AS IF YOU WERE EXPENDING ALL THE POWER BEHIND YOUR WILL TO LIVE!
OOOH! NOW THIS IS A VIOLENT RHYTHM!
AH, HYA! HYA! HYA! HYA! HYA! HYA! HYA! HYA! HYA! HYA! HYA!
BAP BAP BAP
BAPPOW BAP BAP BAP
OH, COME ON! YOU'RE NOT VANISHING AT ALL!
I MEAN, IF ANYBODY SAW ME LIKE THIS...
KACHIK
AH!
YOU...
ARE YOU ALL RIGHT?
GLEEM GLEEM

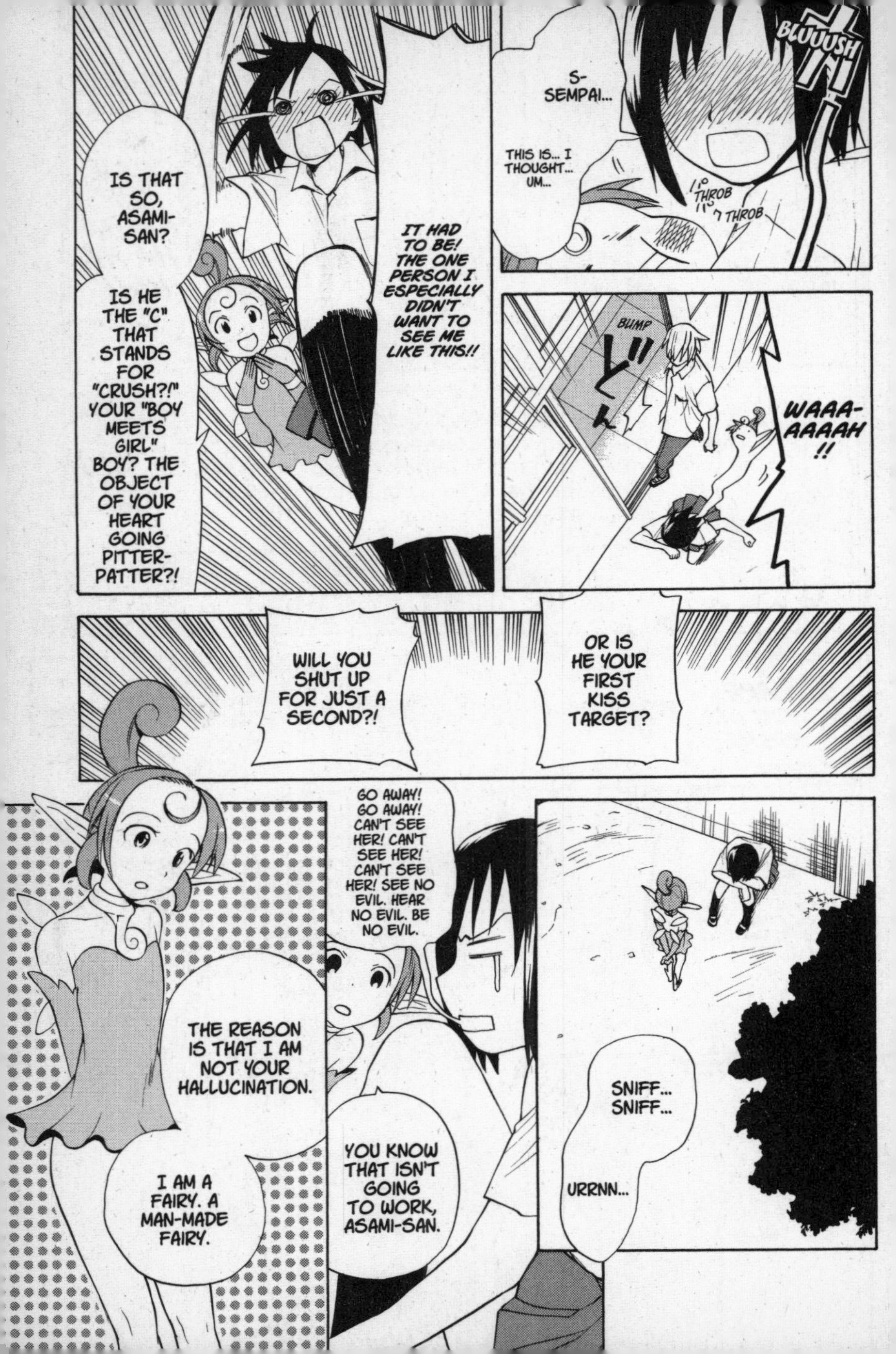
BLUUUSH
S-SEMPAI...
THIS IS... I THOUGHT... UM...
THROB THROB
BUMP
WAAAAAAAH!!
IT HAD TO BE! THE ONE PERSON I ESPECIALLY DIDN'T WANT TO SEE ME LIKE THIS!!
IS THAT SO, ASAMI-SAN?
IS HE THE "C" THAT STANDS FOR "CRUSH?!" YOUR "BOY MEETS GIRL" BOY? THE OBJECT OF YOUR HEART GOING PITTER-PATTER?!
OR IS HE YOUR FIRST KISS TARGET?
WILL YOU SHUT UP FOR JUST A SECOND?!
SNIFF... SNIFF...
URRNN...
GO AWAY! GO AWAY! CAN'T SEE HER! CAN'T SEE HER! CAN'T SEE HER! SEE NO EVIL. HEAR NO EVIL. BE NO EVIL.
YOU KNOW THAT ISN'T GOING TO WORK, ASAMI-SAN.
THE REASON IS THAT I AM NOT YOUR HALLUCINATION.
I AM A FAIRY. A MAN-MADE FAIRY.

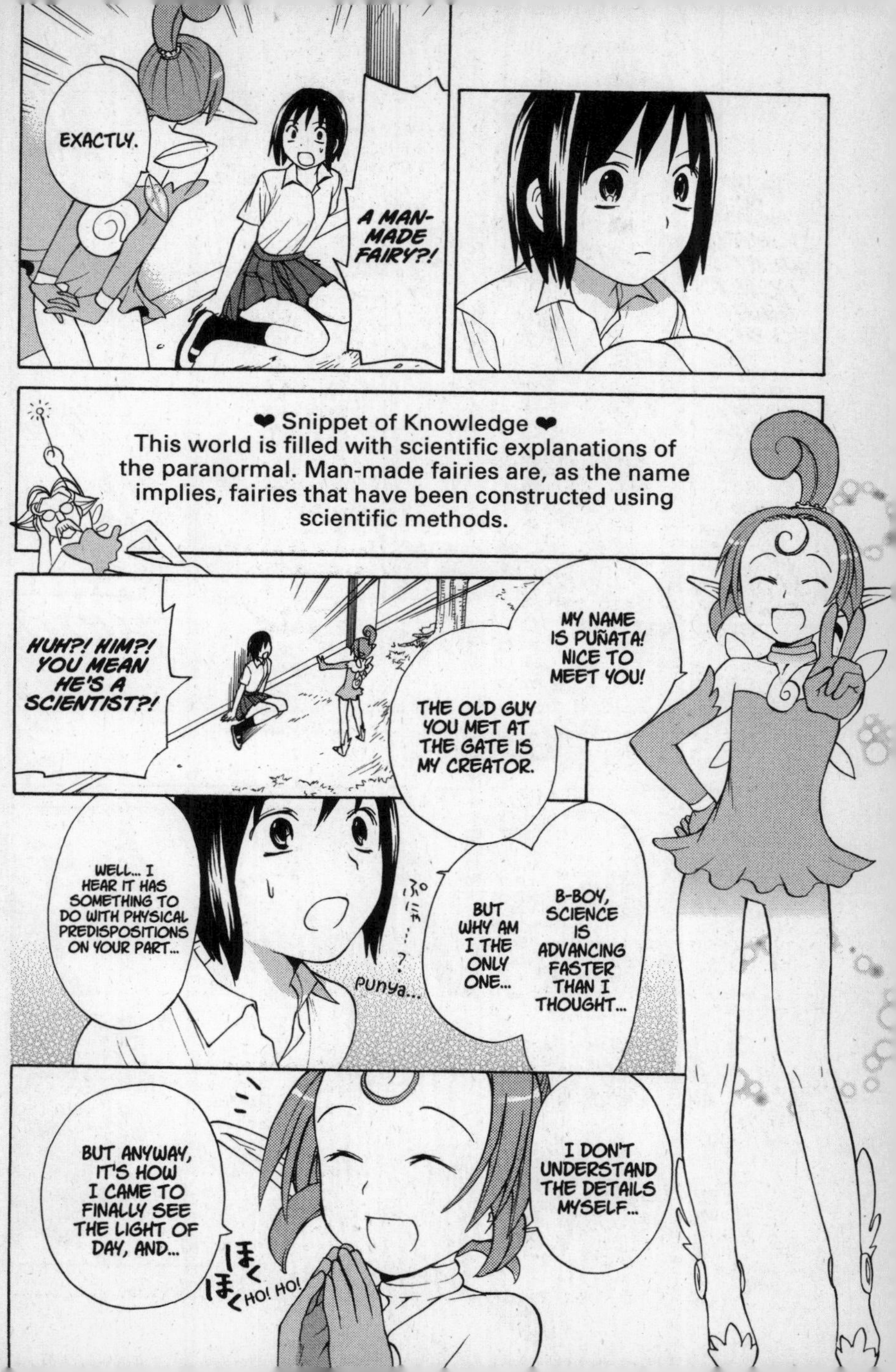
A MAN-MADE FAIRY?!
EXACTLY.
❤ Snippet of Knowledge ❤
This world is filled with scientific explanations of the paranormal. Man-made fairies are, as the name implies, fairies that have been constructed using scientific methods.
MY NAME IS PUÑATA! NICE TO MEET YOU!
THE OLD GUY YOU MET AT THE GATE IS MY CREATOR.
HUH?! HIM?! YOU MEAN HE'S A SCIENTIST?!
B-BOY, SCIENCE IS ADVANCING FASTER THAN I THOUGHT...
BUT WHY AM I THE ONLY ONE...
ぷにゃ…?
Punya...
WELL... I HEAR IT HAS SOMETHING TO DO WITH PHYSICAL PREDISPOSITIONS ON YOUR PART...
I DON'T UNDERSTAND THE DETAILS MYSELF...
ほく ほく
HO! HO!
BUT ANYWAY, IT'S HOW I CAME TO FINALLY SEE THE LIGHT OF DAY, AND...

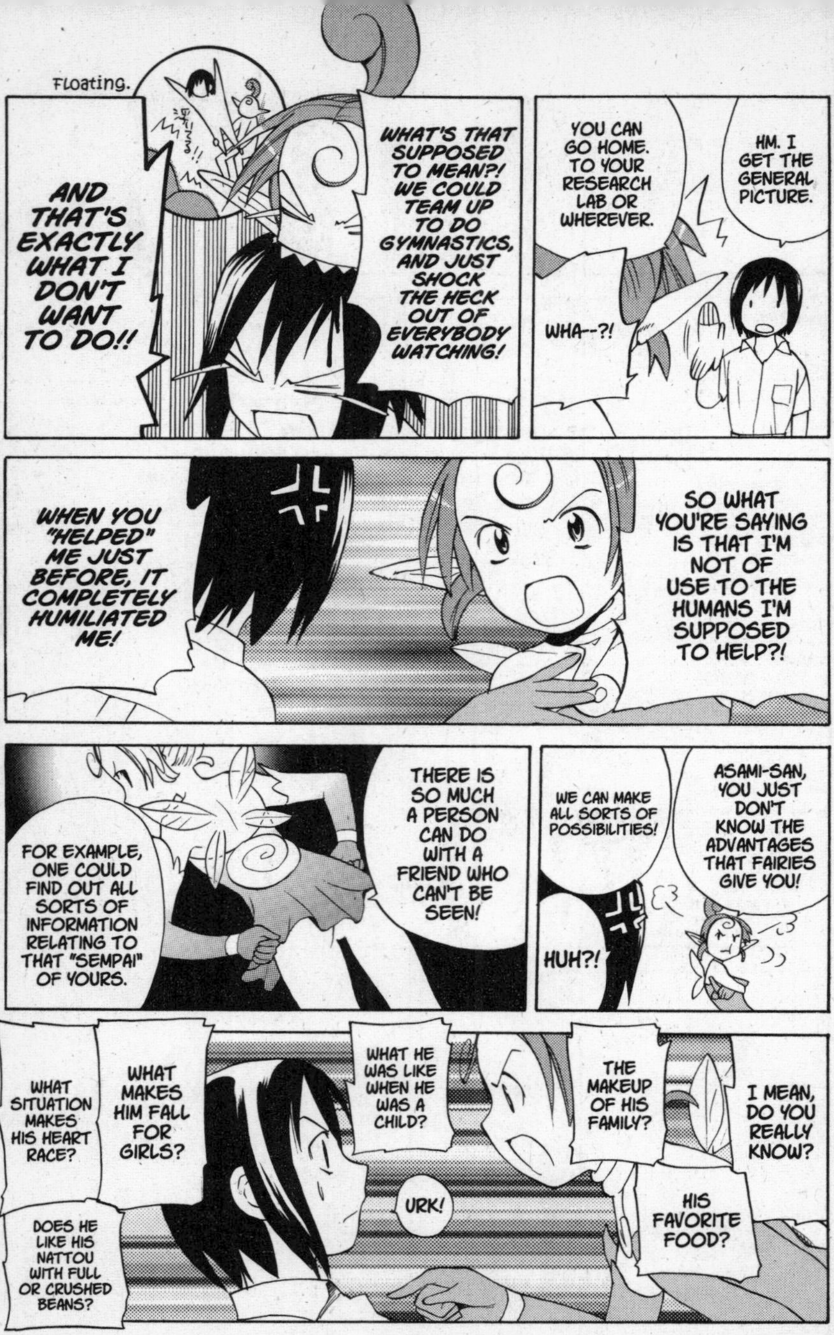
HM. I GET THE GENERAL PICTURE.
YOU CAN GO HOME. TO YOUR RESEARCH LAB OR WHEREVER.
WHA--?!
Floating.
WHAT'S THAT SUPPOSED TO MEAN?! WE COULD TEAM UP TO DO GYMNASTICS, AND JUST SHOCK THE HECK OUT OF EVERYBODY WATCHING!
AND THAT'S EXACTLY WHAT I DON'T WANT TO DO!!
SO WHAT YOU'RE SAYING IS THAT I'M NOT OF USE TO THE HUMANS I'M SUPPOSED TO HELP?!
WHEN YOU "HELPED" ME JUST BEFORE, IT COMPLETELY HUMILIATED ME!
ASAMI-SAN, YOU JUST DON'T KNOW THE ADVANTAGES THAT FAIRIES GIVE YOU!
WE CAN MAKE ALL SORTS OF POSSIBILITIES!
HUH?!
THERE IS SO MUCH A PERSON CAN DO WITH A FRIEND WHO CAN'T BE SEEN!
FOR EXAMPLE, ONE COULD FIND OUT ALL SORTS OF INFORMATION RELATING TO THAT "SEMPAI" OF YOURS.
I MEAN, DO YOU REALLY KNOW?
THE MAKEUP OF HIS FAMILY?
HIS FAVORITE FOOD?
WHAT HE WAS LIKE WHEN HE WAS A CHILD?
URK!
WHAT MAKES HIM FALL FOR GIRLS?
WHAT SITUATION MAKES HIS HEART RACE?
DOES HE LIKE HIS NATTOU WITH FULL OR CRUSHED BEANS?

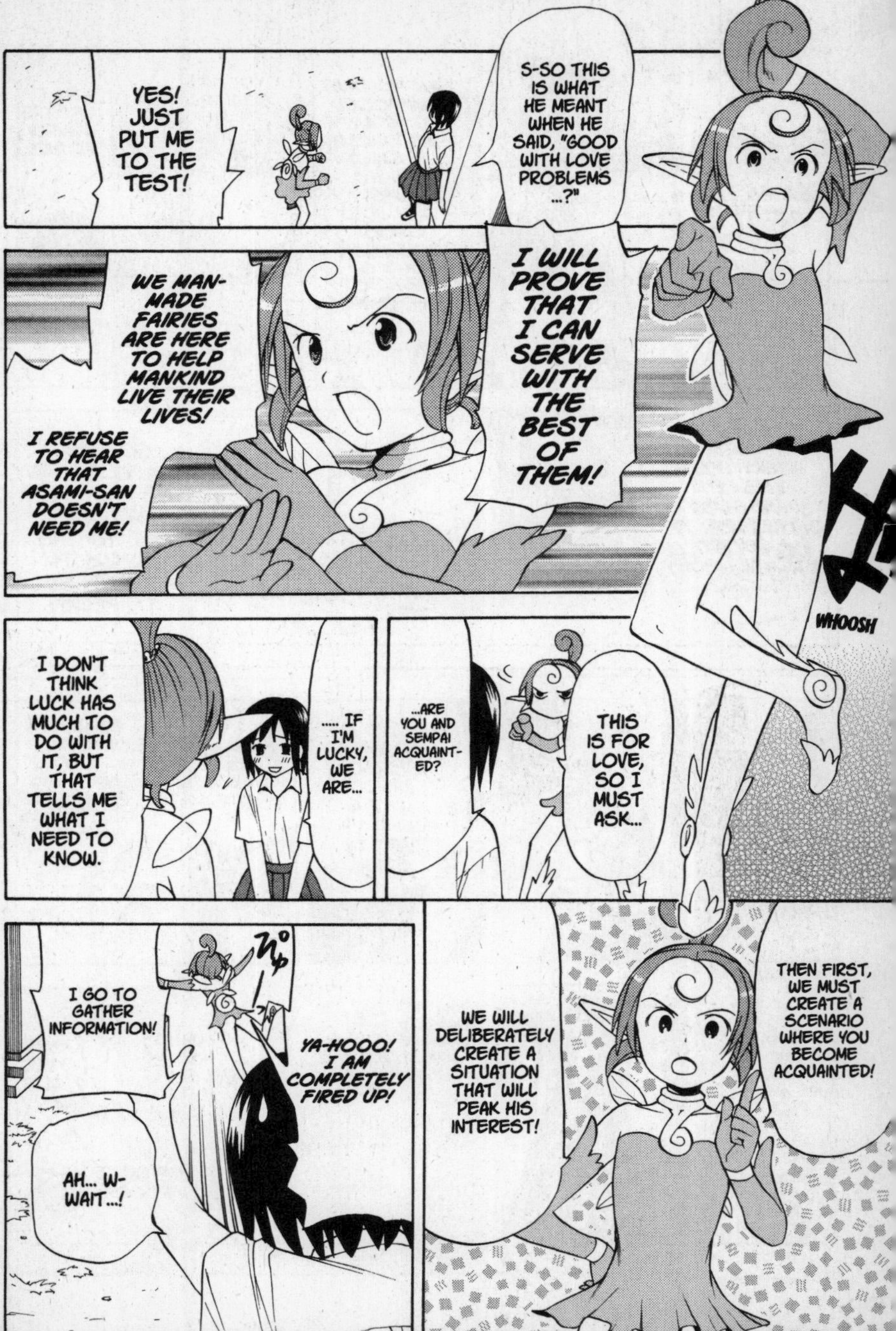
S-SO THIS IS WHAT HE MEANT WHEN HE SAID, "GOOD WITH LOVE PROBLEMS ...?"
I WILL PROVE THAT I CAN SERVE WITH THE BEST OF THEM!
WHOOSH
YES! JUST PUT ME TO THE TEST!
WE MAN-MADE FAIRIES ARE HERE TO HELP MANKIND LIVE THEIR LIVES!
I REFUSE TO HEAR THAT ASAMI-SAN DOESN'T NEED ME!
THIS IS FOR LOVE, SO I MUST ASK...
...ARE YOU AND SEMPAI ACQUAINTED?
..... IF I'M LUCKY, WE ARE...
I DON'T THINK LUCK HAS MUCH TO DO WITH IT, BUT THAT TELLS ME WHAT I NEED TO KNOW.
THEN FIRST, WE MUST CREATE A SCENARIO WHERE YOU BECOME ACQUAINTED!
WE WILL DELIBERATELY CREATE A SITUATION THAT WILL PEAK HIS INTEREST!
YA-HOOO! I AM COMPLETELY FIRED UP!
I GO TO GATHER INFORMATION!
AH... W-WAIT...!

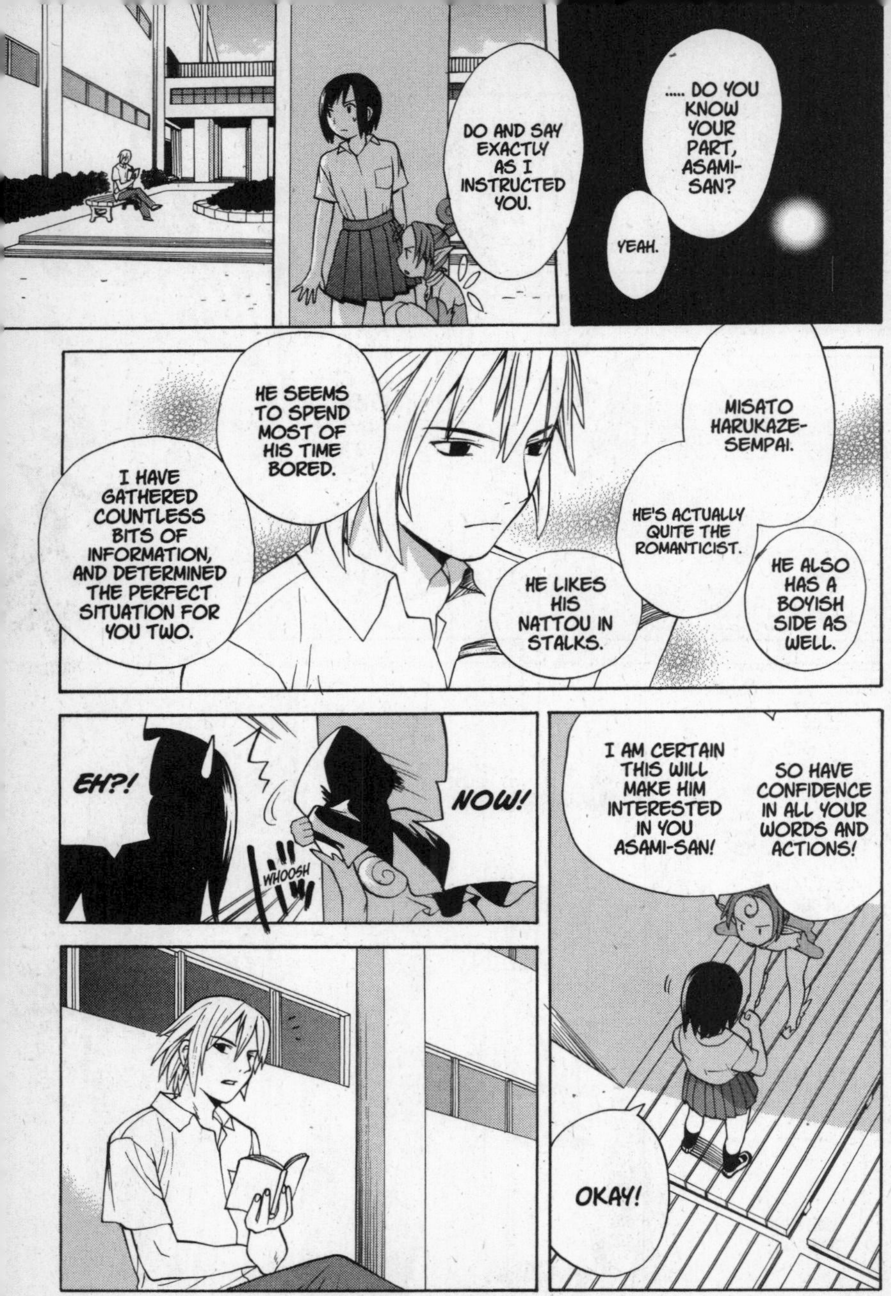
..... DO YOU KNOW YOUR PART, ASAMI-SAN?
YEAH.
DO AND SAY EXACTLY AS I INSTRUCTED YOU.
MISATO HARUKAZE-SEMPAI.
HE'S ACTUALLY QUITE THE ROMANTICIST.
HE ALSO HAS A BOYISH SIDE AS WELL.
HE LIKES HIS NATTOU IN STALKS.
HE SEEMS TO SPEND MOST OF HIS TIME BORED.
I HAVE GATHERED COUNTLESS BITS OF INFORMATION, AND DETERMINED THE PERFECT SITUATION FOR YOU TWO.
I AM CERTAIN THIS WILL MAKE HIM INTERESTED IN YOU ASAMI-SAN!
SO HAVE CONFIDENCE IN ALL YOUR WORDS AND ACTIONS!
OKAY!
NOW!
WHOOSH
EH?!

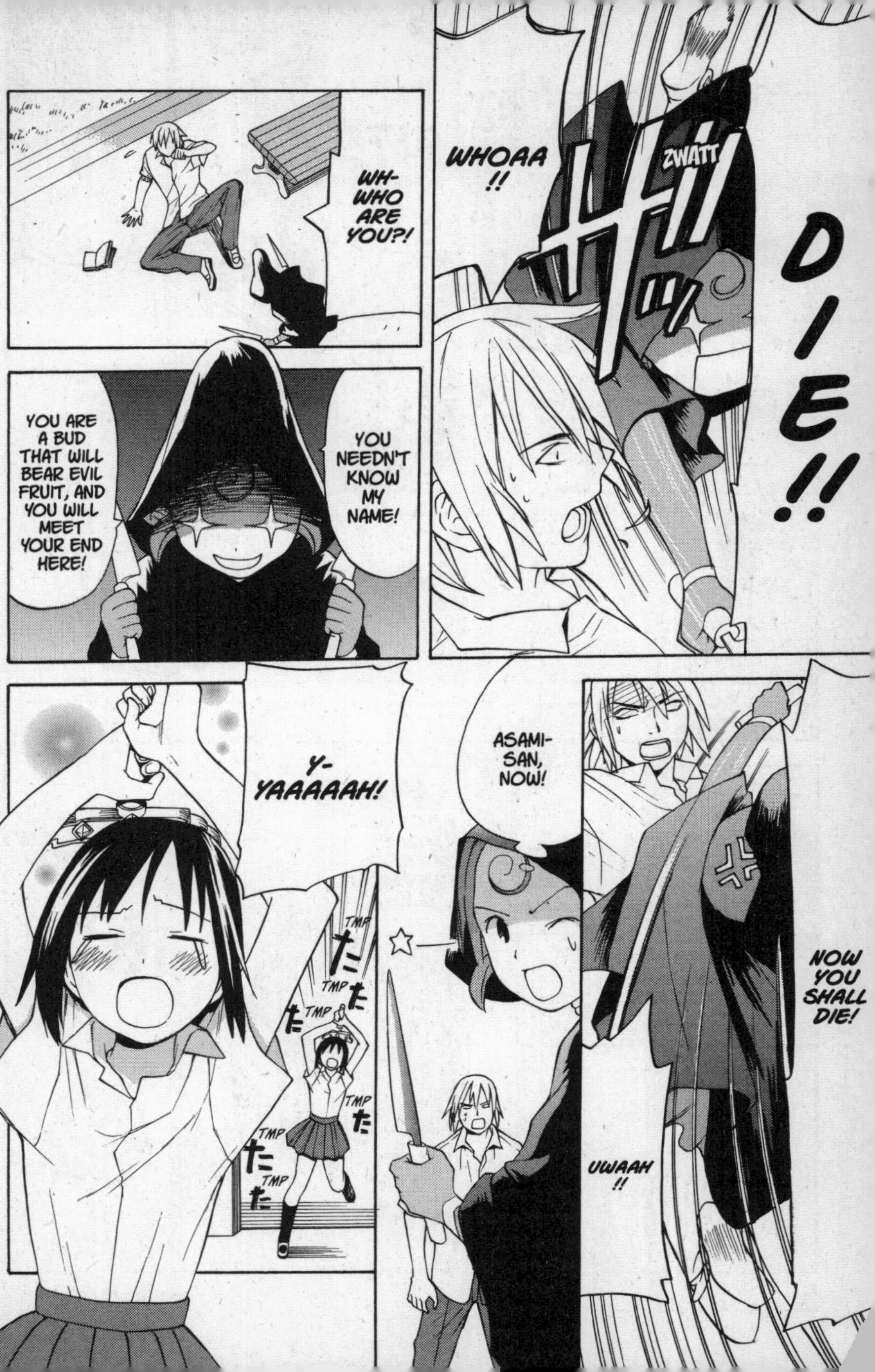
ZWATT
WHOAA !!
DIE!!
WH- WHO ARE YOU?!
YOU NEEDN'T KNOW MY NAME!
YOU ARE A BUD THAT WILL BEAR EVIL FRUIT, AND YOU WILL MEET YOUR END HERE!
ASAMI-SAN, NOW!
NOW YOU SHALL DIE!
UWAAH !!
Y-YAAAAAH!
TMP
TMP
TMP
TMP
TMP
TMP

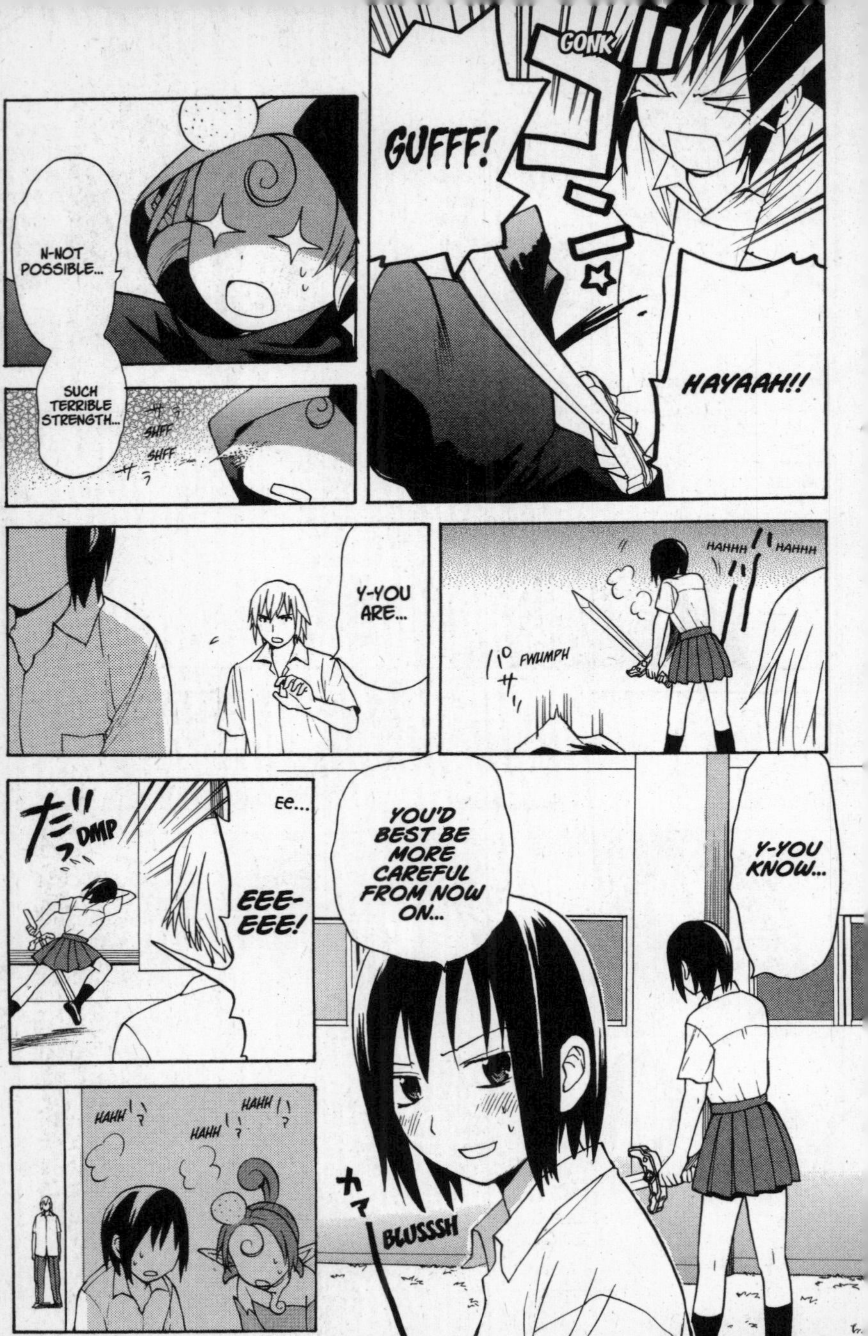
GONK
GUFFF!
HAYAAH!!
N-NOT POSSIBLE...
SUCH TERRIBLE STRENGTH...
SHFF
SHFF
HAHHH
HAHHH
FWUMPH
Y-YOU ARE...
Y-YOU KNOW...
YOU'D BEST BE MORE CAREFUL FROM NOW ON...
BLUSSSH
Ee...
EEE-EEE!
DMP
HAHH
HAHH
HAHH

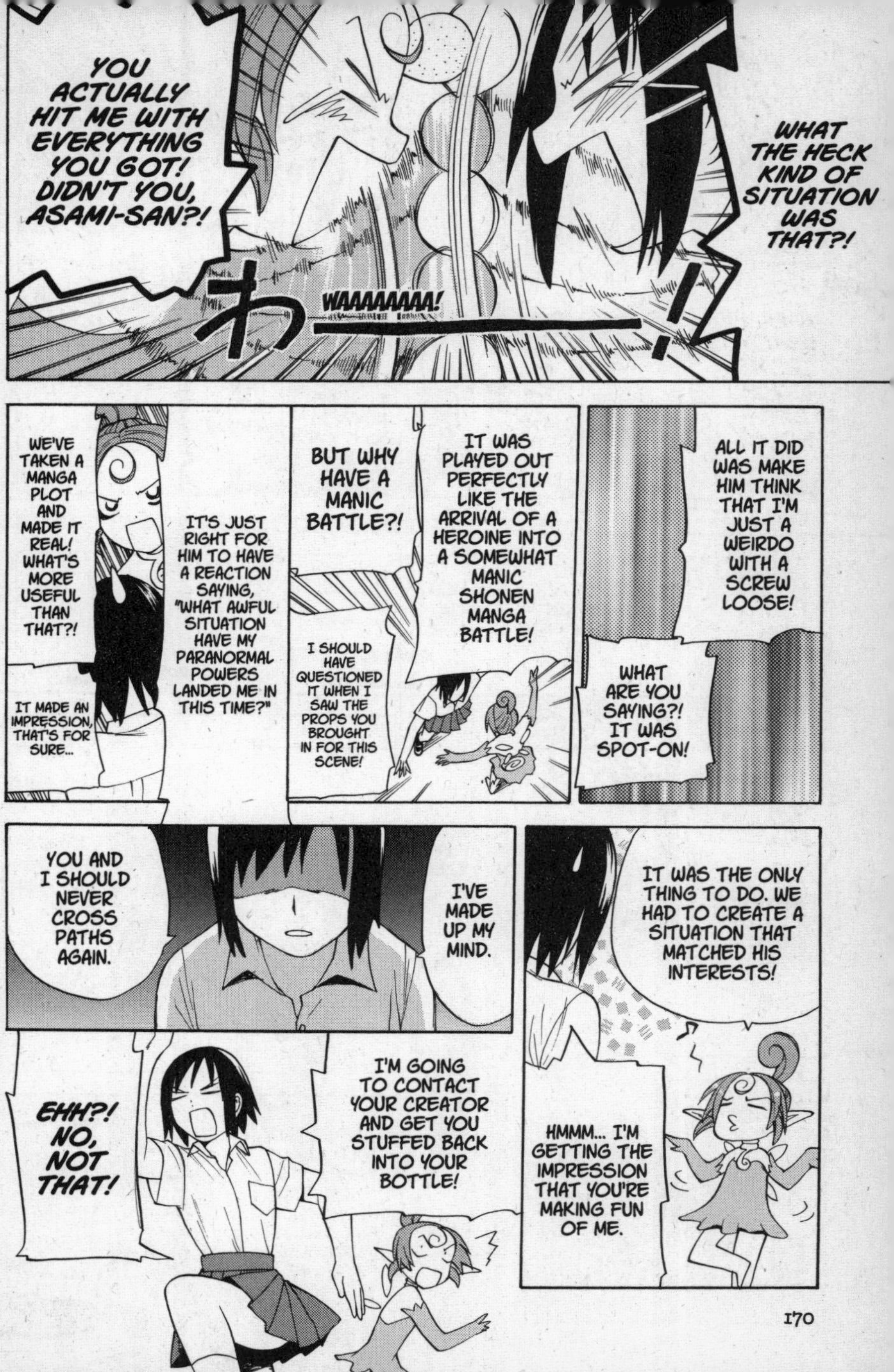
WHAT THE HECK KIND OF SITUATION WAS THAT?!
YOU ACTUALLY HIT ME WITH EVERYTHING YOU GOT! DIDN'T YOU, ASAMI-SAN?!
わーーー!
WAAAAAAAA!
ALL IT DID WAS MAKE HIM THINK THAT I'M JUST A WEIRDO WITH A SCREW LOOSE!
WHAT ARE YOU SAYING?! IT WAS SPOT-ON!
IT WAS PLAYED OUT PERFECTLY LIKE THE ARRIVAL OF A HEROINE INTO A SOMEWHAT MANIC SHONEN MANGA BATTLE!
BUT WHY HAVE A MANIC BATTLE?!
I SHOULD HAVE QUESTIONED IT WHEN I SAW THE PROPS YOU BROUGHT IN FOR THIS SCENE!
IT'S JUST RIGHT FOR HIM TO HAVE A REACTION SAYING, "WHAT AWFUL SITUATION HAVE MY PARANORMAL POWERS LANDED ME IN THIS TIME?"
WE'VE TAKEN A MANGA PLOT AND MADE IT REAL! WHAT'S MORE USEFUL THAN THAT?!
IT MADE AN IMPRESSION, THAT'S FOR SURE...
IT WAS THE ONLY THING TO DO. WE HAD TO CREATE A SITUATION THAT MATCHED HIS INTERESTS!
I'VE MADE UP MY MIND.
YOU AND I SHOULD NEVER CROSS PATHS AGAIN.
HMMM... I'M GETTING THE IMPRESSION THAT YOU'RE MAKING FUN OF ME.
I'M GOING TO CONTACT YOUR CREATOR AND GET YOU STUFFED BACK INTO YOUR BOTTLE!
EHH?! NO, NOT THAT!

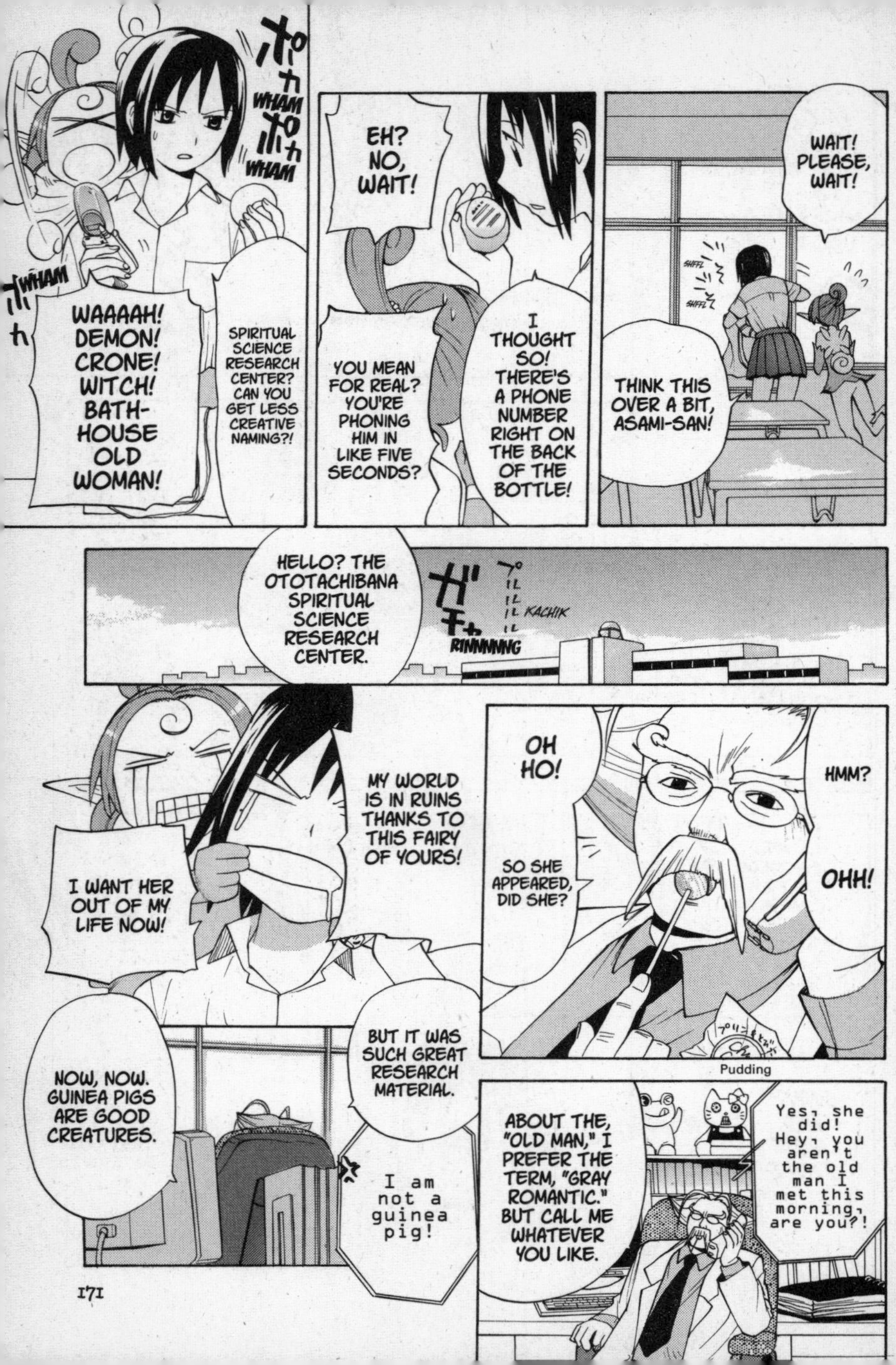
WAIT! PLEASE, WAIT!
SHFFL
SHFFL
THINK THIS OVER A BIT, ASAMI-SAN!
EH? NO, WAIT!
I THOUGHT SO! THERE'S A PHONE NUMBER RIGHT ON THE BACK OF THE BOTTLE!
YOU MEAN FOR REAL? YOU'RE PHONING HIM IN LIKE FIVE SECONDS?
WHAM
WHAM
WHAM
SPIRITUAL SCIENCE RESEARCH CENTER? CAN YOU GET LESS CREATIVE NAMING?!
WAAAAH! DEMON! CRONE! WITCH! BATH-HOUSE OLD WOMAN!
KACHIK
RINNNNNG
HELLO? THE OTOTACHIBANA SPIRITUAL SCIENCE RESEARCH CENTER.
HMM?
OHH!
OH HO!
SO SHE APPEARED, DID SHE?
Pudding
MY WORLD IS IN RUINS THANKS TO THIS FAIRY OF YOURS!
I WANT HER OUT OF MY LIFE NOW!
Yes, she did! Hey, you aren't the old man I met this morning, are you?!
ABOUT THE, "OLD MAN," I PREFER THE TERM, "GRAY ROMANTIC." BUT CALL ME WHATEVER YOU LIKE.
BUT IT WAS SUCH GREAT RESEARCH MATERIAL.
I am not a guinea pig!
NOW, NOW. GUINEA PIGS ARE GOOD CREATURES.

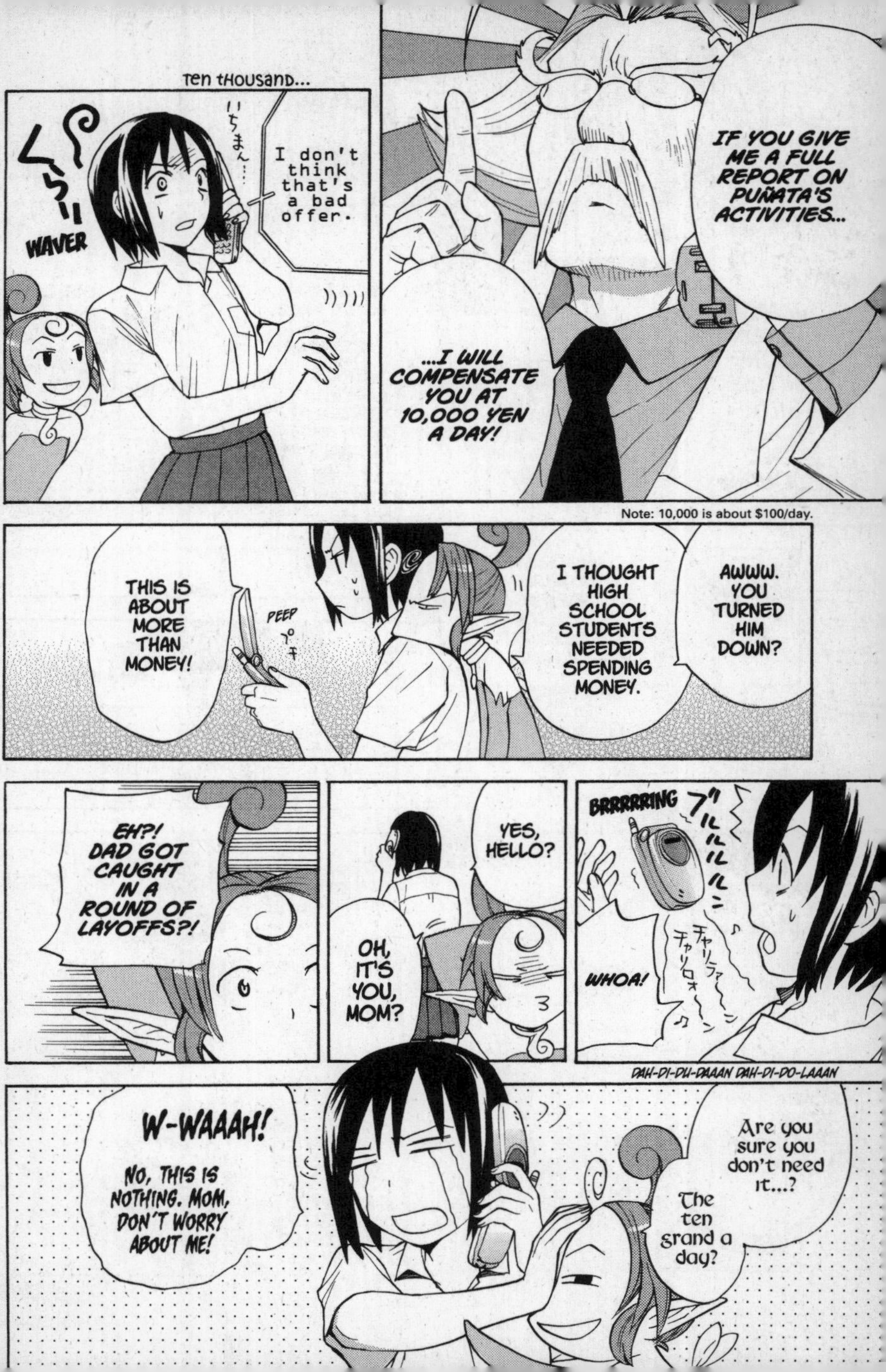
IF YOU GIVE ME A FULL REPORT ON PUÑATA'S ACTIVITIES...
...I WILL COMPENSATE YOU AT 10,000 YEN A DAY!
TEN THOUSAND...
いちまん…
I don't think that's a bad offer.
くらぃ
WAVER
AWWW. YOU TURNED HIM DOWN?
I THOUGHT HIGH SCHOOL STUDENTS NEEDED SPENDING MONEY.
PEEP
ピチ
THIS IS ABOUT MORE THAN MONEY!
BRRRRRING
ブルルルル
WHOA!
チャリラァ〜ン
チャリロォ〜ン
DAH-DI-DU-DAAAN DAH-DI-DO-LAAAN
YES, HELLO?
OH, IT'S YOU, MOM?
EH?! DAD GOT CAUGHT IN A ROUND OF LAYOFFS?!
Are you sure you don't need it...?
The ten grand a day?
W-WAAAH!
NO, THIS IS NOTHING. MOM, DON'T WORRY ABOUT ME!

Note: 10,000 is about $100/day.

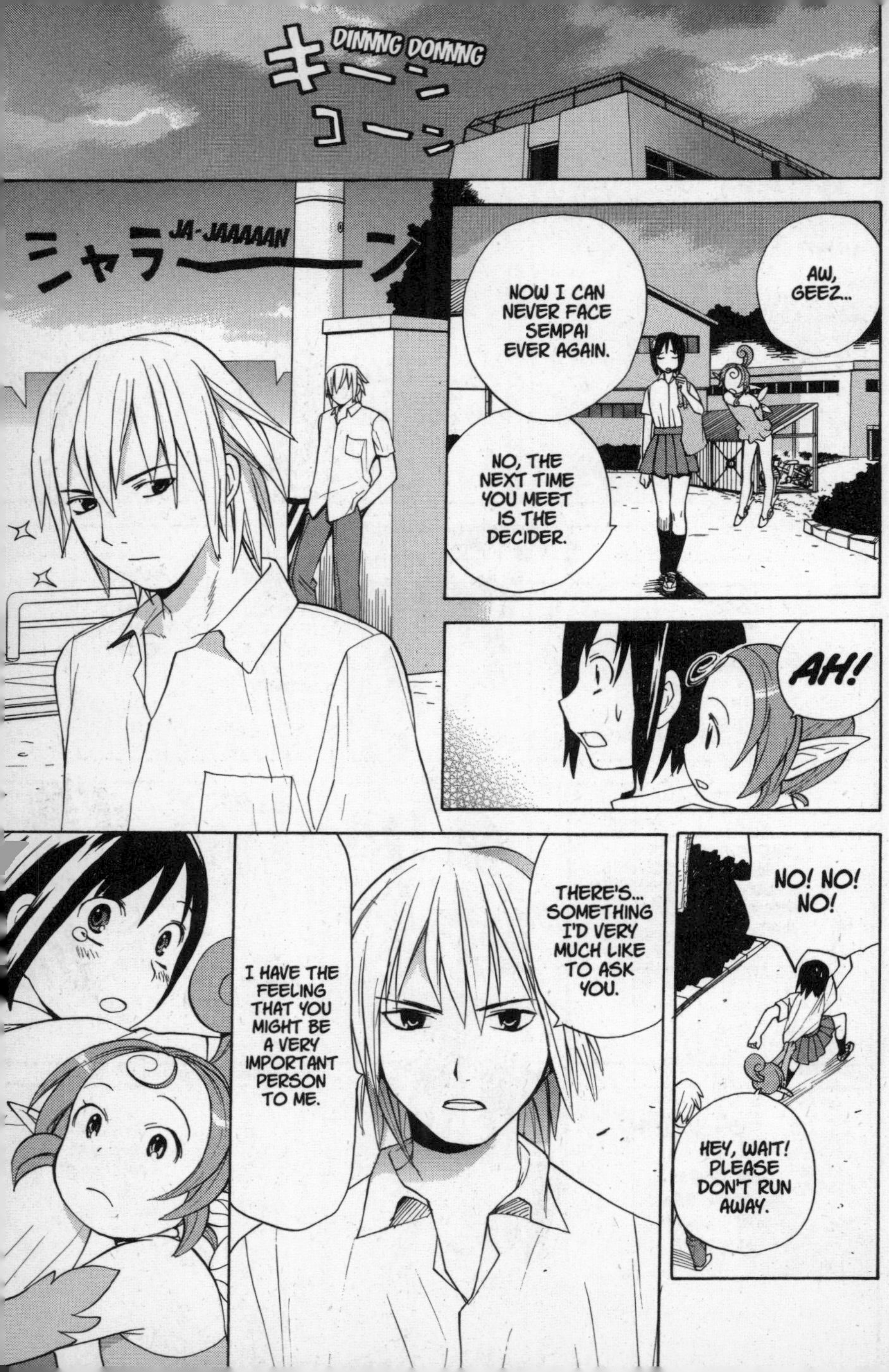

キーーン
コーーン
DINNNG DONNNG
AW, GEEZ..
NOW I CAN NEVER FACE SEMPAI EVER AGAIN.
NO, THE NEXT TIME YOU MEET IS THE DECIDER.
AH!
シャラーーン
JA-JAAAAAN
NO! NO! NO!
HEY, WAIT! PLEASE DON'T RUN AWAY.
THERE'S... SOMETHING I'D VERY MUCH LIKE TO ASK YOU.
I HAVE THE FEELING THAT YOU MIGHT BE A VERY IMPORTANT PERSON TO ME.

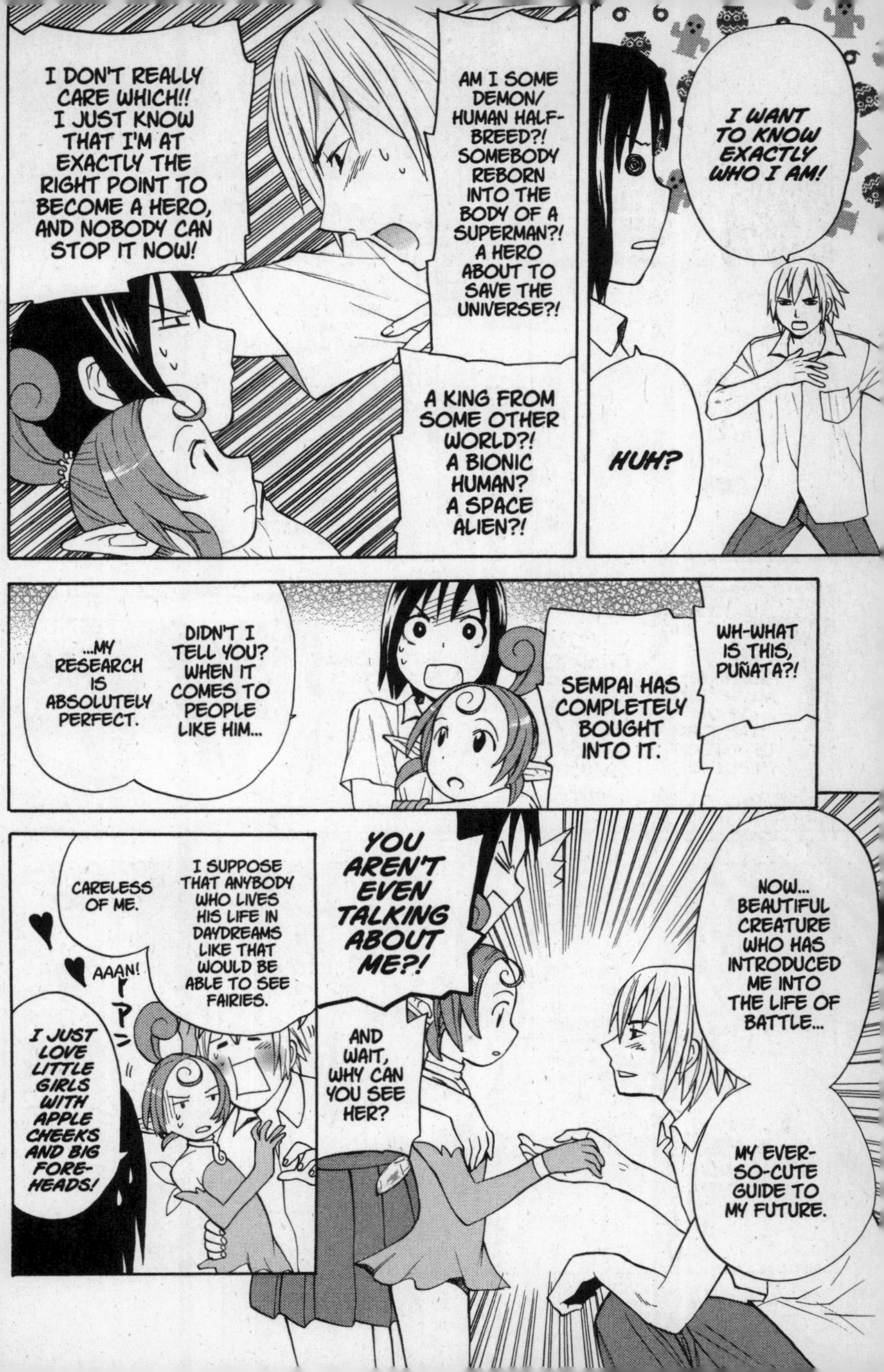
I WANT TO KNOW EXACTLY WHO I AM!
HUH?
AM I SOME DEMON/ HUMAN HALF-BREED?! SOMEBODY REBORN INTO THE BODY OF A SUPERMAN?! A HERO ABOUT TO SAVE THE UNIVERSE?!
A KING FROM SOME OTHER WORLD?! A BIONIC HUMAN? A SPACE ALIEN?!
I DON'T REALLY CARE WHICH!! I JUST KNOW THAT I'M AT EXACTLY THE RIGHT POINT TO BECOME A HERO, AND NOBODY CAN STOP IT NOW!
WH-WHAT IS THIS, PUÑATA?!
SEMPAI HAS COMPLETELY BOUGHT INTO IT.
DIDN'T I TELL YOU? WHEN IT COMES TO PEOPLE LIKE HIM...
...MY RESEARCH IS ABSOLUTELY PERFECT.
NOW... BEAUTIFUL CREATURE WHO HAS INTRODUCED ME INTO THE LIFE OF BATTLE...
MY EVER-SO-CUTE GUIDE TO MY FUTURE.
YOU AREN'T EVEN TALKING ABOUT ME?!
AND WAIT, WHY CAN YOU SEE HER?
I SUPPOSE THAT ANYBODY WHO LIVES HIS LIFE IN DAYDREAMS LIKE THAT WOULD BE ABLE TO SEE FAIRIES.
CARELESS OF ME.
AAAN!
I JUST LOVE LITTLE GIRLS WITH APPLE CHEEKS AND BIG FOREHEADS!

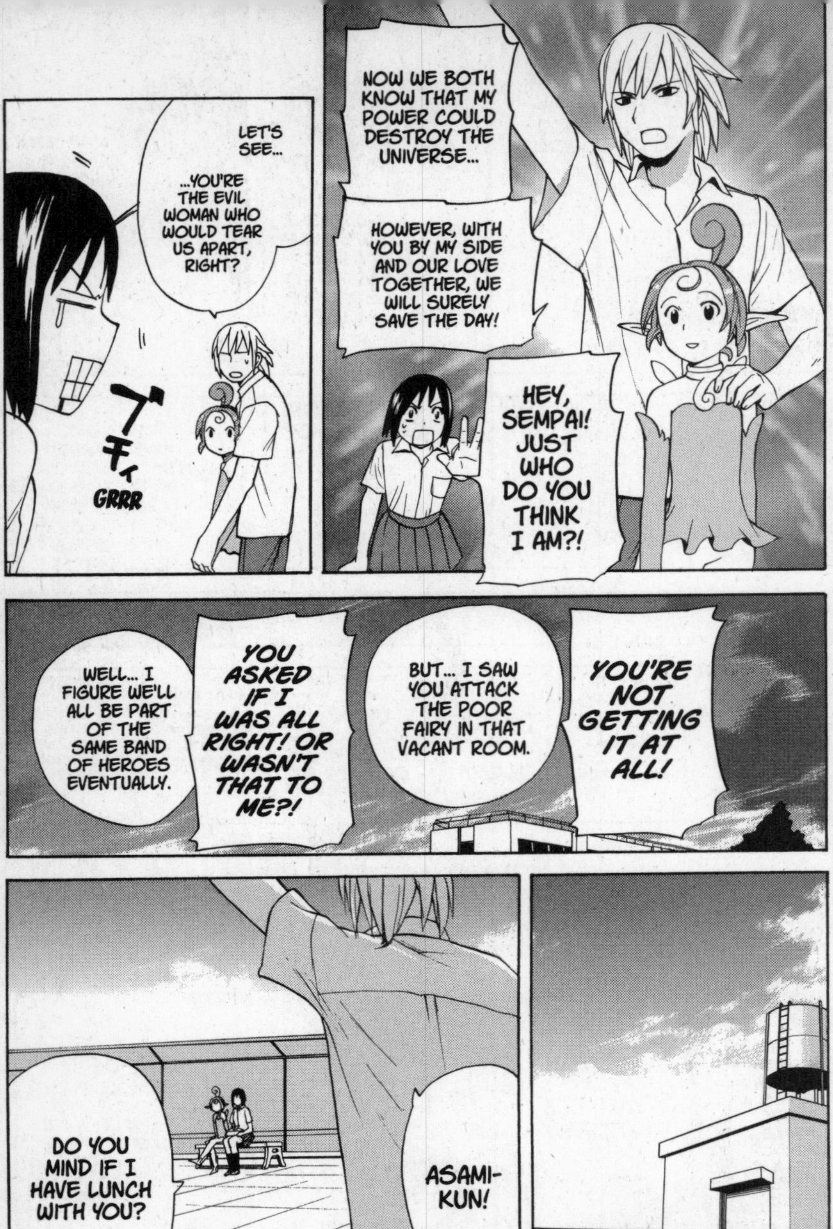
NOW WE BOTH KNOW THAT MY POWER COULD DESTROY THE UNIVERSE...
HOWEVER, WITH YOU BY MY SIDE AND OUR LOVE TOGETHER, WE WILL SURELY SAVE THE DAY!
HEY, SEMPAI! JUST WHO DO YOU THINK I AM?!
LET'S SEE...
...YOU'RE THE EVIL WOMAN WHO WOULD TEAR US APART, RIGHT?
ブチィ
GRRR
YOU'RE NOT GETTING IT AT ALL!
BUT... I SAW YOU ATTACK THE POOR FAIRY IN THAT VACANT ROOM.
YOU ASKED IF I WAS ALL RIGHT! OR WASN'T THAT TO ME?!
WELL... I FIGURE WE'LL ALL BE PART OF THE SAME BAND OF HEROES EVENTUALLY.
ASAMI-KUN!
DO YOU MIND IF I HAVE LUNCH WITH YOU?

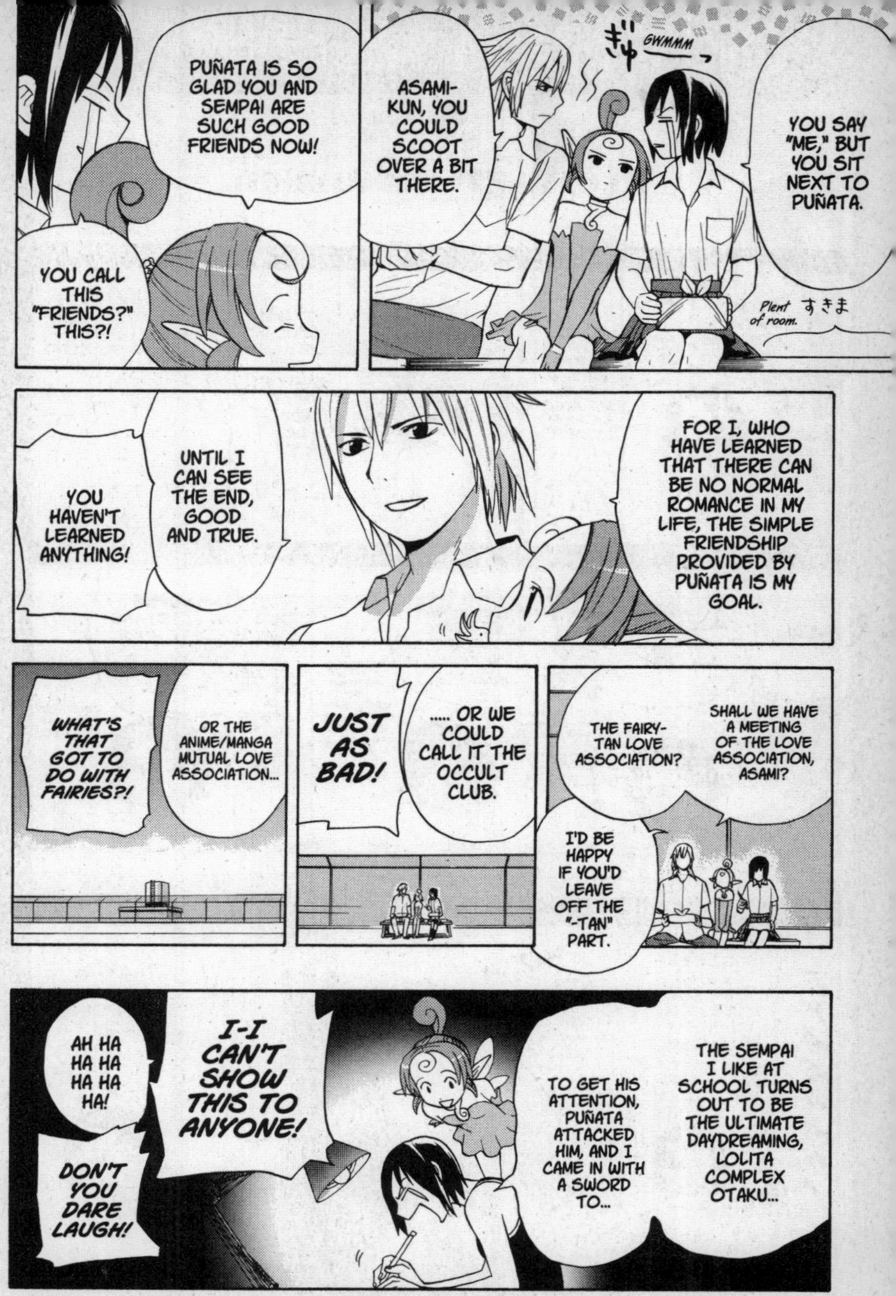
YOU SAY "ME," BUT YOU SIT NEXT TO PUÑATA.
ぎゅ GWMMM
ASAMI-KUN, YOU COULD SCOOT OVER A BIT THERE.
すきま Plent of room.
PUÑATA IS SO GLAD YOU AND SEMPAI ARE SUCH GOOD FRIENDS NOW!
YOU CALL THIS "FRIENDS?" THIS?!
FOR I, WHO HAVE LEARNED THAT THERE CAN BE NO NORMAL ROMANCE IN MY LIFE, THE SIMPLE FRIENDSHIP PROVIDED BY PUÑATA IS MY GOAL.
UNTIL I CAN SEE THE END, GOOD AND TRUE.
YOU HAVEN'T LEARNED ANYTHING!
SHALL WE HAVE A MEETING OF THE LOVE ASSOCIATION, ASAMI?
THE FAIRY-TAN LOVE ASSOCIATION?
I'D BE HAPPY IF YOU'D LEAVE OFF THE "-TAN" PART.
..... OR WE COULD CALL IT THE OCCULT CLUB.
JUST AS BAD!
OR THE ANIME/MANGA MUTUAL LOVE ASSOCIATION...
WHAT'S THAT GOT TO DO WITH FAIRIES?!
THE SEMPAI I LIKE AT SCHOOL TURNS OUT TO BE THE ULTIMATE DAYDREAMING, LOLITA COMPLEX OTAKU...
TO GET HIS ATTENTION, PUÑATA ATTACKED HIM, AND I CAME IN WITH A SWORD TO...
I-I CAN'T SHOW THIS TO ANYONE!
AH HA HA HA HA HA HA!
DON'T YOU DARE LAUGH!

Genius Fairy Puñata The End.

Afterword Bonman.

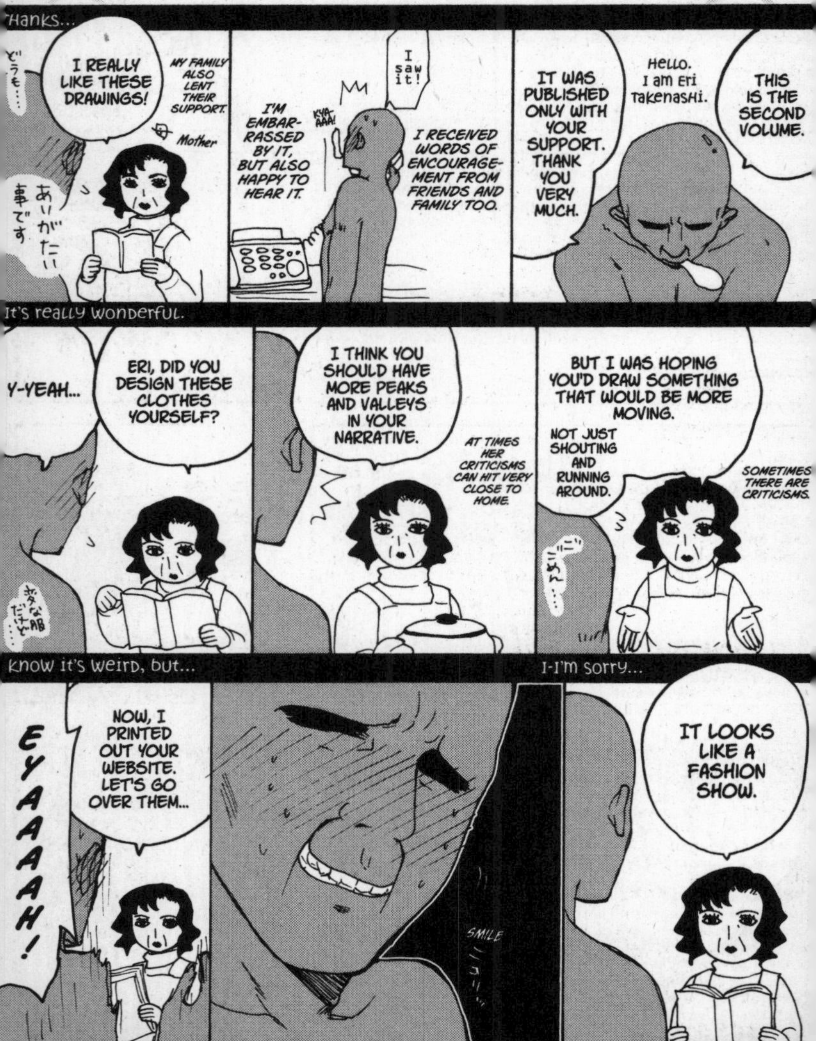
Thanks...
THIS IS THE SECOND VOLUME.
Hello. I am Eri Takenashi.
IT WAS PUBLISHED ONLY WITH YOUR SUPPORT. THANK YOU VERY MUCH.
I RECEIVED WORDS OF ENCOURAGEMENT FROM FRIENDS AND FAMILY TOO.
I saw it!
KYAAAA!
I'M EMBARRASSED BY IT, BUT ALSO HAPPY TO HEAR IT.
MY FAMILY ALSO LENT THEIR SUPPORT.
Mother
I REALLY LIKE THESE DRAWINGS!
どうも…
ありがたい事です
It's really wonderful.
SOMETIMES THERE ARE CRITICISMS.
BUT I WAS HOPING YOU'D DRAW SOMETHING THAT WOULD BE MORE MOVING.
NOT JUST SHOUTING AND RUNNING AROUND.
ごめん…
AT TIMES HER CRITICISMS CAN HIT VERY CLOSE TO HOME.
I THINK YOU SHOULD HAVE MORE PEAKS AND VALLEYS IN YOUR NARRATIVE.
ERI, DID YOU DESIGN THESE CLOTHES YOURSELF?
Y-YEAH...
変な服だけど…
I-I'm sorry...
know it's weird, but...
IT LOOKS LIKE A FASHION SHOW.
SMILE
ニコー
NOW, I PRINTED OUT YOUR WEBSITE. LET'S GO OVER THEM...
EYAAAAAH!

[translator's notes]

Shinto Religion
This story is heavily influenced by the native religion of Japan, Shintoism. Shinto is an animist religion where Gods (called Kami) protect and influence events under their domain. Most Shinto shrines are to local deities, although there are some national deities. Local deities are often (though not necessarily) enshrined in natural places such as unusually large or remarkable trees, prominent rocks, natural water springs, etc., and Gods are believed to inhabit these places. Small shrines may be maintained by the local population and have no specific Shinto priest attached, where as larger shrines may be maintained by a priest and his family (priests may marry and raise families) living on site. In most cases, the Gods and their histories are recorded by those who keep the shrines. However, it is not unheard of for that history to have been lost, and the shrine to be dedicated to an unknown deity.

The books of Shintoism are mainly records of the myths of Japan and are not canonical scripture. There is no founder, and the rituals can vary from region to region. Unlike many other religions, Shintoism does not require that its followers abandon other religions -- in fact, Shintoism and Buddhism have lived together in harmony in Japan for more than a millennium.

Shrine Maidens
Also called miko, these are generally unmarried young women (usually the Shinto priest's daughters) who help in the performance of Shinto rites as well as having rites of their own to perform. Miko have a very long tradition dating far back into prehistory.

p.25 Umainbou
This is a slightly misspelled version of Umaibou, a corn-based snack sold in all sorts of venues but most often in convenience stores. The basic stick is like a long, thick Cheeto flavored with nearly twenty different types of seasonings. On the packaging is Umaemon, a Doraemon look-alike.

p. 25 Sauce
When one says "sauce" in Japan, one is referring to a brown sauce that is popular to pour on meats (and some vegetables). It is considered uncouth to pour sauce onto plain bread or rice, but sauce lovers have been known to do just that.

p.32 Signboards
Called "shikishi" in Japanese, these are paper especially made for receiving autographs or sketches from celebrities, authors, artists, etc. They are a little over one foot square with heavy card stock backing and are suitable for framing. Basically the ultimate type of paper for autograph seekers.

p.49 Mourning Otoko
In Japanese, this was Mo-Otoko, using the kanji "mo" meaning "mourning" attached to the kanji "otoko" for "man." This is Internet otaku slang, where the "mo" originally meant "mottenai" which means "not having a girlfriend," but then the "mo" was changed into a kanji that means something even more self-deprecating. This trend is also noted with the word "fujoshi" below in these notes.

p.56 Yakisoba Bun
Yakisoba is Japanese for fried noodles. Usually it's noodles fried with meat and veggies, flavored with a special yakisoba sauce, and served up on a plate. But most cafeterias (as well as bakeries, convenience stores and shops that serve take-out lunches) carry yakisoba fried up and piled into a thick hot dog-style bun. It is one of the more popular sandwiches sold at lunchtime in Japan.

p.76 Hageshima
As he says himself, Hagashima (a common Japanese name) is his actual name. Hageshima is a derogatory nickname. Hage means bald in Japanese.

p.84 Milk in Miso Soup
Putting milk in your miso soup just isn't done very much. There is a similar trick of pouring milk into a bowl of ramen to make something similar to "tonkotsu ramen" (pork bone ramen) which has a milky-white broth, but straight milk into normal miso soup just isn't a popular choice in Japan.

p.90 Saman• Thava•
First, in manga and other entertainment, when one wants to indicate a brand name, but doesn't want to use its full name (for trademark reasons, etc.), syllables are commonly replaced by substitute characters like the "bullet" used in Kannagi. The actual brand name is Samantha Thavasa, a Japanese maker of handbags and purses which are endorsed by celebrities such as Nicky Hilton and Jennifer Lopez.

p.97 Imusanjo
Imusanjo-sensei is a manga artist who also publishes a manga series in the same magazine as Kannagi, Rex Comics (thus prompting the "in-joke" response from Takako). His series Lollipo Unlimited centers around maid café maids at the top of their game, in competition with each other.

p.99 Restraining Order
Okay, she didn't go quite so far as to say the words "restraining order" in Japanese, but she did say "legally stare" at the maids.

p.102 Fujoshi
There is a common word in Japanese, "fujoshi" which simply means females (encompassing both old and young women). The female otaku of Japan use self-deprecating humor by replacing the first kanji character "fu" (usually meaning "wife") with a different kanji character "fu" meaning "rotten" to describe themselves as female otaku (the same style of self-deprecating humor used in Mo-Otoko above in these notes). The passage should really have had a pun to replace the Japanese pun, but American female otaku are more and more calling themselves by the Japanese term, "fujoshi," and no other term seemed to fit the situation.

p.103 OL
The letters, pronounced "oh-eru" in Japanese, is short for "Office Lady." It is generally a term given to women who have graduated from either two-year or four-year colleges and have entered the workforce. The mental image conjured is a woman in her twenties, living at home, with plenty of disposable income to spend.

p.104 Welcome Back
This is a peculiarity of maid cafés. The maids are supposed to act as one's personal servant, so when entering the café, they act as if welcoming the master of the house back to his mansion. Other businesses use "irrashaimase" ("Welcome to our shop"), but maid cafés use "okaerinasai, Go-shujin-sama" ("Welcome back, Master.").

p.112 Candid Camera
Although the name of the program that Jin is referring to in the Japanese was "Dokkiri," it was almost exactly the same type of program as the American TV show, Candid Camera. A hidden camera show where normal people are caught in weird situations.

p.125 Stormy Wuthering Heights
This title was named after the Japanese title of Emily Brontë's book, Wuthering Heights (Arashi-ga-oka.) In English, the word wuthering means "blustery winds," but in Japanese, "arashi" means "storm." So both the "forbidden love" (such as Catherine's and Heathcliff's) that Daitetsu imagines and the actual storm outside are both referenced in the Japanese title. In English, I imagine there are many readers who do not know what "wuthering" means, although they may understand the relation of the book to forbidden love.

p.126 Honshu
This is the main island of Japan where one can find nearly all the major cities of the nation.

p. 126 Drying the Laundry
Although there are clothes dryers in Japan, they are not as prevalent as in western households. Most houses and apartments only have space for one machine which, for most, is the clothes washer. Drying laundry is hung on racks or rods usually located right outside the southern windows. When it rains, the clothes don't dry as fast, so storms and the rainy season are a point of annoyance for most Japanese people.

p.137 Boil-in-the-bag
The Japanese call boil-in-the-bag foods "ritoruto" (from the Dutch word, "retort" which is a glass tube used for distillation), and they are sold all over Japan as an easily made meal to serve over rice. Boil-in-the-bag curry is the most popular dish, but there are many different varieties available in supermarkets and convenience stores.

p.171 Bath House
Viewers of the Oscar-winning anime, Spirited Away, may remember the villain, Yubaaba. This translates out to bathhouse old woman, and it is one of the insults that Puñata throws at Asami.

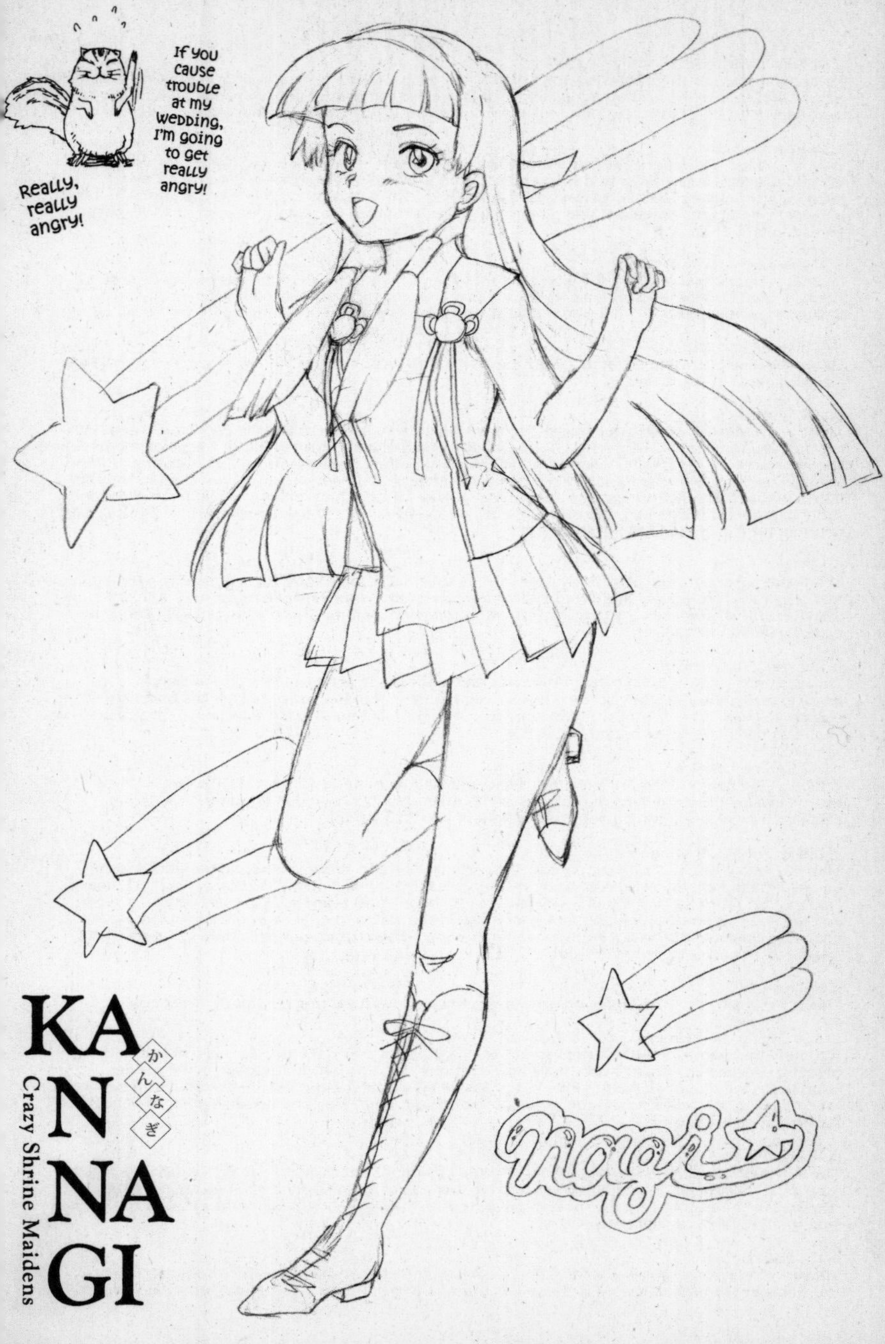
If you cause trouble at my wedding, I'm going to get really angry!
Really, really angry!
KANNAGI
かんなぎ
Crazy Shrine Maidens
nagi

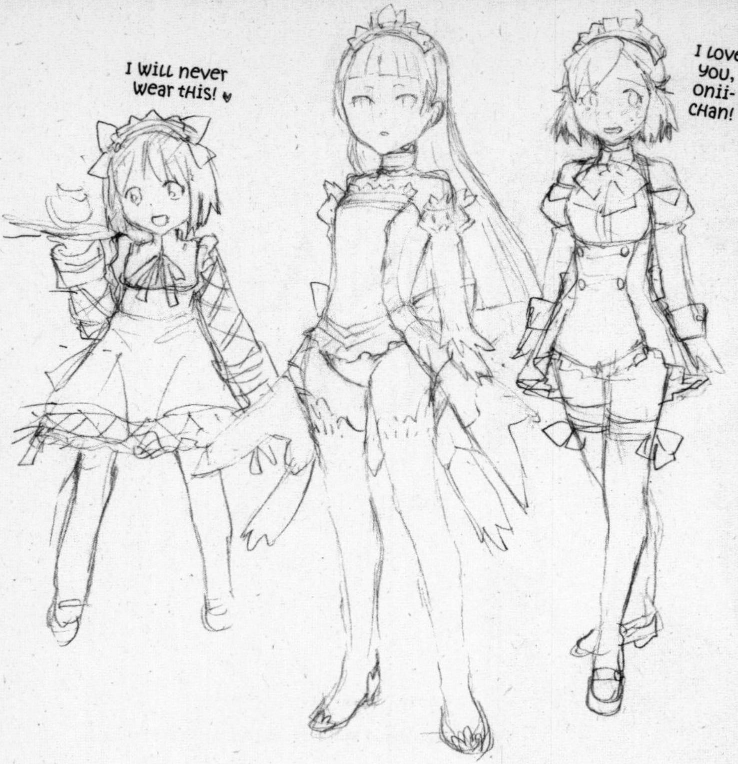
I love you, onii-chan!
I will never wear this! ♥

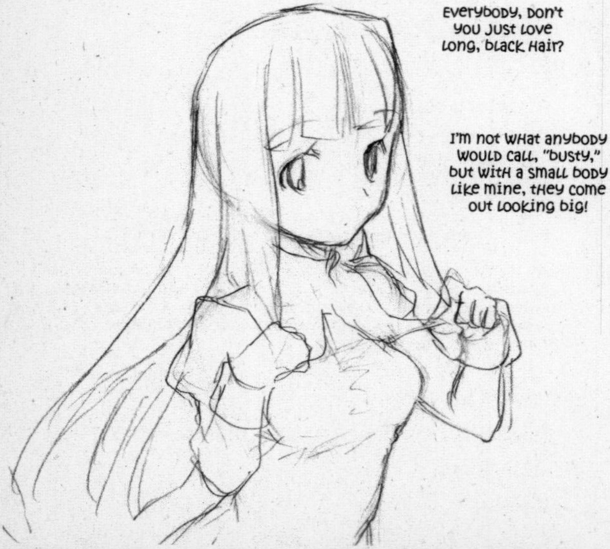
Everybody, don't you just love long, black hair?
I'm not what anybody would call, "busty," but with a small body like mine, they come out looking big!

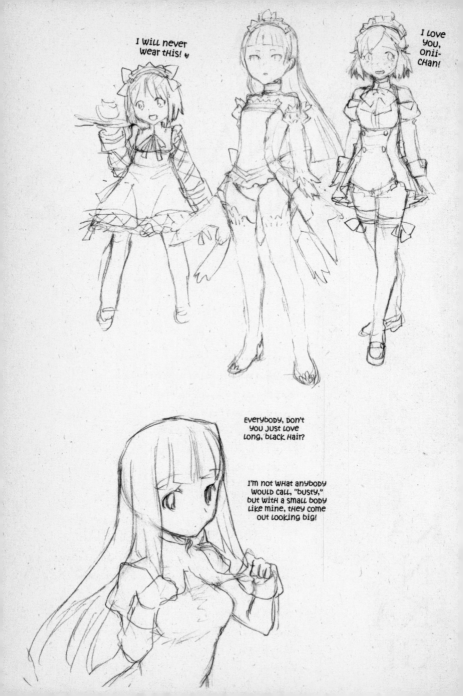

KANNAGI

Crazy Shrine Maidens

2

BY ERI TAKENASHI

English Production Credits

Translated and Adapted by William Flanagan

Production by Jose Macasocol, Jr.

Cover Production by Kit Loose

Copy Edited by Lucy Huang and Taku Otsuka

Edited by Robert Place Napton

Published by Ken Iyadomi

KANNAGI Vol. 2
©2007 by Eri Takenashi
All rights reserved.
Original Japanese edition published by Ichijinsha Inc., Tokyo.
English translation rights arranged with Ichijinsha Inc.

ISBN-13: 978-1-60496-268-0

First BANDAI ENTERTAINMENT PRINTING: SEPTEMBER 2011

10 9 8 7 6 5 4 3 2 1

Printed in Canada

CODE GEASS: LELOUCH OF THE REBELLION - KNIGHT VOL. 3

COMING SOON!

CODE GEASS: LELOUCH OF THE REBELLION - KNIGHT VOL. 4

COMING SOON!

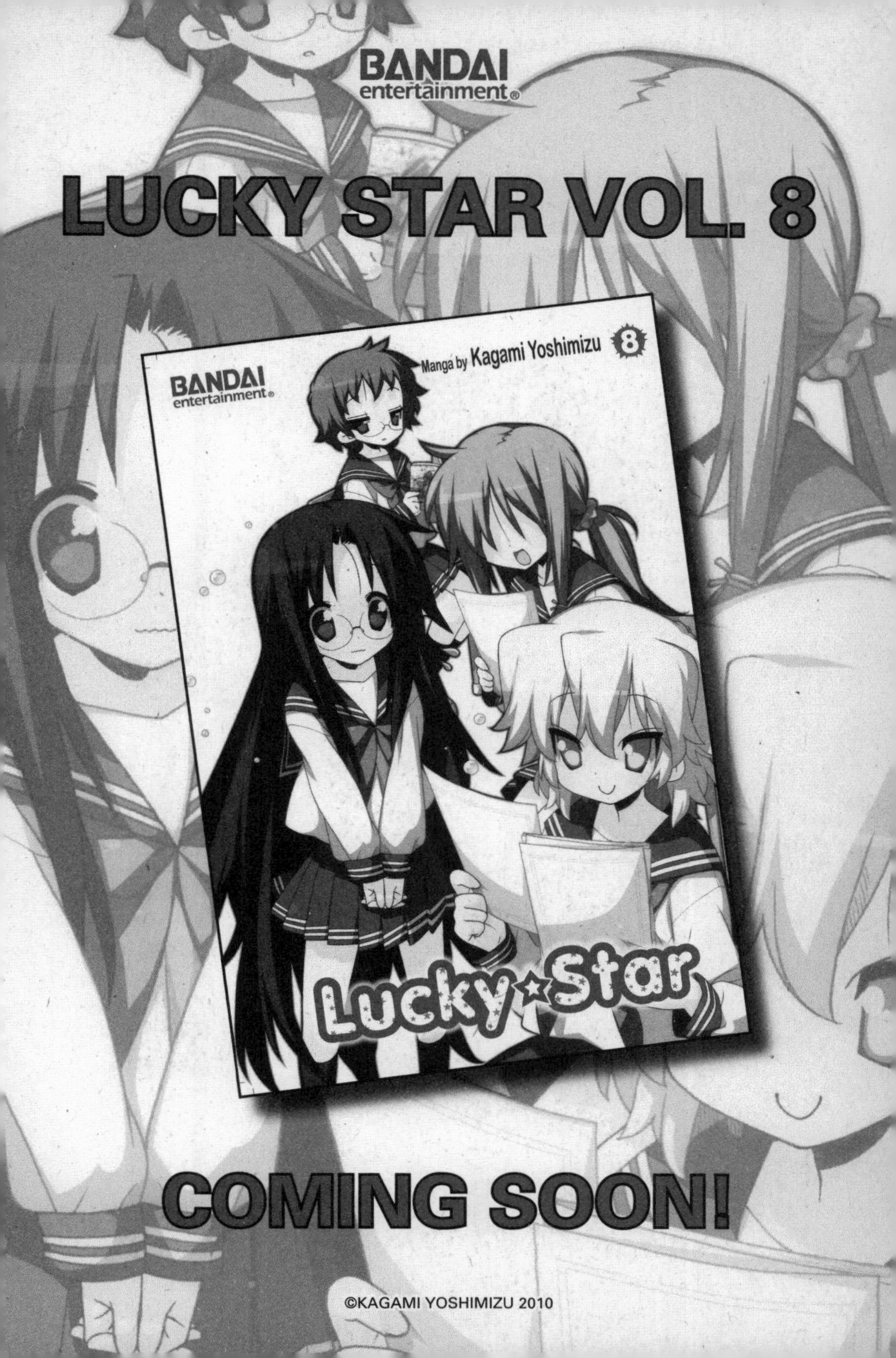
BANDAI entertainment
LUCKY STAR VOL. 8
BANDAI entertainment
Manga by Kagami Yoshimizu 8
Lucky Star
COMING SOON!
©KAGAMI YOSHIMIZU 2010

BANDAI entertainment®

GURREN LAGAAN VOL. 6

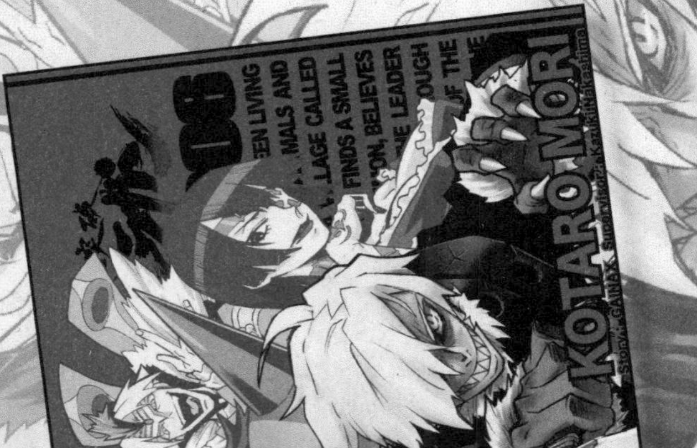
KOTARO MORI
Story: GAINAX Supervisor: Kazuki Nakashima

COMING SOON!

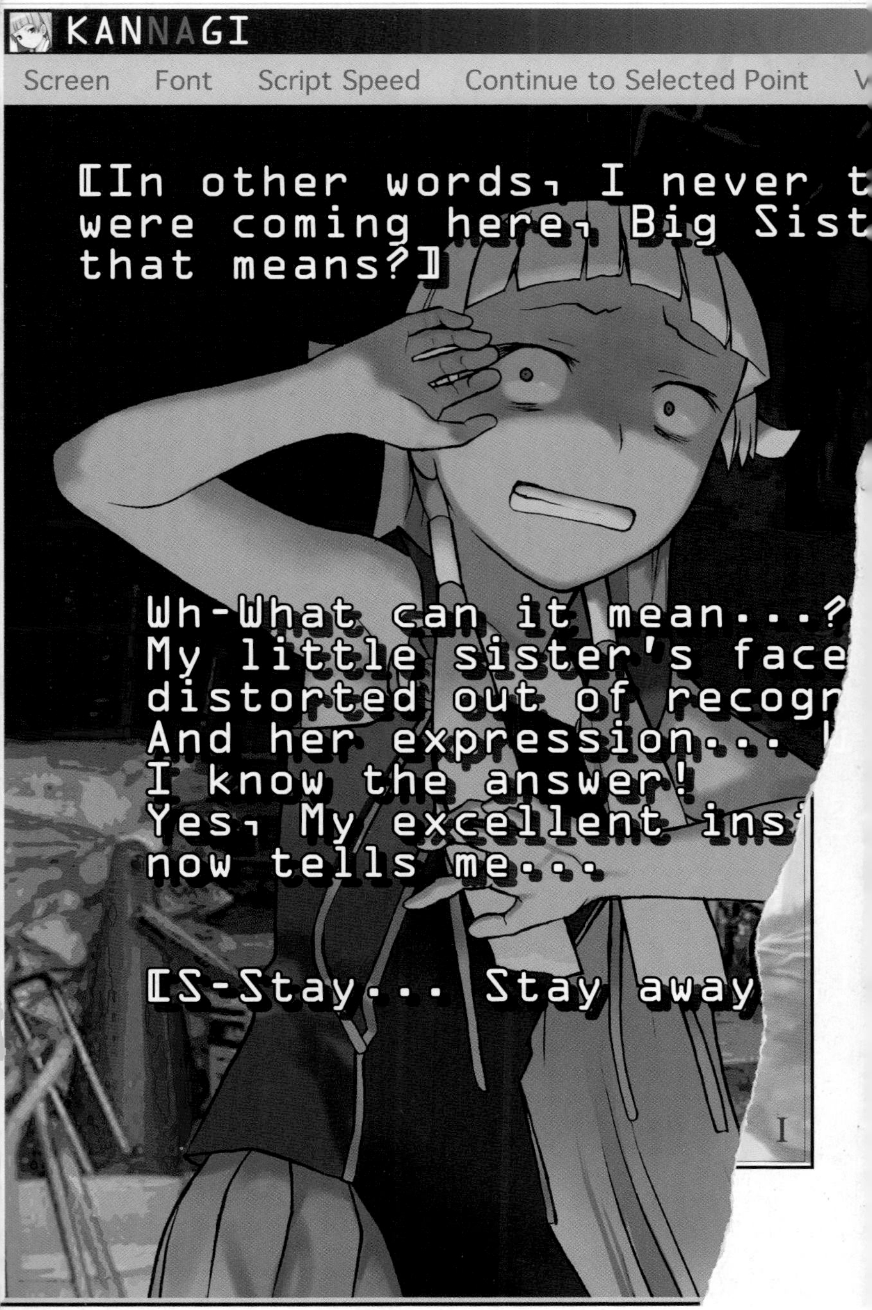
KANNAGI
Screen Font Script Speed Continue to Selected Point
『In other words, I never
were coming here, Big Sist
that means?』
Wh-What can it mean...?
My little sister's face
distorted out of recogn
And her expression...
I know the answer!
Yes, My excellent ins
now tells me...
『S-Stay... Stay away